ARROWS
IN THE DARK

ARROWS
IN THE DARK

David Ben-Gurion, the Yishuv Leadership,
and Rescue Attempts during the Holocaust

VOLUME 2

Tuvia Friling
Translated by Ora Cummings

THE UNIVERSITY OF WISCONSIN PRESS

This book was published with the support of Ben Gurion University of the Negev and the Shalem Center in Jerusalem.

The University of Wisconsin Press
1930 Monroe Street
Madison, Wisconsin 53711

www.wisc.edu/wisconsinpress/

3 Henrietta Street
London WC2E 8LU, England

Library of Congress Cataloging-in-Publication Data

Friling, Tuvia.
[Hets ba-arafel. English]
Arrows in the dark: David Ben-Gurion, the Yishuv leadership, and rescue attempts during the Holocaust /
Tuvia Friling [translated by Ora Cummings].
p. cm.
Includes bibliographical references and index.
ISBN 0-299-17550-2 (hc)
1. World War, 1939–1945—Jews—Rescue. 2. Holocaust, Jewish (1939–1945)
3. Jews—Palestine—Politics and government—20th century. 4. Ben-Gurion, David, 1886–1973. I. Title.
D804.6 .F7513 2003
940.53′1835—dc21

2003008907

In memory of my father, Haron Ben-Avra'am, and my mother, Ida-Yehudit
May they rest in peace

Contents

ARROWS
IN THE DARK

8

"A One-in-a-Million Chance"

Attempts to Rescue Hungarian Jewry and Negotiations at War's End

On 19 May 1944 a German plane landed in Istanbul. Two men disembarked. The first was a small-time industrialist named Joel Brand, a daredevil rescue activist and member of the Aid and Rescue Committee in Budapest, founded by a group of Hungary's Jews. The second was our rather dubious friend Bandi Grosz, a Jewish convert to Catholicism, a thief and smuggler of goods and foreign currency, and a partner in various straw companies. He worked for both the Abwehr and the Hungarian military intelligence services, was one of the agents handled by Kollek and Avriel, and was an agent in the Dogwood web. Without a doubt, he was a multifaceted character.[1]

Brand and Grosz each bore messages from the Germans. Brand had known Grosz in Hungary, but he was only to learn the purpose of his present journey sometime later.[2] The arrival of Brand and Grosz opened a second act in a painful and multifaceted drama lasting exactly two months (until 19 July 1944), ending in a bitter fashion when Brand's ransom proposal[3] was leaked to the Western press. The drama had its good and bad guys, high and low spots, moments of hope and despair, trust and suspicion, and a dramatic plot that stretched across four continents. In the final analysis, the Brand plan did not materialize. The Jews of Hungary, the largest group still remaining in Europe, were led at breakneck speed to Auschwitz, where some 437,000 were slaughtered by the end of the occupation. Some of those who remained died during the infamous "death march" of November 1944.

Notwithstanding all the research into this subject, there is still no clear answer to the question of how substantial Brand's proposal really was. However, documentation of the affair clearly shows Ben-Gurion's deep involvement in decision making, initiation and direction of the operation, devising general policies, and grasping the minutest details.

The various problems involved in efforts to rescue Jews seemed to have been reached a peak during the weeks following Brand's arrival from Hungary. Since Brand's ransom plan was the third of its kind, the JAE behaved and reacted in accordance with previously created patterns.

Among the active groups, the American JDC and the War Refugee Board played a prominent role. The JDC, a non-Zionist philanthropic society, was willing to participate secretly in activities that violated American law. The War Refugee Board, on the other hand, entered the campaign with a display of courage, but its involvement ended within a relatively short time with a show of weakness.

For about a year prior to Brand's arrival in Istanbul in May 1944, the Yishuv emissaries had been experiencing unfortunate results while operating a dubious courier network in collaboration with the Americans and the British in Istanbul. By late 1943 Avriel was called for a review following the discovery that Germans had infiltrated the web. Structural faults in the secret collaboration with the Allies were also apparent by the time Brand's proposal was discussed.

A mysterious invitation sent to Menahem Bader to visit Berlin was another important sign of this tortuous affair, which was linked to similar contacts made in the Iberian peninsula and Sweden. In studying this labyrinth of events, I shall examine the JAE's policies in order to determine if it did indeed shoot "an arrow in the dark," as Kaplan put it, so long as there was even a one in a million chance of rescuing Jews.

Much has been written about this ransom plan, in the form of newspaper articles, memoirs and eyewitness testimonies, a documentary-style book, and stage plays.[4] Many unsolved riddles remain despite state-of-the art research, which only adds to the enigma. In this respect, one must carefully distinguish between what we know today in hindsight and what the heroes and decision makers knew at the time about the situation in Hungary and the motives and plans of the Nazis.

This methodological distinction is also valid with regard to shorter time periods, including weeks or even days. One should be guided by this fact when analyzing the various stages of what was known to the story's participants. Thus, the information at Brand's disposal upon his arrival in Istanbul differed from that at his departure for Syria. What he knew in Aleppo (Syria) was different from what he knew when he submitted various versions of later testimony.

The ransom proposal presented by Brand and the developments it led to departed in significant ways from the original defined boundaries. The repercussions of earlier ransom plans were more moderate. The offshoots of the affair and the chain reaction it caused seriously affected the lives of those who were involved in it and even altered the history of the State of Israel. In addition, the affair was of great importance as a dramatic and concentrated symbol of the tragic absurdity facing the Yishuv in its effort to rescue the Jews of Europe. It reveals the inherent reasons for failure and illustrates the way in which the Yishuv and its leaders faced insurmountable obstacles whenever they attempted to halt the Nazi murder machine.

THE BRAND AND GROSZ AFFAIR

On 19 March 1944, exactly two months before Brand and Grosz arrived in Istanbul, German armies invaded Hungary (Operation Margarete). The process began of turning Hungary from a "paradise" for its Jews[5] into a land in which the "final solution" was put into action. The four or five months preceding the summer were filled with attempts to rescue Hungary's Jews—none of which succeeded.

An outstanding proposal was variously known as "goods for blood" (German "Blut gegen Waren" or "Waren für Blut") or the Brand plan, named after the emissary who brought it to the notice of the Yishuv leadership. Its main points were first disclosed to the rescue emissaries in Istanbul on 19 May 1944. It is more than likely that it was proposed by Heinrich Himmler himself.

It was the third ransom plan to be received by the Yishuv. Joel Brand, a key member of the Aid and Rescue Committee in Budapest,[6] arrived in Istanbul on 19 May 1944 and presented the main points of the plan to the local Yishuv emissaries. They decided to send Venja Pomeranz home immediately, and five days later he arrived with his report on the proposal. From then until it was given to the press and removed from the agenda (19 July 1944), it was examined from all angles and every effort was made by senior members in the Yishuv to put it into action. Ben-Gurion was deeply involved, as were Kaplan, Sharett, Gruenbaum, and the rest of the JAE members. All the senior emissaries were involved, together with the head of the Yishuv's secret apparatus.

IN THE SHADOW OF THE GERMAN OCCUPATION OF HUNGARY

The fate of Hungarian Jewry under German occupation was discussed in two JAE meetings held on 26 March and 2 April 1944. The March debate took place one week after the invasion, which Ben-Gurion defined as a "sign of new calamity." He felt that pressure must be leveled against Britain to increase the quota of certificates for the rescue of Zionists from Hungary and Jews from the Balkans. To this end, the Yishuv delegation had to be reinforced with a special emissary, Dr. Mordechai Eliash, and ex-Romanian or Hungarian Jews. Ben-Gurion also proposed increasing the rescue budget. Shortly afterward the JAE decided to allocate an intermediate sum equal to 100,000 Palestinian pounds.

Ben-Gurion may have referred to the Zionists in Hungary (as opposed to the Jews of the Balkans), under the assumption that, notwithstanding the death sentence hanging over Hungarian Jews in general, the assimilated among them were not yet fully aware of the need to escape. In addition, there was a preference for Zionist activists. When the line to leave got longer, this became the way out for everyone in the Jewish nation.[7]

This debate and several more in the JAE and other Yishuv bodies took place under the growing pressure of ex-Hungarian Jews in Palestine. Ben-Gurion met with one of them four days after the invasion, when he was asked to increase the immigration certificates allocated to Hungarian Jews, to increase financial aid sent by the Yishuv, and to urge the pope to exert diplomatic pressure against Hungary ("since the Hungarian nation is very orthodox"). He was informed of the need for self-defense and the fact that Tito and his people could help.

Various types of cooperation were discussed with Tito both before and after the German invasion. One of the more important discussions—Weizmann's talks with Churchill on the aid requested by Tito for Hungarian Jewish refugees—began as a proposal sent by Joseph to Sharett on 22 March 1944, a day after Ben-Gurion's meeting with the representatives of ex-Hungarian Jewry. Joseph also suggested that the JAE in London ask the Allies to warn the Hungarian government that it would be punished for aiding in the persecution of Jews.[8]

Acquiescing to some of the requests, three days later Ben-Gurion proposed increasing the number of certificates and the budget, since "the entire nation is not poisoned and something can sometimes be done with the money." He also supported the proposal to involve the West and the pope in preventing the murders. In March 1943 Kaplan had asked Vatican staff member Angelo Roncalli to pass along a similar request to the

pope. In Ben-Gurion's speech to the JAE on 26 March 1944, therefore, he combined past activity with future plans. The more secret issues, such as self-defense, were mentioned very generally and only briefly.[9]

The Palestine office in Hungary was also a focal point for pressure and criticism. Thus, Hungarian Po'alei Zion members demanded of Ben-Gurion, Kaplan, and Dobkin, representatives of their sister party in the JAE, that staff changes be made in the Budapest office. Their letter reflected political tensions among the Zionists, who comprised no more than 5 percent of the entire Hungarian Jewish population.[10]

Throughout this period reports kept flowing into Ben-Gurion's office from various sources concerning Germany's decision to treat Hungary's Jews "the way [they did the Jews] in Poland." First steps in this direction had already been taken: Jews were either concentrated in ghettoes or transferred to areas under fire; their property was confiscated; and veteran Zionists were arrested.[11] Public protests and fund-raising in the wake of this news have already been discussed.[12]

GRUENBAUM SUGGESTS MAKING CONTACT WITH THE DEVIL

Brand's proposal was not the first to suggest the possibility that the rescue of the Jews of Hungary might be accomplished through negotiations with the Germans. At a JAE meeting held on 2 April 1944 Yitzhak Gruenbaum, chairman of the Rescue Committee and one of the General Zionists' leaders, proposed that the JAE contact the German representative in Istanbul to determine the cost of "halting the extermination of all the remaining Jews in Europe." The German invasion of Hungary was, of course, the immediate backdrop to this proposal.

The Gruenbaum proposal constituted the dying embers of the Europa Plan, which had been removed from the agenda several months earlier and had also referred to all the surviving Jews in

Europe. Gruenbaum assumed that persons could be found in the shaky Third Reich who cared about their own personal future and that of their country. This assessment was based on earlier feedback from political and intelligence sources and upon contacts with people within the Nazi hierarchy itself. Ben-Gurion, Sharett, and Kaplan even gave strict instructions to Bader to "make contact with the devil" if necessary.[13]

Gruenbaum proposed that Jewish Agency people in the United States urge the Roosevelt administration to suggest to Germany that it "refrain from deporting to Poland the Jews of the Balkans that are now falling into their hands," concentrate them in special camps, and give them the "status of 'enemies' imprisoned during the war period." The Yishuv would finance their upkeep. Such an idea had been raised in 1943 and was again discussed several times thereafter. It can be assumed that Gruenbaum hoped that such pressure would prove fruitful in the United States, where President Roosevelt hoped to be reelected for a fourth term. A War Refugee Board had been established only four months previously in response to domestic political pressure and it was believed at the time that it would be an effective body.

The JAE's reactions were mixed. Some members objected for emotional reasons. Dobkin felt that Gruenbaum's proposal to negotiate directly with the Nazis was "simply shameful." He asked rhetorically, "Could we be offering pity to the Germans?" Dr. Werner Senator rejected in principle the possibility that "a Jew should appear before von Papen," Germany's ambassador to Turkey.

There was a great distance between the worlds of Zaslani, Kollek, and their colleagues, who acted on instructions issued by Ben-Gurion, Kaplan, and Sharett, and that reflected the sentiments of Dobkin and Senator. Within three months history would make them all a laughingstock by placing Dobkin himself face to face with a similar proposal for direct negotiations with the Nazis in Lisbon.

Moshe Shapira and David Ben-Gurion took a moderate stand. Shapira, who belonged to the Hamizrahi party, did not reject outright the idea of contact with the Nazis, suggesting it be done through Ira Hirschmann, the representative of the War Refugee Board (WRB) in Istanbul. Ben-Gurion opposed Gruenbaum's proposal. The superpowers' policies, which demanded the unconditional surrender of Germany, negated any chance of their supporting such a proposal. Moreover, they would blame us, claiming that "for the sake a few Jews we were willing to forgive the Germans for everything."[14]

Ben-Gurion supervised the activity of Zaslani, Kollek, and Avriel. One can therefore safely assume that his words here were a pretext for getting out of this debate. Furthermore, Gruenbaum's proposal was adopted to a significant extent. The JAE decided to seek indirect channels to the Germans through Hirschmann, who had to "find ways of presenting things to the enemy's representatives in Ankara." It was decided to instruct the Palestine office in Istanbul to "ask the German government not to deport Jews from the Balkans to Poland, but rather to concentrate them in special camps under the supervision of the Red Cross." Gruenbaum's proposal to apply to the Americans was not adopted. It is not impossible that the version of the conclusions consulted is incomplete, and it is quite possible that decisions were reached that were not recorded in the minutes or were not mentioned at the meeting itself. These were the sorts of subjects that were meant to be hidden from the eagle-eyed British.[15]

Pomeranz arrived in Palestine on 24 May 1944. The information he presented concerning a new ransom plan completely altered preparations for coping with the threat to Hungarian Jewry.[16] There was an air of urgency in Istanbul. As soon as the emissaries had decided to send Pomeranz home, they attempted to inform the Yishuv that he was on his way and to report back on the new proposal. Chaim Barlas asked Steinhardt, the

U.S. ambassador to Turkey, to help in dispatching the information, and Avriel and Schind asked the same of their friends Whittall and Gibson.[17]

A NOTE HIDDEN IN A TUBE OF SHAVING CREAM AND POMERANZ'S REPORT

Without the help of the Americans or the British, there was no quick way to reach Palestine or pass along a message. The information was conveyed through several channels, one of which was Pinkerton, the American consul in Jerusalem, who phoned the JAE on 24 May with a message for Sharett. "Be waiting at Lod for a special mission regarding Hungary. Prepare an urgent meeting of the JAE on Wednesday evening. Prepare for a sudden trip to Kushta [Istanbul]."[18]

The British proposed that Pomeranz fly to Cairo and make his way from there to Palestine. Pomeranz hesitated, consulted with Avriel, and finally decided to reject the offer for fear of being held up in Cairo. He preferred to travel by way of Beirut and then on to Palestine.[19] This clearly reveals that Pomeranz and his friends had no faith in their British and American colleagues. As we shall see, their suspicion was not misplaced.

Pomeranz arrived in Palestine, visited briefly with his family in Kibbutz Ramat Rachel, and was immediately accompanied by Teddy Kollek to a night meeting with Ben-Gurion and Sharett. He handed them a note, hidden in a tube of shaving cream, in which the emissaries outlined the reasons for his sudden appearance in Palestine:

> The emissary's journey is suddenly urgent, with regard to the arrival of [Comrade] Brand, who has brought the most distressing news of the situation of the Jews in Hungary. That which we have dreaded has befallen us in a way that we could not have imagined. Indeed, the plan, which is aimed at alleviation and rescue, is presented to us in the form of a satanic plan that we were unable to discuss without first showing it to you. The [comrade] emissary will give you all the details, which speak and cry out for themselves, and you must consider the

Venja Pomeranz (Ze'ev Hadari)
(courtesy Venja Pomeranz).

situation and inform us immediately of your decision whether to start negotiations or—because of our inability—to stop. We are waiting, brokenhearted, for your decision, on which many thousands of lives may depend, although we are not at liberty to make it. [Comrade Brand] will wait here until we receive your telegram.

Barlas intensified the message by asking:

a. What should we answer the slave drivers? With regard to goods or with regard to ransom money?
b. Is one of the JAE coming here and, if so, which one?
c. Is it fitting to send him [Comrade Brand] to Jerusalem and can his immediate return be assured, since these are the conditions of his mission?
d. Should negotiations take place in Ankara, too, apart from his [Barlas's] private conversation with Avni [Steinhardt] for his [Steinhardt's] information alone?

He stressed the urgency of the matter and recommended that Sharett or Gruenbaum come to Istanbul. It is possible that fateful decisions would have to be made and there would be no time to wait for a reply from Jerusalem or from the London branch. Barlas also asked for the replies to be signed.[20]

The meeting went on all night. Pomeranz was very agitated. He reported on the details of the proposal and gave his impression of Brand. Ben-Gurion was the first to be included in the secret, as happened in the case of the Transnistria Plan (and probably also the Europa/Slovakia Plan). There is no record by Ben-Gurion of this dramatic conversation, but it can reconstructed from later reports.[21] Ben-Gurion and Sharett decided to convene the JAE immediately for an extraordinary session. This took place the following day (24 May 1944) and became the first in a series of meetings to discuss the Brand Plan. Ben-Gurion made no opening speech and turned the proceedings over to Pomeranz.

"The matter I am about to speak about is both extremely grave and extremely unbelievable," Pomerantz began, and went on to describe events in Hungary since the German invasion on 19 March 1944.[22] Three hundred thousand Jews were imprisoned in concentration camps established by the Germans and the Hungarian Fascists in Carpatho Russ and Transylvania. Eight thousand Jews were sent to death camps in Poland, and preparations were being made to deport twelve thousand Jews a day starting the end of May or early June. Occasionally some of the Hungarian Jews were able to postpone the deportations, said Pomeranz.[23]

He then went on to describe the beginning, according to Brand, of the negotiations between the Nazis and the Relief and Rescue Committee in Budapest. The committee was a kind of emergency leadership established in early 1943. Besides Israel (Rudolf) Kasztner, Brand, and Samuel (Samo) Springmann, the committee also included Otto Komoly, Moshe Krausz, Eugen Frankel, and Ernst (Erno) Szilagyi. Kasztner, Brand, and Springmann were not originally members of the Hungarian Jewish community. Their three colleagues were the ones who gave the committee a sense of "authentic Hungarianism."[24]

Pomeranz brought an inaccurate and garbled description of what Brand had told him in Istanbul. He did not grasp the complexity of the personalities, the organizations and the general background to the plan brought by Brand. Nonetheless, this was the information that Pomeranz placed at the disposal of the Yishuv's leadership, and it was based solely on this information that the Yishuv had to make up its mind.

He told them that negotiations had begun only recently. Joel Brand and Dr. Kasztner had been called to Gestapo headquarters in Budapest. Adolf Eichmann took part in the conversation, as did Hermann Krumey, a senior staff member on his team, Dieter Wisliceny (Willi, or "Count Willivon," of the Slovakia Plan), plus other SS officers. Eichmann began by asking his guests if they knew who they were facing, reminding them that he was the man who has managed "to execute three and a half million Jews."

The rest of the conversation was "businesslike." The Jewish Agency and the JDC were offered a deal: "Instead of blood—goods." The Gestapo was willing to exchange a hundred Jews for one truck and a total of one million Jews in return for ten thousand trucks. The latter were meant for the SS, all of whose transport vehicles might break down at any moment. Also, they were asking for eight hundred tons of coffee and an equal quantity of tea, two hundred tons of cocoa, and two million bars of soap. The Gestapo was willing to supply a commitment that the trucks would be used only on the eastern front. Another condition was that released Jews be sent to Spain or Portugal, not to Palestine.

According to Brand, three or four more conversations subsequently took place. Eichmann and his people agreed to accept money instead of some goods—between four and five hundred U.S. dollars per person—and to exchange Jews for German prisoners. Eichmann agreed to release ten thousand Jews once the agreement was signed in principle and before payment was made. He was even willing to release six hundred Jews with immigration certificates and to allow them to leave for Palestine—a sign that his intentions were serious and that he had "good will."

Brand was sent to Istanbul in order to deliver Eichmann's proposal directly to the Yishuv's representatives. The Gestapo allotted him two weeks and instructed him before his departure. They allowed him to travel to Portugal, Switzerland, and even Palestine, as necessary, and told him the operation was being monitored at the highest levels in Germany. He was issued a German passport with the assumed name of Eugen Band and traveled from Budapest to Istanbul by way of Vienna,

always under the watchful eyes of the Gestapo and with a personal and "respectable" escort.[25]

According to Pomeranz, on Friday, 19 May 1944, Brand arrived in Istanbul, together with another envoy: Andre Giorgi (alias Andor Bondy or Bandi) Grosz, a Hungarian Jew.[26] (We now know that it was Grosz who carried the more important message, a fact that was not known to Pomeranz at the time of his report.) Again according to Pomeranz, Brand stressed the importance of conducting negotiations even if only to halt or postpone deportations to the death camps. He reckoned that Brand's German handlers might agree to a delay in his return to Hungary if they felt that the proposal was being seriously considered. The main question was whether the negotiations could bring about a halt in deportations, which were taking place at the rate of twelve thousand people a day. Other questions concerned whether Brand could come to Palestine, whether the Yishuv could send an emissary to Hungary to conduct negotiations, and whether the talks in Budapest were indeed being held under the auspices of the SS high command and senior officials in the Nazi regime.[27]

In the debate following Pomeranz's report, Ben-Gurion said that although the proposal was indeed "something quite implausible," nevertheless "we should not underestimate its seriousness." Clearly, "the Nazis have one objective—to exterminate the Jews," but it is nonetheless undesirable at this time "to talk about demonic plots." There is no easy way out of the dilemma, causing one to grasp at the scheme's feeble chances of success. "If there's a one in a million chance, we must take it," said Ben-Gurion.

He described in brief what had to be done immediately. First, a JAE member had to be dispatched to Turkey and Ben-Gurion preferred that it be Sharett. Second, the secret must be shared with the governments of Britain and the United States through their ambassadors. Third, the London branch had to be put into action in an effort to obtain Britain's support for the proposal.

Sharett also emphasized the chances of success versus the risks involved in the proposal: "Although the plan appears incredible, [I have] no doubt that a positive reply can save many Jewish lives." He said that "the matter must be handled with great urgency and daring." Nonetheless, Sharett advised against sending anyone to Istanbul at that time, and even to avoid direct contact with the Germans. He preferred to employ the Red Cross as mediators. He warned against conducting negotiations for the purpose of buying time and nothing more. The main objective was to rescue Jews from Europe, and postponing deportations was limited in that it would help only a few.

Gruenbaum was convinced that Eichmann's proposal was "satanic provocation," aimed at diverting attention from the Nazis' real objective, which was the "slaughter of the Jews of Hungary." Still, "[We] must keep playing the game for as long as we can . . . to show that we appear to be doing everything possible in that direction." Gruenbaum also clarified what he meant by "doing everything possible." First, negotiations of some sort would be conducted only if deportations came to a complete halt. Second, the first thousand Jews permitted to leave Nazi-controlled territory would be from Poland, not Hungary. These two conditions constituted a test of the seriousness of the proposal from Hungary.

Kaplan likewise said that the JAE had heard from Pomeranz "a story that arouses speculation," but he stressed that it was the JAE's duty to do "everything possible to rescue the Jews of Hungary." Expressing sentiments similar to those of Ben-Gurion, he concluded, "If there is even a shadow of hope, we must not relinquish it." He also supported the immediate dispatch of Sharett to Turkey.

The main source of disagreement in the debate concerned the question of whether to share the secret with the British. It was unconnected to the facts, since British intelligence personnel and the American ambassador had already been told of the plan by the emissaries in Istanbul. Sharett had been informed of Pomeranz's urgent arrival by Pinkerton, the U.S. consul general in Jerusalem. The emissaries at first hesitated and then decided that, in any event, it would be impossible to conceal the proposal from either the British or the Americans. They realized that there was a very good chance of the matter becoming known through other channels. Moreover, the emissaries knew that it would be impossible to carry out the proposed ransom plan without British and American political, military, and intelligence cooperation, so that they saw no practical reason to hide the information from them.

Ben-Gurion said that he thought the proposal should be taken to the high commissioner, the Colonial Office, and the Foreign Office because "we cannot make a move without help from the government," and because the plan had already been made known to the British and Americans by the emissaries in Istanbul. The argument was hollow, as far as he was concerned (American and British documentation proves he was right). Sharett, Kaplan, and Dr. Emil Schmorak held similar views. Gruenbaum and Dobkin, on the other hand, proposed sharing the secret only with the Americans for the time being.[28]

The JAE rejected Gruenbaum's proposal and decided to inform the Mandatory authorities of Eichmann's proposal—and hence the British government in London—and to ask them to keep the matter secret. The JAE also decided to dispatch Sharett to Turkey and to ask Weizmann to start gathering support within British and American government circles.[29] Thus, the JAE adopted Ben-Gurion's version, namely, to brush aside all doubt for the time being and to give the impression that the JAE was considering a positive reply, that the proposal was being carefully examined, and to weigh how serious the Nazis were—if, indeed, it were possible to save Jewish lives.

THE HIGH COMMISSIONER:
FIRST ROUND

Immediately after the meeting, Ben-Gurion and Sharett requested an interview with Sir Harold MacMichael, the high commissioner of Palestine, who responded forthwith. The meeting took place the following day (26 May). Ben-Gurion and Sharett described the plan down to its tiniest details as well as the sequence of events as they understood them up to that point. They told the high commissioner about Pomeranz's arrival in Jerusalem, Brand's reliability, and the obscene character of "watchdog" Bandi Grosz, who Brand had brought with him. They were still unaware that Grosz had not been sent to guard Brand, or that he bore the main part of the message the Germans wanted to pass along to the West.

Ben-Gurion and Sharett stressed the terrible threat hanging over the heads of a million Jews in Hungary, Romania, Czechoslovakia, and Poland. They made sure to inform the high commissioner that the Nazis had stipulated that the million Jews thus released would, under no circumstances, be allowed to go to Palestine, but rather to Spain and Portugal. It is worth noting that Ben-Gurion and Sharett had no reservations about this condition of the Nazis, which would become significant in the debate that subsequently developed regarding the JAE's position on the issue of evacuating Jews to destinations other than Palestine.

Ben-Gurion and Sharett told MacMichael about the "goods"—trucks, coffee, tea, cocoa, and soap—that the Nazis demanded in return for Jewish "blood," and of their willingness to immediately release up to ten thousand Jews upon signing an agreement in principle and even before delivery of the goods. Ben-Gurion and Sharett told him that the slaughter would continue if the Nazis' proposals were rejected. They told him about the escalated deportations— twelve thousand Jews a day starting on 12 May 1944—and said that this data was supported by reliable sources other than Brand. The Nazis de- manded that Brand return within four days with a reply—and that date had obviously passed.[30]

Ben-Gurion and Sharett told MacMichael that the entire affair seemed incredible to them. Still, they stressed that everything had to be done on the assumption that the proposal was bona fide. In his report to the government in London, the high commissioner chose to quote this point exactly as it had been raised at the meeting:

> They firmly hope that the magnitude and seemingly unbelievable character of the proposition will not deter high Allied authorities from undertaking a con- certed and determined effort to save the greatest possible number. They fully re- alize the overwhelming difficulties, but asked to avoid any move that would cause a bad impression that would lead to catastrophe.

Ben-Gurion and Sharett asked the high commissioner to treat the matter with utmost secrecy, to arrange the swift departure of Sharett to Istanbul, and to pass along the main points of their conversation to his government, to the U.S. administration, to Weizmann, and to Nahum Goldmann of the JAE branch in the United States.

That same day the British government had news of the meeting in Jerusalem. Among other things, the high commissioner wrote that he had asked Ben-Gurion and Sharett if additional steps should be taken and they replied that nothing should be done until after Sharett's clarifications in Istanbul. This fact is important in understanding the JAE's future position, when it was awaiting the British government's official response. MacMichael started working on Sharett's visa into Turkey and tried to get more information on the proposal and on Grosz's movements. He contacted Brigadier R. G. Maunsel, British intelligence chief in the Middle East, who was in Jerusalem at the time, and Maunsel promised to look into the matter.[31]

The fact that Ben-Gurion and Sharett spoke to the high commissioner clearly reflected the importance attached to the affair by the Yishuv leadership. By not ignoring the fact that Eichmann's proposal was incredible they maintained their own reliability and probably avoided having the proposal rejected out of hand. In their conversation with the high commissioner they tried to present themselves as responsible and serious.[32]

Three days later (29 May) the JAE received a report on the meeting with the high commissioner. Sharett summed up his impressions by saying that he "did not know the degree of authenticity the high commissioner related to the proposal, but he considered it seriously and promised to pass it on to London." Sharett described the efforts to obtain a visa for him and mentioned the possibility that he might leave for Turkey without one, perhaps in three days' time. Turkey did not wish to get involved in the new affair, which made it difficult to obtain a visa. When Turkish archives are opened to researchers, it will be possible to get a fuller understanding of that country's position. After the debate, Ben-Gurion noted: "In my opinion, the most urgent issue is Mr. Sharett's trip to Turkey. No opportunity must be allowed to slip by. We must also ask Dr. Weizmann for his response. If the possibility exists to leave for Turkey without a visa, I recommend this be done." This was wishful thinking rather than a real possibility. A man like Sharett, who was well know among all the intelligence and political circles in the region, could hardly enter Turkey without a visa.[33]

The emissaries refused to give up. They cabled Ben-Gurion with the demand that a senior JAE executive be sent to Turkey.[34] They also hinted that they were arranging a visa for Sharett through friends in Turkey, and that they had sent cables to Budapest to calm things down there and to create the impression that the proposal was indeed being seriously considered.[35]

INTERIM AGREEMENT A

Sharett saw that his trip to Turkey was being held up and feared that the Nazis would view the delay as disdain for or even rejection of their proposal. He therefore cabled the emissaries with the suggestion that Brand return to Budapest and inform the Nazis that the proposal was being considered at the highest levels of the Yishuv leadership and that an official response would be forthcoming shortly.[36]

Brand refused. As far as he was concerned, it would be suicidal to return without an agreement and without Grosz. His talks with emissary Menahem Bader led to a new idea, namely, to compose a letter of response to the Nazi proposal, a kind of interim agreement between "Moledet" (homeland, or the Zionist movement) and the Nazis, which Brand would take with him to Budapest. It would be similar to the letter written in Slovakia in the name of Ferdinand Roth (who, it will be recalled, did not exist). The document would create the impression that the Jews were adopting Eichmann's proposal, thereby permitting Brand to avoid being murdered and perhaps bringing about a halt in the deportations, which had been continuing at a horrific rate.

Bader apparently devised the forgery and Brand adopted the idea under great duress. They jointly composed the following agreement:[37]

1. The deportations will cease forthwith, in return for a million Swiss francs, to be transferred at the end of each month.
2. Immigration to Palestine of people chosen by us will be permitted and made possible in return for an advance payment of $400,000 for each transport of one thousand people [$400 per immigrant].
3. Emigration overseas, via temporary camps in neutral countries (such as Spain), will be permitted in return for an advance payment of $1 million per transport of ten thousand people.

4. A supply of food, clothing, shoes, and medicine will be permitted to the camps and the ghettos. In return for each train carriage full of supplies to the ghettos and the camps, the partner will receive another carriage.

5. Until the decision and final agreement on point 2 of this obligation, Mr. Joel Brand will have power of attorney in the name of Moledet [the Yishuv and the Zionist Movement] to decide upon the various issues that may arise, in the spirit of this obligation.[38]

The agreement was signed on 29 May 1944, following a night of coaxing and exerting pressure on Brand. In the course of that night Brand claimed that by sending him to Budapest with the agreement, Bader in effect was "sentencing him to death" and that Bader "would not have demanded the same of himself."

A new development occurred just as they were preparing for Brand's return to Budapest. Whittall and Gibson, British intelligence agents stationed in Istanbul, told their friends Schind and Avriel that if Sharett could not come to Istanbul, they were willing to arrange a journey for Brand to Palestine, where he could present Eichmann's proposal to the JAE. They promised that Brand would be able to return to Turkey and from there to Hungary.

This changed things considerably. Brand began preparing for a trip to Palestine. It was decided to send the interim agreement to Dr. Kasztner in Budapest by way of a Swiss courier, who arrived in Istanbul at about that time. The letter that accompanied the agreement specified that the Jewish Agency representatives were authorizing Brand to inform his dispatchers that they agreed in principle to the proposal and were interested in negotiating with the Germans. According to Kasztner, the agreement and letter only arrived in Budapest on 10 July 1944 and was handed over to the Nazis. If this is true, then the agreement did not achieve its objective, since it arrived too late to bridge the interim period following which the situation could be clarified. Was the agreement sent to Jerusalem for confirmation before being sent on to Budapest? Nothing in the documents I have examined corroborates this. There is some evidence that the agreement was sent to Jerusalem, but it is unclear when.[39]

In any event, it was a quite a daring step. The emissaries had no guarantee that they would be able to obtain the superpowers' support for an agreement of this sort, nor was there any backup for the vast sums of ransom money they promised to pay. Bader and his colleagues were soon to repeat this pattern when, in order to buy time, they would be forced to forge another interim agreement.

It is worth mentioning a condition apparently requested by the leaders of the Zionist movement and its emissaries concerning the allocation of funds for the rescue of Jews and the intention of the rescued to immigrate only to Palestine. As the years passed, there were those who linked this condition to the Zionist leadership. In both the Nazi proposal that was being considered in Jerusalem and in the interim agreement initiated by the Yishuv's rescue emissaries in Istanbul, mention is made of evacuating Jews to countries other than Palestine.

THE DANGLING SWORD OF DEPORTATION

Brand's and Grosz's permits to remain in Turkey were doubtful and problematic. Grosz carried a special Hungarian passport and Brand had a travel visa. Brand was traveling under the alias Eugen Band. Turkey was not interested in getting caught up in the affair, and on 25 May Grosz was arrested on suspicion of smuggling and Brand was arrested for illegally entering Turkey. They were interrogated and their movement was restricted.

On 31 May the Turkish authorities revealed their decision to deport Grosz and Brand to

Hungary. Shortly afterward they announced a change in plan: the two could choose between deportation to Hungary by way of Bulgaria or deportation to Syria. It is not completely clear who was behind this change in the Turkish decision. Could it have been Britain or Germany? Did the Turkish authorities take pity on them? Nor is it clear who was behind the decision to deport Brand and Grosz to Syria in the southeast.

Brand was undecided. He feared that his deportation to Hungary at that time, when he had no real achievement to his credit, would damage the illusory image of an omnipotent world Jewry. The Nazis believed their own propaganda, and in their talks Eichmann mentioned this distorted image as if it were a factual description. In any case, Brand himself was sure that it was this image that prompted the Nazis to initiate the ransom proposal, so that any weakening of it might jeopardize the plan. Brand also suspected the British. He was not sure what lay behind their willingness to help and to permit his entry into Palestine. It would later turn out that his suspicion was not unfounded.[40]

In Istanbul the emissaries were also undecided, and their indecision increased after Sharett cabled them detailed instructions to continue to hold Brand in Turkey and prevent his arrival in Palestine, where he would fall under British jurisdiction. Sharett's reasons: The British might arrest Brand in order to prevent him from returning to Hungary, thereby foiling his mission. Brand was a citizen of an enemy country—however ironic that sounded—and the British were able to arrest him under the pretext that if he returned to Hungary he would supply the enemy with classified information.[41] Sharett treated the British with deep suspicion and attributed a measure of cruel cynicism to them even though he was entrusted with maintaining close ties with them concerning their secret collaboration with the Yishuv.

Sharett's directive was unprecedented in Turkey. The Turkish authorities pressed Brand to

decide within a few days what he was going to do. Brand and the emissaries decided that he would make his way southeast to Syria. His decision relied on promises the emissaries had been given by their friends Whittall and Gibson. The alternative was not to remain in Turkey, as per Sharett's orders, but rather to return to Hungary with no real reply. Although Sharett banned Brand from leaving for Palestine, this ban was based upon a mistaken assumption that Brand could remain in Turkey for the time being. It would therefore appear that the emissaries' and Brand's decision to ignore Sharett's ban and to leave for Syria was correct.

Nonetheless, Barlas, Avriel, Schind, Bader, and others shared Sharett's fear of a British trap: Brand would be arrested, the mission would be foiled by Britain, and the British could breathe a sigh of relief at having their worst fear—a million Jews clamoring to enter Palestine or the Western states—dissolve. Wishing to prevent Brand's arrest or delay, with the excuse that he had seen secret military installations, or had gained wind of other secrets, the emissaries proposed to the British that Brand meet Sharett in Aleppo, close to the Syrian/Turkish border. British agents in Istanbul checked the information and agreed to this arrangement. Sharett, too, received similar approval from the Mandatory government's secretary general in Jerusalem and from Brigadier R. G. Maunsel, head of British military intelligence in the Middle East.[42]

Sharett reported to the JAE on 4 June 1944 on the failure to obtain a visa to enter Turkey. He said that he was warned not to try to enter without a visa and declared that the Mandatory government had "made extraordinary efforts" to arrange his journey. The Turkish consul in Palestine also tried his luck, with no success. Sharett explained that there was momentary confusion in Jerusalem, where it was believed that Brand was returning to Hungary. (It must have become known that Turkey had decided to deport Brand and Grosz.) It later transpired that Brand was about to travel east. At first it was thought he would come to Palestine, but now there was to be a meeting in Aleppo. Sharett said that Brand would set off for Aleppo the following day, and he did not know if his return to Turkey was assured. (Sharett feared that Brand might not be allowed to return.)

It is important to note that the Yishuv leadership remained in the dark at the time, which is why I have presented the indeterminate situation surrounding Brand's plans in great detail, that is, in order to reflect the way in which the JAE in Jerusalem became aware of all events. In time it would be alleged that the JAE jointly conspired with the British to thwart Brand's mission—Brand himself alleged this in one of his testimonies—but the historical documentation utterly refutes these allegations.

At that same meeting Gruenbaum, the Rescue Committee chairman, hinted at his predicament: he was obliged to hide the entire affair from his fellow committee members for about twenty days and yet had to counter the allegation that nothing was being done to rescue the Jews of Hungary. Ben-Gurion replied that he was leaving it up to Gruenbaum whether or not to tell the committee about Brand's mission.[43]

On 5 June Brand and Avriel set off for Aleppo on the Taurus Express, the trans-Turkey railway. Several hours before their departure, they again feared a British double-cross. These fears heightened the already charged atmosphere during a passport control check on the way out of Turkey, leading them to suspect that the British were "waiting" for Brand.[44] Sharett set off on the same day for the meeting with Brand in Aleppo. He was joined by Meirov, Zaslani and Schechter. Sharett was buoyed by fresh promises from the high commissioner and Brigadier Maunsel that he would be allowed to meet with Brand.

As promised, Brand was indeed permitted to disembark at Aleppo. But, in violation of all promises, he was immediately arrested and hidden by British intelligence services. Zaslani, who actually headed the Political Department's secret operations, tried to make use of his ties in the intelligence services to locate those responsible for Brand's arrest and to arrange for the meeting to take place after all. Several days of feverish activity—with letters, cables, and telephone calls being sent by Zaslani and Sharett—came to an end on 10 June when instructions arrived from the British Foreign Office to allow the meeting between Sharett and Brand to take place.[45]

WASHINGTON AND LONDON: HOW NOT TO GET MIXED UP IN THE AFFAIR

Information concerning the Brand plan was transferred to London and the United States through two main channels: intelligence and diplomatic personnel in Turkey and the high commissioner's office in Jerusalem. While efforts were being made in Palestine to hear Brand's proposal firsthand, the British government in London began to discuss the plan's consequences at the end of May 1944.[46]

A typical response is the opinion of Robert M. A. Hankey of the Foreign Office's Eastern Department. Hankey declared that it was a dubious proposal, a trick, part of Germany's political warfare; it was clear to them, after all, that it would not be possible to transfer a million Jews from eastern Europe by way of France to Spain and Portugal without upsetting the course of the war on the western front. Such an operation would strain Britain's relations with Spain and Portugal, upset supplies there, and would require the allocation of ships for the transportation of refugees and food supplies across the Mediterranean and the Atlantic—all at the expense of the war. The handover of large numbers of trucks would seriously hamper the Allied forces' transportation needs in the course of the war.

Hankey assumed that the Brand plan would damage Britain's relations with the Arabs. The introduction of large numbers of Jews into the Middle East would lead to a further source of friction, rioting would break out, and Britain would be obliged to divert army divisions to the area instead of using them to fight the war. He also mentioned the potential precedent of giving in to the extortionate demands of the enemy, which might be followed by similar demands on the part of the Poles, French, Dutch, and others. His recommendations were unambiguous: "The Foreign Office will respond that we are unwilling to discuss a proposal such as this through such channels, and everything possible has already been done in order to prevent the extermination of Jews and the other nations subject to German rule. . . ." He even recommended denying Ben-Gurion's request to pass along details of the plan to Weizmann and Goldmann.[47]

The main points of Hankey's opinion were accepted at an urgent meeting of the British Ministerial Committee on Refugee Affairs on 31 May. Participating at that meeting were: Anthony Eden, secretary of state for foreign affairs (for most of it); Stanley, the colonial secretary; and Lord Selborne, the minister for economic warfare, who was also responsible for part of the British espionage system; George Hall, under-secretary of state; and Alec Randall, head of the Foreign Office's Refugees' Department. The committee decided to refrain from discussing the German proposal, which was "no more than another, more sophisticated, form of war against the Allies."

The reasons given reiterated Hankey's for the most part. The committee's conclusions also claimed that such a proposal could lead to a similar one that "would burden Britain with an even larger number of Jews." Britain was not in a position to alter its immigration quotas if, after a while, Spain and Portugal proved unable to contain so many Jews, and evacuation through Turkey was liable to cause pressure for increased immigration certificates to Palestine "in an especially critical period."[48]

The following day these conclusions were presented to the War Cabinet. Churchill and the cabinet members approved them. Thus, a few

days after reaching London, the Eichmann proposal was discussed and rejected at the highest government levels. The sting of rejection was not dulled by the following clause, added by the cabinet members: "The British government will do its best to care for small groups of Jews that Germany is willing to release, if this does not interfere with military preparations."[49]

It is worth dwelling on the supposedly moderating condition attached to the clause. It expressed one of the principles that governed the management of the war, namely, that there should be no splitting of the main effort. As far as the Germans were concerned, they could not have chosen a better time for making deals— if they actually had any intention of honoring them. Discussions on the proposal were conducted a week or two before the Normandy landings and in the midst of the huge Soviet spring attack. This is the background to the cabinet's mention of war preparations.[50]

The decision in London largely explains events in Istanbul, Ankara, Aleppo, and Jerusalem. There were people in British intelligence circles and within the political hierarchy who deliberately misled Ben-Gurion, Sharett, and the emissaries by informing them that the issue was being seriously considered when it was already clear that the proposal would be rejected.

Details of Brand's plan were ultimately passed on to Weizmann and Goldmann despite recommendation to refrain from doing so. The British probably realized that it would reach them one way or another, and withholding it would only increase the bitterness of the Jews and their supporters. On 5 June Randall and Hall delivered details of the proposal to Weizmann, and on 7 June Weizmann met with Eden and asked him to arrange an urgent visit for Sharett in London and not to reject the proposal out of hand.

Weizmann promised Eden that the Jewish Agency would do nothing on the matter without the knowledge and agreement of the British government. It was a far-reaching promise similar to the one Weizmann gave during discussions of the Transnistria Plan. This time, too, Weizmann hinted that the Zionist movement would not try to take advantage of concessions aimed at advancing rescue operations by turning them into precedents in its political discourse with Britain. Eden promised Weizmann that the "door would remain open." He may have taken into consideration the possibility that the Americans might wish to examine the proposal.[51]

The British Foreign Office passed the Nazi proposal on to the United States, together with the War Cabinet's reservations. On 3 June Eden approved the text of the cable sent to Lord Halifax, Britain's ambassador to the United States. The latter showed the cable to Edward Stettinius Jr., acting U.S. undersecretary of state, including the stipulation that Britain would not enter into any negotiations based on the proposal, which was a "monstrous proposal . . . part of an overall system. . . ." Halifax advised the Americans not to give Weizmann a clearly defined response before the position of the Allies was clarified and to warn him against independent negotiations with the enemy. He promised that the British government would not "close the door" to any honest proposal for rescuing Jews.[52]

The Americans had known of the plan as soon Brand arrived in Istanbul. Barlas had rushed to pass on the main details to Laurence Steinhardt, the U.S. ambassador to Turkey, and even asked him for help in passing the information on to Jerusalem. Steinhardt had instructed Pinkerton, the U.S. consul in Jerusalem, to pass the information on to the JAE's Political Department, and he himself made sure it reached Washington.

Grosz, who had arrived with Brand, was an old acquaintance of the Americans, who had handled him directly through the Dogwood network. It will be recalled that Kollek himself served as an intermediary between them and Grosz. When Grosz arrived in Istanbul, he informed his contacts in American intelligence of the main points of the message from the Nazis and provided his own evaluation. Grosz was aware that the ground was beginning to give way and made sure to rescue his wife, who was with him in Istanbul.

Grosz also reported to the British on his mission. He asked them to get him out of Turkey, which they agreed to do. They were no doubt interested in interrogating him regarding his activity on behalf of the Germans and their satellites. A few days before Brand departed for Aleppo, they sent Grosz east and then south in order to arrest and interrogate him upon his arrival in their territory.

Thus, no secrets were hidden from the British and Americans at this stage of the affair. They had information from various sources, which reached them at about the same time it reached the Yishuv in Palestine, its emissaries in Istanbul, and its leadership in Jerusalem. Information was also sent to Washington, where discussions commenced immediately to map out an American position.[53]

Dr. Goldmann, the Jewish Agency's U.S. representative, received information on the affair by way of the Yishuv's communication channels and started promoting it. He tried to persuade Stettinius to support a reply to the Nazis that would give the impression that their proposal was receiving serious consideration. This kind of response arrived from John Pehle, executive director of the War Refugee Board, who met with President Roosevelt and persuaded him that it was imperative to create an illusion of progress.

This set in motion a series of conflicting gestures on the part of the Americans. Although the impression was conveyed that negotiations with the Germans were under serious consideration, there was no real basis for this belief. For example, Roosevelt agreed that Ira Hirschmann, a representative of the WRB, immediately be sent to meet Brand in Istanbul, thus signaling to the Germans that the Americans were willing to discuss their proposal, but it was made very clear to

Hirschmann that he was not authorized to conduct any negotiations. To take another example, on 10 June instructions were cabled to Steinhardt that "all efforts must be made to persuade the Germans that this government [U.S.] is quite concerned by this problem and is willing to evaluate real proposals aimed at rescuing Jews," but Steinhardt was told that he was not to agree to Brand's proposal except after "consultations with the British government and with that of the Soviet Union."[54]

The U.S. administration instructed Averell Harriman, its ambassador to the USSR, to report the details of the proposal to the Soviets and the U.S. position on it, but it also told him to stress that nothing had been decided and that any action would be taken only after consultations and agreements of the three superpowers. The essence of this position was also cabled to London on 19 June: the proposal should not to be rejected out of hand, since it may be the forerunner of other, more feasible proposals. Since mere negotiations might delay the extermination process, the U.S. was prepared to promise the Germans that the Allies would provide temporary asylum to any Jew who was released.[55]

If one were to compare Britain and the United States in terms of their willingness to create an illusion that the proposal was being given serious consideration—and, by doing so, to buy time—it would appear that the United States was superficially more willing than Britain. However, it is worth remembering that the United States wasted no time in informing the USSR of the proposal, and that by doing so the plan might come to naught.[56]

It is possible that the interim position that emerged from American decision-making circles was what softened Britain's position and persuaded it to permit the meeting between Sharett and Brand, who had "disappeared" in Aleppo. Britain did not go back on its rejection of Eichmann's proposal, but it may have sensed the atmosphere in the United States on the eve of the presidential election, in which Roosevelt would be returned to office for the fourth time. The British realized that this was not the time for them to be the sole naysayer, opposing a plan that would almost certainly collapse for a myriad of reasons and not necessarily because of Britain's objections. They therefore moderated their policy to some extent and preferred to present a united front with the United States.[57]

THE MEETING IN ALEPPO: A TURNING POINT IN UNDERSTANDING THE PROPOSAL

To return to the meeting in Aleppo, the following senior Yishuv staff involved in secret activity had left for the Syrian town: Sharett; Meirov, who headed the illegal immigration operation; Zaslani, who was responsible for the Political Department's secret activity, including secret ties with Britain; and Schechter, who was in charge of preparing the parachutists at the time. The senior status of the representatives is additional proof of the importance attached to this meeting. The composition of the delegation, which included senior political officials and heads of the professional units, made it possible for the delegation to examine the new information and decide what to do with it on the spot.[58]

After several tense days of waiting, Sharett met Brand on 11 June. A German-speaking British officer was present at the meeting, which lasted about six hours, and Schechter recorded the minutes. This meeting was followed by several others, lasting an additional twelve hours.[59] Brand described at length the various stages of negotiations with the Nazis in Budapest before he and Grosz set off for Istanbul. He summarized the situation of Hungary's Jews and discussed plans for self-defense.

The Yishuv team returned to Palestine following talks with Brand, who continued to be held prisoner by the British in blatant defiance of their earlier promises. They took him by way of Palestine to a prison in Cairo, where they interrogated him for several months. Grosz was already locked up in a Cairo jail.

Ben-Gurion and the rest of the JAE were given the minutes of the talks with Brand in Aleppo. They also received a report on the talks at a special meeting at Ben-Gurion's home on 14 June.[60] Information on Grosz's real mission constituted the main new information obtained by Sharett in Aleppo, but before examining it I wish to dwell on Brand's report of negotiations with the Nazis.

The report revealed the names of other Nazis who participated in the negotiations from the very beginning until Brand left for Istanbul. Brand and the Sharett team did not know for certain the true identities and importance of these Nazis since they were unfamiliar with the hierarchical yet anarchic organizational structure of the Nazi regime.

Among the names mentioned by Brand in Aleppo were Dr. Josef Schmidt, who, according to Brand, belonged to a German military institution in Budapest (we now know that he was a member of the Abwehr); Gerhard Clages, described by Brand as a member of the SS in Budapest under Eichmann (he was commander of the SD in Budapest, which handled SS security services, and headed Unit F); Hermann Krumey, likewise an SS man under Eichmann's command.[61]

According to Brand, another man by the name of Schröder took part in the negotiations. Brand added that this was not his real name, which he was forbidden to disclose. Schröder was none other than Fritz Frantisek Laufer, alias "Iris" of the Dogwood network. It will be recalled that Laufer was a Prague-born Jew, an agent of the Abwehr, and one of the couriers that Kollek and his men, as well as Schwartz-Dogwood, handled out of Istanbul. Laufer had been in Istanbul in 1941 and became familiar with the emissaries during 1943. He carried out his first mission for Kollek shortly after the latter's arrival in Istanbul in late spring and early

summer 1943. And here he was, a senior member of a group of Nazis negotiating with the Hungarian Aid and Rescue Committee.

His real handlers, the Abwehr, had sent him to the Americans in Istanbul with a proposal to exchange Jews for trucks. Schröder was a slippery character. He had other names as well, such as Ludwig Mayer and Karl Heinz. The Sharett team was unable to distinguish between Schröder, a key personality in the SS team (not the Abwehr) in Budapest, and the courier Laufer, who served them and the Dogwood network and was exposed as an Abwehr agent who had previously infiltrated the Czech underground.[62]

Brand believed that Schröder, together with Clages, was primarily involved in the commercial aspects of the negotiations in Hungary. At the time of Sharett's talks with Brand, it was not possible to correctly determine the jobs of each of the Nazi counterparts of the Aid and Rescue Committee, a situation that remained relatively unchanged even later. We now know that Clages was in charge of the intelligence rather than the commercial side of the affair.[63]

The invasion of Hungary was already being felt in the air a week before it took place—so Brand told Sharett—and members of the Aid and Rescue Committee in Budapest began establishing ties with the SS group under the command of Wisliceny. They were working under the assumption that Wisliceny had "deferred the deportation of Slovakian Jews in return for large sums of money." He also had in his possession letters of recommendation from the Slovakian Working Group. Brand and his colleagues wanted to interest Wisliceny in a ransom plan for Hungarian Jews, but these first feelers were unsuccessful.[64]

Brand was arrested the same day the Germans invaded Hungary. He believed the arrest was carried out by Schmidt, who headed what Brand thought was the Abwehr in Budapest. The arrest was apparently aimed at preventing the Aid and Rescue Committee from forming ties with other elements within the German camp and to supply the Abwehr group in Budapest with a good source of intelligence deals and easy money. Brand barely touched on the complex relations between all the parties involved, but he was unable to describe their significance.

Brand was released on the third day of his imprisonment. Several days later (24 March) he and Israel Kasztner, succeeded in meeting Wisliceny. Kasztner was a subchairman of the Aid and Rescue Committee in Budapest (the chairman was Otto Komoly). This meeting was also attended by Schmidt and several SS men, one of whom was Kurt Becher. Kasztner and Brand asked the Germans to halt the executions of Jewish prisoners and asked for a German commitment to end the ghettoization and deportations and permit the immigration to other countries of those Jews with entry certificates.

Wisliceny was generous enough to accept a cash deposit of two hundred thousand dollars in Hungarian currency. Two million dollars appeared to him too small a sum for the entire transaction. The Jews were worth more, so he said, and the sum would not be sufficient to pay for all the Jews able to escape extermination—in other words, not only the Jews of Hungary but also those of the Balkans. He was sure that negotiations could be conducted to save the lives of about two million Jews.

Wisliceny was prepared to promise that there would be no exterminations. "The current German system," he said, "is not to kill Jews but to exploit their labor power." Deportations to the camps in Poland depended solely on the Germans and not on any local factor, and the Germans were not interested in deporting Jews from Hungary at that time. He was prepared to promise that there would be no concentration of Jews in ghettos or camps, but this promise did not include Jews from rural areas who were being concentrated in larger towns. He said that the Germans were interested in the large-scale emigration of from 150,000 to 160,000 Jews and asked for a practical program.[65]

Kasztner and Brand jumped at this and presented a proposal for the emigration of an equal number of Jews to Palestine. They arrived at this figure by manipulating the remaining immigration certificates from the White Paper quota in the possession of the Jewish Agency. Around 30,000 were left over, which were identified as intended for heads of families and multiplied by 5 people within each family.[66] Kasztner and Brand also asked that an additional 750 people be allowed to leave Romania, since a ship was anchored in Constanța that could take them to Turkey.

NEGOTIATIONS WITH EICHMANN

Brand told Sharett and his team in Aleppo that there would be another meeting a few days later. Wisliceny said that his superiors would permit the exit of 750 people, as requested. He handed over money and letters from Nathan Schwalb, the Hehalutz representative in Geneva. His men had confiscated them and he was delivering them unopened to their intended recipient as a symbol of his and his superiors' willingness to cooperate.

This was, of course, a baseless lie. While negotiations were being conducted, rural Jews were being rounded up in camps. In the larger towns Jews were forced into ghettos. Basing their complaints on Wisliceny's promises, the representatives of the Jews lodged a formal protest. His reply was that the Hungarians were responsible for this cruelty, not the Germans.[67]

Toward the end of April the rank of Nazis involved in the negotiations rose when Eichmann took over as chief negotiator and the ransom price went up. He was assisted by Krumey, Clages, and Edmund Veesenmayer, the new German minister plenipotentiary of the Reich. According to available documentation, this change was pivotal in the SS's attempt to undermine the Abwehr group.

Brand attended the first of four meetings with Eichmann. (We now know that in his reports Brand mixed up the order and contents of the meetings.) He told Sharett that Eichmann had told him that he was willing to give him "all the Jews" and added that he understood that Brand and his handlers would want "the young Jews first of all, the men and women who could give birth to children."

That meeting and the ones following produced an even clearer picture of what Brand described as a "satanic plan that could have bared the excuse to the justification to the world for the swift annihilation of the remaining Jews of Europe." The ten thousand trucks that Eichmann demanded were meant to replace the SS fleet, whose heavy transport vehicles were in dire need of repair. Upon his return from Germany, Eichmann took the trouble to emphasize that he had visited Berlin and Berchtesgaden, Hitler's highly guarded country residence, where his ransom proposal was approved at the highest levels.

The talks with Eichmann also clarified the reasons for determining the destinations to which the released Jews were to be sent: Spain, Portugal, or North Africa (west of Tunisia), but not Palestine. First, the SS assumed that Turkey would not permit the transit of so many Jews across its territories. Second, the Germans did not wish to annoy the Arabs with so large a wave of Jewish immigration. Third, having no desire to establish an overly strong Jewish Yishuv and wishing to prevent a concentration of Jews in Palestine, where they could become a strong and consolidated force, they warned: "If you establish a large force in Palestine, then in a given matter of time we shall be in conflict with you again." Fourth, since the SS believed that the Jews were a malignant plague, by dispersing them in countries belonging to the Allies they hoped to infect their enemies with the plague.

Eichmann told his Zionist counterparts that as far as he was concerned it would not be a tragedy if, for military reasons, one or two ships arrived at the coast of Palestine, but that "on the whole the flow of migration should not be directed at Palestine." He entrusted the Jews themselves with arranging visas to their destined countries, since "they are in control of the whole world and all the American senators leap to carry out their orders," so "they won't have any trouble obtaining entry permits." Eichmann also touched on the issue of transportation, stressing that the Germans were arranging necessary transport for concentrating Jews in transit camps in Germany, "so as to turn them into German merchandise," from which they would then be transferred, by way of France, to Spain or Portugal.

Eichmann himself even permitted the representative of the Aid and Rescue Committee to leave for Switzerland or Turkey in order to get the proposal off the ground. He refused Brand's request to stop deportations while negotiations were being conducted. These continued in full force, twelve thousand people a day, in order to pressure the Jews into speeding up negotiations.

Only afterward did Krumey promise that none of the deportees would be killed until Brand's return to Hungary. He also promised that deportations to the camps would cease as soon as news arrived of the real chance of Jewish support for the plan. At such time Jews would begin being transferred to transit camps in Germany, where emigrants would be chosen. Krumey also promised to release all Jews trapped in Germany and the rest of Europe at that time.[68]

MAIN OBJECTIVE: A SEPARATE PEACE WITH THE WEST

The main novelty in Brand's testimony in Aleppo consisted of information on Grosz's mission.[69] The JAE was now faced with a much more complex picture than they had at first anticipated, although the information they received was still neither accurate nor complete. They were gradually being made aware of the labyrinthine structure of the Nazi and Hungarian authorities. Even before the invasion, ties had existed between the Hungarians and a German group within Hungary (we now know that this was the Abwehr) under the tyrannical, pro-German government. Other ties were also maintained with Hungarian military offices. In both cases the name of the contact person was the same: Bandi Grosz.

Brand described Grosz to Sharett and his team in Aleppo as being a man with connections within the Hungarian establishment as well as with the Nazis, especially with Clages and Schröder. Brand believed that Grosz was sent to accompany him in order to hide the real objective of his journey. He did not know at first what Grosz's real task was, but various signs led him to believe that it was something beyond mere chaperoning. Grosz's mission gradually became clearer while they were waiting to be interrogated in Istanbul. Apparently Grosz had been entrusted with establishing a "connection between American and British institutions and certain German institutions on the matter of conditions for peace."[70]

Based on this assumption, said Brand, the proposal sparing Jewish lives in return for trucks, merchandise, and/or money merely camouflaged Grosz's mission and provided an excuse for beginning negotiations between Nazi Germany and the West. The ransom plan was aimed at proving to the United States and Britain that certain groups in Germany were willing to change direction on the Jewish issue, but the main objective of these groups was to bring about an end to the war between Nazi Germany and the Western powers.

Signals such as these had already been received in the past. Franz von Papen, former prime minister, German ambassador to Turkey, and one of the leaders of the conservative opposition to Hitler, had long been pointing in this direction. Hatz and Schröder had also offered such proposals. This time the signal came from within the Nazis' inner circle, from senior SS and SD officers, but it is hard to know how far the Yishuv team was able to distinguish among the various groups. The tendency was to apply the term "Gestapo" to all of Germany's undercover organizations.[71]

Sharett thoroughly interrogated Brand in Aleppo, as did other members of his team.[72]

Among other things, Brand was asked if he believed the Germans were serious about their ransom proposal. He said he was not absolutely sure, but he assumed that the goods were very necessary to them; according to his evaluation, some or all members of Eichmann's group were trying to obtain an alibi for themselves for the end of the war and they may even have been trying to gain some points for Germany as a whole. The Nazis treated Brand as if he were a "very important person," and the attention they lavished on him was one of the things that testified to the seriousness of their proposal.

Sharett's team asked Brand his opinion as to what could be anticipated in three cases: his return to Hungary with a positive reply; his return with a negative reply; or his nonreturn to Hungary. Brand replied that after learning of the political aspect of the plan—Grosz's part in the mission—the reply was made much more complicated. If he were not to return at all, he expected that all his friends and most of his family would be murdered. The few who were spared would be held for ransom, "victims of the evil Brand who deserted them to save his own skin." If he returned with a negative reply, he had no doubt that "the immediate annihilation of the Jews of the Balkans would begin."[73]

He replied positively to the question of whether the Eichmann group could carry out such an emigration program with the agreement of the "top brass in Germany." Still, he believed that Eichmann and his people would need the approval of Himmler and perhaps Hitler himself. Indeed, Eichmann had already told him that he had discussed the matter at the highest government levels during a visit to Berlin and Berchtesgaden.

Brand was also asked about the possibility of money being substituted for merchandise. He pointed out that such a possibility had been raised and that various kinds of currency had been mentioned. As for the kinds of Jews the Nazis were willing to release, Brand informed

Eichmann that he could not decide this issue; he was not prepared to desert any single group of Jews and was interested in taking them all. He added that in the meantime he had learned—from an agreed upon signal from his wife—that the deportations had ceased.

Brand recounted how Hungary's Jews were preparing to defend themselves and described their underground, which was led by Moshe Schweiger. His replies to Sharett's questions on these issues were detailed and to the point. Sharett, Meirov, Zaslani, and Schechter were in need of this information since they were preparing a plan to help protect the Jews of Hungary and the Balkans, having even approached Tito to this end.[74]

Sharett and his team wanted to know how to give the Nazis the impression that their proposal was being considered seriously. They also wanted Brand's evaluation of Germany's reaction if the United States demand the release of the Jews. Brand replied that such a demand could be beneficial. They also asked for a cable to be sent periodically to his wife in Budapest to prove that negotiations were being conducted. Brand said that if he went back with positive signs of possible separate negotiations with the West, feeble though these might be, this would demonstrate to the Eichmann group that it was worth taking him seriously and it would grasp at the opportunity.[75]

Upon Sharett's return, the previously mentioned special meeting was convened in Ben-Gurion's home.[76] Ben-Gurion conducted the meeting and allowed Sharett to speak first. Sharett repeated in detail what he had heard from Brand in Aleppo and emphasized the main points: "The matter is more complicated and complex than we had foreseen. It became even more complex with the intervention of the [British] authorities." He told them that his impression was that the proposal to release Jews was no more than a small piece of bait dangled by the Gestapo in order for them to arrange meetings

with the United States and Britain, where they could discuss "other issues altogether"—an attempt to arrive at a separate peace agreement with the West. "There is no doubt" said Sharett "that Brand's companion [Grosz] revealed the entire mission to the British."[77]

At the end of the debate, Sharett recommended the following course of action: to prevent the British from claiming that the main objective in Eichmann's proposal was "separate peace talks with the Nazis" and thereby extricate themselves from Brand's plan; to stress "the possibility of rescuing Jews and to put off deportation without making any commitment"; to attempt to increase the number of those willing to support a plan for "purchasing Jews." Sharett proposed asking Sir Herbert Emerson, chairman of the Inter-Governmental Committee on Refugees (IGCR), to have his organization negotiate the ransom plan with the Germans in a neutral country. Sharett also recommended doing everything possible to get Brand back to Hungary, to report to the high commissioner on the talks in Aleppo, and to send a JAE representative to Cairo and from there to London, where negotiations could be held with British and American leaders.

The JAE did not discuss Sharett's report and recommendations, which seems puzzling. It learned for the first time that, as far as the Nazis were concerned, the message they sent with Grosz about their desire for a separate peace was the main one and not the ransom proposal. Why, then, did no debate take place? Were most of the members too shocked to react? Given the complexities and failures of the Slovakia and Transnistria plans, this seems unlikely. Perhaps the minutes do not reflect the JAE's real feelings.[78]

No documents exist that might provide answers to these questions. The fact remains that after Sharett's report, only Kaplan and Ben-Gurion gave short speeches. Kaplan announced that Weizmann had met Eden. He supported Sharett's recommendation to report to the high commissioner on the talks in Aleppo and to send a JAE representative to Cairo. Ben-Gurion uttered a single sentence: "The main thing now is to visit London." The minutes makes no mention of a debate or a vote on other parts of the report. According to available records, the JAE simply voted on the proposal to report to the high commissioner; there was no preliminary debate.[79]

A "COMPLETELY SUPERFLUOUS" WARNING BY THE HIGH COMMISSIONER

The following day (15 June) Ben-Gurion and Sharett held an urgent meeting with Mac-Michael, the high commissioner of Palestine. The high level of the consultations and the fact that Ben-Gurion and Sharett were in such a hurry to meet with MacMichael again signaled to Britain that the JAE attached supreme importance to the ransom proposal. The meeting was as long as its predecessor had been.[80] Sharett related to the high commissioner all that he had heard in Aleppo. He stressed Brand's reliability and the emissary's impression that the Eichmann plan was a "serious proposal by high-ranking Nazis,"[81] a result both of Germany's real need for the goods and its need for an alibi, based on the assumption that "if they prevent the murder of another two million, they would be exonerated of the murder of six [million]."

Sharett also passed along to MacMichael the Nazis' unambiguous demand that Jewish refugees would not come to Palestine. He probably chose to expand on this point in order to reassure the British that Palestine would not be flooded with Jews. Sharett told the high commissioner of Eichmann's promise that children and old people rather than young people and potential fighters for Zionist objectives in Palestine would be the first to be released.

Sharett demanded that Britain and the United States discuss the Brand proposal with the Nazis and suggested employing Emerson for this purpose because his committee's activity did not obligate any particular government. Emerson's involvement in the negotiations would not constitute accepted agreement for the concept of a separate peace between the Germans and the Allies.[82] Alternatively, Sharett suggested making use of the International Red Cross or the American War Refugee Board, whose rules permitted direct contact with the enemy.

If these possibilities were unworkable, said Sharett, he believed that the governments of Britain and the United States would know how to organize such a meeting. He issued a firm demand that Brand, who was imprisoned in Cairo, be allowed to return to Hungary, as had been promised to Sharett himself; otherwise the Germans would assume that their proposal was rejected and continue to murder the remaining Jews remaining of Europe. Sharett asked that Weizmann, in London, be given the high commissioner's report and that his own urgent visit to London be scheduled immediately.

MacMichael listened carefully to Sharett, although in some places he seemed impatient. When Sharett mentioned the promise to Brand that he would be allowed to return to Hungary, MacMichael reminded him that "this is wartime" and that Sharett should "not impose too many complaints." The high commissioner went out of his way to stress that "Sharett made no mention of the fact that this plan was part of an organized campaign against us, aimed at embarrassing us."

In his report to London, MacMichael pointed out that he had decided against mentioning the connection between the Eichmann proposal and the Nazis' inclination to detach the Soviets from Britain and the United States, thereby isolating them as Europe's new enemy. He substantiated this by saying that Sharett did not even raise this point in his report on the Aleppo meeting. He stressed Sharett's opinion with regard to the urgent and immediate need to examine Eichmann's proposal and to halt the murder of Jews by giving the Nazis the impression that the Allies were giving the proposal serious consideration.

MacMichael wrote that Ben-Gurion supported his assessment that the entire proposal was solely aimed at extorting money from the Allies and embarrassing them. He pointed out that, like Weizmann (according to information from London), Ben-Gurion did not even hesitate to suggest that the proposal was only a "trick," although Sharett avoided such an assessment. MacMichael was also impressed that Ben-Gurion was dissatisfied with Sharett's report on the talks in Aleppo, noting that he became

> a little restive at Shertok's rather tendentious cleverness in dealing with each aspect of the matter in turn, then took charge of the conversation and spoke with obvious sincerity, dignity and appreciation of the dangers. He said that there were probably things which I could now tell them and he hoped that I would do so. For the rest, if there was anything which could humanly be done in such a way as not to be of any advantage to the enemy or prejudice the war effort he pleaded that it should be done.

The high commissioner promised to pass on all the requests to London and asked the Jewish Agency leaders to bring to his notice their decisions regarding the affair. In response to Ben-Gurion's request for information, MacMichael said that he could pass along only what the British ambassador in Ankara ordered him to give to Sharett, were he to go there. At the end of the meeting MacMichael warned Ben-Gurion and Sharett against associating with the enemy. Ben-Gurion remarked that the warning was "absolutely superfluous."[83]

"A CLEAR OPINION IS ESSENTIAL FROM ALL THE MEMBERS"

At the weekly JAE meeting three days later, Ben-Gurion and Sharett reported on their last meeting with the high commissioner and a heated debate took place. Things that had been suppressed at the previous meeting at Ben-Gurion's home surfaced at this one, which was marked by anger and pain and feelings of helplessness and frustration.

After Sharett had reported on the meeting and the subjects discussed, discussion shifted to other topics. Much attention was devoted to the issue of whether it had been wise to pass along information to the British on the Eichmann proposal. Most of the speakers were in favor of this action. For example, Dr. Emil Schmorak said, "I still think that contacting the high commissioner and handing over the information was the right thing to do." He held this view despite the danger that the JAE might be accused of thwarting the mission because of the emissary's nonreturn to Hungary, and would consequently be held responsible for the annihilation of Hungary's Jews.[84]

Shapira and Kaplan discussed the role played in history by the supernatural. "It was a miracle that we did not hide the fact of the emissary from the government," said Shapira. Expressing similar sentiments, Kaplan added, "We are lucky to have chosen the correct path and immediately reported the matter to the government." They both agreed that had the matter reached the British by any other means—and there was no doubt that it would have, since "there is a second emissary [Grosz], who told the British everything"—both the mission and the Yishuv would have "suffered badly."

At first Gruenbaum rejected the proposal to report to Britain on Brand's mission. Steadfastly maintaining his position, he added with bitterness, "I do not believe the governments on matters of rescue." He said that the British had no intention of helping in the rescue of Jews, and that all their actions thus far proved this. They would take advantage of any information they received in order to thwart the plan. In the end, the debate was a hollow exercise, since the Eichmann proposal was already known to the British from their own sources.

Another question considered was whether the British should be required to allow Brand to return to Hungary, as they had promised, and whether it was appropriate to force him to return against his will. Schmorak believed that, because the Jewish Agency was intimately involved in bringing Brand to Aleppo, it should be responsible for his safe return; otherwise it would be blamed for thwarting his mission. Kaplan agreed with Ben-Gurion and others that "the only person able to decide on this is the emissary himself," and that the JAE had to "help him carry out his decision." He was relying on recently received information from Istanbul and assumed that Grosz, who was being held prisoner in Cairo, would not want to return to Hungary. Kaplan had already uncovered Grosz's shady personality when he was in Istanbul in 1943, and even more dedicated characters than Grosz would not have been in a hurry to risk returning to the Nazis empty-handed, with no indication of success.

Shapira believed that it had been a mistake to remove Brand from neutral Turkey to a British-controlled zone in Syria, which he felt was the result of the emissaries' inexperience. Brand was surely aware of what awaited him upon his return to Hungary. It was therefore better to leave the decision to him. Shapira shared Kaplan's opinion that Grosz had no plans to return. Shapira's criticism of the emissaries was unfounded, since Brand could not have stayed in Turkey, where he was under threat of deportation, and the alternative to being taken to a British-controlled zone was deportation to a region under German jurisdiction. Brand's journey to Syria was not a naive act. The emissaries considered the possibility that the British proposal to bring Brand to Syria was a trap and decided to adopt it only after it became clear that Sharett was unable to come to Turkey. With no meeting between Sharett and Brand, and with no authorized reply from the Yishuv, there was no point in returning Brand to Hungary.[85]

Joseph insisted on Brand's return but feared his execution or his exploitation for "other matters" (most likely espionage or propaganda).

Sharett said that Brand had expressed his willingness to return even if this meant his own death; he still hoped he would be able to save Jewish lives. Sharett added that Brand's return without Grosz would harm his reliability and influence. This may have been based on the assessment that the willingness of several Nazi groups to grasp at the straw of a "separate peace" with the West was behind the proposal that the latter purchase the lives of Jews. Grosz's return with no British response would remove the reason to prefer the sale of Jews over their murder.

Gruenbaum was doubtful that the British would agree to return Brand, and even insisted that, once the emissary was taken to Cairo, there was no point in demanding his return, since "his return meant—certain death." He said that in Brand's place "I would not have left Hungary, so long as the deportations had not ceased." It was clear that he had no understanding of how miserable was the situation of Joel Brand and his counterparts in Hungary. Nonetheless, Gruenbaum agreed that it was up to Brand himself to decide if he wanted to return.

The participants at the meeting discussed the most suitable framework to conduct negotiations. Three possibilities were repeated: negotiations could be conducted by Emerson or someone on his behalf; a Red Cross representative; or a representative of the American War Refugee Board in Istanbul, Geneva, or Stockholm. (In Stockholm feelers were also being sent out to determine the possibility of separate negotiations with the West.) Gruenbaum was also opposed to the Yishuv's tendency to allow Britain and the United States to serve as go-betweens. He wanted a British government official to conduct negotiations on ransoming the Jews. Moreover, he insisted that all negotiations with the Nazis were dependent on an immediate halt to deportations.

Ben-Gurion reminded the speakers that the subject was "grave and bitter" and that "a clear opinion is essential from all the members." The JAE members were asked to engage in soul-searching and to make difficult decisions. He added a few details on the meeting with the high commissioner, outlined his own evaluations, and asked for the opinions of his colleagues.

Ben-Gurion decided that the main negotiations would take place in London, not Jerusalem or Cairo, and that it was imperative that Sharett leave immediately. In Jerusalem and Cairo the main issue involved matters "connected with the war" and cooperation with the Yishuv focused only on intelligence and operations. London, on the other hand, was where matters of state were discussed, and there was a good chance that the ransom plan might be given greater consideration there. Ben-Gurion told his colleagues that Sharett was needed in London, if only to provide support to the London branch of the JAE.

These facts are important in light of the bitter debates that took place years later concerning the position taken by the JAE on the rescue issue in general and Brand's mission in particular. If Ben-Gurion and his colleagues were seeking a way of extricating themselves from Brand's proposal, why was Ben-Gurion eager to have Sharett travel to London in order to break the stalemate?

On the matter of Brand's return, Ben-Gurion made the question even more pointed. He said that if the British were to allow Brand to return, he would indeed do so and could expect "death through horrible torture." It was worth remembering that the emissary was fully aware of the nature of his mission and what he could expect if he failed, and the question he faced concerned "the rescue of his nation, not only that of his wife and children." Thus, "we would not tell him to go or to remain, but we shall help him to return, since he insists on this," and this had to be done "even without knowing if this act of ours was useful or not."

Ben-Gurion rejected all preliminary conditions to beginning negotiations. He objected to Gruenbaum's provision that no negotiations be conducted unless deportations were halted, or to the return of Brand to Hungary. He also rejected

Gruenbaum's criticism of the sharing of information: "After all, the matter depends on England and America agreeing. What does Mr. Gruenbaum suggest—that we tell the emissary to go home because we do not wish to negotiate with the government?" Ben-Gurion told Gruenbaum that "I would never undertake such grave responsibility." Even if there was no hope, or just the slender hope of buying more time and holding up the murders, it is the JAE's duty "to do everything—to go to the government, to inform them of the matter and demand their help."

Ben-Gurion was outspokenly critical of what Sharett had said to MacMichael and denied the assumption that it was possible to conceal from the superpowers the risks involved in Eichmann's proposal. "We must speak to the government as people who are aware of their fears of the enemy's dirty dealings," and on this basis we must insist on help. He also objected to Gruenbaum's demand that negotiations be conducted directly by a British representative. Ben-Gurion asked him, "Does it depend on us?" After all, Britain and the United States would be the ones to appoint their representatives and they would act in accordance with their own best interests. Any emissary would be a "government emissary and the mere existence of the mission would be of benefit to us by putting off the slaughter. The main thing is that the negotiations don't stop and the enemy knows that [people are] willing to speak to [him] about saving Jews."[86]

Ben-Gurion believed that the high commissioner had not transmitted all the information he possessed concerning developments in the affair. Sharett reported that MacMichael had promised to help arrange his flight and entry into England. On the other hand, MacMichael had refused to arrange Brand's return to Hungary and said he would check with his superiors.[87] Sharett also reported that he had explained to the head of the British Criminal Investigation Department in Palestine that Brand must be considered an emissary on a mission to rescue Jews and that there was no reason to mix him up in investigations or other things that could be used as justification for refusing him reentry into Hungary.

The deep frustration of the JAE members is tangible, the result of the cumulative failure of one plan after another over a period of eighteen months—ever since news of the annihilation of Jews in Europe reached the Yishuv and the rest of the world. There was a feeling in the JAE that the same miserable end could be expected for what might be the last chance to save Jews. It was thus possible to understand Gruenbaum's pain and even his tendency to blame himself regarding the passing of information to Britain. Ben-Gurion's reaction somehow led Gruenbaum to apologize and to say that the dissent was the result of the fact that "the others were not as deeply entrenched in the affair as he was. There is no document on the matter of rescue that he has not looked at." He may not have wanted to appear overly sensitive as compared to his peers.[88] The JAE approved the following summary of the debate by Ben-Gurion:

a. The JAE will cable London and America and ask the members to do something to prove to the enemy that people are willing to negotiate with him over the rescue of Jews.
b. The JAE will try to speed up Mr. Sharett's journey to England to the best of its ability.
c. The emissary sees himself as the ambassador of a million Jews who are under the sentence of death—and if he wants to return, it is our duty to help him carry out his wish.
d. The JAE will do its best to hold a meeting with Mr. Hirschmann in Jerusalem or Cairo.[89]

On 21 June Pinkerton informed Sharett that Ira Hirschmann, the WRB representative, was about to arrive in Cairo, so Sharett flew to Cairo the next day to meet him. Hirschmann had already met Brand and was favorably impressed. President Roosevelt and Stettenius, the undersecretary of state, had dispatched Hirschmann on an urgent mission as soon as they heard of the ransom plan.[90] The British tried to keep Hirschmann from Brand. They looked into the possibility of sending Brand to London and perhaps burying the affair there. Their meeting was permitted only under pressure.[91]

Sharett found that Hirschmann was "a man with a heart—and a Jewish heart." His attitude toward the rescue of Jews "was deeply touching" and he had a "fine mind," although there was something "hasty about him, and he did not see many hardships and complications." Hirschmann was willing to synchronize positions with the JAE and shared Sharett's evaluation that the plan, if it were to succeed, would require unconventional action. This was a significant (albeit temporary) return to Sharett's attitude toward Hirschmann. At the beginning of the month a member of the OSS in Jerusalem had reported that Sharett was sharply critical of Hirschmann and the War Refugee Board. To this day, said Sharett, not a single Jew had been saved as a result of this organization.

The meeting with Hirschmann in Cairo encouraged Sharett. Hirschmann agreed to cooperate with him in composing the summaries to be sent to London and Washington, which would contain an unambiguous demand for Brand's return to Hungary, armed with a letter of intent concerning his serious desire to conduct negotiations on behalf of the superpowers. He believed there was no need to complicate matters by involving other international bodies. Hirschmann probably wanted to go down in history as a rescuer of Jews. He was not the only one. In one of his letters Menahem Bader wrote to his family in Palestine that the line in Istanbul of such Jewish saviors was long.[92]

Zaslani was in Cairo at this time promoting the "self-defense plan." In the course of his meetings with members of the secret services, he discovered the source of the order to arrest Brand

and take him to Cairo, which was not issued by Lord Moyne, the resident minister, but by the Security Intelligence Middle East (SIME), one of Britain's major intelligence branches in the region. Sharett's own way in Cairo was strewn with obstacles laid down by an anonymous British hand, which tried to prevent a meeting between him and Brand in Cairo, held up the dispatch of a cable from him to Barlas, and delayed the issuance of a permit for his flight to Britain for five days.[93]

THE POSSIBILITY OF ACTING INDEPENDENTLY: A DISCUSSION IN CAIRO

A new attempt was made to implement an idea that had been raised during previous discussions on earlier ransom plans. The Cairo meeting was attended by Hirschmann, Joe Schwartz, the JDC director in Europe, and Sharett. The three examined the possibility of independent action in the event that the United States and Britain became hesitant or evasive. They discussed preparations for raising a large sum of money in a location from which it would be possible to transfer funds into occupied Europe, so that the Nazis would be paid in money rather than in trucks and merchandise. The Nazis had agreed to accept money instead of merchandise and, during preliminary negotiations in Hungary, had even gone so far as to stipulate a price per life saved.[94]

Schwartz and the American-Jewish aid organization he represented in Europe had already shown a willingness to join an independent rescue operation even if this meant violating American law or contradicting the wartime policies of the United States and its allies. Hirschmann was an official of the United States, representative of a committee that was given far-reaching authority to make contact with the enemy. An American Jew and a senior manager in the Bloomingdale's department store in New York, he carried a personal letter from President Roosevelt authorizing him to act on behalf of the remaining Jews of

Europe. It may be assumed that Hirschmann's official status and personal self-confidence reinforced Schwartz's disposition to plan and participate in rescue activity that skirted legality.

Hirschmann wanted to adopt the working concepts used by the Yishuv's rescue emissaries in Istanbul. "Great guys" was how he described them to Schwartz and Sharett in Cairo, claiming that they were the only ones who were doing anything to save Jews.[95] Sharett was sure that this was meant to encourage Schwartz to take unconventional action. Indeed, it could be that some internal stocktaking among various elements of American Jewry was at work here. Hirschmann was a supporter of Hillel Kook and his group in America,[96] whereas Schwartz represented a non-Zionist philanthropic organization, the epitome of conservative and cautious behavior. Schwartz's secret activity following news of the annihilation tends to dispel this image. On the other hand, it becomes progressively clearer that there was no real cover to Hirschmann's self-confidence, and that he had no ability to act independently.[97]

Sharett, Schwartz, and Hirschmann discussed the proposal that the JDC deposit funds into a closed account in Switzerland, where the money would be available for disbursement, instead of ten thousand trucks and goods. Thus, the head of the Jewish Agency's Political Department, the JDC representative, and the representative of the U.S. administration's WRB were examining alternative options according to accepted British and American administrative practices. It was a semiautonomous alternative based on the assumption that the U.S. and British governments would turn a blind eye at first and cooperate only at a later stage when the deal was sealed.

Pinkney Tuck, the person in charge of American interests in Egypt at the time, contributed to the general atmosphere. Already in 1942 he had devised a plan for rescuing Jewish children from France.[98] Tuck accompanied Hirschmann on his visits in Cairo and was responsible for supplying logistical support and communications services for this alternative plan. Judah Leon Magnes, the JDC representative in Palestine, was brought in on the secret plan and was supposed to leave with Schwartz for Istanbul. He wanted to be sure that Schwartz was not overstepping the mark, so he reported on the plan to the JDC president in New York.[99]

Hirschmann also reported to Steinhardt, the U.S. ambassador to Turkey, on the semiautonomous alternative plan and asked him to arrange Schwartz's entry into Turkey. Lord Moyne, a senior M. P. and resident minister in the Middle East, was also privy to this secret. Hirschmann asked him for his opinion on the plan's chances of success and Lord Moyne replied that he was not sure his country would oppose it. When Lord Moyne asked if he was permitted to report to London on the idea, Hirschmann suggested that he refrain from spreading it about before it was discussed with Steinhardt and his superiors in the U.S. administration.[100]

Since the arrival of information from Hungary, the JAE had been active in both the diplomatic channel and what I have defined as the semiautonomous approach. In meetings in Jerusalem, Washington, and London, the JAE tried to get the authorities to approve Brand's return and to jump-start negotiations with the Nazis on their ransom proposal. In no way did the JAE disregard the unrealistic nature of the proposal, but it insisted that Britain and the United States create at least the illusion of a positive reply; in doing so, the deportations of Jews to death camps might be forestalled. At the same time, the Yishuv offices and their American Jewish partners were accumulating money for a semiautonomous operation in the event that the superpowers withdrew explicit support for Brand's proposal while turning a blind eye to the efforts of the Yishuv and American Jews to implement it.

The JAE often received firsthand information. After Sharett's meeting with Brand in Aleppo, the JAE had all available information. It appears that efforts at involving an American representative proved successful, and Hirschmann was duly appointed. Likewise, efforts to return Brand to Hungary also looked promising. Hirschmann managed to prevent Brand from being sent to London and was about to get Washington to act on his behalf.

It can be concluded that the JAE did its best to promote the possibility of rescuing Jews, which presented itself in the form of Eichmann's proposal, or at least to delay the slaughter by means of negotiations on the proposal. The JAE's activity thus far does not support the negative image that has developed over the years. On the contrary, the JAE showed no hesitation in implementing the proposal brought by Brand. Although it was regarded with suspicion—Ben-Gurion and others had doubts about its practicality—the JAE did everything in its power to adopt the ransom plan, or at least to fool the Nazis into entering into negotiations whose sole objective was to hold up deportations.

Immediately following Sharett's return from talks in Cairo, the JAE convened an extraordinary session on Saturday, 24 June 1944, at nine o'clock at night. It was the third such meeting at which the Brand mission was discussed. (Sharett was to depart for London the following day.) Ben-Gurion conducted the meeting, which commenced with Sharett's report of his activity in Cairo.

During his talks with Lord Moyne in Cairo, Sharett became aware of a real danger: the British Foreign Office intended to make public information on Brand's mission. The air was still rife with the bitter experience of the Transnistria proposal, whose exposure thwarted the effort (if it had any chance of success in the first place). Sharett naturally objected to the plan being made public, since this would mean the end of it, and Hirschmann seconded him. Sharett demanded that the British Foreign Office await his arrival in London. Lord Moyne promised to pass the request on to London and Sharett was thus obliged to get there in time.[101]

Ben-Gurion determined that Sharett would stay in London until the end of the affair and would not return to Palestine unless positive developments demanded his return for consultations and decisions. Dr. Werner Senator, the non-Zionist representative in the JAE, objected to this: The JAE and the Zionist Actions Committee were then seeking important political clarifications from the British over the Jerusalem Plan (the amended Biltmore Program). It was thus essential that Sharett return immediately following clarifications on the Brand affair. Ben-Gurion refused to budge:

> We have held clarifications. Mr. [Sher-tok's] opinion is known and we can continue the clarifications in his absence. . . . It is not, of course, possible to foresee the development of events in Europe. It is hard to imagine the Nazis being able to hold up on three fronts [on 6 June the Allies landed in Normandy, opening up a third front] and it is possible that surrender will come suddenly, so it is imperative that one of our people remain permanently in London and act there.

He concluded the meeting without calling for a vote on the issue: "In the name of the JAE, we wish Mr. Shertok 'bon voyage!'"

Sharett made no mention in his report of the semiautonomous operation he had discussed with Schwartz and Hirschmann in Cairo. This is strange, since it was reported to Lord Moyne and other British and American officials. Magnes even reported on it to the JDC president in New York. Still, it appears to have been decided not to raise the matter at the JAE session that evening, or at least not to include it in the minutes.[102] The reason for this decision is not clear. Perhaps it was motivated by a fear of leaks to other sources who might wish to thwart the plan.

The following day, at the regular JAE meeting, there was again no mention of the Cairo talks. Ben-Gurion reported that Sharett had left for London on rescue matters. The participants approved his proposal to send Dobkin to the United States to promote the Brand plan. Dobkin was in Lisbon at the time, involved with rescue matters in Spain and Portugal.[103] Ben-Gurion continued to maintain that Washington and London constituted the main front and that the Yishuv should take direct action in Washington instead of waiting for help to arrive from Hirschmann or Steinhardt.

All the procedures carried out up to the time the main effort was relocated to London clearly show that Ben-Gurion and others in the JAE put all their weight behind efforts to rescue the Jews of Hungary. They did this despite their real fear that the proposal brought by Brand was nothing more than a hoax and given the risks involved in trying to have it accepted by Britain and the United States.

WEIZMANN AND SHARETT IN LONDON

In the meantime, reports on the affair were flowing into London. The British officials were undecided as to how to reply to Brand and the JAE without implicating themselves too deeply. Another question was whether to allow Sharett to come to London, as the JAE had requested. The British officials even tried to cater to the differences in style and position between Ben-Gurion and Sharett—if such differences even existed.[104]

Robert M. A. Hankey, in the Foreign Office's Eastern Department, played a pivotal role in solidifying Britain's opposition to the ransom plan by stressing the differences between Ben-Gurion and Sharett. According to him, Sharett was "worried," a "poor fellow" who "was trying to save as many Jews as possible from the claws of the Nazis" and to bring them to Palestine without taking into consideration the situation in the Middle East or "the cost of this effort."

Hankey warned against accepting the plan and made no mention of the Nazis' ban on transporting Jewish refugees to Palestine. This ban actually negated his main reason for rejecting the plan. Ben-Gurion was "more extreme," according to Hankey, although he did concede that Ben Gurion exhibited a "clearer view" of the affair. Hankey was referring to the fact that Ben-Gurion recognized the possibility that the plan might be a Nazi hoax, but he ignored the rest of Ben-Gurion's statement on the issue, namely that even if the proposal were a hoax, it must be discussed with the Nazis in order to delay the slaughter.

Hankey pointed to a large number of people—including British and American ambassadors in Ankara; MacMichael, the high commissioner; Lord Moyne, the resident minister; and General Harlold Rupert Alexander, the commander in chief of Allied Forces in the Middle East—who shared his view that in its presumptuousness the proposal was a brazen attempt at extortion. "Ben-Gurion and apparently Weizmann, too, accept this opinion with sympathy," said Hankey. He suggested delaying a reply as long as possible, in coordination with the Americans, and ultimately demanding that the proposal be dealt with through the usual channels.[105] Another British official complained that his people were "busy passing fantasies from one Zionist to another."[106]

At the conclusion of that chapter in Britain's internal consultations, George Hall, undersecretary of state for foreign affairs, wrote to Weizmann about Sharett's meeting with Brand. He told him that Brand felt the proposal was a serious one, having originated among top-ranking German authorities, and that Sharett had been impressed with Brand's reliability. The letter included the JAE's request for the proposal to be evaluated and that a meeting with the German representatives be contemplated. Hall even mentioned the three channels proposed by the JAE in which negotiations could take place and informed Weizmann that the possibility of Sharett's visit to London was being checked out. He himself noted that the sincerity of the proposal and its origins were dubious and that "Ben-Gurion had stressed the possibility [to the high commissioner] that the entire matter might be no more than a hoax."

The notes on the draft copy of the letter, added during consultations among Foreign Office officials, reveal the working methods of the British Foreign Office. On the back of the draft Hankey wrote that the motives behind the proposal were understandable and were aimed at upsetting relations with the USSR. Ben-Gurion, who had spoken to the high commissioner, believed the whole matter was a hoax. Hall's written reply was that it would be wise to heed Ben-Gurion's concern.[107]

Sharett arrived in London on 27 June 1944. The information from Hall had reached Weizmann by then, as had information from Alec Randall, head of the Foreign Office's Refugees' Department, and from Nahum Goldmann of the Jewish Agency's American branch. Randall had informed him that they were awaiting Sharett's arrival, after which a decision would be forthcoming on Brand's release and return. He demanded that the Zionists "not make use of Brand's imprisonment in Cairo to hint that His Majesty's government was giving insufficient attention to the plan to rescue Jews suffering under the Nazi threat."[108] On 24 June Goldmann sent Weizmann suggestions for action. Among other things, he proposed concentrating Hungary's Jews in camps, to be run by the International Red Cross or the Swiss government, and said the Jews would finance their upkeep.[109]

All this information reached Weizmann through British channels, but once Sharett arrived in London he was able to report directly to Weizmann and others, eliminating deletion or editing of his information. This vastly improved source of information probably escalated the Zionists' activity in London. Until then Weizmann had managed to meet with Foreign Secretary Eden and to exchange a few letters with senior officials.[110]

The day after his arrival, Sharett sent a reassuring message home: it appears that Brand and Grosz will be allowed to return to Hungary, Hirschmann will most likely be called for consultations and, finally, "there is no intention of going public." He also added that "the meeting with the Germans depends on Russian approval," a fact that had definite negative implications with respect to the plan's chances of success.[111]

Two days later (30 June) Weizmann and Sharett met with Hall and reiterated their demand to return Brand to Hungary and to report to the Germans (through Brand) that the proposal was being reviewed at the highest possible levels and that the Allies were prepared to negotiate with Germany's representatives over the release of as many Jews as possible. Weizmann and Sharett also raised several other proposals, including the issuance of warnings. Hall replied that the matter was being reviewed in the War Cabinet, which would reach a decision at the earliest possible moment.[112]

Immediately after his meeting with Hall, Sharett cabled Ben-Gurion and outlined the main points discussed. That same day he sent him a lengthy, detailed report that Ben-Gurion received only ten days later.[113] Ben-Gurion received another personal and detailed report at a meeting with Gershon Agronsky (Agron), editor of the *Palestine Post*. Agronsky set out for London equipped with a questionnaire, prepared by the Political Department, consisting of forty-five questions primarily involving the Brand affair and the "Self-Defense Plan." Upon his return, Agronsky told Ben-Gurion that Sharett had responded positively to Hall's question as to whether the JAE believed it worthwhile to conduct negotiations with the Germans, and had suggested appointing and authorizing a representative of the American War Refugee Board to negotiate with the enemy.[114]

From Agronsky's description it appears that Sharett added his own emphases to the JAE's decision, informing Hall that "any hint at conversa-tion must be accompanied by the provision that deportations cease." Thus, Sharett adopted Gruenbaum's repeated demand, which Ben-Gurion and the JAE had rejected. Gruenbaum had not given up and insisted on its importance in his cables to Sharett in London. Based on newly acquired data, he described the murderous pace of deportations of Jews from Hungary, which Sharett subsequently quoted in his conversation with Hall.[115]

Hall summed up the meeting by making the following three points: there was no time to lose; the War Cabinet was discussing the issue; and all action was to be coordinated with the United States and all real action would not take place without the USSR.[116] These promises had a bittersweet quality. Although it was stressed that time was of the essence and that the matter was being discussed at the highest possible levels, the provision regarding the USSR actually hinted at an impasse.

INVITATIONS TO BUDAPEST AND BERLIN AND TALKS IN STOCKHOLM

Several days before Agronsky's conversation and before the arrival of the comforting cable from Sharett, Ben-Gurion decided to report to his colleagues in the JAE on recent developments.[117] He told his colleagues that Menahem Bader had informed him from Istanbul that the Germans had asked the local Yishuv emissaries to negotiate with them directly. Bader had received this proposal on 10 June, at the height of Brand's mission, thus adding to the convoluted drama that was unfolding.

Ben-Gurion described developments in great detail. The Hungarian military attaché in Istanbul (his second in command, it would appear), a man named (or nicknamed) "Feri," suggested to Bader that a Yishuv emissary conduct negotiations directly with the Nazi leaders. At 8:00 A.M. on 10 June, following an exchange of telegrams between Istanbul and Budapest, it was

Menachem Bader, one of the senior emissaries in Istanbul
(Haganah Archive).

revealed that Brand's mission was in trouble. "Feri" said his proposal had come from SS officer Hermann Krumey, the "head of the anti-Jewish activity in Hungary," who was "a 'fair' man in his opinion." Krumey asked why a Yishuv emissary shouldn't come to Hungary to conduct direct negotiations. He stressed that such an emissary would be assured safe conduct home.

Ben-Gurion went on to report that Bader did receive a telegram from Budapest on 23 June in which he was invited to conduct direct negotiations. The telegram closed with a promise that further details would arrive soon. Zaslani in Istanbul sent out all this information on 28 June,

several days before Ben-Gurion decided to report to the JAE.[118] From this point on the affair underwent endless ramifications, and to this day there is much that is still unknown.

"Feri," about whom the Yishuv emissaries reported to Ben-Gurion, was none other than Ferenc Bagyoni, emissary and aide to the Hungarian military attaché in Bulgaria, Lieutenant Colonel Otto Hatz, the Abwehr agent known as "Jasmine" who had managed to infiltrate the Dogwood network. Hatz's close relations with the Germans became clear toward the end of summer 1944, which signaled one of the main nails in the web's coffin.[119] Bagyoni was also attached to the Dogwood network, where he was given the name "Pink." As we shall see, Bagyoni's name was also linked to an attempt to open another channel for the rescue of Jews from Sweden at the end of 1944.

The third member of the group of Hungarian agents was Lothar Kövess,[120] who introduced himself to Kollek and Avriel during 1943. After Hatz was discovered, Kövess replaced him in the Dogwood network and was assigned the name "Jacaranda." Kövess, who belonged to a politically prominent Hungarian family, was a British agent and had excellent connections among the Nazi agents. He worked for the Socony Vacuum Oil Company in Istanbul, whose general manager was Archibald Walker, a member of the American OSS.[121]

Following the German occupation of Hungary, the SS played a central role in the new administration and took control of organizations formerly managed by the local Abwehr. In April 1944, shortly after the invasion, the SS summoned Hatz, Bagyoni, and Kövess to Budapest. The three were arrested on 3 May and released on 26 May. Among other things, the SS was interested in locating pro-West cells in Hungary in order to destroy or utilize them for their own ends.[122]

After their release, the three probably became agents on behalf of the Budapest SS group. This is important for a proper understanding of the future stages of the affair and, in particular, for deciphering the meaning of Bagyoni's (Feri's) messages. Who handed them over to the SS and who helped set them free? Probably "Direktor Schröder"(Laufer), who had made great inroads in the new Hungarian administration. Beginning as a double agent handled by the Abwehr in the British, American, and Yishuv espionage networks in Istanbul, Laufer had risen to a position of importance in the Budapest SS group.

Laufer knew everyone within the German, Hungarian, and Jewish Yishuv systems. He was intimately familiar with their agents and couriers, their operational norms, and knew the subtle distinctions between one type of loyalty and another that had been sold elsewhere. If one wishes to name the independent sources of intelligence used by Britain and the United States, one should place Hatz alongside Grosz in this respect. Hatz belonged to a group of ex-Abwehr agents (the others were Laufer, Bagyoni, and Kövess) who were now in the employ of the SS in Budapest.

The Nazi counterparts to this group also included the shadowy "Consul Stiller," a mystery man who had attached himself to the German consulate in Istanbul. As we shall see, Stiller also approached Bader with a similar proposal to hold direct negotiations between the Yishuv and authorized Nazi officials. Stiller invited Bader to Berlin rather than Budapest.

A review of the German camp in Istanbul, Hungary, Germany, and other countries reveals a very motley bunch of senior Nazi officers and officials. One of them was Bruno Peter Kleist, who had been sent to Stockholm by Joachim von Ribbentrop, Germany's foreign minister, and was apparently also in the service of Heinrich Himmler. He was letting it be known, to a greater or lesser degree, that certain circles in the Nazi hierarchy were interested in developing a dialogue with the West through discussions with the Jewish Yishuv in Palestine or other Jewish organizations.[123]

THE FIRST PROPOSAL RECEIVED BY BADER ARRIVES IN JERUSALEM

To return to Ben-Gurion's report to the JAE regarding Bader's invitation to enter into direct negotiations in Budapest, about which he had learned a few days earlier from Zaslani in Istanbul,[124] Ben-Gurion pointed out that this development had to be reported to the regional intelligence unit and from there to the command in Cairo. Ben-Gurion chose not to disclose to his colleagues that Tony Simmonds, who sympathized with the Jewish and Zionist issue, was the one to forward Zaslani's letter. The practical significance of such a service was quite clear at this stage of the war and the rescue attempts: at least some of the British secret service personnel were aware of the letter's contents even before carrying out Zaslani's request to pass it along to the regional intelligence unit.

After pointing out Zaslani's request, Ben-Gurion made two comments that are crucial to a proper understanding of future developments. The first revealed that "our people in Kushta [Istanbul] were not sufficiently tight-lipped, and this might place us in an uncomfortable situation." The second, an aside, noted that "Mr. Shaul Meirov is leaving for Kushta today and he can take our reply with him," and added that Kaplan was scheduled to leave three days later.

Ben-Gurion raised Bader's question of whether to accept the invitation to Hungary. After registering his own opposition, he gave his colleagues a chance to have their say, since Sharett was still trying to persuade Britain and the United States to negotiate with the Nazis. (That very morning news had arrived from London that the proposal was being given serious consideration.) Ben-Gurion also said that the Foreign Office might allow Brand and Grosz to return to Hungary, and the British had not ruled out a meeting with the enemy. He was also convinced that as long as the superpowers had not totally rejected the possibility of Brand returning with a reply of some sort, the JAE should not contemplate entering into independent negotiations with the enemy.

Gruenbaum was also opposed to Bader's journey and had not changed his position since the beginning of the affair: no negotiation with the Nazis as long as the deportations continue. According to recent information, said Gruenbaum, thirty-five thousand Jews remained stranded in Hungary at that time. If his demand was not met, he feared that it would be a short while before there would be no one left to negotiate over. Ben-Gurion, who also objected to Bader's journey as long as there was a chance of agreement with the Americans and the British, rejected both the claim on which Gruenbaum based his objection and the

very idea of making demands: "Mr. Gruenbaum appears to have forgotten that we are dealing with wild animals here. Our men can only point out that continued deportations might complicate negotiations."[125] Kaplan was similarly opposed to Bader's trip to Hungary. The JAE decided to turn over the new information to the Mandatory government in Jerusalem and to Sharett in London, to instruct Bader to await Kaplan's arrival in Turkey, and to ban him from going to Hungary for the time being.[126]

A BAN OR A CONTINGENT BAN?

That same day Ben-Gurion cabled Sharett in London regarding new developments in Istanbul, but from this document and from the little that was said at the JAE meeting it is to be assumed that more decisions were almost certainly reached, as were other conclusions that were not recorded or discussed in official forums in the presence of more than a few people.

This can be gleaned from several clues. First among these are the obvious hints at the difficulties involved in concealing Bagyoni's offer to Bader. Recall that Ben-Gurion pointed out the difficulty involved in keeping the new development secret and expressed considerable dissatisfaction at the transparency of the Istanbul operation. He probably already knew quite a bit about that crowded city. Zaslani himself had given orders to forward this classified information to the British and even used them himself to pass along "information." As in earlier cases, he had no choice and Ben-Gurion knew this. It is even possible that Zaslani had discovered that the British already knew about Bader's invitation from its own sources. Zaslani did not "volunteer information." He passed on only what he considered was already known or would soon be known from other sources. Under the circumstances, this was not an unfounded assumption, nor was it easy to keep such information classified either. Britain and the United States were "on the tail" of the Yishuv leaders in Tel

Aviv and Jerusalem, especially with regard to these subjects. [127]

It is obvious that Ben-Gurion was extremely uncomfortable conducting a debate on so charged an issue where the opening steps were exposed to the British. There can be no doubt that he was reluctant to conduct it in such a public arena as the JAE. A possible conclusion here is that Ben-Gurion was obliged to present the appearance of being openly opposed. The emissaries' activity was transparent to the British because they depended on the latter's services. Moreover, it is almost certain that Britain and the United States knew of Bagyoni's offer to Bader from their own sources. Thus, it was important not to appear irresponsible, not to act like someone capable of helping the enemy "in his narrow objectives" and by doing so to play into the hands of hostile groups within the American and British administrations at a time when no decision had yet been reached in London and Washington.

On the other hand, past experience had proven that no faith should be placed in the United States and Britain on the issue of rescuing Jews. Thus, Ben-Gurion was obliged to engage in a subtle juggling act: to give Britain and the United States the information—it might already be in their possession and not sharing it could complicate the Yishuv's relations with the West, whose help was essential in all stages of the rescue operation—while at the same time examining a semiautonomous plan, based on developments involving Bader, in the hope of supplying the contumelious superpowers with a "pre-cooked dish" they would be hard-pressed to reject (thus the term "semiautonomous," since without their help no possibility existed of rescuing Jews).

Thus, parallel to the "naive" presentation of the material to the West, a step was taken that was not documented but appears to be broadly hinted at in Bader's subsequent communications to Ben-Gurion. (As we will see, Bader wrote that Kaplan had explained to him the reasons for the ban against his trip to Budapest).[128] Juggling of this sort could only succeed only if the British and American friends of the Yishuv emissaries had no inkling of its classified aspect, which contradicted its obvious one. This would explain Ben-Gurion's heightened insistence on secrecy at this stage.

There was nothing really new in all this. The Yishuv leaders had behaved similarly on other issues, such as concealing weapons, military training of the Palmah, the illegal-immigration operation, land purchase, and long-term economic planning. Although the Jewish Agency proclaimed that it was not involved in illegal activity, it most certainly was. Here, too, it presented itself as a partner with "clean hands," but in reality it was secretly making plans for semiautonomous action. A typical example of this is the case of the emissary who was captured on his way to Greece.

A second clue was Meirov's and Kaplan's mission to Istanbul. Although this had been planned beforehand—several days after Sharett's report on the meetings in Aleppo they were already making plans for a higher-level political and operational headquarters in Istanbul—it is not farfetched to assume that the news of Bagyoni's proposal to Bader speeded up these preparations. A top-ranking team was again being assembled in the Turkish city: Kaplan and Meirov were about to set off; Zaslani had preceded them; Avriel (leader of the courier web, who accompanied Brand to Aleppo and then came to Palestine) and Pomeranz were preparing to return to Istanbul. Having learned of the Bagyoni proposal, Sharett, Zaslani, Kollek, Schind, and others attempted to convince their counterparts in the American and British espionage services in Palestine, Cairo, and Istanbul to arrange urgently needed entry and transit permits to Turkey.[129]

This speeded up deployment of top-ranking individuals would not have been necessary unless those involved were planning a far-reaching operation. This is proof that the Yishuv was determined to salvage something from the affair. It was thus necessary to bring together top-level decision makers at a location close to the hub of activity. But how can one ascertain whether this speeded-up deployment was also intended to leave open the possibility that semiautonomous action might be necessary if the superpowers ducked out of the other option? This can be determined from Bader's correspondence with Ben-Gurion after his conversation with Kaplan in Istanbul. Bader's eyes were opened to Ben-Gurion's and his colleagues' real intentions when he heard from Kaplan about the secret plan to take semiautonomous steps. This conclusion is based on a large body of testimony and highly significant indication.

A third clue can be found in Ben-Gurion's telegram to Sharett. Ben-Gurion had instructed Sharett to cable him from London any new information or changes in the situation with respect to the JAE and to cable directly to Kaplan in Istanbul, who was authorized to decide on the spot. Information from London would help Kaplan decide if the Yishuv would keep its activity secret from Britain and the United States and perhaps even whether to pretend to be negotiating on behalf of both.

In other words, based on factual and circumstantial testimony, I am assuming that Ben-Gurion was acting both on overt and covert levels. Superficially—things he said to the JAE; the contents of his cables to Sharett and Bader—he was opposed to Bader's desire to bargain directly with the Nazis. On the other hand, he appears to have instructed Kaplan and Meirov to clarify for Bader verbally what he himself was prevented from writing (for fear of disclosure), and authorized Kaplan to decide from Istanbul whether to pursue further contact with the Nazis. The secret summary instructions were meant to be carried out when it became obvious that the British were once again leading the Yishuv down the garden path and were about to jeopardize new possibilities of rescuing Jews.[130]

According to my assessment, Ben-Gurion's objection to Bader's trip to Hungary was limited to a certain circumstances. Once the British got wind of Bagyoni's conversation with Bader, there was no reason to deny or conceal it. He was constantly wary of appearing irresponsible. At a time charged with anticipation over the reply of the superpowers, he chose a path of controlled disclosure. The withholding of such sensitive information could have upset the delicate relationship with Britain and thereby further reduced the already small chances of rescue. Nevertheless, parallel to his efforts to present the Jewish Agency as cooperating with the British and Americans, Ben-Gurion was giving orders to prepare secretly for a semiautonomous act. It would appear that the fear of an information leak meant that even the majority of the JAE were unaware of this directive.[131]

Ben-Gurion was well aware that he himself and the major Yishuv units were under constant surveillance, although even he could not have know to what extent. Just a few days after Agronsky's meeting with Ben-Gurion, during which Weizmann's and Sharett's activity was discussed, the information was reported in detail to American intelligence services. It was clear to Ben-Gurion that, because this operation involved the rescue of so many Jews, British and American intelligence services would make every effort to discover what the JAE was up to.[132]

BADER'S SECOND INVITATION, INTERIM AGREEMENT B, AND THE KLARMAN-GRIPPEL PROPOSAL

While the emissaries in Istanbul were still awaiting the JAE's response to Bagyoni's invitation to Bader, another call came from Budapest asking if Bader intended to come. This reinforced the emissaries' impression that the proposal was serious. Fearing that an important opportunity to save Jewish lives might be missed because of a delay in responding, they decided to take independent action. Their plan was intertwined with a step that was being devised in Cairo by Hirschmann, Schwartz, and Sharett—and, in my opinion, was probably also linked to Ben-Gurion's secret deployment.

At this stage of the affair, Hirschmann and Schwartz had just arrived in Istanbul and joined the rescue activists on the spot. Magnes came with Schwartz. After some indecision, the emissaries decided to tell Hirschmann about Bader's invitation to visit Budapest. The meeting took place in a hotel room. Hirschmann was sick and in a foul mood. Upon his return to Istanbul, Steinhardt informed him that Washington had instructed him not "to having anything more to do with the Brand affair."

The apparent change in American policy was the result of Lord Halifax's influence on the American Foreign Office. It was a blow to Hirschmann, who had arrived in Istanbul in a "Bergson"-style fighting spirit. Obliged to contend with denials from Washington, little remained of the self-image he had affected for himself in Cairo, where he reprimanded Schwartz for being too moderate and for fearing accusations of "dual loyalty." Hirschmann, who had said in Cairo that he felt himself humbled in the presence of those courageous emissaries, was obliged to repeat that he would do all he could to help even though his "hands were now tied."[133]

Another interim agreement was proposed during the meeting with Hirschmann, under the assumption that the previous agreement had been received in Hungary and had achieved its objective, namely, to keep the proposal simmering while it was being discussed in London and Washington. They wished to reiterate an "agreed upon" reply on behalf of the "homeland"—to reiterate that the Yishuv was willing to take independent action and to transfer money in return for Jewish lives, and that, if the Nazis were agreeable, Bader would go to Budapest to finalize the negotiations. Magnes and Schwartz, the JDC representatives, promised that this time there really would be money available. Schwartz was thus ad-

hering to the position he adopted in his talks with Sharett and Hirschmann in Cairo. It was decided that Hirschmann would not report on this new move to Steinhardt and that attempts would later be made to involve him in the process and perhaps even to try to mobilize the more senior players in Washington.[134]

The entire process was shrouded in secrecy. The people in Istanbul did not wish to jeopardize Weizmann's and Sharett's efforts in London. It was clear that Britain was not willing to cooperate with the Zionist movement in implementing the Brand plan, but the emissaries were not aware of this yet. While awaiting Kaplan's arrival in Istanbul, they were told that Gruenbaum's arrival was also imminent and that Barlas had arranged entry permits for both of them.[135]

In the meantime, another daring proposal was raised by two "oppositional" members of the council of rescue emissaries in Istanbul: Ya'akov Grippel of Agudat Israel and Joseph Klarman of the Revisionists.[136] They proposed sending two Yishuv emissaries from Istanbul to Hungary in the interim until permits were obtained for Brand and Grosz, the earlier couriers. These emissaries would serve as living proof that serious attempts were being made to examine the ransom plan. Following discussion, the matter was dismissed, but it was decided to raise it again once the second interim agreement had achieved its objective.[137]

All these clarifications and discussions took place between 25 and 30 June. On 29 June Schwartz's proposal was adopted and on 30 June telegrams were sent to Vienna and Budapest announcing that the Yishuv was ready to enter negotiations on a financial basis.[138] This was the second interim agreement, representing a further attempt at bypassing the obstacles and buying time. On this occasion it was the result of cooperation between the emissaries and the JDC. Hirschmann was let in on the secret, but he acted behind the scenes. The second agreement reached Budapest, was eagerly accepted, and probably set the stage for the next step—which arrived from Berlin.

To return briefly to the explanation Bader heard directly from Kaplan concerning instructions from Jerusalem, a few days after their talks in Istanbul, Bader wrote to Ben-Gurion. Right at the outset of the letter, the "verbal doctrine" instructions were obvious, lurking behind Ben-Gurion's open refusal, together with that of the entire JAE, to acquiesce to the new proposal:

> I have received your telegram demanding a halt to further activity regarding the invitation to Budapest and to await Eliezer's [Kaplan] arrival. In the meantime, Eliezer also came and reported on the reasons for this cable. Pity that the friends [the British intelligence people who passed along the message] once again didn't keep their promise to Ze'ev [Schind] to pass along the cable to HQ [in Jerusalem] to prevent it from falling into the hands of another department.[139]

The discomfort at being so transparent to the British is obvious. The cable's sentence order leads to the conclusion that this transparency is the basis of the "reasons for this cable," in other words, the reasons that motivated Ben-Gurion to pretend that he was totally opposed to Bader conducting negotiations without the knowledge of Britain and the United States.

Since the cable's contents had immediately been leaked to the British—both to the political units and to the intelligence services—and since the intelligence services maintained an ambivalent attitude toward the Yishuv—specifically cooperation with the Yishuv, for there were those who opposed this—Ben-Gurion was unable to openly support this step. He left it to Sharett and Weizmann to do their persuading in London, while simultaneously laying the groundwork for a semiautonomous action if the superpowers decided to drop out. The two important steps were financial preparation (which was discussed in

Cairo by Schwartz, Hirschmann, and Sharett) and Bader's departure to negotiate with Kaplan's approval. Indeed, Kaplan arrived with instructions and briefed Bader on the logic behind the plans and the parts that were classified. How else is one to understand Bader's statement to Ben-Gurion that "I had no intention of acting without your consideration and decision" and, in the self-same letter, informing Ben-Gurion about his so-called forbidden connections?

THE THIRD ROUND: BADER-STILLER

Several days after the second agreement was dispatched to Vienna—following Kaplan's arrival in Istanbul and talks with Bader, and while the emissaries and Kaplan were awaiting a letter from London or Jerusalem containing the decision of the superpowers—Bader received a new proposal. Ben-Gurion was once again the first person to receive information on it. As Bader related the event to Ben-Gurion, on 8 July (a Saturday morning) he received a call from the German consulate in Istanbul asking him to attend a meeting. The speaker introduced himself as "Consul Stiller" and told Bader that he had been trying to locate him for two days. Bader talked to Kaplan and other emissaries and it was decided to agree to a meeting.[140]

"Consul Stiller" invited Bader to attend negotiations in Berlin. A special plane would be sent that would wait for him for three days. Bader explained that he was unable to leave Turkey without the proper exit permits issued by the Turkish and British authorities. He asked for an extension in order to weigh his options. Bader was trying to buy time in order to check the credentials of the mysterious emissary and the legitimacy of his proposal. He wished to consult with his colleagues and obtain their approval to conduct direct negotiations with Berlin. Nonetheless, he did not wish to miss an opportunity that might not be repeated, and stressed that he could probably go if suitable permits were forthcoming.

Kaplan's explanations provided Bader with enough confidence to inform Stiller that his trip to Berlin was not out of the question. This approach was adopted by Bader and his colleagues throughout the interim period, namely, to create the impression that "the door was open to negotiations." Bader also used this logic in the previously mentioned letter to Ben-Gurion.

"Consul Stiller" suggested that Bader obtain a passport from a neutral state and promised that he, too, would search for ways of overcoming technical difficulties. They arranged for another meeting in three days' time, which was the longest delay Bader was able to obtain. The consultations in Istanbul were attended by Kaplan, Meirov, Schind, and Barlas. Some of the meetings were also attended by JDC representatives Schwartz and Magnes, as well as by Hirschmann, who represented the War Refugee Board in Istanbul. All were party to the financial accords discussed in Cairo and to what has been defined here as Interim Agreement B.

In a report to Jerusalem, Bader recalled that after each consultation it was decided to pass along new information—as well as doubts—to Ben-Gurion in Jerusalem and Sharett in London, and to leave all final decisions to them. Bader even stressed that he had no pretensions regarding his authority to make decisions, but that it was his duty to add that "this [is] now a very serious stage, which shows is revealed by the fact that they [the Nazis] had moved the discussion of the issue to a central location—Berlin rather than Budapest or Vienna." He was prepared to leave even though the proposal might turn out to be a trap.[141]

Two days later (10 July) more information was sent to the Yishuv. Jewish underground circles in Budapest had been informed of Bader's invitation, and they were awaiting his arrival. On 11 July a further meeting was planned between Bader and a member of the German consulate. It was decided that Bader would buy time by saying that he was awaiting instructions. Ben-Gurion

and the JAE were asked to reach an immediate decision for or against.[142]

In Jerusalem the picture became clearer thanks to another report, written on 8 July, whose arrival was delayed. The telephone call Bader had received inviting him to the consulate came directly from the German consulate in Istanbul. After Bader refused, the speaker suggested a meeting at a private house, and once again Bader refused the invitation. In the end they agreed to meet that same morning at 11 a.m. at a German-owned bookstore. The man told Bader that a special plane had been waiting for him at the airport, but, since he could not be located, the plane returned to Berlin. He added that it would return in exactly one week's time for the same purpose. Bader reminded the man that he was a Jew and was therefore unable to fly to Berlin. The man told him he did not know this. He had thought that Berlin was requesting a citizen of a neutral state. They agreed to meet again within a couple of days.

The emissaries wondered about transferring information on these new developments to Palestine and to Sharett in London. Kaplan asked why they should not try to do so through the British embassy in Ankara. Schind explained that experience had taught them that the British followed two paths: doing everything in their power to save the lives of Jews and doing everything in their power to thwart any attempts at rescuing Jews. Based on our knowledge of attempts to transfer information about the "Feri" proposal, we now know that Schind was right. In the end it was decided to try to enlist Hirschmann's help despite the fact that Washington had imposed a ban on his activity.

Hirschmann reiterated to Kaplan that he and the American embassy in Ankara were forbidden to get involved in the matter. Kaplan asked him to at least "forget the whole thing." After a fruitless meeting with Hirschmann, Kaplan said that he would issue instructions within a few hours. Four hours later he announced that he had decided to cable Ben-Gurion through the friends of the Yishuv in the British or American secret services. He hoped that the cable would arrive within a couple of days—and that only Ben-Gurion would receive it.[143]

MYSTERY AND DECODING

There is a great mystery surrounding the double attempt to approach Bader, involving Lieut. Col. Otto Hatz, the Hungarian military attaché, and his aide Ferenc Bagyoni (Feri), accompanied by Lothar Kövess and Bandi Grosz—all double or triple agents who at that stage were already representing the SS in Budapest. These men were taking orders from the SS in Berlin and would almost certainly have been connected to the SS branch in Vienna. As we have seen, shortly after the occupation, the Abwehr agents underwent a retraining program at the SD (the SS security and espionage service) facilities in Budapest.[144]

In early summer 1944 the British and American secret services and the Yishuv rescue emissaries were still unaware of the complex conflicting loyalties of these people, but what they did know was already leading them to ask questions. Who, in fact, was Bagyoni representing in the Nazi jungle in Budapest? Was he perhaps representing elements in the Hungarian intelligence services? Who was the mysterious "Consul Stiller" and whom did he represent? Bagyoni said he was bearing a message from Herman Krumey, an SS officer in Budapest. Stiller said that he had been sent by people in the German Foreign Office in Berlin. What, then, could have been behind the proposal to rescue Jews in return for money? Was this yet another attempt to open an additional channel of communication with the West, following the difficulties in the Brand-Grosz mission? It may well have been. But then what is the connection between the invitation to Bader by Bagyoni to travel to Budapest and "Consul Stiller's" invitation to Bader to go to Berlin?

In order to answer these questions, one must return to Budapest and examine the responses to the two interim agreements sent by the emissaries. Paul L. Rose, one of two researchers (the other being Yehuda Bauer) who have examined this matter in detail, discusses only the first interim agreement. According to his findings, this agreement reached Budapest at the end of the first week in July. Only then did it begin to arouse interest in Budapest and subsequently in Berlin. Both Rose and Bauer have determined that responses to that interim agreement ultimately led to, among other things, the opening of additional channels for direct negotiations between Jewish groups and the Nazis in Istanbul, Switzerland, the Iberian Peninsula, and Scandinàvia.[145]

I share Rose's and Bauer's estimation of the importance of that first interim agreement, but I am convinced of the existence of two interim agreements. Each of the agreements had a single central objective. The fact that the Yishuv sent out two separate agreements explains why Bader received two invitations. Both the available documentation and the timetable and developments of the period lend support to my theory.

To briefly review the events: On the night of 29 May Bader and Brand formulated the first interim agreement, which was sent by courier the following night to Dr. Israel Kasztner in Budapest.[146] Interim Agreement A was intended to save Brand and his mission and to cover the fact that no significant developments had taken place that could have permitted Brand to return. It was an initiative devoid of any financial, logistical, or political foundations. Bader and Brand took a chance, hoping that the Yishuv and the superpowers would ultimately supply the necessary cover for the false offer presented in Agreement A.

This agreement arrived in Budapest after Dr. Kasztner and Hansi Brand (Joel Brand's wife) had been released from prison, having been arrested by those unfamiliar with the current state of communications between the various Nazi authorities and the Jewish Aid and Rescue Committee in Hungary.[147] Upon its arrival in Hungary, the agreement was passed on to Kasztner's

Nazi contacts. Although they had reservations about the Istanbul "partners," they nevertheless decided to signal that their "business" intentions were sound and sent Bagyoni to invite Bader to Budapest on behalf of SS officer Hermann Krumey.

Bagyoni delivered the invitation to Bader on 10 June, only a few days after the arrival of the agreement in Budapest. On 23 June Bader received confirmation of the invitation in a cable from Budapest, which informed him that he was indeed invited to conduct direct negotiations and that additional details would follow. All this information was sent to the Yishuv on 28 June by Zaslani.[148]

If one rules out the possibility that Bader was invited to Budapest in response to Interim Agreement A, it becomes hard to explain why he, of all people, received the invitation and why the latter specifically arrived in early June. Bader was a coauthor of Agreement A. Thus, the agreement achieved its objective: the Nazis accepted it, offered a counterproposal, Brand's family was not liquidated, and his mission was extended. Today it is easier to gain a more complete picture of the background leading up to all this: certain Nazi circles were looking for contacts in the West and were in no hurry to burn their bridges.

Interim Agreement B was devised in Istanbul during the five days between 25 and 30 June. Brand was already imprisoned in Cairo at that time, while the emissaries in Istanbul were still waiting for final permits that would enable Bader to set off for Budapest. This proposal was much more serious because it was based on the guaranteed financial backing of the JDC and Lord Moyne and the Americans gave it their silent approval—or so it seemed at the time.

The objective of Agreement B was completely different, the issue no longer being the fate of Brand or his family—although the Yishuv still hoped that Brand would be released and allowed to return home, there was already a growing suspicion that the superpowers would prevent this

once again—but rather the establishment of a secret basis for direct negotiations between the Yishuv and the Nazis. Something along these lines was whispered in Bader's ear by Kaplan and Meirov. In Istanbul they supplied Bader with top-level political and military support. In this respect Agreement B also differed from Agreement A. The main points of Agreement B were cabled to Vienna and Budapest on 30 June. It was emphasized that the Yishuv was prepared to enter into direct negotiations to rescue Jews in exchange for money. The dispatch of the cable to Vienna is noteworthy.[149]

The actual document containing Interim Agreement B was only sent by courier on 5 July (it appears that no reliable courier was available before that date) and reached Kasztner in Budapest two days later.[150] The Interim Agreement B document and the cables to Vienna and Budapest that preceded it probably precipitated the next step taken by the Nazis from Berlin, namely, Stiller's overtures to Bader.

GANGS AND CONSPIRACIES UNDER TOTALITARIAN CAMOUFLAGE

In order to sort out the various elements in this merry-go-round, one must elaborate somewhat on the relations between the SS and the Abwehr, specifically the absorption by the SS of the Abwehr station in Budapest and the Abwehr's inability to comprehend that the SS had taken it over.

The roots of the conflict can be traced to the early days of the Third Reich. In 1935 the Abwehr, the military intelligence unit, was headed by the nationalistic Admiral Wilhelm Canaris. From the very beginning a bitter feud was waged between Canaris and Reichsfuhrer Heinrich Himmler, the commander in chief of the SS.

The feud was conducted between the army and the Nazi party, between the military intelligence and its commander, Canaris, and the party's security units (the SS, SD, and the Gestapo), which were subject to Himmler's authority. The personal issue was the decisive one here. The leaders of various organizations fought for power and status. Conflicts also developed over the character of Germany under Nazi party rule. There was friction between the traditional elite and the new elite, which had been elevated by the party from the masses, as well as disagreement over definitions of the central foe and ways of conducting the war. Conflict even surrounded the political issue with respect to the Jews and various ways of carrying out the "final solution."

There were similar underground organizations supporting Germany's former prime minister, von Papen (now German ambassador to Turkey), against the Hitler government. One of the few outward expressions of this oppositional activity was the conspiracy to murder Hitler. The Canaris-von Papen-von Ribbentrop circles and the group of conspirators who wished to kill Hitler were among the right-wing elements that Hitler inherited from the previous regime. His rise to power was based, among other things, on a confederacy with some of them, which explains the relative influence they maintained in Germany.

Besides Himmler, the bitter struggle was waged by other young stars, including SS Obergruppenführer Ernst Kaltenbrunner, Walter Schellenberg, and Obergruppenführer Heinrich Müller of the Gestapo. They all strove to take over the Abwehr—including its connections, webs, and resources—and to subordinate it to the Nazi party's security units. This struggle continued throughout the war in all the countries under Nazi occupation, including its satellites. SS personnel also strove to take control of Abwehr agencies in neutral states such as Spain, Portugal, Sweden, and Turkey.

Toward the end of 1943 and during 1944, a certain advantage was accorded the SS. The Abwehr's status was reduced primarily because of its failure to obtain and analyze intelligence, but it was Hitler who decided against the organization. He was convinced that Canaris and his men were

undermining his authority and decided to subjugate them to more loyal units. In February 1944 Canaris was fired and Himmler succeeded in abolishing the Abwehr's autonomous existence by linking it to the SD, the SS security and espionage services.[151]

When the SD people arrived in Hungary following the occupation, they therefore came as bosses, as commanders, not as junior partners. This fact did not immediately register at all levels of the Abwehr in Hungary and elsewhere. It took time for the various cells and stations to understand that their bosses had been replaced within that centrist feudal establishment.

Gerhard Clages, who was mentioned by Brand in his reports, was the SD commander who "swallowed up" the Abwehr in Budapest, together with all the attendant officers and agents, even if this fact was not yet common knowledge. Schröder-Laufer was then his aide. The Nazi murder machine was also active in Budapest—the Sondereinsatzkommando under the leadership of Adolf Eichmann of the Gestapo, which was an authority within the Reich Main Security Office (RSHA) within the SS.

Edmund Veesenmayer was also active in that system. He was German minister plenipotentiary of the Reich, and after the occupation he became the de facto governor of Hungary. Veesenmayer simultaneously belonged to two opposing groups in the disintegrating Reich: he was an ambassador on the Foreign Office staff and was thus subject to Foreign Minister von Ribbentrop, one of Himmler's enemies; but he also held a position in the SS, Himmler's organization. Before Veesenmayer was sent to Budapest, Hitler met with his two superiors, von Ribbentrop and Himmler, and tried to coordinate their activity in Hungary. Hitler was in no hurry to place all the power in Himmler's hands even when faced with von Ribbentrop (which partially explains why he defended Canaris for such a long time). Some historians are convinced that Himmler opposed Veesenmayer's appointment to Hungary and that

Hitler forced him to accept it. Whenever there was even a hint of dissent between Veesenmayer and the SS, he would claim that he had in his pocket a kind of insurance policy, a personal letter from Hitler appointing him to the post.[152]

All these elements within the Nazi establishment, together with the Hungarian civilian and military intelligence services, were struggling with the question of how to maneuver through the political and military minefield that was evolving in Europe at that time, as reflected in the dispatch by Brand, the invitations to Bader, and the activities of such agents as Laufer and Grosz.[153]

MORE ON THE STILLER AFFAIR

Concerning the new invitation issued to Bader in Istanbul by "Consul Stiller," the question arises as to why Bader was invited. Bader was again chosen because the Nazis considered him instrumental in formulating the first and second interim agreements. Their agents were present in Istanbul and heard about the Yishuv rescue emissaries, Bader included among them.

Information on Interim Agreement B, which was sent by the emissaries from Istanbul, could have reached Berlin through one of two channels: directly by way of Vienna (with no Jewish intervention) or through Kasztner in Budapest. Kasztner related that as soon as he received the cable he met with Eichmann and Kurt A. Becher, Himmler's special representative. A document of this kind was instrumental to the Aid and Rescue Committee in obtaining a delay in the deportation to death camps of Hungary's Jews. It was equally important to Kasztner's German counterparts and to senior members of the Nazi establishment, who could have interpreted it as a position signal to the supporters of a "separate peace" with the West.

By this time Himmler believed that Germany could suffer a defeat if it continued the war on two fronts. It is clear, therefore, why Becher hastily departed Hungary to present the informa-

tion on Interim Agreement B to Himmler (according to Kasztner).[154] Once the information reached Berlin, Stiller was dispatched on his mission. It is almost certain that the two invitations received by Bader from Bagyoni and Stiller were linked to the interim agreements.

It can be assumed that information on Interim Agreement B reached Berlin through two possible channels, but definitely by way of Vienna. When the document arrived in Vienna, preparations were set in motion that led to Stiller's invitation to Bader. The arrival of the information from Becher—by way of Budapest—resulted in a growing tendency to enter into negotiations with the Yishuv emissaries in Istanbul. My hypothesis also relies on Stiller's remark that he had been searching for Bader[155] since 6 July, in other words, before the full content of Interim Agreement B had reached Kasztner and, of course, before his meeting with Becher.

To summarize, after Brand left for Istanbul, his Nazi handlers waited for replies. When Brand failed to return, they put pressure on Kastner and Hansi Brand and their friends. They urged Istanbul to supply an immediate response to Eichmann's proposal. On the night of 29 May Brand and Bader wrote a false response, in the form of Interim Agreement A, in order to save Brand's mission. The agreement was dispatched on 30 May and arrived in Budapest several days later. Krumey and his cronies in Hungary took the agreement seriously since they had nothing to lose by accepting it. They then sent Ferenc Bagyoni, one of the agents they had inherited from the Abwehr, to Istanbul and issued an invitation to Bader to visit Budapest. Bagyoni handed the invitation to Bader on 10 June.

In the meantime Brand was taken to Cairo. The Zionists were unable to persuade the British to permit his return to Budapest with a response that would provide a platform for negotiations with the Nazis. Financial discussions were simultaneously held in Cairo in preparation for a semi-autonomous Jewish rescue operation. Schwartz and Hirschmann, Sharett's partners in that discussion, arrived in Istanbul and, together with the Yishuv emissaries, took part in composing Interim Agreement B. The main points of the agreement were cabled to Vienna and Budapest on 30 June. A reply followed swiftly. On 8 July Stiller invited Bader to Berlin. We do not know who he was to meet.

Although Bader reported that the invitation originated in the German Foreign Office, or circles close to von Ribbentrop—one might easily assume that Veesenmayer or someone else tipped von Ribbentrop off with regard to Interim Agreement B—it is my opinion that after learning of Interim Agreement B from his people in Vienna and Budapest (Becher), it was probably Himmler who was behind the invitation to Bader to negotiate in Berlin.

Lacking sufficient information and not always knowing what to expect, the Yishuv leaders still had to make important decisions, but even current researchers equipped with a wealth of data and sufficient hindsight have been unable to decipher the entire story. How much did the emissaries know about "Consul Stiller"? A friend in American intelligence informed them that Stiller was indeed Germany's consul in Istanbul, but my own examination of the list of German functionaries in Istanbul does not confirm this. Was there a connection between that "consul" and von Papen, the former German chancellor, who was involved in anti-Hitler activity at the time? Could Stiller have been sent by Clages, SD commander in Budapest, who handled former Abwehr agents in various German consulates?[156] Was the invitation to Germany a test to determine the Yishuv's and the West's response or was it merely a form of provocation aimed at exposing traitors and collaborators?

Neither Ben-Gurion and his JAE colleagues nor the Yishuv's secret service personnel and emissaries in Istanbul—not even Brand, who had arrived in May 1944 with information—could make heads or tails of the complex relationships

and loyalties within the Nazi hierarchy. Ben-Gurion and the Yishuv did realize that the double invitation issued to Bader reflected Nazi authorities engaged in some sort of power struggle. First, they assumed that some of the signals regarding a willingness to negotiate had come from Himmler, who was very close to Hitler in the Nazi hierarchy, and that others had come from the Foreign Office. Second, they assumed that this willingness to negotiate reflected the realization within certain Nazi circles that Hitler was leading Germany to disaster and that they had to be rid of him and to strive for a "separate peace" with the West. Third, they assumed that they could make use of the situation to rescue Jews. They tried to pass their conclusions along to the Allies, since without such cooperation it would have been impossible to take advantage of these new developments within the Nazi camp to rescue Jews.

HIDE-AND-SEEK IN LISBON: DOBKIN AND SCHWARTZ RECEIVE INVITATIONS TO BERLIN

Bader was not the only one to be invited to Berlin. Around the same time (early July) invitations were also extended to JAE member Eliyahu Dobkin and JDC European chief Joe Schwartz. Dobkin was in Lisbon at the time, dealing with rescue issues. The JAE had recently decided that he would set off for the United States, where he would try to gain support for negotiations with the Nazis concerning the Eichmann proposal. Kasztner cabled Dobkin several times that the Germans were hoping to meet with him and with Schwartz. The SS was prepared to send four delegates for this purpose to any location chosen by Dobkin and Schwartz.

The two men were not unknown to each other. Dobkin had helped lead negotiations with Schwartz in August 1943. The two men had formulated a secret agreement between the JDC and the JAE. The JDC agreed to participate in the funding of a ransom plan on condition that the fact be kept secret that an American-Jewish organization was violating the laws of its own country.

Dobkin was quick to report to Sharett in London and the JAE in Jerusalem. He saw this invitation to Berlin as an important development, perhaps reflecting an attempt to simplify the conditions of the deal by accepting money instead of trucks.[157] Dobkin asked Sharett to determine if London was willing to discuss the money option, or goods that had no military value, with the Germans. Sharett was making plans to come to Lisbon to oversee rescue preparations, and now Dobkin suggested that he move his visit up and personally conduct negotiations with SS agents in Lisbon.

Dobkin was unhappy about meeting with SS agents without Sharett's prior approval. It should be noted that he had been very reserved about independent negotiations with the Nazis when the issue was discussed in the JAE immediately after the occupation of Hungary.[158] He had undergone a significant change in attitude, his fear having nothing to do with principles. Dobkin had no desire to interfere with the efforts of the Yishuv's rescue emissaries and the Zionist movement in London, Istanbul, and Jerusalem, who would have found it hard to persuade the Allies of the necessity of negotiating with the Nazis over Eichmann's proposal were it to become known that the Yishuv was conducting independent negotiations with the Nazis in Lisbon.

Dobkin tried to evade Nazi observation and to stall the meeting until he had more official data on developments. His attempts proved useless: Gestapo agents managed to locate him and informed him that their superiors were prepared to meet him in Switzerland and would send a plane to take him there.[159]

At the same time, Eichmann informed Kasztner and his colleagues in Hungary that he would permit fifteen hundred Jews to leave Hungary by train for Switzerland. Through this offer he may have been hinting that the hosts in Berlin were actually planning to bargain over the release of Jews. Kasztner reported this to Istanbul and to Dobkin and asked the latter to prepare for the arrival of refugees.[160] Just a few years later, the selection of those fortunate enough to board that train would become one of the focal points of a wretched court trial known as the "Kasztner Affair."

In London Weizmann and Sharett were awaiting Britain's final official decision on Brand's return and on the response to the Nazis. All this time new information and data had been streaming in from the Yishuv, Portugal, and the United States indicating that the deportation of Hungarian Jews to death camps was continuing, as well as news of the invitations extended to Bader, Dobkin, and Schwartz to visit Berlin.[161] Weizmann and Sharett were convinced that the Nazis were serious about conducting negotiations, and that it might still be possible to save some Jews. They demanded a meeting with Foreign Secretary Eden.[162]

This meeting took place on 6 July 1944. Weizmann and Sharett discussed the gravity of the situation in Hungary: four hundred thousand Jews had already been deported to extermination camps (mostly to Birkenau) and an additional three hundred thousand were about to be sent in their wake. They recognized the fact that "the Gestapo's proposals were not devoid of foul intentions," but they understood that there would be no choice but to pay the ransom. Although the Yishuv leadership's proposals were "neither conservative nor routine," they had to be adopted in the face of the "terrible calamity." Weizmann and Sharett told Eden about the two invitations to Berlin and Budapest and hinted that they might signal that the Nazis were indeed prepared to discuss the release of Jews. They went on to ask the Allies to supply the Europe's Jews with safe-conduct permits, to warn the Hungarians against involvement in the murders, and to bomb Auschwitz and the railway lines leading to it.[163]

Weizmann and Sharett felt that Eden was sympathetic to their cause. They sensed no evasion when he expressed the view that "the enemy was obviously playing a devilish game" and that one needed to proceed with care, coordinating everything with the Americans and the Russians. Eden told them that the Bader invitation had to be discussed by the British War Cabinet. Sharett reported on the meeting to Ben-Gurion that same day.[164]

Eden's comments were couched in the kind of understatement that Weizmann and Sharett did not manage to comprehend. They did not yet realize that Britain and the United States had already "buried" the ransom plan. By the time the matter was fully understood, several more developments had taken place and the invitation received by Bader underwent a few more transformations. From Jerusalem Ben-Gurion, together with the emissaries in Istanbul, tried to move the plan forward. Nonetheless, Ben-Gurion's remarks during those days (mid-July) showed that he no longer hoped for help from Britain and the United States in rescuing Jews.[165]

Magnes, the JDC representative, returned from Istanbul with firsthand information and personal impressions regarding the invitation received by Bader. He handed this information over to Ben-Gurion and Gruenbaum. Magnes pointed out that the second invitation had been issued by Nazi circles within Berlin itself. Additional details were known to Ben-Gurion from other sources. Magnes stressed that the invitation was still valid, so Ben-Gurion hurriedly cabled Sharett (13 July 1944) that the invitation stood and pressed him to demand that the British authorities allow him to leave for Berlin. He also sent Sharett a long and detailed memo that Magnes had given him concerning recent developments in the affair.[166]

A CLEAR REFUSAL ON THE PART OF THE BRITISH

Sharett received the cable the following day and passed it on immediately to Alec Randall, head of the Refugees' Department in the Foreign Office. By way of explanation, Sharett stressed that the proposal to fly to Berlin was proof that "the matter is still valid because the Germans have something to offer and because they are prepared to discuss the proposals."[167]

It was a desperate and futile attempt. Sharett already knew by then what Britain's position was on the issue, and he was not optimistic about his appeal. That same day he cabled some bad news to Ben-Gurion: "The Foreign Office has vetoed Brand's return . . . Menahem's proposal . . . negative." Sharett also pointed out that, as agreed, he had cabled this information directly to Kaplan in Istanbul.[168]

Sharett based his information on Randall and Ian Henderson, both senior officials in the British Foreign Office. They met with him on 12 July 1944 (the day before Ben-Gurion sent his cable) and told him that Bader would not be permitted to fly to Berlin, that there was no point in Brand returning to Budapest, that the idea of supplying Jews in Nazi-occupied areas with documents that would grant them Allied support was ridiculous, and that arranging a safe haven for several thousand people was impossible and impractical. Eden's pleasantries had masked an attitude of cold indifference.

On 15 July Randall officially informed Sharett that this was indeed the firm position of His Majesty's government.[169] His reasons for this decision were based on information received from Grosz and the fact that Churchill had determined that the ransom plan was not to be taken seriously, since it was a "plan that had come through the most dubious of channels . . . and was itself of the most dubious character."[170]

Sharett tried to return to the proposal that had been raised at the beginning of the affair, namely, that Britain and the United States send representatives of their own, or an official from one of the international organizations, to negotiate in order to buy time and, at the very least, delay the murders. He cabled Ben-Gurion and Kaplan with details of the new proposal: Gustav Kullman, a Swiss citizen and deputy chairman, under Sir Herbert Emerson, of the Inter-Governmental

Committee on Refugees would be sent to Budapest to investigate the possibility of negotiating the fate of the Jews. The proposal was presented to the United States and the USSR; as Sharett reported, he himself had presented it to Randall and it was currently under review.[171]

On 16 July Ben-Gurion recounted the latest developments to his colleagues in the JAE. He detailed the course of the invitations received by Bader and said that Magnes had clarified the picture upon his arrival in Jerusalem. He pointed to the connections with the German Foreign Office, as expressed in "Consul Stiller's" involvement and the fact that Bader was actually invited to Berlin, which he believed made the matter all the more suspect as a "Nazi trick," by which he may have meant that one of the parties backbiting in Berlin had used the invitation to set up a trap for its adversaries.[172]

Ben-Gurion also singled out the change from enthusiasm to reserve experienced by Ira Hirschmann, of the American War Refugee Board, as a result of instructions "not to have further dealings with the Brand affair."[173] Sharett cabled Ben-Gurion twice on the decision against the ransom plan, but the two cables only reached their destination after the JAE meeting (one that same day and the other the following day). Thus, at the meeting Ben-Gurion could relate only to Hirschmann's behavior and signs of heel-dragging.[174]

THE LEAK

From this point things started moving quickly. Within three days it became clear that the worst possible thing had happened. The plan had been removed from the Allies' agenda (as the Transnistria Plan had earlier) through leaks to the press. On 19 July the matter was published in the *New York Herald Tribune* and the following day it was common knowledge throughout the free world and Palestine.[175] Within a few days it became clear both in Palestine and among the emissaries in Istanbul that the ransom plan that Brand had brought with him from Hungary was dead and

that it was time to investigate other rescue options.[176]

Responses were grim. Gruenbaum defined the leak as an "indescribable provocation. The Gestapo offers a secret proposal, this proposal is rejected, and then publication is made of what the Gestapo offered us . . . an unprecedented injustice, in which the blood of our brothers is given no consideration. . . ." Schind characterized Brand's mission as "the miserable plan" and lashed out in all directions—including at himself—for the fact that tens of thousands of Jews could have been saved if only the British had not been approached and if negotiations had begun immediately following Brand's arrival in Istanbul not two months later. All this second-guessing was unfounded, although it was voiced by a man experienced in undercover activity. I have already demonstrated that Britain and the United States had known of the plan from their own sources and kept its progress under close surveillance. Sharett said that the British did all they could to thwart the rescue plan, fearing "a flood of Jews in the event that anything came of it."[177]

Ben-Gurion did not respond directly to the leak. Nine days before the leak, he expressed his sentiments in an extremely outspoken public statement.[178] By contrast, his words in the tension-filled debate that followed the leak were devoted to refuting self-blame and were mainly aimed at Gruenbaum, who accused the JAE of being partly responsible for the plan's failure because of its decision to share information with Britain and the United States.

Gruenbaum's speech followed Kaplan's report of his journey to Turkey. It is worth dwelling on the speech within the context of his complex relationship with Ben-Gurion.[179] In the third chapter I touched on this relationship in the context of Gruenbaum's complex and thankless position as head of the Rescue Committee. Gruenbaum's ire was now aroused by the way in which Kaplan went straight from reporting on the Brand plan to demanding that Britain ensure the entry into Palestine of any Jew who managed to make it to Turkey. According to Kaplan, preparations had to be made for the immigration of thousands of Jews, and Britain had to allow them to enter.

Gruenbaum was furious. Hadn't the JAE learned from the Brand affair that Britain was not to be involved in rescue issues? Gruenbaum rightly pointed to the British government's announcement in the summer of 1943 that any Jews who managed to reach Turkey would be allowed to immigrate to Palestine, and he insisted that there was no need for debate, since the British were "using all kinds of tricks and intrigues to hold up the arrival of Jews in Palestine." "No further questions must be asked" that might lead to the British "placing obstacles in our way and making it impossible for us to rescue those that it is still possible to rescue." It was obvious, as it had been in the Brand affair, that nothing would come of it.

In linking the two issues Kaplan was mistaken both in terms of substance and strategy. First, the question of Jews arriving in Turkey being given automatic permission to immigrate to Palestine was very different from the Allies' attitude toward a complex process like the ransom plan, which could impact the management of the war and influence relationships among them. Second, from a tactical and rhetorical point of view, it was a mistake to even mention the words "permission from the British" in the current atmosphere of anger and frustration following Britain's thwarting of the plan to ransom the lives of Hungary's Jews. Third, there was no point in permitting Britain to "resell" a commitment to the Jews that they had already taken upon themselves.

"Have we committed a crime?" Ben-Gurion demanded in the midst of Gruenbaum's polemic. "We did what we had to do." Gruenbaum continued to complain bitterly that his conscience was not at rest, linking other allegations to this issue. He insisted that the JAE did not protect him when he and the Rescue Committee were at-tacked for inaction. When he spoke out, insisting that there was little chance of rescuing Jews, he was viewed "even by this desk" as not wishing to save Jews.[180]

Ben-Gurion called on Gruenbaum not to launch accusations: "We are all men of conscience here," and it would be best to avoid hinting at misdemeanors on the part of the JAE on the Brand issue. Even if errors had been made—insofar as "members of the JAE were mistaken" in the same way that Gruenbaum had made mistakes—there had been no bad intentions but simply a desire to help born of deep personal concern.

Kaplan, too, rejected Gruenbaum's accusations and called on him "not to complicate the debate with other things—important or not." Following a detailed and comprehensive investigation of the matter, he could declare that in the Brand affair the JAE had acted "correctly, out of political conscience, according to the best interests of the Hungarian Jews and those of the Jewish people. . . ." Kaplan knew whereof he spoke, having been intimately involved in the secret collaboration, the plan for rescuing children, the ransom plans, and having just returned from Istanbul.

In summing up his sentiments at the end of the debate, Gruenbaum may have realized that he had overstepped the mark in his unfounded accusations. "On the matter of conscience, I of course had no desire to offend [anyone]. I referred only to my own conscience. I said that my own conscience was not appeased."[181]

HORTHY'S ANNOUNCEMENT

On 20 July 1944, one day after the Brand affair was made public, the world press published an announcement by Hungarian dictator Admiral Miklós Horthy that Hungary was prepared to halt the deportation of Jews to Poland and to allow them to escape across its borders.

It is worth noting that at the time of this announcement Hungary had already been under

Nazi occupation for four months. It would appear that Horthy's change of heart grew out of a feeling that the Reich's days were numbered and that it was a shadow of its former self. This was plain to everyone, and it now seemed that this was the last chance to side with the victors. Horthy feared that the local gendarmerie, energetically rounding up Jews for deportation, might topple him from power. The Hungarians were especially fearful that reprisal would take the form of an air attack. The world press was filled with news of Auschwitz and the annihilation of Hungary's Jews, President Roosevelt's warning to Horthy, and the bombing of the railway station in Budapest—all of which increased Hungary's fears. The pope and the neutral states also influenced the situation, as did the willingness of various countries and organizations—such as the International Red Cross and the American War Refugee Board—to aid in the rescue of Jews.[182]

News of the Brand affair and Horthy's announcement created a new situation. It was hard to conduct such complex negotiations when all the details had been made public. Horthy's announcement also aroused certain hopes—for a few weeks at least—that a large-scale, aboveboard rescue operation would obviate the need for secret negotiations. Despite this hope, rescue activists were still concerning themselves with the invitation issued to Bader and proposals by German agents that Dobkin meet with SS people in Spain or Portugal, and another that Gustav Kullman of the Inter-Governmental Committee on Refugees negotiate with the Germans over the fate of the Jews.

Sharett wrote to the JAE that he was about to meet with someone in the British Foreign Office in order to discuss Kullman's mission. When Britain expressed displeasure about the latter proposal, Sharett suggested the International Red Cross as an alternative. He planned to put pressure on Britain through the Americans and asked the JAE to instruct Nahum Goldmann to be active once again in the United States. Sharett

also reported that Kasztner had told Dobkin of the Germans' willingness to meet him and Schwartz in Lisbon.[183]

The emissaries in Istanbul also tried to breathe new life into the plan by suggesting sending Bader to Hungary or Germany or arranging a meeting between Dobkin and Schwartz with representatives of the SS. Once again they informed the JAE of the Germans' willingness to meet in Spain and demanded a reply within ten days concerning the possible location. The emissaries reiterated that "Menaḥem's journey was imperative" and added that Schwartz had left Turkey en route to Jerusalem and would be held up there for a while on his way to Spain, probably to synchronize positions. They asked for this information to be passed along to Sharett in London.[184]

In late July (ten days after the leak) Pomeranz and Bader reported to the JAE from Istanbul concerning a cable Kasztner had sent them on 28 July. Kasztner wrote that the Germans proposed holding a meeting with the "black" (Schwartz) at the French-Spanish border and they wanted to set the date. About twelve hundred of the seventeen hundred people Eichmann had permitted to leave were now at Bergen-Belsen and five hundred were leaving soon for Spain. A man called "Schröder" was among the German representatives who would be coming to the French-Spanish border. We do not know if he was the same Frantisek Laufer involved in earlier incidents.[185] In the end Dobkin failed completely in his efforts to obtain permission from the British and Americans for him and Schwartz to meet with the Germans. They were told that there would be no negotiations, neither involving goods nor money.[186]

Horthy's announcement raised hopes because it was public, the result of pressure on Hungary, and because it was preceded by a remission in deportations to the death camps. The hope was tangible in Sharett's cable from London to Jerusalem:

In light of Horthy's announcement, we recommend (1) the immediate renewal of the Swiss and Swedish proposals for [rescuing] children; (2) increasing the number of immigration certificates to Palestine; (3) [supplying] Adler-Rudel with financial resources for the Swedish project; (4) further review of the Kullman idea, based on the evacuation of Hungarian Jews.[187]

What was Sweden's role in all this? Earlier in this study I described the attempt to rescue Jewish children by transferring them to neutral Sweden. The plan was examined at the beginning of 1943, shortly after the official news of the annihilation.[188] Now, nine months later, the possibility existed that the plan might be realized. In fact, on 1 July (just under three weeks before Horthy's public announcement) Sweden had contacted the JAE in Jerusalem with the promise that Jewish refugees from Hungary would be permitted to enter Sweden.[189] Sweden therefore was destined to be the country of refuge for those Jews leaving Hungary following Horthy's announcement. Schlomo Adler-Rudel, the Jewish Agency emissary, was again sent to Sweden to lay the groundwork for the operation.[190] This course of action offered more promise than sending Bader to Berlin to spite the Allies.

BAGYONI AND KLEIST IN STOCKHOLM

From this point on Sweden became the focal point of rescue attempts for the Jews of Hungary. Even in this northern geographical shift of activity there is more hidden than aboveboard. At least two of the earlier leading players (Bader and Bagyoni [Feri] were involved in events concerning Sweden. Bagyoni arrived in Sweden in September, shortly after Adler-Rudel. The object of his visit was not at all clear, but he brought with him a recommendation written by Bader plus letters to Adler-Rudel and Dr. Marcus Ehrenpreis, the chief rabbi of Sweden's Jews. Bader wrote that "Feri" had served the rescue emissaries in Istanbul and that he could be relied upon to help in the matter of "Ezra hagar," the code name for the rescue of Hungary's Jews.

Adler-Rudel asked for confirmation from the JAE that connections with Feri were conducted with its authority and asked if Barlas was also familiar with Feri and supported Bader's recommendation. After meeting with Bagyoni, Adler-Rudel wrote Bader that he had not supplied him with any special proposal or new details. Bader's reply, in the form of three cables, assured Adler-Rudel that Bagyoni aided Kasztner in his efforts to rescue Hungary's Jews and stressed that for over a year and a half he and his colleagues had worked with Bagyoni and that he could be trusted.[191]

Bader's report to the JAE in Jerusalem on the "match" Bader made between Adler-Rudel and Feri dispels some confusion. There was a prevailing fear that the Nazis' death throes would reflect on the Jews—especially those remaining in Poland—in the form of "blitzkrieg attacks that would leave no trace," and Bader hoped for Feri's help in thwarting them. Bader further reported that Adler-Rudel had told him that he was awaiting "the arrival of an Ashkenazi [German] with whom to negotiate . . . and it was possible that negotiations similar to those of Sali [Mayer] were being conducted on other fronts." The Ashkenazi mentioned was Dr. Bruno Peter Kleist, whose negotiations and those conducted by Sali Mayer in Switzerland are discussed elsewhere.[192]

Bagyoni's arrival in Stockholm and the ties between him and Adler-Rudel were known to the Americans, who were aware of all developments, including Bader's cables to Adler-Rudel and Ehrenpreis's and Adler-Rudel's meetings in Stockholm. They read the cables sent by the Yishuv's rescue emissaries in Istanbul and already saw in Bagyoni and his colleagues intelligence objectives. A further source of information was the report Adler-Rudel himself sent to the British ambassador and to Count Folke Bernadotte, then deputy chairman of the Swedish Red Cross.

What worried the Americans? First of all, they were unable to understand what Bagyoni was doing in Stockholm. They recalled that Bagyoni had worked for Otto Hatz, Hungary's military attaché in Bulgaria and an agent in the Dogwood network, which was already known to be serving many masters. They also knew that Bagyoni worked with Lothar Kövess, a member of the colorful Hungarian enclave in Istanbul, who was a double agent subject to the close scrutiny of the Americans.[193] Of course, the Americans also had an ongoing interest in keeping tabs on Zionist plans for mass immigration.

Another mystery surrounded Peter Kleist's mission in Stockholm. A businessman in his late thirties, he was the emissary of German Foreign Minister von Ribbentrop, but he also acted on behalf of the SS and even served the Abwehr in his spare time. There were connections, intentional or otherwise, between his assignment and those of Brand and Grosz. For example, Bader and Bagyoni were implicated in both missions.

Kleist visited Stockholm several times during the summer and autumn of 1944. Iver Olsen—the financial attaché at the American embassy in Stockholm and a representative of the American War Refugee Board who was also attached to the OSS in Stockholm—enlisted his services. Kleist bore a double message: a proposal for separate negotiations with the West and a willingness to release Jews from the Nazi murder machine.[194]

Kleist had already begun conducting preliminary talks and had sent messages between von Ribbentrop and representatives of the West from 1942 to 1943. During these visits he also met with Count Folke Bernadotte.[195] At that time he was already offering to release Jews (two thousand Latvian Jews in return for two million dollars) to improve relations between Germany and the West. He later lowered the price to the equivalent of two million Swedish crowns (half a million dollars) in foreign currency on the condition that

Germany be allowed to buy supplies—especially medicine—in Sweden. It is hard to ignore the similarity between this idea and the earlier overtures to Hungary.[196]

As Kleist testified after the war, at the beginning of 1944 he met Hillel Storch, chairman of the Swedish branch of the World Jewish Congress. At this meeting they discussed the possibility of rescuing thousands of Estonian Jews as well as the fate of other Jews imprisoned in German concentration camps. During these visits in Stockholm—some of which took place around the time of Brand's and Grosz's departure for Istanbul—he also met with Adler-Rudel, the Jewish Agency's representative in Sweden, and an anonymous Jewish businessman (probably Eric Warburg, a Jewish banker from Stockholm).

Most researchers are convinced that the motive behind Kleist's proposal was similar to that of the other proposals, namely, a desire to open a separate communications channel with the West through discussions concerning the fate of the Jews. Particularly on the eve of defeat, the Jews were practically the only "goods" the Germans were able to offer the West. They discovered that the West was not about to go out of its way to purchase these "goods." It can be ascertained that Kleist's mission, like other steps taken by Germany at the time, originated within Himmler's circle—or at least was based on the latter's knowledge and tacit approval.[197]

Adler-Rudel arrived in Stockholm equipped with a list of Hungarian Jews, supplied by the JAE in Jerusalem, for whom he was to arrange Swedish "safe conduct" certificates—the selfsame idea that Randall and Henderson of the British Foreign Office had told Weizmann was ridiculous (12 July 1944). The Jewish Agency's *modus operandi* was obvious: when one channel appeared blocked, it approached the matter from another direction. The emerging picture, therefore, does not confirm the subsequent negative image of the Jewish Agency as inactive regarding the rescue of Jews.

Immediately following his arrival in Stockholm, Adler-Rudel heard from Storch about Kleist's activity. Storch had already met Kleist on several occasions and had proposed that the Nazis release several thousand Jews being held in Bergen-Belsen and supply them with South American passports. Included in this group were thirteen hundred Jews from the famous "Kasztner train," who had left Hungary and were being held temporarily in Bergen-Belsen. Another three to four thousand Jews from the Balkans were being held in German forced labor camps, and an additional three hundred Jewish women were imprisoned in a camp near Tallinn in Estonia.[198]

As with negotiations concerning Latvian Jews, Kleist at first demanded a million dollars but later agreed to accept a million Swedish crowns, with which the Nazis would buy medicine from Sweden. Adler-Rudel was thus involved in activity that had begun before his arrival. He apparently made a point of reporting to the British embassy and to Count Bernadotte to prevent this activity from interfering with his main objective in Sweden, namely, the rescue of Jewish children. Of course, he also reported to the London branch of the Jewish Agency and to the rescue emissaries in Istanbul, where his information was transferred to Jerusalem.[199]

It is not entirely clear which Nazi figure was behind the proposals discussed in Stockholm. Here, too, there were many players. The emissaries sent by the Germans secured their own interests amid the tenuous reality that surrounded the chaotic German government. They reported to whichever side seemed sufficiently important and strong enough to protect them. Kleist, who was sent by von Ribbentrop, secretly reported to Ernst Kaltenbrunner, then head of the Reich Main Security Office (RSHA). Apparently he also reported to Himmler, Kaltenbrunner's patron and von Ribbentrop's enemy.[200]

Was there any connection between these feelers being put out in Stockholm and other initiatives being bandied about around the same time in Istanbul, Spain, Portugal, and Switzerland? How significant is it that in all these locations one finds representatives from the Yishuv, American Jews, members of the JDC or the WJC, representatives of the WRB (in Switzerland, this was Rosewell McLelland), as well as various emissaries from the Nazi side?[201]

What is clear from this set of complex coincidences is that the JAE had been trying to put into action an initiative—part of the plan to rescue children—since early 1943. Also obvious are the threads connecting the Yishuv leadership and the Zionist movement in Jerusalem and London with their operative arms in Jerusalem, Istanbul, Lisbon, and Stockholm. Also apparent is the involvement of the JDC (both with and without the Jewish Agency) at that time. Equally well known is Adler-Rudel's mission in Sweden, namely, to transform the Swedish government's promises and Horthy's declaration into a workable system for rescuing Jews.

On the other hand, it is not at all clear how Bagyoni, arriving in Stockholm on a German transit permit, figured in these activities. Was there any connection between Horthy's declaration and Bagyoni's mission? Was Bagyoni enlisted to escalate the release of Hungary's remaining Jews thanks to his connections within Hungary? Were certain persons interested in sending a loud and clear message that Horthy's proposal was practical and that the Hungarian establishment was indeed looking for a way of breaking free of the German stranglehold? If so, how was it possible that American intelligence services knew nothing of a plan in which the United States was purported to be a central player, forcing it to make inquiries worldwide about Bagyoni's journey to Stockholm?

Moreover, it is unclear whether there was a connection between Kleist's mission and the two invitations received by Bader to Budapest and Berlin. Bagyoni was indeed involved in Bader's invitation to Budapest, which was almost certainly sent by the SS, but it would appear that this time he had come to Stockholm at another's bidding. Perhaps he did so with the intention of creating a convenient alibi for a time when the West had won the war. It is also possible that he was sent by his superiors in the Hungarian intelligence services. Then again, he may simply have escaped to Stockholm to distance himself from his betrayed handlers in the multilateral espionage operations he and Otto Hatz were mixed up in. It is also possible that he was sent by German intelligence to ferret out anti-Nazi activity in Stockholm and to close ranks against the impending disintegration of the Nazi camp.[202]

Why did Bader recommend that Adler-Rudel cooperate with Bagyoni? One cannot be certain since everything was linked to everything else: intelligence, rescue, and smuggling. In any event, it is clear that after the rejection of Brand's ransom plan, attention shifted to Horthy's announcement, and it was hoped that large-scale, aboveboard, government-initiated rescue operations would now go into effect. Thus, the possibility of Bader conducting independent negotiations with the Germans was shoved to the sidelines.[203] Furthermore, the open and clandestine negotiations conducted by various representatives of the Nazi camp with Adler-Rudel and Storch and with Mayer and Kasztner would have made Bader's journey to Berlin superfluous.

NEGOTIATIONS BETWEEN MAYER AND KASZTNER AND BECHER AND KRUMEY

During the summer and early autumn of 1944, the two arenas in which the fate of Europe's Jews was discussed were Sweden and Switzerland. In Switzerland negotiations focused on transferring Jews through Switzerland to the Iberian Peninsula. In many ways these talks resembled those that had preceded them: they expressed the desire of elite Nazi groups to sell Jews in return for money and the opening up of channels to the West; representatives of the Nazi camp were usually the same people and all had ties to Himmler's camp; and they faced a motley collection of Yishuv activists and representatives of the JDC, the World Jewish Congress, the American War Refugee Board, as well as others representing the United States and Britain.

In both Switzerland and Sweden Jewish forces tried to jump-start negotiations, if only to halt the extermination process and save as many Jews as possible before the Nazis were defeated. Allied forces were constantly advancing on all fronts into the heart of Europe, and negotiations for the rescue of Jews through Sweden actually took place after the Allies had already liberated several concentration camps inside Germany itself.

While the Germans were sending out feelers to the West, they continued to murder Jews. Beginning on 8 November 1944, the Nazis' arsenal of destruction was expanded to include the horrific "death march." Thirty to fifty thousand of Budapest's Jews marched along the Budapest-Vienna highway some 180 kilometers toward the Austrian border, while the Nazis picked out the weaker ones on the way and shot them to death. The extermination, therefore, continued virtually up to the final moments before the collapse of the Nazi government.

Negotiations over the rescue of Jews through Sweden were conducted at a time when the Third Reich was breathing its last. This might explain why in April 1945, only days before the final collapse, a meeting took place in Berlin between Reichsführer SS Himmler and the Jewish representative of the World Zionist Congress. This meeting played a very minor role in Ben-Gurion's agenda and that of the Yishuv's intelligence establishment, the reasons for this being twofold. First, from the Yishuv's point of view negotiations with the Nazi camp thus far had proved that they were no more than wishful meanderings and that Britain and the United States would prevent any real results from emerging. Second, toward the end of the war Ben-Gurion and his colleagues focused their efforts on attempting to reach those Jews who had survived the Nazi withdrawal.

Ben-Gurion and his colleagues in the JAE strove to collect the Jews in the liberated zones, care for them, and prepare them for immigration to Palestine or for the anticipated political struggle following the war. These tasks seemed to be more practical to the Yishuv, although they, too, involved political and economic problems. Senior members of the operational hierarchy were responsible for carrying them out, and the Yishuv's leaders devoted most of their attention to them.[204] It is for this reason that Gruenbaum and the Rescue Committee were involved in the later ransom plans on behalf of the Yishuv. Most probably the Political Department and the illegal immigration operation had little faith that any positive results would emerge from negotiations in Sweden and Switzerland.[205]

Before briefly describing the main points of these negotiations, I wish to draw the reader's attention to the connection between the possibility of acting semiautonomously (discussed by Sharett, Hirschmann, and Schwartz) and Sali Mayer's plan in Switzerland. The former discussions, held in Cairo in June 1944, focused on establishing a large monetary fund and conducting direct negotiations—which was precisely Mayer's objective in Switzerland.

On 21 August 1944 five people met on the bridge spanning the Rhine canal between Saint Margareten in Switzerland and Höchst in Austria. These included Sali Mayer of the JDC, Dr. Israel Kasztner of Hungary, and three SS officers—Kurt Becher, Hermann Krumey, and an unidentified officer. Most of them had been involved in previous ransom plans. The meeting was aimed at examining another ransom plan involving those European Jews who had survived the Nazis. There was nothing new in terms of the concept, the method, or the participants.[206]

Mayer gambled. Like the Yishuv emissaries who forged two "agreements" and were not in possession of the money the sellers of Jews were demanding of them, Mayer was forced to manipulate and maneuver. The American authorities agreed that he could create the illusion he was negotiating in order to buy time and to hold up the extermination process, but they forbade him from negotiating over a plan that was similar to the one Brand had brought from Hungary. He was also expressly forbidden to turn up at a meeting as the official representative of the United States and to offer the Nazis money or goods. These bans were issued from Washington by Rosewell McClelland, the representative of the War Refugee Board in Switzerland. The JDC center in New York also placed severe restrictions on Mayer's negotiations with the Becher-Krumey group. When Schwarz arrived in Switzerland, he, too, was forbidden to conduct negotiations.[207]

Mayer ignored the ban and entered into negotiations. The first meeting took place in August on the aforementioned bridge that connected Switzerland to Austria—and for a very prosaic reason: The Swiss government was reluctant to permit the entry of Nazi officers into its neutral territory. The Nazis proposed that the Jews supply ten thousand trucks to be used for agricultural purposes, and in return Jews would be released to the United States.[208] As the negotiations dragged on into September, October, and early 1945, the Nazis asked for goods. Mayer tried to offer money, but even the sums he talked about were not at his disposal. He had no more than what he had actually managed to collect in Switzerland.

In October and November these negotiations were joined by local Jewish initiatives in Hungary and Switzerland. Until then Mayer had successfully transferred both money and tractors, and at one point he even obtained permission from Stettinius, the U.S. secretary of state, to transfer twenty million Swiss francs from the JDC center in New York to their account in Switzerland, but Stettinius forbade him to hand the money over to the Nazis. The deposit, meant to serve as a signal that the negotiations were serious, gave Mayer a chance to buy precious time.[209]

The last meeting between Mayer and the Nazis took place in February 1945. Mayer showed them the bank slip confirming the transfer of twenty million francs from the JDC in New York. He tried to bring the Jews under the auspices of the International Red Cross. The Jewish negotiators in Sweden had also tried a similar maneuver.[210]

What were the results of Mayer's negotiations? He appears to have brought about a softening of Nazi policy toward the Jews. It is possible that the holdup in deportations of Budapest's Jews during August 1944 resulted from these negotiations. He may also have effected a positive change in attitude toward the Jews being held in several camps, and may even have paved the way for a "smooth" transfer of the camps to the Allies.[211]

It is worth mentioning that Walter Schellenberg, Himmler's close associate and one of the SS heads, was also active on the Nazi side, as was Clages, SD commander in Budapest, who took a leading role in the Brand affair. Clages had been party to dealings with Mayer since September. Schellenberg's involvement was another sign of Himmler's presence behind the Nazi negotiating team.[212]

To return to Palestine and Ben-Gurion, when Kaplan returned from Turkey, he brought preliminary information on negotiation attempts in Switzerland. At a JAE meeting Kaplan told those present: "We are at the beginning of a momentous event that could be very large." He also informed them that Schwartz, the JDC chief in Europe, had left Istanbul for Lisbon "in order to make attempts from the other end," and that Adler-Rudel had been sent to Stockholm. Kaplan also reported that he had taken certain steps in order to ensure the availability of money for the evacuation of Jewish children to the Iberian Peninsula.[213] More detailed information had already reached Ben-Gurion's desk on 22 August 1944, a day after the meeting in Saint Margareten. Ehud Avriel reported from Istanbul on additional Nazi signals in the direction of Switzerland: "The Germans want another meeting on this matter in Switzerland. Any other plan, as well as the carrying out of Horthy's declaration on immigration to Palestine, depends on this meeting. Some 2,000 [people on Kasztner's train] have been taken to Bergen-Belsen—probably for exchange or release when the meeting takes place."[214] Two days later Jerusalem sent this message to Sharett in London and asked for his intervention.[215] In October 1944 Ben-Gurion met with Brand and mentioned negotiations in Switzerland. Brand had just been released from custody in Cairo. Ben-Gurion told him of the efforts to rescue the remaining Jews of Hungary and expressed his hope for positive results from Mayer's and Kasztner's negotiations in Switzerland.[216]

A JEW CONFRONTING THE MURDERER OF HIS PEOPLE

Similar negotiations were being held in Sweden. This time they were centered around Felix Kersten, personal masseur to Himmler, who was conducting negotiations with members of the Swedish branch of the World Jewish Congress. Kersten, a German of Baltic origin with a Finnish passport, had managed to assuage certain of Himmler's physical pains and thereby gain his trust, eventually becoming his confidant.[217]

Kersten arrived in Sweden in 1943. From the beginning he tried to mediate between Himmler and the West. In Himmler's name (or so he alleged) Kersten proposed that the American OSS representative in Stockholm fly to Berlin for a meeting with Himmler.[218] During 1944 and 1945 Kersten established connections between Himmler and Hillel Storch as well as other representatives of the World Jewish Congress. Sweden's steadfast involvement in attempts to rescue Jews—especially from Hungary—served as a backdrop to these activities.

Like Bader, Dobkin, and Schwartz, Storch was also invited to Berlin, this time for a meeting with Himmler himself. In early March 1945 Kersten delivered the invitation directly from Himmler. At the same time, Himmler promised to release ten thousand Jews to Sweden or Switzerland. Storch consulted with the Swedish Foreign Office, which told him that his journey was imperative, an opinion shared by Count Folke Bernadotte—affiliated with the Swedish Red Cross at the time —who was about to set off for Berlin on rescue missions. Another player on the Nazi side was Schellenberg, who had established contact with Mayer and other Jews in Switzerland.

Storch made sure to report his own activity and developments in the negotiations to several people. Gruenbaum received these reports, as did Adler-Rudel (who had returned to London in the meantime) and Josef Linton, the experienced secretary of the London branch of the Jewish Agency. He also reported to Stephen Wise, Nahum Goldmann, and Arieh Tartakover, all members of the World Jewish Congress in the United States. Wise and Goldmann were also members of the Jewish Agency's American branch, and both organizations worked in close cooperation. Storch, who asked that his journey be kept a secret, wrote that Himmler had stressed that any leak of such a program would point up Germany's weakness and force him to renege on his promises.[219] Four days later (31 March) Storch informed those same colleagues that he had also consulted with Rabbi Ehrenpreis and that they were both convinced that time could be bought by holding negotiations with Himmler. Storch therefore decided to set off for Berlin.[220]

Kersten sent out feelers throughout April. In early spring 1945 the Jewish side in the negotiations decided that Norbert Masur would go to Berlin. Masur was the chairman of the Stockholm Zionist society and was also treasurer of the local chapter of the World Jewish Congress.[221] On Saturday, 20 April 1945, ten days before Hitler's suicide in a Berlin bunker, Masur met Himmler at Kersten's estate near Berlin.

The meeting lasted more than two and a half hours. Masur demanded that Himmler stop deporting Jews to extermination camps and allow all the survivors to remain where they were or to leave Germany with the help of the International Red Cross. Moreover, he demanded that Himmler order all camp commanders to treat the Jews humanely and, over time, to hand over the camps to the advancing Allied forces. Masur also supplied Himmler with a list of Jews whose immediate release was being demanded by the World Jewish Congress.

Himmler said that the Nazis had recently been responsible for the release of large numbers of prisoners from several camps. The Allied forces had released prisoners from other camps, including Bergen-Belsen and Dachau. Himmler complained that the Allies had made public the sights they encountered upon entering the liberated camps in Germany. This was propaganda, remonstrated Himmler.[222]

Masur reckoned that this group included several dozen Norwegian Jews from the list he had given Himmler; Swedish Jews from another list; a thousand Jewish women who had been transferred to Sweden from the Ravensbrück camp; and several Jews from Theresienstadt. He also expected Himmler to place an unequivocal ban on murdering Jews in the camps and allow the Red Cross to provide food and medicine.

Himmler's single condition was that the entire transaction be kept secret, that no details would be reported on the reasons behind the releases, and that the latter would not be linked to Himmler or his people. According to Masur, one of the participants at the meeting told him that Hitler was still firmly opposed to any concessions to the Jews, and that if he were to get wind of the decisions reached at that meeting he would probably thwart them. The man told Masur that even just three weeks before the end of the war, Himmler was not about to defy Hitler even if he had the ability to do so.

In the course of the meeting, Himmler tried to spread lies, but Masur did not place much faith in his commitments. Nonetheless, Himmler definitely appeared to be trying to salvage something at the last moment. Masur believed that Himmler might exterminate the few Jews who remained, but that there was a chance that he would fulfill some of his commitments. All this information was sent to the JAE in Jerusalem and to Adler-Rudel and Linton at the London branch. After the war, Adler-Rudel reckoned that twelve hundred Jewish women were indeed released from Ravensbrück on Himmler's orders.[223]

It can be established that Ben-Gurion and his colleagues in the JAE and the London and U.S. branches were aware of the discussions being held in Switzerland and Sweden.[224] Although they were supplied with reports on the main developments, they were not as involved as they had been in the Brand mission and its ramifications. As far as they were concerned, the talks in Switzerland and Sweden were a continuation of previous efforts that had produced virtually no results.

The negotiations and communications had thus reached a peak with the meeting between a Jew and an archmurderer, Reichsfuhrer SS Heidrich Himmler, second in command in an administration whose objective was to dehumanize and exterminate "the Jew." Himmler met with a representative of the World Jewish Congress and the Zionist movement. It was a dramatic and even pathetic and absurd finale to a horrific event. It was under such circumstances that the curtain fell on the final act, which was marked by an array of attempts to rescue Jews during the Second World War, all of which were complex and daring but none of which had a strong enough grasp of reality.

Ben-Gurion was deeply involved in the Brand affair, which constituted the main effort to rescue the Jews of Hungary and the surviving Jews in other European countries, a rescue plan riddled with all the problems characteristic of previous efforts. He played a central role in determining general policies and tactical strategies. In the JAE debate held on 2 April 1944, two weeks after the Nazi invasion of Hungary, he did not reject direct

negotiations with the Nazis over the release of Jews. Nonetheless, his expectations for the success of such negotiations were none too high because the Allies were unwavering in their demand for an unconditional German surrender. When the Brand plan was placed on the JAE's desk, he declared that it was "quite implausible" and that the Germans clearly had "one objective—to exterminate the Jews." He did not seek the easy way out of this pessimistic evaluation and determined that "if there's a one-in-a-million chance—we must grab it."[225] As the affair moved forward, Ben-Gurion emphasized that as far as the Jews were concerned, the main objective was to hold up the extermination by entering into negotiations even if this proved futile. He skillfully used artifice to convince the Nazis that their proposals were being given serious consideration and to motivate them to put off the murders.[226]

The Brand affair illustrates the way in which Ben-Gurion was forced to maneuver in order to maintain the necessary operational freedom of movement in the face of the reality of the Yishuv in Palestine: subservient to a foreign power that kept close tabs on every move made by the local leadership; confronting a world war and the extermination of the Jews of Europe. This necessitated the emergency procedures adopted by Ben-Gurion, such as not recording debates, conclusions, or instructions attached to certain decisions that were relayed by "word of mouth," and even bypassing the JAE, which unwittingly found itself approving decisions made by Ben-Gurion and his confidantes.[227]

As we have seen, this need to maneuver between extreme extenuating circumstances forced Ben-Gurion to establish a "parallel system" of debating, planning, and decision making alongside the leadership's "formal" bodies. The fingerprints of this system are apparent throughout the Brand affair, at the center of which was the leadership triumvirate—Ben-Gurion, Sharett, and Kaplan. These men proved outstanding. These men motivated a group of young, courageous, and devoted helpers who admittedly lacked operational experience and professional training. This group was headed by Meirov and Zaslani. Others included: Epstein, Kollek, and Avriel; Schind, Bader, and Pomeranz.

Even this parallel system was not always as coordinated as it should have been. It was often disorganized and riddled by conflicting loyalties. It grew out of a pluralistic, involved public composed of diverse bodies, movements, and political parties, immigrant organizations, and trade unions. Thus, the *modus operandi* of this parallel system involved improvisation and even operating within "gray areas."[228]

Most of the members of this secret group were aware of events before they became known to the JAE. Sometimes they were even aware of activity carried out without JAE approval or that contradicted its (recorded) policies. As we have seen, the JAE records make no mention of two major funding agreements between the Jewish Agency and the JDC or of a report of debates, held by representatives from the two organizations, concerning JDC aide to Jewish plans involving semiautonomous activity against the Nazis.[229]

The Brand affair also illustrates the way in which the Yishuv's intelligence channels operated. The latest information first landed on Ben-Gurion's desk and that of the parallel system surrounding him. Venya Pomeranz arrived in Palestine on 24 May 1944 and immediately reported to Ben-Gurion and Sharett. According to one source, upon his return from Aleppo Sharett reported first to Ben-Gurion. Agronsky returned from London and reported first to Ben-Gurion only on Weizmann's and Sharett's activity regarding the Brand issue and the "self-defense plan." This was also the pattern followed by Judah Magnes and Harry Vitals of the JDC and Kaplan and Eliash upon their return from Turkey. News of the Nazis' invitation to Bader first reached Ben-Gurion and only later was shared with his colleagues.[230] Ben-Gurion was the first to receive information about unfolding developments from London and Istanbul even if it was addressed to Cohen or Kaplan. This is also obvious from information contained in Ben-Gurion's reports to the JAE.

The members of this secret group usually deferred to Ben-Gurion's authority. He was the senior political leader, chairman of the JAE, and head of the Zionist Labor movement's major political party (all members of the group belonged to the labor movement). Since Ben-Gurion, Sharett, and Kaplan were more attentive than their colleagues to special wartime needs, Ben-Gurion established a special relationship, based on mutual respect, with the people involved in the Yishuv's secret activities.

Ben-Gurion's tendency was to uphold, as far as possible, the rules of democratic leadership even during a state of emergency, and he strove to involve the JAE in all strategic decisions. After Brand's arrival from Hungary, he convened the JAE for three extraordinary sessions. On 25 May he called his colleagues together for a hearing on Pomeranz's report; on 14 June they met at his home in Tel Aviv, following Sharett's return and his report on the Aleppo meeting; on 24 June they met to discuss Sharett's Cairo meetings with Hirschmann, Schwartz, and Moyne prior to Sharett's departure for London. The JAE also continued to hold regular Sunday meetings, which were devoted, in part, to discussions on the Brand affair and its ramifications. On one of these occasions Ben-Gurion demanded that his colleagues confront these complex dilemmas, and for the first time since the ransom issue was placed on the agenda they were all required to air their views. From the very beginning, he had also activated the JAE's branches in London and Washington, represented by Goldmann and Weizmann, whom he instructed to win the support of the two superpowers.[231]

Ben-Gurion also acted on a tactical level. For example, as soon as the Brand affair became known to him, he insisted on sending Sharett to Istanbul (even without the necessary entry permit) and from there to London. It was Ben-Gurion who insisted on including the United States and Britain in the secret plan, and he was also the person who passed along all new information to Sharett in London.[232] As we have seen, Ben-Gurion was the one who oversaw the Yishuv's and the Zionist movement's tactics throughout the Brand affair.

Important operational partnerships developed in the course of the Brand affair. Political and ideological differences among the large Jewish organizations were pushed aside. Dr. Magnes of the "Brit Shalom" and the JDC, who visited Turkey on an aid-and-rescue mission, brought back with him up-to-date information on Bader's invitations, which he handed over to Ben-Gurion. The JDC cooperated with the Zionist leadership and even considered the possibility of the Jewish side secretly allocating money for independent negotiations with the Nazis.

These secret discussions express a certain measure of independence. Even if plans that were debated did not materialize, it was not the consequence of a non-creative thought process but rather because the rescue of Jews—supposing the Nazis were to agree to release them—was wholly dependent on the West. The Yishuv leaders welcomed the intervention of Hirschmann, who represented an American government–affiliated body and was an enthusiastic supporter of the Bergson (Kook) group, although instructions from Washington forced Hirschmann to withdraw his offer to lend a hand in unconventional rescue procedures. Unlike Hirschmann, who had to follow the orders of those who were indifferent to the fate of the Jews, one can contrast the relative independence of certain Jewish people who acted on behalf of the Zionist movement and such organizations as the JDC and the World Jewish Congress. Both organizations also cooperated with the JAE in negotiations held in Switzerland and Sweden, which was reflected in the fact that Zionists such as Stephen Wise and Nahum Goldmann carried out a joint mission on behalf of the Jewish Agency and the World Jewish Congress.

Unlike the two previous ransom plans, no information was leaked to the public concerning the JAE's secret discussions of the Eichmann proposal and its repercussions—a clear sign of maturity. Despite tactical differences among members of the JAE and notwithstanding heavy pressure placed on them by the Yishuv's ex-Hungarian population, the issues discussed by the JAE were not sensationalized.

The Brand affair raises a painful question: Did Ben-Gurion and the Yishuv leadership make their participation in plans to rescue the Jews of Europe contingent on the refugees coming only to Palestine? In other words, did they refrain from taking part in rescue plans that provided refuge outside of Palestine? There clearly was no such stipulation, since the proposal to rescue Hungary's Jews was based on a ban against sending them to Palestine. (Eichmann himself provided five reasons for the ban.) All the plans discussed in the wake of Brand's mission and even afterward never suggested that refuge be restricted to Palestine.

It could, of course, be claimed that Ben-Gurion was conducting himself like a savvy politician who, though realizing he had to come to terms with the ban, also knew that most of the Jews sent to Spain, Portugal, Sweden, and Switzerland would ultimately end up in Palestine because at that time there weren't many "takers" for Jewish refugees.[233] Even if one were to accept the dubious logic behind this allegation, there is no denying the fact that Ben-Gurion made no conditions and acted to the best of his ability to rescue the Jews of Hungary. His involvement in the Brand affair was so great that Gruenbaum complained that Ben-Gurion was undermining Gruenbaum's own efforts.[234]

The Brand affair also revealed Ben-Gurion's susceptibility to pressure from immigrant organizations, typically those that had not been contained by the Rescue Committee, his "lightning rod." On 23 March 1944 he met with an important delegation of ex-Hungarians and did his best to fulfill most of their requests. He also met with leaders of the Jerusalem Sephardic community, discussed the possibility of rescuing the Jews of Greece, and hinted at "negotiations with the devil," who did not distinguish between Ashkenazic and Sephardic blood. Ben-Gurion asked his counterparts to pull together and calm things down in their respective communities. This meeting took place in the wake of the polemic Gruenbaum was involved in at the time.[235]

A review of the Brand affair clearly shows the obstacles the Yishuv's leadership faced in deciphering the enormous complexity of the various procedures involved. On the one hand there were the Nazis with their labyrinthine chain of command, their conflicting intentions, and the gap between what they said and what was actually happening. On the other hand there was Ben-Gurion and his colleagues, taking a stand against Britain and the United States, who were offering the Yishuv sympathy and promising tactical cooperation while doing their utmost to thwart any attempt at a mass rescue of Jews. One should also not forget the Russians as a primary player. They were terrified of a German conspiracy with the West, which as early as 1943 had been an option among certain circles in the Nazi establishment. Moreover, the Russians were not overly enthusiastic about rescuing Jews.

PERPLEXING QUESTIONS

Ben-Gurion was required to ask the right questions in real time, based on fragmentary information that was often misleading and riddled with contradictions, without having at his disposal any retrospective knowledge. Thus, he and his colleagues were unsure whether Germany really intended to carry out its promise to "sell" a million Jews. The Nazis may have intended to release small groups at a high political or personal price. Perhaps Ben-Gurion and his colleagues assumed that Nazi Germany could hold on only if

it managed to spread confusion among the Allies, leading to open conflict, with Russia leaving the pact.

Simply leaking information on these negotiations would have been sufficient for the Russians—who were by nature suspicious—to become quite agitated. Whoever designed the ransom plan may have intended to cast a shadow over the superpowers by suggesting a "separate peace" with the West and continued war against the USSR, or did they intend to use to such a revolutionary process to counter the old/new threat against the world, namely, communism? The Germans probably intended to sow dissent among their enemies by manipulating the "omnipotent" Jews into pressuring the superpowers, to embarrass them with an apparently far-reaching proposal to rescue Jews, to maneuver them into refusing and then claiming that they put the Jews at their disposal but they didn't want them. Perhaps the Nazis hoped that such a process would improve their position in the peace talks following the war.

But if this was a blatant act of propaganda, why did it take place in secret? Why, for example, was the proposal not broadcast over Radio Berlin? After all, the pressure on Britain and the United States would have been so much greater, the confusion would have increased, and it would have been harder for anyone to wriggle out. These feelers may have been aimed at overturning the economic embargo to which Germany was subject. Those behind the proposal probably assumed that by sending out ships bearing coffee, cocoa, and other goods, the Western powers would be indicating to other countries wanting to do business with Germany that the embargo had been lifted.

It is also possible that the objective of the ransom proposal was to frustrate the Allies' plans to open a new battlefront against Germany from the west. An imminent invasion from the west, coupled with a million Jews on their way west and southwest to Spain and Portugal, would have blocked the main highways, bridges, and all major access roads, possibly halting the invasion altogether.

It is possible that the Nazis simply hoped to achieve some quiet in Hungary and to extort money from the Jews there—to instill in them the false hope that a solution was close at hand in order to prevent them from rebelling or preparing their self-defense, as they had done in Warsaw, and leaving the arena clear for annihilating them in peace. Such trickery had its horrific precedents, with names such as "resettlement," "transferring to the east" and other euphemisms.

It was hard to understand the discrepancy between Eichmann's proposal and the continued deportation of Jews from Hungary to Auschwitz. Nor did they stop after June, when Bader was invited to Budapest. Another long list of questions could be posed regarding the intentions of the Hungarians and the Nazis and the origin of the Eichmann's ransom proposal. No simple response suffices, since it would have been hard to assume that anyone on the German side could have supposed that Britain or the United States would have agreed to send the Germans ten thousand trucks at that stage in the war.

Even today there is still no consensus among historians on a number of major issues. For example, was Eichmann serious about his proposal? Was he acting under instructions from Himmler or had he misinterpreted Himmler's intentions? Was he acting out of a desire to thwart, once and for all, Himmler's tendency and complete the "final solution" at any cost? How can one conclude that the West would agree to pay the Germans in trucks (for use on the eastern front), food supplies, or a substantial sum of money in return for Jewish lives? What are we to make of Wisliceny, who came armed with recommendations and an unauthorized promise that there would be no ghettos, deportations, and murders. How were the leaders to interpret the choice of Grosz, who served all parties, with his devious and unsavory personality? Did the choice of such an emissary prove that the plan itself was dubious, or was Grosz selected because of the complex nature of his mission?

An American secret service agent in Turkey voiced these concerns in a cable he sent his commanding officers: "If the idea of a separate peace is to be taken seriously, are a minor industrialist from Hungary [Joel Brand] and a well-known double agent the most suitable emissaries to pass on the message even in its earliest stages?" In that case, what was a leader to do when faced with a situation that was as obscure, multifaceted, and poorly understood as this one? Even today researchers remain divided.[236]

It was also possible, from the Yishuv's standpoint, to raise such questions with regard to other incidents, such as the invitations extended to Bader, the negotiations conducted by Mayer, and the activity of Kleist and Kersten. If Himmler's people in the SS—Schellenberg, Krumey, Becher, Clages, among others—intended to sell Jews and to gravitate toward a deal with the West, why did they send out contradictory signals? Why did Himmler stand by Hitler almost to the very last moment and refrain from freeing himself both publicly and practically? If they were really prepared to carry out a deal, why did the meeting between the Reichsführer and the Jewish representative take place only when the Allied forces were virtually at the entrance to Hitler's Berlin bunker? Why didn't the Nazis conduct any serious negotiations in Istanbul? These questions were posed by the Yishuv leaders at the time, but like researchers today they were unable to supply any real answers.

VIEWING THE SITUATION THROUGH BEN-GURION'S EYES

How did Ben-Gurion interpret all this? He understood that the source of the Nazis' proposal lay in Germany's deteriorating situation and assumed that the supplicants were seeking a way out for themselves or for Nazi Germany. He believed, in other words, that the proposal should be accepted. He also realized that the proposal revealed a lack of consensus among the various Nazi authorities and actually indicated that the chaotic situation that existed in the Nazi camp was what made the proposal possible. This assumption was reflected in his opinion concerning the invitations received by Bader. After the meeting in Aleppo, it was clear to Ben-Gurion that the central issue was the proposal for a "separate peace" that Grosz had brought with him. He gathered from this that there was no chance of the plan succeeding, since Britain and the United States would reject it out of hand. He therefore proposed that negotiations be undertaken—even if these proved futile—in order to raise Germany's hopes and cause it to delay exterminations.

Ben-Gurion believed that the superpowers were not enthusiastic and that the slight chance of enlisting them in the "buying time" strategy depended on their goodwill, so it became essential for the Yishuv not to be caught conducting independent activity behind their backs. In any case, the bitter experience leading up to the Brand affair and the logistical hardships involved in the mass rescue of Jews placed the plans in the realm of fantasy.

Ben-Gurion veered from these assumptions when he considered sending Bader to conduct negotiations and questioned the Yishuv's financial ability and the JDC's willingness to participate in semiautonomous activity. He prepared the groundwork for a last-minute procedure if it turned out that Britain and the United States responded negatively. The Yishuv had nothing to lose under such circumstances and could attempt to fool the Nazis without the support of the superpowers—and might even manage to rescue a few Jews as a result of the negotiations.

In fact, Ben-Gurion had no choice and was quite desperate. His wavering activity reflected his unresolved position. His hands as well as those of his close associates were tied and they did their best to get something for nothing, which was clearly impossible because there was no con-nection between the goodwill invested in the plans and whether they would bear fruit. In time an increasing sense of guilt within certain segments of Israeli society would result from this discrepancy—as well as accusations in the wake of the Kasztner affair.

The Grünwald-Kasztner trial provided strong support for the allegation that Kasztner had collaborated with the Nazis, an allegation that was first heard among that part of the Jewish community that had been involved in the attempts to rescue the Jews of Hungary, and would later spread throughout the young state of Israel. The first part of the trial and the controversy surrounding it also resulted in an unprecedented hypothetical comparison: Kasztner collaborated with the Nazis just as the Jewish Agency and Mapai, under the leadership of Ben-Gurion, collaborated with the British. European Jewry in general, and the Jews of Hungary in particular, were left to fend for themselves, according to the accusers, in order to achieve personal or Zionist objectives. This allegation, based on material discussed in the Kasztner affair, contributed most forcefully to the negative stereotype surrounding Ben-Gurion and the Holocaust.[237]

In fact, it was the Nazis who murdered, the Hungarians who collaborated, and the superpowers who did their best to evade and mislead the Yishuv leadership. Ben-Gurion and his colleagues were aware of the limits of their offer of cooperation. If the Yishuv leaders did not overstep these limits—the extent to which they remained within those limits is not at all clear—it was because they had no alternatives for rescuing European Jews. In the face of British and American opposition, no rescue plan was achievable. The meager results proved that Ben-Gurion and his colleagues in the JAE were fighting insurmountable obstacles.

Ben-Gurion left no clear-cut response to the failure of the plan to rescue the Jews of Hungary. Still, in his rejection of Gruenbaum's self-blame it is possible to see the way in which he coped with it. He devoted little time to discussions of the degree of wisdom and initiative displayed after Brand's arrival. In late 1944 Ben-Gurion devoted most of his efforts to rescuing the surviving Jews in the liberated areas[238] and to the political activity he anticipated after the war. The death of Berl Katznelson in August 1944, which came as a harsh blow, also caused him to withdraw and avoid being caught up in any controversy. Ben-Gurion personally tried to explain to Joel Brand, following his release from British custody on 7 October 1944, that the Yishuv leadership was not to be blamed for the failure of his mission. He wanted Brand to be included in aid and rescue activity and even to be given secret missions.

BRAND'S TEMPESTUOUS REACTION

Brand was convinced that the Yishuv leadership had worked with the British to thwart his mission. Upon his release, he lashed out in all directions—even targeting Ben-Gurion—verbally and in print. After being released, Brand was held in a British intelligence camp near Cairo under the guise of a British officer. He bitterly announced to the JAE that he had exposed its conspiracy against him. Brand declared that he was lifting the yoke of obedience placed on his shoulders by Sharett in Aleppo and threatened to start acting independently. Responsibility for the results of his activity would fall on the JAE.[239]

As soon as Brand arrived in Palestine, Kollek brought him to Ben-Gurion. Here is how Brand summarized this meeting:

■ At long last I found myself in the presence of the JAE Chairman. I vented my bitterness, which had accumulated for several months while I was incarcerated in prison.

■ What have you done, Comrade Ben-Gurion? . . . How could you have permitted me to sit for five months in a Cairo jail while our brothers in Hungary were being exterminated? Who else is still alive?—For the time being, everything is in order. We have re-

newed negotiations and everything will be all right.

■ Who are the negotiators?

■ Sali Mayer, representative of the JDC in Switzerland, a man of much experience. I was filled with fury. And you, Comrade Ben-Gurion, say it with complete calm? Are you aware of the kind of person Sali Mayer is? He is old and untalented. He is unequipped to conduct negotiations of this kind. Sali Mayer is a disaster for us all.

Brand later wrote that he had been impolite to Ben-Gurion. Ben-Gurion replied. "There are missions to which an old man is more suited than three youngsters." Ben-Gurion did not share Brand's negative opinion of Mayer. Brand asked about events in Hungary, to which Ben-Gurion replied: "The situation is better than you think. We have had many achievements. Hundreds of thousands will be saved." This was an expression of the hope that the Yishuv's various activities, combined with those of the JDC, the International Red Cross, Sweden, and others, would soon prove fruitful. Brand asked for permission to leave for Hungary and Ben-Gurion replied that Kollek would take care of him and "see to everything."[240]

Ben-Gurion ordered that information be placed at Brand's disposal on all the procedures relating to his case from the moment it became known. He probably wanted to supply Brand with data that would substantiate the complex picture he himself had of the affair. This order clearly reflects Ben-Gurion's opinion that neither he nor his colleagues had anything to hide regarding the Brand affair. Ben-Gurion also instructed Kollek to ask the Rescue Committee to supply Brand with copies of all cables relating to Hungarian Jewry and that of other European countries. He wanted to involve Brand in activity on behalf of European Jewry in order to help him overcome his powerful sense of guilt.[241]

After a while, Brand was invited to participate in the activities of the Political Department and the Yishuv's intelligence circles, especially preliminary activity in rooting out war criminals and bringing them to trial. In March 1945 Kollek introduced Brand to Lieutenant Colonel Hunloke, a senior British intelligence officer (MI5) in the Middle East. Brand told him that he knew many war criminals, their organizations, and their modus operandi, and that he was prepared to leave for Europe if he was permitted to meet his family in Hungary.[242]

Brand summed up his evaluation in a letter addressed to the JAE and Ben-Gurion. He described his movements from the moment he left Budapest and offered his opinion of the JAE. Concerning his prison experience he wrote: "I assume that during my absence the Jewish Agency did everything possible to help the Jews of Europe." The blame for not being able to return to Hungary was placed squarely on the shoulders of "some of the British authorities," but also, to some degree, on the JAE's decision, which was based on information from Hungary. He signed off with a series of suggestions for possible activity, some of which had already been adopted.

Brand was thus not convinced that the JAE and Ben-Gurion had done their utmost to rescue the Jews of Hungary. He made do with a reserved "I assume" to describe his feelings regarding the JAE's activity during his imprisonment. He insisted that the JAE was opposed to his return—which it was not. On the contrary, Ben-Gurion led the JAE to adopt a position that left Brand to make up his own mind as to whether to return to Hungary. When Brand was arrested, the JAE acted to obtain his release and demanded repeatedly that he be permitted to return to Hungary if he so chose. People worked on his behalf in Jerusalem, Cairo, and London, and on several occasions Sharett appealed to various individuals in Palestine, London, and Cairo. None of this proved effective because of Britain's objections.

During his imprisonment Brand was visited by members of the Jewish Agency's Political Department's secret services, by Kollek, Zaslani, and Schechter—all of whom checked on his condition and saw to his needs. They talked to him and encouraged him by stressing the importance of his mission and achievements, attempting to dispel his deep sense of guilt. They also promised to help his family, saying that his children would be among the first to be evacuated from Hungary, and they did indeed try to fulfill this promise. They attempted to rescue his mother, wife, and other members of his family by way of Switzerland. According to the instructions that accompanied this effort, "All expenses involved in this will be reimbursed," While he was still in prison, they even examined various ways of involving him in operations following his release, including the possibility of his returning to Hungary after all.

It is unlikely that the JAE's behavior reflected a fear of what Brand would find out. On the contrary, even after details of the plan were leaked, Zaslani and Kollek consulted first with the Istanbul rescue emissaries and then with the Jewish leadership in Hungary on the possibility of Joel Brand returning to Hungary.[243] Another option was to send Brand to the United States and South Africa on a fund-raising drive.[244] Had there been the slightest fear of Brand and what he knew, the JAE would probably have behaved differently toward him and refrained from sharing information on their activity in the wake of the proposal he had brought from Eichmann.

On the question of a possible conspiracy, a report sent on 8 June by what I choose to define as the "Special Tasks Section," headed by Zaslani, mentions a journey to Aleppo by Sharett, Meirov, Zaslani, and Schechter whose objective was to meet with Avriel and Brand: "We expect their return from Aleppo either tomorrow or the day after. We do not know, for the time being, if Avriel will return with the Yishuv people to Palestine from Aleppo, or if he will accompany Brand back to Istanbul. One way or the other, you cannot imagine how eager we are to receive the information they are bringing with them. . . ." Thus, when the delegation set out for Aleppo, its members had no idea how things would develop, and the most obvious thing would have been for Brand to return to Istanbul and from there to Hungary.[245] If there had been a conspiracy between the Yishuv leaders and the British to arrest Brand and, in doing so, destroy his mission, it must have been so secret that the JAE itself had no idea of its existence.

Brand's position kept changing. This sprang not solely from an impartial analysis of testimony and documentation but from the deep sense of pain and frustration that plagued him and the many good people involved in the rescue operations, who shared Brand's sense of guilt.[246]

The weight of responsibility may also have affected Brand's judgment, which oscillated between overestimating his own power to influence the fate of Hungary's Jews and sinking into a morass of self-blame. He may also have adopted the stereotype of "the Jews who govern the world." After all, the Nazis believed this and repeated it constantly in their conversations with Brand. Even Kasztner nurtured it as a kind of wishful thinking ("the Jewish Agency will find a way"), on the one hand, and a way of tricking the Nazis, on the other. Brand did not delve deeply into the complex relationship between the Allies and found it hard to comprehend the real—miserable—position of the Yishuv, the Jews of Europe, and the Jews of the world within the multiple considerations that guided the Allies in the war. To repeat, he was not the only one not to have thoroughly grasped it.[247]

BEN-GURION'S LETTER TO YEHOSHUA KASZTNER

The documentation I have examined does not express Ben-Gurion's fierce attempts at deflecting criticism. Even on previous occasions he had not invested too much effort in this area, although he was often not averse to firmly and publicly siding with positions that were hard to support. He may even have left the job to others,

but he appears to have avoided controversy because he saw no reason for it at a time when the wounds were still fresh.

In time Israel Kasztner met with Ben-Gurion. His legal problems were at their worst and he came to Ben-Gurion's Negev home in Sede Boqer. After the visit, Kasztner told his brother, Yehoshua, that Ben-Gurion had a profound understanding of the matter and "the day will come that the prime minister of Israel will stand in the Knesset and supply the correct evaluation of all my and my colleagues' actions and declare the whole truth before the entire nation." In early 1958, after Kasztner was murdered and the High Court of Justice had found Kasztner's accusers guilty of defamation, Yehoshua Kasztner asked Ben-Gurion to fulfill his brother's wish. Ben-Gurion replied: "I am in receipt of your letter and I respect your concern for the honor of your brother, who was murdered by base criminals and whose honor was trampled upon in his lifetime and at his death by villains, who have adopted the guise of guardians of decency." But the time had not come to clear Kasztner's name. Ben-Gurion went on:

> Nor do I agree with the judges' proposal to convene a public tribunal to look into the terrible events of the Holocaust. I do not believe that it is possible nowadays to establish a tribunal whose only objective would be to unearth the truth. Partisan political interests are exploiting the Holocaust—they would no doubt leave their traces on any public tribunal dealing with this tragic affair—and only historians, responsible for their consciences, would be able to clarify the matter in the future.

Ben-Gurion thus exhibited great practicality by rejecting attempts at explaining something that was inexplicable, given the circumstances surrounding the generation that had experienced the Holocaust.[248]

Ben-Gurion may also not have tried to fend off criticism because he was aware of the enormous conceptual discrepancy between those who grasped the total picture and those who glimpsed only part of it. Even the most experienced Istanbul emissaries, who were geographically and operationally closest to the rescue efforts, found it hard to believe that there had been no neglect on the part of the JAE. The complexity of the plan and its feeble chances of success resulted in skeptical responses. Even members of the Aid and Rescue Committee in Budapest were reserved when Brand first told them of Eichmann's proposal. It was only a short distance to believe doubts to lead to neglect. Even some of the Yishuv's rescue emissaries were caught up in these doubts, which were logical but had no basis in reality.[249] Ben-Gurion understood that it would have been impossible to explain away the depth of the tragedy and its absurdity. He realized that no explanation could dispel the strong tendency to gravitate toward self-blame or to accuse the leadership.

In order to grasp Ben-Gurion's position regarding the Brand affair and to understand his feelings, it is worthwhile to examine his direct appeal to Roosevelt eight days before the Eichmann proposal was leaked to the press. On 11 July 1944 Ben-Gurion sent Roosevelt an eleventh-hour plea to intervene and save the ransom plan. In a long cable Ben-Gurion outlined the main points of the affair. He told Roosevelt that the Nazis had agreed to release a million Hungarian and Romanian Jews "according to certain conditions known to the American State Department" and stressed that the JAE had suggested conducting negotiations with those making the proposal. He did not sweep aside "certain doubts" that accompanied the proposal "in its current state," nevertheless insisting that haste must be taken in entering into negotiations "with representatives of the enemy circles that initiated it."

Ben-Gurion also pointed out Brand's imprisonment in Cairo and called upon the president to adopt the JAE's proposals to the British government: "First, to hint to the other side, through suitable channels, . . . of the willingness to appoint a delegate who would discuss the rescue and transfer of as many Jews as possible." Second, to hint to the Nazis that a "prior condition" to any debate would be an "immediate halt" to the deportation of Jews to their death.[250]

A second cable, sent from Jerusalem the same day, asked Roosevelt to permit representatives of the War Refugee Board to meet people "from the Budapest group" in Istanbul in order to take action to permit Brand to return immediately to Hungary and to entrust him with the news that the Allies were prepared to negotiate over proposals to release Jews and stop the murders. Alternatively, Roosevelt was asked to motivate the British into allowing Brand to return immediately and to entrust him with the announcement that the proposal he had brought was being "discussed in the most senior circles and that action could be expected soon."[251]

I have been unable to uncover any response from Roosevelt in the available documentation. This should come as no surprise. Who was Ben-Gurion, after all, and what was his power at that time? He was ignored. Although one has no way of knowing how the U.S. administration viewed him, one thing is certain: it rightly reckoned that the Jewish side it was facing was helpless.

Both of Ben-Gurion's cables to Roosevelt, the symbol of power in the free world, were sent after all the information on Bader's invitation to Berlin was already at Ben-Gurion's disposal. This information increased the hope that it was still possible to delay exterminations through negotiations. At the same time, frustration increased as time was slowly running out while Britain and the United States prevaricated, isolating themselves, and remained so obtuse as to refuse to help in coaxing the Nazis into false negotiations whose sole objective was to hold up the extermination of Jews. The cables also prove that Ben-Gurion and the entire JAE membership shared Gruenbaum's position and that now any negotiations with the Nazis were contingent on a halt in deportations to death camps. This possibly testifies to their feeling that the final moment had arrived and that they no longer had anything to lose: if the annihilation did not stop now, it would not stop until the fall of Germany.

On 10 July, one day before cabling Roosevelt, Ben-Gurion delivered an impassioned speech and hurled accusations at the Allies. He was care-ful not to reveal details of the recently received proposal from Hungary or to recall the frustrat-ing appeals to Britain and the United States. The public was able to comprehend the full meaning of Ben-Gurion's words when, only a few days later, the affair was leaked to the press. Only now was it possible to understand that by then Ben-Gurion was already mourning the demise of the ransom plan.

9

Bombing to Deter and Stultify

Applying various forms of pressure in order to undermine confidence in the enemy's home front, shaking its morale, destroying its economic infrastructure to punish or deter—such tactics resembled those applied during the war itself. The warring sides in the Second World War merely perfected most of these methods but did not invent them. These included: destruction of the economic infrastructure and blockades; striking at industrial complexes, transport facilities, and civilian populations; threatening prisoners and hostages with bodily harm; and announcing trials and severe punishment once the war was over. The Nazis had no compunction about using any or all of these methods both before and during the war. An outstanding example was the blitzkrieg against Britain; even Tel Aviv was under threat of bombing by the Axis powers. The Nazis' considered their (ultimately unsuccessful) attempt to develop V-2 missiles and launch them against civilian populations in Britain an important strategic move.

Aerial bombing, especially of civilian populations, was one method used by the Allies to undermine the ability and will of their adversaries to fight, as well as a means of punishment and deterrence. Outstanding examples include the bombing of Dresden and the destruction of the Japanese cities of Hiroshima and Nagasaki by atomic bombs. Among the central issues in the present discussion is the fact that the Allies could have announced that the bombing of enemy cities also constituted punishment for the treatment of the Jews and could have threatened to keep up the bombing until the annihilation ceased. Another issue is that the Allies could have stopped the annihilation by bombing and destroying the enemy's death camps and the roads, bridges, and railway tracks leading to them.

As soon as the Jews in Palestine, the United States, and the rest of the free world were aware of the situation in Europe, the question became how to put an end to the extermination through sabotage. One suggestion was to bomb the camps or the roads leading to them. This could have taken the form of straightforward bombing of specific targets, or the camps could have been included in larger bombing operations involving important military objectives. Such an operation could have been included in the "small rescue," which involved operations aimed at improving the Jews' chances of surviving Nazi persecution, as opposed to the "large rescue," whose objective was to free them from Hitler's clutches.

SHOULD WE DEMAND BOMBING? LATE 1942–LATE 1943

After they razed the Bohemian village of Lidice, the Nazis were warned by Roosevelt (June 1942). Roosevelt and Churchill jointly issued a further warning after the Nazis murdered hostages in France, with Churchill threatening revenge for the Nazis' use of poison gas. These warnings had nothing to do with the plight of the Jews, notwithstanding the fact that it had been common knowledge since the summer of 1942 that the Jews were victims of a particularly gruesome form of persecution.

Even before the Yishuv officially announced that Europe's Jews were being systematically annihilated, Richard Lichtheim of the Jewish Agency in Switzerland asked for warnings to be issued to the Nazis—or at least to their satellites—that they would be punished for persecuting Jews. Lichtheim appended this appeal to his first revelations from Geneva regarding the murders. In September 1942 the London branch of the World Jewish Congress also appealed to the rest of the world to warn the Nazis.[1]

In the summer of 1942 a number of direct warnings were issued to the satellite countries by General Wladyslaw Sikorski, former prime minister and head of the Polish government-in-exile; Shmuel Zygelboym, Bund representative on the Polish National Council, a parliament in-exile; and Cardinal Arthur Hinsley, archbishop of Westminster, against persecuting Jews or collaborating with others who persecuted Jews. Cardinal Hinsley broadcast a speech, specifically aimed at Roman Catholics, denouncing the persecution of Jews. In another radio broadcast Professor Pieter Sjoerds Gerbrandy, prime minister of the Dutch government-in-exile, also condemned the expulsion of Jews from Holland.[2]

More specific, practical suggestions were also proposed. In June 1942 General Sikorski demanded that Churchill order the confiscation of German property and intensive bombing raids on nonmilitary targets inside Germany to "pay back for German cruelty." Vyacheslav Molotov, the Soviet foreign minister, declared that his country would try all Nazi leaders for war crimes, and the Soviet Union established a special international court for this purpose.[3]

The necessity for pressure to be applied to Germany and its allies was discussed repeatedly in the JAE, the National Council, Mapai, and other Yishuv political bodies as soon as news emerged from Europe. Suggestions put forward included: Allied governments broadcast by radio or any other means a clear and uncompromising message to Germany that it could expect "retribution and revenge for its crimes, including financial reparations"; execute Nazi leader Rudolf Hess, who was imprisoned in England; execute German citizens residing in the United States; round up German nationals residing in Palestine and announce that they would be executed if the Nazis did not stop annihilating Jews; establish a Jewish air squadron as part of the U.S. forces, with the express purpose of bombing civilian populations in Germany.[4]

Immediately after the announcement of the annihilation, Dov Joseph cabled the American Emergency Committee for Zionist Affairs and the Jewish Agency's London branch to request that they press Roosevelt and Churchill into issuing warnings to Germany and the satellite states. The Yishuv's chief rabbi was asked to meet with the envoy of the Catholic church in Jerusalem to demand that the church publicly condemn the extermination of Jews and warn that all those assisting in the murders would be punished.[5]

At a JAE meeting held a week after the announcement (29 November 1942) the participants discussed the kinds of pressure that could be exerted on Germany and the Axis powers. Ben-Gurion supported the proposal to "demand that the Allies warn the Nazis that they would face collective punishment for murdering Jews." He offered no details of the kind of collective punishment he envisioned, but he considered this demand among the few available practical options.[6] He was also in favor of establishing a Jewish air squadron: "I am sure the American government will agree at once to the establishment of special units of Jewish pilots, as it agreed to special units of Norwegians, with the clear intention that these would be the first to invade Norway.[7]

Ben-Gurion repeated the call to action in a dramatic speech at a special meeting (30 November 1942) of the Elected Assembly, arguing that Germany's military leaders and the German people must be warned "that they will be held responsible for the bloodshed."[8] This sentiment was echoed at a JAE session held on 6 December 1942, where he stressed the distinction between the German people and their leaders and went into a lengthy and detailed description of his own views on the efficacy of the warnings. In his earlier speech to the Elected Assembly he presented a lengthy analysis of Hitler's murderous nature and convinced his colleagues that "warnings to Hitler alone are worthless," but that warnings aimed at the German army might prove effective. Ben-Gurion pointed out that his modest request expressed the Yishuv's and the Jewish nation's impotence and helplessness, in so "sorry a state as to have to appeal to Roosevelt to carry out our missions, and there is no knowing if he will do so or not."[9]

At that session the JAE adopted a number of resolutions concerning rescue operations, which Ben-Gurion then translated into operational directives in letters to JAE branches and activists in Britain and the United States. In these letters he elaborated on his views of the various forces involved in exterminating the Jews:

> [I] doubt if Hitler himself can be influenced to any great degree, but reports indicate that the actual massacres are not being carried out by the army but by the Gestapo and special storm trooper divisions of the Nazi party, which makes it conceivable that firm warnings on the part of President [Roosevelt] to the German military commanders that they will be held personally responsible for the atrocities may have some effect.

He also mentioned the possibility of influencing the satellite states: "Special action must be taken to rescue the Jews in the Balkan states, Hungary, Romania, and western Europe, where there is no direct Nazi rule, or where the Nazis are still not as cruel as in eastern Europe. An American warning to the governments of Hungary, Romania, and Bulgaria might have some effect even though they share a pact with Hitler."[10] In a letter to Berl Locker, stationed in the London branch, Ben-Gurion reiterated this point:

> As far as we know, the butchering is being carried out without military participation by the Nazi special police, and although it is doubtful if any warning would influence Hitler, we are sure that warnings to army commanders that they will be held personally responsible for the murders probably will prove effective. We suggest applying to the British government

with the request that it issue a warning to the German military leaders.

Ben-Gurion even went so far as to suggested how contact could be made with people in the countries that had received these warnings:

> We suggest you ask the [British] government to allow us to [fly over Poland in special aircraft to drop leaflets to the Jews to show that we] stand with them in this calamity, to rescue whoever can be rescued, and to tell them that the Jewish people in Palestine, England, America, and other countries are doing their utmost to rescue them. We also suggest that the British government distribute leaflets in Germany to the German people, telling them about the murders and the atrocities, that the entire civilized world is appalled and calling upon them, the Germans, to stop the murderers. There is a special need to apply to the governments of Hungary, Romania, and Bulgaria, which, although Hitler's allies, must be held responsible if they lend a hand in the massacre perpetrated by the Nazis against the Jews of Poland."[11]

At a Mapai meeting Ben-Gurion claimed that leaflets might help disperse the smokescreen the German government was using to conceal its activity. The German people and the soldiers would become aware of the atrocities, as would the people of Poland, who would be asked to stop the murderers and be warned against collaborating in them.[12]

On this issue Ben-Gurion was approached by people who suggested specific action, and he was obviously affected by the public's sentiments. Here is one typical example from a Tel-Aviv resident: "The German people and their allies, especially the German women, have little idea of the vile atrocities being perpetrated by the Gestapo and Hitler's henchmen." Here is another: "Publicity must make the issue known, via radio broadcasts to the German people and their allies, and one must protest the atrocities being committed in their countries by sadistic lunatics, who are worse than wild animals in their cruelty, by issuing warnings against complying with unforgivable crimes."[13] Another letter contained a suggestion that Ben-Gurion draft a petition—to be signed by all the Jewish male and female soldiers serving in the British armed forces, as well as all the Jewish men and women working in industrial plants directly connected with the war effort—asking Churchill, Smuts (the South African leader), and Roosevelt to issue an unequivocal warning to Germany that it could expect severe punishment if the extermination did not cease immediately.[14]

The Near East division of the Polish republic's press association also wrote to Ben-Gurion expressing sympathy for the Yishuv's pain and full solidarity with the Jewish people's demand that the Allied governments take immediate action against the unprecedented annihilation of the Jewish nation. The Polish press shared the Yishuv's view that "acts of retaliation were necessary as the only means of halting the barbaric cruelty of the Germans in Poland and other occupied countries."[15]

On 17 December 1942 the Allies condemned the Nazis' "bestial" policies and "cold-blooded annihilation." Such actions, they said, only reinforced the determination of all freedom-loving nations to crush Hitler's barbaric tyranny. They warned the Germans that the "perpetrators of these crimes will not go unpunished." The JAE had mixed feelings about the declaration. Some members felt it may have been insufficient and that a more aggressive warning should have been issued.[16] The majority, however, tended to approve of the declaration. "It is the first time our appeal to other governments has received attention," said Ben-Gurion, adding, "There is moral satisfaction in that Israel's cry of agony has been heard."[17]

We now know that the declaration was completely ineffective. Nor should it be supposed that many of the Yishuv leaders actually believed that any practical results would emerge from verbal threats unless some were implemented. In any event, the declaration was widely publicized in the press and on the radio and was followed by other declarations. Poland's ambassador to London, the Czech foreign minister, and Radio Free Belgium all declared their support. To some extent, it was a moral achievement for the Jews.[18]

The Allies' declaration also roused Britain's Jewish community to action. The *Jewish Chronicle,* for example, repeated the Yishuv's demand for warnings to be issued to the Germans over the radio or through leaflets dropped over Germany. Prof. Selig Brodetsky of the JAE's London branch made the same demand at a late December meeting with Richard Law, the parliamentary undersecretary of state for foreign affairs.[19] The Allies threatened to punish perpetrators of crimes against the Jews but offered no refuge to the persecuted Jews, nor did they promise any tangible aid. The impression was that the Allies' concern was not entirely sincere, which made their threats somewhat unconvincing. The declaration did not induce the Germans to soften their attitude toward the Jews, nor did it reassure those in the West who sympathized with the plight of the Jews. Indeed, beginning only a few days after the declaration and continuing throughout 1943, there were repeated calls for more severe condemnations and a more sophisticated means of placing pressure on the Nazis and their accomplices.[20]

During January 1943 the JAE twice discussed asking the Allies to bomb civilian population centers in Germany and to announce that these were acts of reprisal for Germany's behavior toward the Jews. Gruenbaum reported that the Polish government-in-exile had suggested to the JAE that they join forces in demanding that the Allies "bomb German cities, not only for strategic reasons" but specifically as retaliation for their persecution of the Jews.

By June 1942 Sikorski had been making such demands of the British and continued to repeat them because the Poles obviously believed that the chances of having their proposals adopted had improved. They were encouraged by the public outcry and the Allies' December declaration to Germany. They must have believed that the warnings were an expression of the Jews' great influence over the West. It turned out to be illusory, but even delusions can sometimes prove effective.

Ben-Gurion's reaction was discouraging: "If Britain can bomb German cities, it will do so, and our demands will make no difference." This view was shared by others in the JAE. Was Ben-Gurion reserved because of a belief that Britain would indeed use all its might to bomb Germany? Was he afraid of making too many demands, choosing to focus on demands that appeared to be more important, such as those pertaining to the mass rescue of Jews, the Transnistria Plan, and the Parachutists' scheme?

Perhaps Ben-Gurion assumed that Britain would bomb Germany anyway, as part of its war effort, but would refuse to declare that the bombings were reprisal for the annihilation of Jews. He may have assumed that Britain would avoid linking the bombings with Jews for fear of being accused of waging a "Jewish war," and that Britain might be willing to make do with anything less than unconditional surrender. Too great an insistence that the Nazis stop the mass murder of Jews might be construed as a readiness on Britain's part to accept a "separate peace" with Germany without unconditional surrender. Documentation sheds no light on the reasons for Ben-Gurion's and his colleagues' opposition to this opinion in the JAE.[21]

The suggestion was again discussed in the JAE following Gruenbaum's report, at the end of January 1943, regarding his meetings with Stanislaw Kot of the Polish government-in-exile, who was on a visit to Palestine at the time. Kot repeated the Polish proposal for joint Yishuv-Polish appeals to the British to allow Polish pilots to conduct bombing raids over Germany in reprisal for Nazi atrocities. His proposal was not discussed.[22]

In January Ben-Gurion again called on the Allies to issue warnings to the German army and general public. He called for a propaganda drive in which leaflets would be dropped over Germany and Poland, explaining that such leaflets could stress the positive examples of other nations, such as the Belgians and the Dutch, who "help [the Jews], often at the risk of their own lives." We now know that Ben-Gurion's view of the Belgians and the Dutch was based on partial and inaccurate information.

In his public announcements Ben-Gurion hinted at the reasons behind his reluctance to ask the Allies to declare that their bombing of German cities was in retaliation for atrocities committed against the Jews. He pointed out that even in their December declaration the Allies ignored the fact that the Nazis had singled out the Jewish people and did not mention rescue operations, which such treatment made necessary.[23]

Ben-Gurion's reservations were fully confirmed. The Polish government-in-exile, undeterred by the JAE's reluctance to cooperate, again appealed to the Allies to carry out bombing raids over Germany. The demand was presented to Churchill and was reviewed by the Foreign Office and Air Ministry, both of which rejected it.

Several fears were aired: Allied bombings defined as reprisals for Nazi atrocities against the Jews would exacerbate Nazi cruelty; by complying and halting the murders, the Nazis would be forcing the Allies to cease bombing civilian German targets; other parties might make demands for Allied reprisals for their own "partisan problems"; the Allies might be accused of competing with Germany in terms of acts of cruelty.

In addition, operational arguments were brought to bear against reciprocal bombing raids.

In retrospect, it is hard to reconcile this with the fact that since early 1943 British and American bombers had been flying missions out of Britain to sow destruction in major German cities and industrial sites. The justifiable apprehension remained that retaliatory bombing would give currency to Nazi propaganda claiming that the Allies were fighting the war on behalf of "world Jewry." These misgivings were common to the Americans, the British, and even the Jews, including those in Palestine. Ben-Gurion shared this concern and did not wish to undermine the fighting spirit of the nations battling Hitler—for anti-Semitism was rife among them, too.[24]

At JAE meetings held early in 1943 suggestions were often made for exerting pressure on Germany and its satellites. Usually demanding that the Allies take unspecified "special steps," they generally did not produce results. A suggestion was also put forth to appeal directly to Hitler to release the Jews. Proposals were made to warn satellite nations, since the war was beginning to look bad for the Axis forces. It would appear that expectations raised by the Bermuda Conference were responsible for postponing the debate on these issues.[25] By May and June 1943, it was quite clear that the conference was not yielding any positive results.

The call to threaten the Nazis with severe retaliation was again raised in August 1943. This time it was addressed to Jan Smuts, South Africa's prime minister. At a meeting with Smuts, Gruenbaum suggested that the former issue a direct demand to Hitler to put a stop to the murders and to accompany this with a stern warning. Smuts was evasive, only agreeing to make an announcement that the Allies had detailed lists of the perpetrators, who would be forced "to pay for everything." Gruenbaum tried to pressure him by recalling Roosevelt and Churchill's recent joint written statement warning the murderers of the Polish farmers on the banks of the Bug River, pointing out that the warning did not contain a single word about the murdered Jews. The fate of the Jews, said Gruenbaum, was clearly of no consequence, and as far as the Allies were concerned, the Nazis could abuse and murder them all. Again Smuts was evasive and asked Gruenbaum for a memo on the subject.[26]

I have uncovered no documentation on a JAE discussion prior to Gruenbaum's request that Smuts threaten the Nazis with reprisal. It is known that Gruenbaum met with Ben-Gurion before departing for South Africa, but the content of their conversation is not recorded. Gruenbaum was most consistent in his tendency to make such demands and to urge the JAE to behave likewise. He may have cleared his appeal to Smuts in advance, but it is equally likely that he made it on his own initiative.

It is also conceivable that Ben-Gurion gave his silent approval to Gruenbaum to float a "trial balloon" in the form of an appeal to Smuts. If the former had adopted Gruenbaum's initiative, he would have suggested to his counterparts on the Allied committee to threaten Hitler with reprisal; even if he did not, the Yishuv would not be faced with a direct refusal from Allied leaders. The Yishuv did not have a "direct line" to Allied leaders and every appeal, to some extent, was made at the expense of another issue.

Gruenbaum's conversation produced no change in Allied bombing policy. In late October 1943 the foreign representatives of Britain, the United States, and the USSR met in Moscow to discuss another declaration by the superpowers. Britain preferred not to refer to the gas chambers. In the end, the declaration signed by Stalin, Roosevelt, and Churchill on 1 November 1943 made no mention of Jews.[27]

The efficacy of the warnings was the subject of much professional debate. Not making them did not necessarily reflect a lack of concern for the plight of the Jews. Several propaganda and psychological warfare departments of the Western espionage agencies expressed doubt as to the efficacy of repeated warnings in the form of radio broadcasts or leaflets dropped from the air. Their value might be diminished and there was even a danger that repeated warnings would achieve the opposite effect: if the Allies appeared to be sensitive to the Jewish issue, the Nazis might consider it best to put pressure on them precisely by stepping up the persecutions.

Everything was subordinated to the main issue, namely, to win the war, and it appeared that focusing on the Jewish problem was not compatible with this objective. Law said that Britain was not able, at that stage of the war, to assign enough importance to the matter as to outweigh other issues of interest to their propaganda machine.[28]

By the end of 1943 it was clear even to Jews subject to Nazi rule that Allied bombings of German targets would only worsen their plight. Some even demanded that pressure be put on the Allies to refrain from such bombing. There were senior Jewish leaders in the free world who were apprehensive as to the possible repercussions of these bombings. Moreover, since May the Allies had been involved in large-scale bombing (known as the "Point-blank Campaign") of Germany's strategic military positions. The large number of aircraft involved in these missions meant that no additional missions, such as retaliatory forays over population centers or extermination camps, were possible.[29]

FROM OPPOSITION TO PASSIVE SUPPORT: 1944

A change in attitude within the Yishuv leadership was discernible by mid-1944, especially with regard to efforts to rescue the Jews of Hungary. Since the several demands to warn Germany had received no verbal support from the JAE. In 1944, too, it was Gruenbaum who was the chief spokesperson favoring such demands: "Does an alternative exist to Hitler being forced by his own people to stop the murders, since he is bringing disaster down upon them? Is anything more suitable to this end than Allied bombing of German cities—and not merely when strategic considerations are involved?"[30]

Immediately following news of the invasion of Hungary in March 1944, support for a demand that the Allies threaten retaliation began to grow. On 22 March the Political Department suggested that Sharett, who was in London, issue a demand that the Allies warn the new regime in Hungary. In view of the new situation in Hungary, the suggestion was cabled to Sharett two days before the JAE actually discussed what action should be taken. Based on the JAE's past pattern of activity, it is safe to assume that this initiative was first examined by Ben-Gurion or another senior JAE leader. In any case, no mention was made of it at the JAE meeting, most likely because it was known that President Roosevelt had issued such a warning three days earlier.[31]

Britain was even more firmly opposed to issuing warnings than was the United States. The reasons remained the same, with only a slight addition: the Allies must not adopt Germany's savage behavior. Britain's indifference on this issue grew stronger. The U.S. government decided to warn Hungary, whereas Britain maintained that the Allies' previous warning (December 1942) had little or no impact whatsoever and the plight of the Jews had actually worsened. There was therefore no reason to believe that further warnings would offer better results. Still, public pressure on Eden, Britain's foreign secretary, in late March 1944 forced him to issue a warning to the murderers and their collaborators.[32]

By April 1944 Gruenbaum remained the only Yishuv leader who refused to make do with verbal warnings and demanded harsh retaliatory bombing attacks against Germany, believing that these would deter the Germans from proceeding with mass extermination. He publicly attacked the Allies' arguments against retaliatory bombing raids. Notwithstanding Britain's reluctance to issue ultimatums, several such warnings were broadcast to the Hungary's government, among others, following the spring of 1944. The Hungarian people were asked to follow Denmark's example by aiding their Jewish fellow countrymen by preventing their deportation to death camps. Nevertheless, Britain remained firm in its refusal to conduct retaliatory bombing raids.[33]

In May 1944 concern mounted in the Yishuv following indications from Hungary that Jews—especially those in provincial towns—were being sent to death camps. Nevertheless, shortly before his return from London, Sharett remained reserved in his replies to journalists and politicians regarding the JAE's position on bombing concentration camps and roads leading to them. He insisted that the JAE still rejected this option.[34]

The third week of May 1944 saw the arrival in Istanbul of Joel Brand. Upon receipt of Pomeranz's information on the ransom proposal, Gruenbaum sent a series of cables to Allied leaders demanding the bombing of railroad stations and tracks from Hungary to Poland. The JAE did not discuss these cables, which were obviously sent on Gruenbaum's initiative in his capacity as Rescue Committee chairman. He was probably leaning on public opinion and the support of David Remez, secretary of the Histadrut.[35]

Gruenbaum was acting independently when, at a meeting on 2 June 1944 with Lowell C. Pinkerton, the U.S. consul in Palestine, he urged Pinkerton to press Washington into issuing a severe warning to Hungary, a request the consul did indeed fulfill. Gruenbaum also asked for the U.S. air force to bomb the death camps in Poland and roads and railway lines leading to them from Budapest, this time not merely as a warning or act of reprisal but to thwart the extermination process.

Pinkerton agreed to pass on the request to his government but expressed concern that such bombing would result in the death of many Jews and that German propaganda would be quick to announce that Americans were killing Jews. In reply, Gruenbaum said that under the circumstances the Jews had nothing to lose and might even gain from the delay that would result from the destruction of death installations. The Germans would probably be unable to build new installations, and it would be difficult to replace death camp staff killed in bombing raids. Also, some Jews might be able to escape the camps in the ensuing confusion. Pinkerton, however, firmly refused to pass on this request to his government and insisted on receiving it in writing. Fully conversant with the Yishuv leadership's inner workings, Pinkerton suspected that Gruenbaum's demand had not been cleared with his JAE colleagues.[36]

A few days after this meeting, Gruenbaum circulated a summary of his request among JAE members. The memo was discussed at the JAE meeting on 11 June 1944, when Gruenbaum reiterated his conversation with Pinkerton and stressed that Jews were being deported from Hungary at the rate of twelve thousand a day (as was stated in chapter 8, this data was inaccurate).

In general, the JAE was firmly opposed to bombing Poland. Not knowing the state of affairs in Poland, Ben-Gurion said that the JAE was not in a position to "make proposals on the matter." Senator Joseph and Schmorak agreed that "we cannot take responsibility for any bombing that could result in the death of even a single Jew." Gruenbaum was rebuked for applying to the American consul in the first place without first agreeing on a united position with the JAE heads. He was criticized even more for raising so controversial a demand with the representative of a major power. As Ben-Gurion concluded, "The JAE holds that no proposals must be made to the Allies regarding the bombing of places in which there are Jews."[37]

It is important to note that the JAE only condemned that part of Gruenbaum's proposal relating to bombing the camps. It did not touch on the demand to bomb the roads and tracks leading to them (which Pinkerton agreed to pass on to Washington). Here, too, documentation is unhelpful because one cannot be sure that the minutes include everything that took place at the meeting. It would be surprising if the proposal to bomb the roads and tracks was not discussed, since such action would not have endangered Jews, making Ben-Gurion's arguments inapplicable.

First, it is possible that, given this heated discussion, the questions of whether to demand the bombing of the camps or of the roads leading to them became intertwined. Second, the American consul had agreed to pass along this demand without delay. Moreover, Gruenbaum had already sent a cable in a similar vein to the United States and Britain and had encountered no opposition on the part of the JAE.[38]

Clearly, the general tension surrounding the Brand affair, as well as the tense period while waiting for replies from Britain and the United States, probably led to the rejection of Gruenbaum's initiatives. His opponents most likely feared that additional appeals to the Allies would influence their willingness to help the Jews. Ben-Gurion and his colleagues may have felt that negotiations based on the Brand plan were a surer way of postponing deportations than Gruenbaum's bombing raids. They may have feared that Gruenbaum's demands would have a negative effect and reduce the already slender chance that the Allies would help the Jews take advantage of Eichmann's offer.

The debate over the bombing issue sealed the chapter on the JAE's opposition to Gruenbaum's sustained and unrelenting efforts. After this, the JAE did an about-face in terms of its position. Although Gruenbaum insisted that the matter was of supreme urgency, he permitted several days to elapse between taking the steps he took listening to Pomeranz's report and raising the issue in the JAE. He probably had to wait several days for an audience with the consul, but it still took him several more days to draft the memorandum summing up the meeting and a few more days to bring the material to the JAE's attention. After all, it was he himself who had claimed that twelve thousand Jews were being led to their deaths daily. Why did he procrastinate?

Then there is the question of how much the JAE actually knew about the situation. The discussion may well have been influenced by a general lack of knowledge of the true situation. Someone said, "There are Jews" in Auschwitz, while someone else said, "There is a large labor camp in Auschwitz." There was no one present to correct these statements. It is worth noting that there was a series of camps at Auschwitz, some of which were labor camps. Another part, Birkenau, contained installations in which Jews from all over Europe were brought to be slaughtered. These installations were expanded to accommodate the Jews of Hungary.

The JAE may thus have been under the false impression that Auschwitz was but one labor camp among many, not associating it with deportations from Hungary or elsewhere, and consequently had no real idea of the destination of the deportees or the type of installation that required bombing.[39] Thus, notwithstanding the wealth of information arriving in Palestine, it appears that both in the Yishuv and in occupied Europe no one really knew for sure the location of the major extermination center or what Auschwitz really was. Auschwitz was not always described as an extermination center, unlike Belzec and Treblinka, which were considered the main death camps. Not only the Jews in occupied Europe and in Palestine but also in countries in the free world and the governments-in-exile in London (with the exception of Poland), thousands of whose citizens were imprisoned in Auschwitz, had no idea at the time of what was happening there.[40]

How ironic, therefore, that a sudden change took place only a few days later, prompted by the escape of two prisoners from Auschwitz, Rudolf Vrba (alias Walter Rosenberg) and Alfred Wetzler, whose stories reached the governments of Britain and the United States, as well as Jewish organizations in Palestine and the rest of the free world.

Consequently, when Gruenbaum placed the issue on the JAE agenda, there was substance to

Ben-Gurion's statement that the Yishuv did not know the real situation in Poland. Also, when Gruenbaum discussed bombing the death camps with Pinkerton, he was, in fact, thinking about camps that no longer existed, such as Chelmno, Treblinka, and Belzec. Gruenbaum emphasized Auschwitz as being the main target for bombing, apparently unaware of its deeper significance.[41]

Meanwhile, there were clear signs of increased public pressure. On the day of the JAE meeting (11 June 1944) Rabbi Binyamin (Yehoshua Radler-Feldman, a member of the Al-domy group), heading a committee of seven public figures, demanded in writing an urgent meeting with Ben-Gurion "re: the rescue of the Jews of Hungary and rescue activity in general." The letter specified nothing more, but it may be surmised that the rabbi wished to review the request to bomb the camps, since this was a subject he had discussed with Gruenbaum on 25 May 1944. Ben-Gurion's meeting with the rabbi took place the following day (12 June 1944). All this pressure may have contributed to the JAE's change in attitude regarding the bombings.[42]

At the 15 June 1944 meeting between Ben-Gurion and Sharett and Harold MacMichael, the British high commissioner, Ben-Gurion said, "If anything possible can be done that will not supply the enemy with an advantage or adversely affect the war effort, he [Ben-Gurion himself] begs that it be done." Ben-Gurion did not explain what he meant by "anything possible."

These words, uttered only four days after his vehement rejection of the proposal to bomb Auschwitz, may have signaled a change in attitude on his part. He was also influenced by public opinion. However, it is not impossible that his change in attitude derived principally from a marked diminution of his hopes (qualified to begin with) to save the Jews of Hungary by means of the proposal brought by Brand. It happened following Sharett's return from Aleppo, when Ben-Gurion realized that a "separate peace" was the main trend among the proponents of the ransom proposals that had

arrived from Hungary. He knew that there was no chance of the Allies swallowing the bait. With a ransom plan that had only the slimmest chance of success, it is easy enough to understand why Ben-Gurion tended to favor the Yishuv's demand that the Allies bomb the death camps and put them out of action. By then there was virtually nothing to lose in presenting such a demand.[43]

Gruenbaum's refused to accept the JAE's judgment regarding his proposal and complained bitterly at two Rescue Committee sessions as well as in a letter to Barlas in Istanbul.[44] But his tactics failed to sway the JAE to adopt his way of thinking. The change was apparently due to new information. Vrba and Wetzler succeeded in escaping from Auschwitz in April 1944, bringing with them reliable firsthand information about what was going on there. They had been working in the camp's registration office and were thus able to supply detailed descriptions of the camp's layout, the names of its officers, and procedures—especially the extermination process. This information was reinforced by additional testimony from two other inmates who had escaped at the end of May.

All the evidence reached Slovakia and was forwarded to Geneva. Local representatives of the Yishuv, the Zionist movement, and the other Jewish organizations published the information in the press and elsewhere. The testimonies were also relayed to representatives of Orthodox Jewish organizations in Switzerland, who in turn informed their counterparts in the United States. The information reached Hungarian Jewish leaders; Anthony Eden (the British foreign secretary); and the U.S. State Department (through Roswell McClelland, of the War Refugee Board, and Wise and Goldmann, who were in the United States). The Yishuv leadership received the information on 18 June 1944 by way of Istanbul, as indicated in the minutes of the Rescue Committee presidency for that date.

In their testimony the escapees pleaded that Germany and Hungary be threatened with retaliatory action by the Allies that the Vatican be asked to issue a severe public condemnation—and, above all, that the gas chambers and crematoria in Birkenau and the railway tracks leading from Slovakia and Hungary to Poland be bombed. A dramatic appeal to "blow up from the air the centers of annihilation" in Auschwitz and the railway lines, bridges, and stations leading to it was made by Rabbi Michael Dov Ber Weissmandel of the Slovakia Working Group.[45] All this information reached Palestine toward the latter half of June. Everything pointed to the fact that Auschwitz was the final destination of those deported from Hungary and that things were moving at a rapid pace.

Gruenbaum intensified his efforts to get his proposal accepted. He sent cables to Sharett, Wise, and Goldmann. Similar cables were sent by immigrant organizations and others in Palestine, all demanding that the Allies bomb Auschwitz immediately.[46] Gruenbaum's persistence was not new, but this time he managed to get Weizmann and Sharett to contact the Allies in London and to convince them to bomb Auschwitz and the roads leading to it. The question, however, was not brought before the JAE plenum until early July. When did the change take place? Who instructed Sharett to reverse the JAE's decision of 11 June 1944?

Sharett was in London at the time, supervising activity on behalf of Hungarian Jewry. He made a point of supplying Ben-Gurion with most of the details of his activity, either by cable or by word of mouth through trusted couriers. Thus, if the JAE's records do indeed reflect the essentials of the discussions, it would seem that at least during the first half of July Ben-Gurion was not divulging to the JAE all the information in his possession. This might have been due to the sensitivity of the Brand affair.

Sharett reported—among other things—that he and Weizmann had delivered the contents of Gruenbaum's cables to George Hall, the British undersecretary of state for foreign affairs,

on 30 June. Ben-Gurion also learned that the two had raised the proposal at a meeting with Eden on 6 July and that the latter had informed them that he had discussed with the Air Ministry the possibility of bombing the camps, and also that he would discuss the suggestion that the railway tracks leading to them be bombed.

Sharett sent Eden a memo summarizing the testimony of the escapees. He vouched for their reliability and reiterated his conviction that bombing was essential in order to hold up the extermination process and the deportation of many thousands still in Hungary "at least until the roads and railway tracks could be repaired and the installations for murder could be rehabilitated." Sharett pointed to the long-term benefits of bombing: it would signal that the Allies were declaring direct war on the annihilation; it would expose the German propaganda lie that the Allies were actually satisfied the Jews were being exterminated (which did not prevent the Nazi propagandists from insisting that the Allies were mercenaries of "international Jewry"); it would dispel doubts prevalent among several of the Allied countries that the reports of genocide were exaggerated; and substance would be given to threats of retaliation for murdering Jews. Sharett even voiced the hope that such bombing would create pressure inside Germany against the continuation of the annihilation. Sharett simultaneously stressed that the JAE was aware of the downside of such acts: the bombing of Auschwitz would harm Jews already there; it was doubtful if this would lead to large-scale rescue. The memorandum was also transmitted to Ben-Gurion, but he delayed informing the JAE about it.[47]

At a JAE meeting held in early July—two days after Weizmann's and Sharett's meeting with Hall—Gruenbaum asked to be allowed to hold a press conference for the foreign press, in which he would update them on events in Auschwitz, the deportations in Hungary, and would demand a halt to such deportations "at all costs." The JAE's and Ben-Gurion's reservations were still evident in the discussion. Brand's ransom plan claimed most of their attention, and they were unwilling to jeopardize it. Schmorak, Senator, and Ben-Gurion were not in favor of a press conference on the grounds that such publicity would be useless and would not put an end to the extermination. "There is no call for a press conference with foreign newsmen," said Ben-Gurion. "Western European reporters have a different mentality, and such a conference will be of no benefit whatsoever to us."[48] He probably did not wish to acquaint the entire JAE with all the information he had received on the activity of Weizmann and Sharett in London. It should be remembered that other options—concerning the invitation received by Bader—were being examined at the same time in Istanbul and Cairo, and these, as far as we know, were also not discussed at the JAE's meetings.

Eden's reply to the suggestion made on 6 July was that the possibility of bombing had already been discussed and rejected, but he added that under the circumstances the matter would be reviewed. In a letter to Churchill the same day, he mentioned Weizmann's request and suggested that it be discussed in the cabinet. Churchill favored the proposal and suggested contacting the air minister before bringing the matter to the cabinet. The following day (7 July) Eden contacted Sir Archibald Sinclair, the air minister, to inform him of Weizmann's suggestion and of his own commitment to reassess it, pointing out that Churchill favored it. Eden hoped that "something could be done."

The explicit backing of the prime minister and the foreign secretary was of no avail. On 15 July Sinclair wrote to Eden that three topics had been examined: the disruption of the railways, the destruction of the extermination installations; and other strikes in the camp. The results were negative: the distance was too great, the operation dangerous and costly, and it was doubtful if it would help the prisoners. He suggested contacting the Americans and not giving Weizmann

a negative reply before allowing them to consider the request, although they would most probably reject it too.

Eden was angry at this response and wrote the following alongside Sinclair's doubts as to the benefit to the victims: "He was not asked for his opinion . . . he was asked to act." The same day Alec Randall, head of the Refugee Department in the Foreign Ministry, told Sharett that the matter of the bombing was "being examined by the appropriate authorities," even though the answer would most probably be negative.[49]

Passing on responsibility to the Americans was typical. Washington had already discussed the request relayed by Pinkerton and similar appeals by the World Jewish Congress and had even managed to reach a negative decision. By 4 July, the Assistant Secretary for War, John McCloy, had determined that the war department considered the bombing plan to be impractical, since it necessitated considerable air support that was required elsewhere. Moreover, even if it were practical, it would likely result in "retaliatory acts by the Germans."[50]

At a JAE meeting on 9 July 1944, Ben-Gurion reported on the information from Sharett and Agronsky, who had returned to Palestine from London. He talked about the Weizmann/Sharett meetings with Hall and Eden and read Sharett's telegram on the meeting with Hall, but he made no mention of the bombing-and-warnings issue. The discussion focused on efforts to proceed with the ransom proposal.

The bombing-and-warnings issue was raised at the JAE only a week later. The reason behind this is clear: the feeling that nothing positive would come of the Brand affair was growing more acute and, in view of the deteriorating situation in Hungary, Gruenbaum's proposal had to be implemented. Gruenbaum reported that recent Allied bombing raids over Hungary had also been directed at railway stations and did not rule out the influence of the Yishuv's demands on the selection of targets.

July 1944 marked the first time that Ben-Gurion did not circumvent the issue of bombings at a JAE session, although his remarks were very brief. He noted that Sharett had indeed "informed us that London had agreed to bomb railway stations between Hungary and Poland." He said nothing about bombing the actual camps.

That meeting ended with no resolution to demand that the Allies issue threats if the Nazi annihilations were not halted. At the same time, it appears that things were taking place outside the plenum. A few days later Lauterbach, the head of the Jewish Agency's Organization Department, sent a proposal to Joseph Linton, the London branch secretary, calling for the Allies to label the crimes against the Jews, including deportations to Poland, as war crimes.[51]

At that mid-July meeting Ben-Gurion did not mention—perhaps because he did not know—that on 11 July the London branch had decided to send a firm, lengthy, and detailed demand to the British government to bomb the death camps and the roads leading to them. (It is possible that he had no knowledge of this decision at the time.) Although the London branch acknowledged in a memo that any bombing of the camps "had little chance of rescuing the victims," it insisted that the death factory "could be destroyed and its personnel killed . . . and it could deal a blow to the apparatus of mass murder" and delay the slaughter of the remaining three hundred thousand Jews trapped in Hungary. It also stressed the moral weight of the bombings. In order to invest the proposal with greater significance, it pointed out that "the Oswiecim camp contains workshops belonging to the German arms corporations Siemens and Krupp," which were bombing targets.[52]

It is obvious that from mid-June to late July 1944 Ben-Gurion experienced a change in position from firm opposition to the Yishuv even suggesting the bombing of extermination camps (not to mention the roads leading to them) to tacitly approving such action. Documentation does not indicate what led to this about-face. Did it happen in Jerusalem, in the wake of the meeting with MacMichael, or in London? Was Sharett instructed in the spirit of the new policy before departing for London, after hearing Ben-Gurion's remarks to MacMichael that everything possible should be done so as not to give the Germans an advantage? More likely, the demand for the bombing was initiated by Zionist movement leader Weizmann and the JAE London branch, with Gruenbaum's vigorous support. It would appear that Sharett backed Weizmann and his colleagues in London to insert the demand into their conversation with Hall and Eden. In any event, Ben-Gurion was the most informed among his colleagues on the JAE concerning the essentials of Sharett's activities in London and he was in no hurry to share his information with them. He did not go out of his way to support the new position, nor did he mitigate against it.

Efforts to prompt the Allies to bomb from the air in order to disrupt the extermination process continued off and on until the end of the year. In the final analysis, they produced no tangible results. Yishuv leaders believed—falsely, at times—that certain bombing forays amounted to compliance with their requests. When, as a result of a deviation in the trajectory of one bombing raid from its target, some bombs mistakenly fell on the Birkenau extermination camp instead of the adjacent Monowitz rubber and synthetic petroleum factories, Sharett was quick to cable Gruenbaum that Britain was acting on his demands.

It was quite natural for Gruenbaum to receive this information, as well the amendment to it that Sharett sent a few weeks later. Even now it was he who stood out in his demands to bomb the camps and the roads and tracks leading to them.[53] Again Gruenbaum sent a series of cables to Wise and Goldmann in the United States, Brodetsky and Sharett at the London branch, Lichtheim and Mayer in Switzerland, Ehrenpreis in Sweden, and Barlas in Istanbul, demanding that they press yet again for the bombing of installations and road and rail tracks leading to them. He also raised these demands in his various speeches.[54]

Gruenbaum did have some support in his tireless campaign. On his visit to Turkey, Mordechai Eliash sent cables to Sweden (on the recommendation of Steinhardt and Hirschmann), the U.S. and the International Red Cross. Sharett instructed Linton at the London branch to continue demanding the destruction of the death camps, since in their current position (summer 1944) the Germans would be unable to rebuild new camps. After Britain claimed they were unobtainable, Linton appended plans and further descriptions of Auschwitz received from the Polish government-in-exile.[55]

Britain and the United States were opposed to bombing the camps and the roads and tracks leading to them. Most modern researchers agree that there was no factual, practical basis to the various arguments they used as excuses. Their negative attitude is obvious. For example, the maps of Auschwitz supplied by Linton were not handed over to the Air Ministry but rather hidden away in Foreign Office files. The British government did not seriously examine additional information offered by the Polish government-in-exile. The RAF general staff "examined" the proposal only because it was instructed by Churchill to do so and could not be rejected without some explanation. Phrases such as "technical difficulties" or "the matter was discussed and examined from all angles" were used as an excuse for not bombing.

These maneuvers by British officials succeeded because Churchill was out of the country from the end of August, and it would appear that he was kept uninformed of the tendency to forestall such operations. Eden, the foreign secretary, did not deal with the matter; he was preoccupied with the crisis in relations with the USSR over the latter's refusal to allow British and American supply aircraft to land during the revolt of the Polish (non-Jewish) underground in Warsaw. The issue was consequently entrusted to Richard Law, the parliamentary undersecretary of state.

Speaking on behalf of Eden, Law gave Weizmann the negative reply in early September 1944. The matter had thus been under discussion for about two months before being rejected as "impractical" and "unwarranted." The system involved dragging out appeals or unpopular requests by passing them from one unit to another until they were no longer valid or those who originally proposed them gave up in despair.[56] In October 1944 efforts were made to revoke the decision. Gruenbaum, Goldmann, representative of Britain's Jewish communities, and others continued to demand bombing, mainly because it was known that targets very near the camps were being bombed at the time.

Another option was to win the agreement of the Soviets. Eliyahu Epstein of the Political Department, who had broad global connections, revived an idea suggested in July and contacted a Soviet embassy adviser in Cairo, requesting that the USSR bomb Auschwitz and the roads leading to it, since Soviet airfields were closer to the target than those of Britain and the United States. The reply was negative, such a proposal being "out of place from a political standpoint." What the adviser apparently meant was that Moscow was not about to worsen relations with London and Washington by adopting an idea rejected by the western superpowers. In London representatives of the Jewish communities asked the Foreign Office to examine the possibility of bombing the camps in conjunction with the USSR. This request was also turned down.[57]

A greater measure of success, though limited in scale, was achieved by those asking that collaborators and war criminals be warned about the punishment they could expect after the war. In October 1944 British radio broadcast to Germany a list of Auschwitz murderers who would be punished after the war. The Polish underground sent the list to its government-in-exile in London and it was also broadcast in Polish, together with an explicit threat of punishment. This approach conformed to Churchill's attitude. He wrote to Eden in October 1944 that he favored the issuance of such warnings because they offered a chance to save the masses affected by Nazi oppression. Still, there was no significant change in British propaganda, which was ultimately found lacking as far as the murder of Jews was concerned.[58]

The last attempt to motivate the Allies into disrupting the extermination process occurred in April 1945, with a typical reply: a cure-all promise to make up for all the suffering in the form of an imminent victory over Germany. On 1 February 1945 Gruenbaum cabled a desperate message to Roosevelt, Stalin, and Churchill, begging them to "raze the death factory in Oswiecim" while their aircraft are "destroying the petroleum, arms, and ammunition plants." He also asked for severe warnings to be issued to the Nazis and their collaborators against any attempts to harm the remaining Jews during the death throes of the Third Reich.

On 10 April a polite letter arrived from Pinkerton, the U.S. consul, acknowledging receipt of the cable on behalf of his president. Although encouraging, Pinkerton stressed that a satisfactory solution to the Jewish problem would come only with the liberation of Europe, when the forces of darkness and death would be crushed. No replies from Churchill or Stalin to Gruenbaum's final appeal have been uncovered to date.[59]

Most researchers agree that the Allies' reasons for refusing to bomb the death camps and the roads and rails leading to them range from utter insincerity to downright lying. Among the operational arguments given were: complexity of mission; lack of available intelligence data; distance of targets from airfields; risk to pilots; difficulty of ensuring accurate hits; and expense. Halting the deportations from Hungary (although there was always the fear that they would be resumed) was also given as a reason for removing the proposal from the agenda. Other reasons involved the fact that annihilation of the Jews was a central issue in Nazi ideology, which meant the Nazis

would soon find another way of carrying it out, and that the Allies were reluctant to play into the hands of Nazi propaganda and be accused of fighting on behalf of the Jews. An examination of flight routes, number of sorties, and scope of bombing over air space close to Auschwitz all lead to the conviction that the oft-repeated refusal to bomb the death camps reflected utter indifference to the fate of the Jews being slaughtered in Auschwitz and elsewhere.[60]

Ben-Gurion's and the JAE's position may be summed up by recalling that there was a broad consensus regarding the need to demand that the Allies issue verbal and written warnings to Germany. Ben-Gurion himself made this demand on numerous occasions in his public speeches and in his directives and remarks in internal discussions. He also included a call for warnings in his many protest speeches.

Until mid-June 1944, Ben-Gurion disassociated himself from the proposal to demand Allied bombing of the camps and roads and rails leading to them. Even when he altered his position, his support was only moderate. He may have believed that efforts should not be divided and that one should concentrate on promoting Brand's plan. He may also have concluded that the Allies would disregard the demand in the end and that it would only harm any chance of obtaining Allied consent on other important issues. He may have feared that insufficient intelligence information meant that more Jews would be hurt in Allied bombings than would be saved.[61] It is clear that until June 1944 Ben-Gurion did not fully comprehend the true nature of Auschwitz, perhaps a result of the highly sophisticated system of misinformation and camouflage developed by the Germans. In any event, Ben-Gurion did not ally himself unequivocally with those few individuals who considered the bombings something symbolic and significant in an effort to shatter the "other planet." He left it to Gruenbaum and the London branch to determine the pace and was content to give his quiet assent to their activity.

PART 3
FINANCING OF RESCUE ATTEMPTS AND ASSISTANCE

10

At the Edge of the Abyss

Financial Maneuvers by Ben-Gurion and Kaplan, 1942–1943

Research has not yet provided a complete answer to the question of how much money was allocated by the Yishuv to the rescue of Jews during the Second World War, especially when the true significance of what was happening in Europe became common knowledge. This is a formidable task since the rescue activities were extremely complex and mostly secret.

Determining the financing of the rescue operation also raises special difficulties. Those allocating the funds and their recipients took care to carefully cover their tracks. Varied methods were utilized to "launder" some of the money and to conceal its movement—for example, by means of "straw companies"—because transferring funds from the free countries into occupied Europe required violating the laws and currency regulations of the Western countries. Some of these activities required the payment of bribes. The conversion of money or diamonds (which were easier to smuggle) into currencies usable in occupied Europe was an intricate process that took place on the black market through couriers or shady moneychangers who made their brokerage conditional on the highest degree of discretion. They did not issue receipts or bills of lading for what was transferred through them or for what they retained for themselves. The principle of acting in secrecy was also applicable in the case of those banks involved in the depositing and the transfer of monies. At times Western spy services helped with the movement of funds, and very often their involvement also had to be kept secret. All of these were matters that people are reluctant to discuss freely even in normal times, let alone during a world war. Nations and intelligence agencies today still practice some of these methods and consequently are reluctant to reveal their past activities. As a result, the paucity of documentation concerning the financing of the rescue operation is not surprising, and it is clear why it is so hard to assess the scope of the funding and its routes.

In part 3 of this book I shall examine how Ben-Gurion and his closest colleagues (particularly Kaplan) raised and allocated funds for the rescue of and assistance to the Jews of Europe. I will attempt to determine if they had a clear financing policy, how much money was raised, and from what sources. In the absence of complete documentation on the allocations, one can learn about funding by tracing the movement of monies in occupied Europe and determining the extent of the activity. It is also important to understand how the funds were transferred, which intelligence agencies followed the transfers and knew of them, and whether there was a reaction to these financial activities by the Yishuv in Palestine.

These are central questions, the financing of rescue activities being one of the main criteria for determining the sincerity of a statesman's pronouncements regarding his intention to adopt a given policy. On the other hand, the funding of such activities can also indicate the presence of an unpublicized policy—perhaps even a practical policy that contradicts official declarations—as well as secret processes for which funds are allocated, and real criteria, as distinct from those reflected in public discourse.

Moreover, it involved violations of the law, and there was even a real danger that allocations of money would be irretrievably lost, would hamper the political activity of the JAE, or would come at the expense of settlement activity and the establishment of an infrastructure for mass immigration. Nevertheless, establishing that funds were allocated and to what extent provide significant testimony to the level of concern or indifference of the Yishuv's leadership regarding the fate of Europe's Jews.

To briefly sketch the background, the allocation of funds from resources of the Yishuv itself was obviously also a function of its economic capability. During the war years, the population of the Yishuv comprised between 450,000 and 475,000 Jews, the majority recently arrived younger immigrants. A small minority belonged to the moneyed stratum or to the well-off veteran Yishuv. The period was characterized by various political upheavals, including the Arab revolt (1936–1939) and the Second World War (from 1939 onward), and a general sense of political and economic instability that existed throughout the world as well.

Beginning in mid-1941 an economic revival was discernible in the economy as a whole as well as in the life of the individual in Palestine. The standard of living of the workers improved, but it was the capitalists and industrialists who mainly enjoyed the fruits of the recovery.[1] Only in hindsight can one know for certain if a particular improvement was the first stage in a process of general and sustained recovery or simply a momentary caprice on the part of the "minister of history" or the "finance minister." Other pictures raced through the minds of the heroes of that period— the capitalists and wage earners—as they read the newspaper headlines: the difficult situation of the United States, "the land of unlimited opportunity," which was only then just beginning to recover from the great economic crisis that had gripped it since 1929; the memory of the severe economic and political crises which completely overturned the established order of things in Europe.

The demands made on the capitalists and wage earners to contribute more money to aid and rescue the Jews of Europe therefore came during a time of economic improvement in the Yishuv but also a feeling of uncertainty. Even in less stormy times, expectations, illusions, feelings of uncertainty—all of these exert a not inconsiderable influence on economic systems.

The significance of the battle of El-Alamein in pushing back the Germans from North Africa was not known at the time the events occurred. Even after El Alamein, and following news of the mass slaughter of European Jewry, the fears of the Yishuv Jews with regard to their own safety were not dispelled. Consequently, they assumed that the Yishuv budget would continue to finance mobilization, fortification, and other defense activities, perhaps to make certain that what happened to the Jews "there" would not recur with such ease a few months later "here" in Palestine. Here one should stress the signal importance of the fact that the Yishuv was based on a volunteerism structure. Most of its political machinery functioned thanks to volunteers. Consequently, the ability of the Yishuv leadership to enforce— for instance, to collect taxes and levies—was limited to various forms of social and organizational pressure. The willingness or indifference of the various volunteer elements carried greater weight than the relatively weak enforcement measures available to the leadership. From this standpoint, the significance of the money raised was greater than that of an equal sum raised and allocated in a sovereign society.

The JAE budget at the time was based on income from three main sources: the fund of the Palestine Foundation Fund (PFF); the Jewish National Fund (JNF); and the Mobilization Fund. Every year they collected donations from individuals and organizations through special appeal campaigns, issued compulsory loans and bonds, and collected direct and indirect taxes and levies.[2]

The official and unofficial exchange rates are an essential element in the present discussion. It is clear that the budgets of the Jewish Agency and the allocations of the various funds were calculated according to the official rate of exchange. However, the value of the sums exchanged on the black market or transferred to occupied Europe was generally lower. Every exchange or transfer transaction required different kinds of "commissions." Thus, the official exchange rate for one

Palestinian pound was four U.S. dollars, but at times it was exchanged for three dollars. Similarly, in Switzerland the official exchange rate for one dollar was four francs thirty centimes, but on the Swiss black market the dollar was only worth two francs seventy centimes. The decline in the value of money as a result of wartime inflation must also be taken into consideration, although the inflation rate in Palestine during the Second World War was very slight.

Another aspect that should be considered is the degree of flexibility of the budget. Discussions regarding the financial dimensions of aid and rescue activity began toward the end of 1942, immediately after reports of the extermination were received and made public. At that time the Jewish Agency budget had already been "up and running" for several months. Anyone who has ever managed a budget—even that of a PTA committee—is aware of the difficulty of coping with a significant and unplanned expense after a part of the budget has already been used up. A new allocation requires that the planned budgetary framework of any organization be increased and may involve the utilization of "reserves" or changes in the apportioning of the budget. However, every allocation reflects the needs and the constant pressure of influential groups on the work program of the organization, making it very hard to alter an approved budget. Toward the end of 1942, the JAE was quite limited in its ability to change the Jewish Agency's current budget.[3] Only beginning with the budget for 1943 did the JAE enjoy relative freedom to adapt the budget to the new situation.

The Jewish Agency's budget—especially its size—is obviously an indicator of the economic state of the Yishuv at that time. Based on this, one can attempt to estimate the dimensions of what researchers refer to as "the Yishuv's capacity" to undertake additional tasks. Discussing what the Yishuv was able to allocate might be less emotional and less demagogic—and definitely more productive from a researcher's standpoint—if one determines these dimensions on the basis of a professional economic analysis.

It is therefore apposite to know that the regular budget of the Jewish Agency in the years relevant to this discussion was as follows: 1943 = 1.15 million Palestinian pounds; 1944 = 1.1 million Palestinian pounds (the regular budget) plus 2.1 million Palestinian pounds (the "irregular" budget, i.e., the addition dependent on future income).

In order to obtain a more accurate picture of the degree of elasticity in the budget, it is necessary to examine the relationship between standard expenses—a component that is very difficult to alter, especially in periods of crisis—and variable expenses. The true significance of changes in the budget, in particular allocations for aid and rescue, can only be properly assessed if one takes into account the relationship between the agency's regular expenses and its variable expenses.

According to Dina Porat, between 1 February 1943 and 1 June 1945 the Yishuv transferred for rescue 1.329 million Palestinian pounds. The sources for this sum are as follows: Mobilization and Rescue Fund = 647,000; JDC = 512,000; various other communities in the free world = 170,000.[4] Based on the value of the U.S. dollar at that time (4 U.S. dollars for 1 Palestinian pound), the Yishuv allocated for rescue 2.588 million U.S. dollars of the funds that were collected by the Mobilization and Rescue Fund (these were not the only funds the Yishuv allocated for rescue). This sum alone was greater than that allocated by other Jewish communities, with the exception of the Jews of the United States. This was a relatively major allocation when one takes into consideration the size of the Yishuv, its demographic structure, and the fact that it was a society still in its formative stage of development.[5] Porat also determined that rescue activity was one of the JAE's four main expenditure items.[6]

According to Akiva Nir's analysis of the Yishuv delegation in Istanbul, the latter spent

188,000 Palestinian pounds in 1943, 247,854 in 1944, and 285,403 in 1945, for a total of 721,257 Palestinian pounds. Based on these figures, it is clear that the money collected in the Yishuv or transferred through the Yishuv, reached the emissaries in Istanbul and was used for aid and rescue activities.

Nir also supplied data gleaned from the official statistical information sheet of the JAE. According to this information, the Mobilization and Rescue Fund raised 827,000 Palestinian pounds in the five years between 1940/41 and 1944/45, but of this amount only 234,000 Palestinian pounds were spent on rescue. The remaining 593,000 Palestinian pounds were spent mainly on funding mobilization and the families of the mobilized troops, with the smallest amount (106,000 Palestinian pounds) transferred to the Kofer HaYishuv fund-raising agency to finance the activities of the Haganah.

If these figures are accurate, and if Nir is correct in stating that a little over 721,000 Palestinian pounds reached Istanbul, and if only 234,000 of them came from the Mobilization and Rescue Fund, then the remainder (487,000 Palestinian pounds) came from other sources—either directly from the JAE budget or from other bodies that allocated money to the Yishuv for rescue, which the JAE then transferred to Turkey.[7]

Menahem Bader, who, among his many duties, served as treasurer of the Istanbul delegation, apparently knew quite a bit about what the delegation transferred to occupied Europe. In summarizing his mission, he wrote that in the years 1943 and 1944 over 1.1 million Palestinian pounds were spent on aid and rescue—much more than was estimated by Nir. (In another summary Bader wrote that the Yishuv transferred 1.3 million Palestinian pounds for the same purpose.) Bader reckoned that if from that same sum of 1.1 million Palestinian pounds one deducted payments for the purchase or leasing of ships (it may be assumed that they were not intended for pleasure cruises between the Bosporus

and the Dardanelles), one arrives at the conclusion that "close to 700,000 [Palestinian] pounds were allocated for purposes which can collectively be called aid and rescue." This is similar to the sum estimated by Nir, minus the payments for the ships. According to Bader, the sum available to the emissaries at the start of their term in Turkey was only 5,000 Palestinian pounds, and the increase in the budget allocated to them was "gigantic and legendary."[8]

Summing up his activities and those of his colleagues in Istanbul, after the war Bader wrote that up to that point approximately 1.3 million Palestinian pounds had been spent on all the items relating to aid and rescue. He detailed the components of the expenditure as follows: the rescue of Jews from Greece and children from Yugoslavia; support for the Jews of Bulgaria and the Jews who suffered from hunger and cold in Transnistria and Tchernowitz in Bukovina; those "who wandered over the snow-covered mountains of Italy and Savoy and the Pyrenees until they found haven and refuge"; and thousands of orphans who were smuggled out of France, Belgium, and Holland. Money was also spent to fund the "Tiyulim," the "trips" Jews made "braving the fire of a thousand dangers from Poland to Slovakia, from Slovakia to Hungary, and from Hungary to Romania," from a dangerous area to a more peaceful, less dangerous area.

Additional monies, Bader continued, were allocated for the acquisition of "forged documents and certificates, bread coupons, and the doors which were opened in prison," as well as "for bribes [?] to delay deportations and to prevent the liquidation of work camps in Novaki, Srat, and Krakow." In addition, money was also allocated following "the diabolical offer of the chief murderer, the man from Sharona," the ransom offer made by Eichmann, who visited the Templar settlement of Sharona, near Tel Aviv. Possibly Bader was referring to funds that were transferred into Hungary as advance payment of one kind or another, perhaps advance payment in support of the first "interim agreement." Bader also mentioned the money allocated for the rescue of seventeen hundred inmates at Bergen-Belsen, the people on the "Kasztner Train," and the twelve hundred rescued from Theresienstadt toward the end of the war. In his summary Bader included allocations for the purchase and leasing of ships for the thousands of survivors who reached Palestine by being "transported in rickety crates from Constanţa and the shores of Greece—across stormy seas and past enemy watches and the suffocating noose of the White Paper."[9]

In this document Bader indicated a still greater funding role performed by the Yishuv: close to two thirds of the 1.3 million Palestinian pounds (totaling a little over 850,00 pounds), or some 150,000 pounds more than his estimate in another summary. According to him, the funds were transferred to occupied Europe

> as a ransom for lives saved—into the darkness they were flung at times, into the fog, into the unknown—to serve as a delaying barrier and wall, and barricade for arms, for the fire of revenge, and a burning flag and for bread, simply for bread to break the hunger, and a warm blanket and bunker, and rescue boats!— one million three hundred thousand Palestinian pounds, divided into 800 days of killing and suffocation and blazing extermination furnaces, and you see what they amounted to, a drop in a raging stormy sea of blood and tears into which five and a half million of our brethren dove and drowned.[10]

Bader's estimate of 1.3 million Palestinian pounds is very close to that of Porat, who estimated that the Yishuv allocated 1.329 million Palestinian pounds to the rescue mission.

According to a report by the Rescue Committee to the Twenty-third Zionist Congress at a meeting in Jerusalem, the budget of the committee totaled 1,756,734 Palestinian pounds. This sum includes all the expenses and income of the committee, but it does not include the additional funds that were transferred for aid and rescue by other groups or without the committee's knowledge. Even so, the budget of the Rescue Committee indicates a considerable level of activity.[11]

There are those who expand the definition of funds allocated for rescue by including funds allocated for a comprehensive solution to the problem of the Jewish people, specifically for the establishment of an infrastructure to create a state. This, it will be recalled, was the overall concept of Ben-Gurion and Kaplan. Since they felt strongly that the establishment of a state would provide a comprehensive solution to the problem, the allocation for an infrastructure was, in their view, a direct and essential contribution to the rescue effort. According to this broader view, the Yishuv allocated a far greater sum for rescue. Kaplan articulated this point with directness and suggested "saving every penny" for the days following the war for the integration of the many immigrants who "will need housing and work," to which one must also add the basic requirements of health and rehabilitation, settlement, education, and so forth. According to figures supplied by Shabtai Teveth, a major part of the budgets of the JNF and the PFF and the entire immigration budget (1,210,360 Palestinian pounds in 1943) were allocated to activities that could be called "long-term rescue."

According to this argument, during the five years of the Second World War about 3.39 million Palestinian pounds (roughly 112.9 million U.S. dollars at today's rate of exchange) were allocated for rescue (in the broadest sense of the word). Teveth further shows that at that time only 1.149 million Palestinian pounds were allocated for the purchase of land by the JNF (about 38.3 million U.S. dollars).[12]

To refute a widespread misconception, contrary to the image which Ben-Gurion himself cultivated, there is no basis for the assertion that he understood little or nothing about economic matters. The establishment of extensive economic systems, management of finances, the creation and management of a budget, raising funds in Palestine and abroad—all these were not foreign to Ben-Gurion. As general secretary of the General Federation of Labor (Histadrut) and (later) chairman of the JAE, he was involved in the establishment of very large economic and financial institutions by Yishuv standards. Ben-Gurion was deeply involved in the activities of the Economic Research Institute and the Planning Committee and its subcommittees (all chaired by experts); he raised funds for the Haganah in Europe and the United States; and before, during, and after the war he managed secret funds that provided him with a degree of operational flexibility.[13] Right from the start of his public career, Ben-Gurion realized only too well the power of money to translate dreams into action. Basic economic concepts were clear to him, or else he could learn them with ease because he was an autodidact par excellence. Consequently, although the treasury and management of the budget were not specifically included in his area of involvement, it is quite clear that he knew everything necessary about the funding of rescue operations.

In economic matters he was assisted by people like David Horowitz as well as other economic experts, particularly by his colleague Eliezer Kaplan, the treasurer of the JAE and a member of the ruling triumvirate (the third being Sharett). He was an efficient treasurer, one of the leaders of Mapai and the JAE, and a confidant of Ben-Gurion. Kaplan, together with Ben-Gurion and Sharett, headed Mapai, the JAE, and the Yishuv.

Ben-Gurion received the bulk of information passed along to Kaplan concerning the financing of aid and rescue, and was also a partner in the main funding decisions made by Kaplan, although he permitted him freedom of action. This last point is one of the premises

adopted in this part of the book, and I feel obligated to justify it.[14] It would appear that Kaplan was a kind of "punching bag." The anger and frustration that characterized discussions of financing the rescue operation were generally directed at him. What Kaplan absorbed Ben-Gurion was spared, but this does not mean that Ben-Gurion did not concern himself with the funding of rescue activity.

When Kaplan returned from his first visit to Istanbul, he likened the action required to the shooting of an arrow in the dark. The financing of the rescue operation was the immediate context of his statement, and there was no one better suited than Kaplan to express the policy of the JAE: money would be collected and transferred—this despite the fear that it would be equivalent to throwing it away—because it was forbidden to overlook any opportunity to rescue Jews.

At the end of 1942 the Yishuv leadership was confronted with the necessity to speedily draw up an orderly plan of action. The pressure was immense. It would not be an exaggeration to say that the reports shocked the leadership and threatened to paralyze it. It did not dictate developments, which demanded a response from it, and frequently had only a very limited degree of control over what was happening in the Yishuv itself. The balance of this chapter will be devoted to an examination of whether the leadership— and, above all, Ben-Gurion and Kaplan—succeeded in formulating a financing policy and acting in accordance with it.

Questions regarding financing—what to finance, how much to spend, and where to find sources of income—appeared straightaway. Precisely at that time the JAE was in the final stages of approving the Jewish Agency budget for the upcoming financial year (1942–1943).[15] The funding of the rescue operation became a pressing question, particularly when three costly rescue plans were presented in succession: the plan to rescue children and two ransom plans.

FINANCING THE PLAN TO RESCUE CHILDREN

This plan—rescuing twenty-nine thousand children from Europe and bringing them to Palestine by utilizing the remaining immigration permits from the White Paper of 1939—demanded exhaustive team effort and important decisions regarding the extent and manner of funding. It aroused greater hope than any other plan—even Ben-Gurion was optimistic—and it seemed at the time that the British were prepared to help in its realization.[16] The two ransom plans presented were the Transnistria Plan—based on a proposal to release seventy thousand Jews from Transnistria in exchange for a ransom—and the Slovakia Plan, from which emerged the broader Europe Plan, or Rabbis' Plan. It should be apparent that a serious organization had to carefully weigh how best to organize itself for operations which were unforeseen and very costly—perhaps even exceeding its financial capability.

Discussions about funding the rescue began immediately following official reports on the extermination. In time it became clear that the rescue of masses of Jewish children was nothing more than wishful thinking, but at the beginning of December 1942 Mapai and the Histadrut, as well as other organizations, had discussed the children's integration. The main question was how the children were to be divided up among the various Yishuv groups. In the background a heated controversy was already developing.

At one of these discussions (9 December 1942) the members of the Mapai secretariat asked about the role of Mapai, the Histadrut, and the kibbutz settlements in integrating the children. Who would provide financing and what system would be followed—private absorption, absorption on agricultural settlements, or absorption by private individuals in various cities? Would world Jewry, through organizations like Hadassah or the Polish government-in-exile, continue to participate in the financing and, if so, what would be the extent of their financial assistance?

The fact that discussions were detailed, with the process of integration stripped down to its component parts based on cost, proves that there was a real expectation of the arrival of thousands of children.

As was described earlier (see chapter 4) the sense of urgency prompted Ben-Gurion to propose that the integration of the children not remain the exclusive responsibility of the Youth Aliyah (Immigration) office headed by Henrietta Szold. He did not flinch from his proposal even though Szold was one of the leaders of Hadassah. A blow to Szold was also likely to put at risk Hadassah's financial support of the Yishuv, and it also had harmful repercussions for Ben-Gurion and Mapai. Another sensitive area concerned the children of those mobilized from the Yishuv. There was a feeling among the families that the Yishuv leadership did not support them adequately—and now it would make a great effort to assist refugee children arriving in Palestine on behalf of the mobilized soldiers.

Ben-Gurion decided that if the need arose the Yishuv would bear the sole financial burden of integrating the first five thousand children. He used their arrival to raise money from world Jewry and viewed the integration of children as a promising event that would give birth to a big settlement enterprise: "We shall have to go to the Jews of America and say to them: we require for these children land, equipment, houses, a new settlement. . . . [T]he calculation has to be based on settlement, not merely temporary refuge." The Mapai secretariat adopted his proposal that a special committee draw up the program.[17]

Ben-Gurion placed the rescue of children within a very broad context. The cost of the enterprise, according to his expanded conception, would far exceed the financial capabilities of the Yishuv, especially when one took into account its participation in the funding of other aid and rescue campaigns and the defense expenditure. His expanded approach reflected a considerable degree of optimism, which in the end was groundless. His desire to present the enterprise as a first stage in the evacuation of Jewish children from occupied Europe was based on the hope that the broad context would contribute to the acceleration of the rescue plan and improve the chances of securing funding for it.

In remarks to colleagues in the Mapai secretariat, Ben-Gurion began by outlining the elements of the policy plan that had been discussed by the JAE on 13 December 1942 and at a session of the special Committee for Child Immigration, which met the following day. At the meetings of the JAE and the special committee (Ben-Gurion was one of its five members) it was decided to announce to the British government that the JAE would fund the integration of the twenty-nine thousand refugee children and was also drawing up "broader plans" in accordance with Ben-Gurion's wishes. The JAE consequently adopted the policy he outlined in the party arena: the Yishuv would bear the financial burden of this large-scale enterprise and the JAE would undertake to finance it and subsequently act to obtain the money.[18]

Ben-Gurion and Kaplan pointed to the potential partners in financing "the rescue of these children and their integration in Palestine": the JDC, the aid organization of American Jewry, which, with certain qualifications, would be included in the financing; and "the Jewish and non-Jewish world." Kaplan explained that the decision to raise money from outside sources did not contradict the JAE's decision to assume financial responsibility "for every child that can be rescued . . . meaning tens of thousands." The significance of this undertaking was that the JAE would guarantee the financial side of the immigration and integration processes through interim funding until money was obtained from other sources; in the worst-case scenario it would finance them from its budgetary reserves or through an increase of its debts.

The JAE thus succeeded in recovering from the initial shock and in formulating a clear policy

with regard to the possibility of rescuing tens of thousands of children. It was decided to initiate contacts with representatives of the JDC and to dispatch Yitzhak Gruenbaum to the United States in order to try to get American Jewry to finance the projected aid and rescue efforts. As will be recalled, Ben-Gurion opposed sending a Yishuv delegation to the United States, but he espoused the suggestion that Gruenbaum should travel alone on a mission of propaganda and fund-raising.[19]

Specific sums were already referred to in a discussion held at the Mapai secretariat toward the end of December. In the plan presented there, those present discussed the rescue of a minimum of ten thousand children. The estimated cost of transport and their integration—including "settling them during their adolescence" in the spirit of the broad conception presented by Ben-Gurion at the previous session—was about five million Palestinian pounds (twenty million U.S. dollars at the then current rate of exchange). Although it was understood that the funds for this operation would not be required simultaneously,[20] all realized that such an enterprise would exceed the Yishuv's financial capability.

Ben-Gurion described to his party colleagues the stand adopted by the JAE in their discussions with the Mandate government and the British government in London: "We want to save 25 thousand children. They asked us: money; plans. We said: 'We take responsibility for the funding.' They were not satisfied with this; we gave an official letter. We thought: afterward we can continue with the discussion." He again stressed that the JAE had assumed total financial responsibility—since bringing the children over and their integration were "the most important consideration of Zionism"—and it intended to obtain the "assistance of all the Jewish people" to finance the enterprise.[21] It is worth recalling that the Yishuv's "capacity for economic integration" was an important element in the restrictions imposed by the British on immigration at the end of the thirties. Now they were raising this subject in the context of the rescue of children; in 1942 and the beginning of 1943 the British were well aware of the fate awaiting the Jewish children remaining in Europe if they were not rescued.

The financial responsibility of the JAE for the transport and integration of the children necessitated that it look to outside funding. The JAE had assumed a risk, having no other choice, and had taken responsibility for an undertaking without any real long-term coverage apart from the ability to provide interim funding. This fact is not in keeping with the accusations subsequently hurled in JAE meetings. A hesitant leadership, one shackled by routine, would not have dared to take such a risk. The general principle laid down by Ben-Gurion and Kaplan with regard to the financing of the JAE was hardly conservative, to say the least: at every occasion that offered a chance of rescue, the JAE would assume financial responsibility for the enterprise and only afterward would it try to find funding. Lack of money would not thwart rescue efforts.

FUNDING THE
TRANSNISTRIA PLAN

The JAE was virtually called upon to finance three rescue projects simultaneously. The second was placed on the agenda in Palestine at the end of December, immediately after the first reports about it reached Jerusalem from Istanbul. As was stated earlier (see chapter 5), the information about this development was first given to Ben-Gurion and Gruenbaum. It was subsequently presented to the JAE at a special session held on 23 December 1942.

Gruenbaum chaired that meeting in the absence of Ben-Gurion. He gave the JAE information concerning the ransom offer and summarized Ben-Gurion's position as expressed during their meeting before the session: Ben Gurion felt that one should consider the proposal and weigh its chances of success, strive for continued negotiations, although he doubted the plan could be implemented, since the Allied governments would most likely not permit funds to be transferred to enemy countries.[22] The amount of ransom demanded was between three and four million Palestinian pounds (equivalent to roughly twelve to sixteen million U.S. dollars) in exchange for seventy thousand Jews from Transnistria. According to another version, the ransom money demanded was more than twice this amount.[23]

Nonetheless, Ben-Gurion stressed that negotiations should continue in order to assess the possibility of implementing the plan, for if it became clear that taking out and transferring the money was the only obstacle, perhaps a way would also be found to overcome this.[24] Kaplan next described the size of the financial burden involved in this proposal and voiced the fear that the whole affair might be nothing more than a form of "financial blackmail." Nevertheless he was determined to pursue the matter to the end even at the risk of losing great sums of money.

As was mentioned in chapter 5, the JAE members discussed the proposal to divide the ransom plan into two parts. It was suggested that one begin with the cheaper operation, namely, evacuating Jews from Transnistria and returning them to Romania, later extricating them from Europe. Eliyahu Dobkin also suggested raising some of the funds from the wealthy Jews of Romania. The Yishuv was then unable to raise such sums from its own resources, and certainly not from the 1942–1943 budget, which was due to be approved at the time. Raising money in Romania itself to rescue Jews in Bessarabia and Bukovina who had been deported to Transnistria would also avoid the necessity of having to violate the prohibition against transferring money to the Axis countries. The JAE therefore approved the proposal to continue negotiations, adding to Gruenbaum's agenda the task of soliciting contributions for the ransom during his U.S. visit.[25]

While the JAE was discussing the funding of the two rescue plans, a third rescue plan was also presented. Each of them required great sums far in excess of the Yishuv's financial capability. The cost of rescuing twenty-nine thousand children and bringing them to Palestine was 4.8 million U.S. dollars—which did not include the cost of integrating and settling them. The financial cost of the Transnistria Plan was at least 12–16 million dollars. Compared to those 16.8 to 20.8 million dollars, the budget of the Jewish Agency in 1942 was 1.15 million Palestinian pounds including fixed expenses, and the projected budget for 1943, which was 1.1 million Palestinian pounds, was increased by 1 million Palestinian pounds in the nonregular section of the budget, totaling 2.1 million Palestinian pounds.

The sum required for the transport of the children alone amounted to the entire budget of the JAE for 1942 plus another two hundred thousand U.S. dollars; according to the lower cost estimate of the Transnistria Plan, it was two or more times greater than the said budget. It would have been difficult to find organizations able to stretch their economic resources to such an extent. Yishuv funding of the rescue plans was nothing more than a pipe dream. Nevertheless, Ben-Gurion and the majority of JAE members decisively favored doing everything possible to implement the plans.[26]

Ben-Gurion paid close attention to the details concerning the funding of the plan to rescue children, which seemed practical, but contented himself with general remarks about funding the Transnistria Plan, which in his view was quite illusory. At the same time, the overall policy of Ben-Gurion and Kaplan also devolved upon the Transnistria Plan, and the JAE decided that lack of funding should not present an obstacle to its implementation.

A NONCOMPLIANT JAE

A short time after the rescue policy had been decided, it became clear that the JAE was incapable of obtaining funding to cover the obligations it had undertaken. Many did not believe that it was actually incapable of obtaining the funding. There were those who maintained that the JAE did not understand what was required, whereas others were of the opinion that it simply did not wish to participate in the rescue operations.

Criticism mounted—and not without reason. The sums allocated by the JAE seemed very small—even ridiculous—totaling twenty-five thousand Palestinian pounds for the year 1942–1943.[27] Criticism came from different quarters: the Budget Committee of the Zionist Actions Committee, the Zionist Actions Committee itself, the Rescue Committee, the Histadrut, Mapai, to name just a few. Critics suggested other ways to obtain the required money, their comments reflecting great confusion. The JAE was criticized on all sides for a lack of understanding, impotence, opposition to finance rescue plans that had only a faint chance of success, and allocating insufficient funds in general. The JAE was also accused of the historic blunder of distinguishing between "Zionism" and "rescue," which, according to the critics, must never be distinguished from one another. They maintained that the JAE had made such a distinction even though, as has been demonstrated, the attitude of the leadership was the reverse.

A large part of the criticism was directed at the JAE's leaders: Ben-Gurion, the chairman; Kaplan, the treasurer, who was not prepared to allocate "even a penny"; and Gruenbaum, chairman of the Rescue Committee. It was not enough, many of the critics argued, to decide upon an overall policy, to extend financial coverage for rescuing children, or to be prepared to assist veteran Zionists. They called for the allocation of at least ten times the amount proposed by the JAE, at least 250,000 Palestinian pounds.[28] It is worth noting that such an expanded allocation was nowhere near the immense sums under discussion at the time.

The criticism leveled at the JAE sheds light on its policy at the time. Since Kaplan, Ben-Gurion, and Gruenbaum were forced to defend themselves, the criticism elicited explanations concerning their financing policy and forced them to be more specific. At the beginning of 1943, a month or two after the reports of the extermination, horrifying reports became increasingly frequent, and it was very difficult to admit that the JAE did not have sufficient money for rescue. The rate of extermination increased and there were reports of deportations of Jews from the Balkans, Holland, Belgium, Germany, and Norway. It became known that Hitler intended to systematically murder five million Jews, and Himmler gave orders to annihilate all of Polish Jewry by the beginning of 1943. The impassioned calls of the Yishuv emissaries in Istanbul, and the words of reproach from those returning from there, fanned the flames.

A characteristic discussion took place at the Mapai secretariat on 10 February 1943. It occurred following a report given by Bader during his visit to Palestine, plus other reports that were circulating. Sharp attacks were made against the JAE, against members of Mapai in the JAE, and particularly against Ben-Gurion. David Remez, the general secretary of the Histadrut, succinctly expressed the criticism welling up in the Histadrut leadership and Mapai when he described the situation where there is apparently "money for every necessity" and, on the other hand, "when it is necessary to give baksheesh of a few thousand lira, we have no money."[29]

Avraham Haft, who was involved with financial matters in the kibbutz and moshav movements and active in the Kofer HaYishuv, stated that Ben-Gurion "does not display the maximum concern in this matter" and expressed the view that the JAE did not allocate sufficient money for rescue because it erred in making a distinction between "the catastrophe" and "Zionism." Haft rejected the tight-fisted approach, which he ascribed without any proof to Gruenbaum, favoring the allocation of "hundreds of thousands of Palestinian pounds." His remarks created the impression that the main

problem was conceptual, a mistaken view that took root in JAE circles, and not simply one of empty coffers pure and simple. Only the atmosphere of those hectic and troubled days can explain how a practical man like Haft, well aware of the difference between wishful thinking and having the required financial capability, could express these sorts of views.

Others called for a halt to "this silence" and urged a constant state of alarm that would open hearts and wallets. Here it is worth recalling the connection between the public's alarm and the raising of contributions based on it. It was further stated at that same meeting of the Mapai secretariat that the allocation of monies should not be made contingent on the guaranteed success of the plans, for "when a person is lying dangerously ill, no man will dare say: 'No medicine will help anymore; it is a pity to spend money on a medical specialist.'"[30] As we have seen, this was indeed the JAE's policy.

The JAE was asked in an accusatory tone what it had done to collect money abroad and in the United States. There were calls to at least save the Yishuv's "Zionist conscience." Golda Meir called on the JAE to concentrate on rescue because "there is now no other Zionism." She demanded that unnecessary confrontations be avoided but nevertheless asked how Kaplan could talk about the allocation of a lot of money for rescue and then argue with the Mobilization Fund over sums on the order of twenty thousand Palestinian pounds.[31]

From the long list of critics and those offering suggestions, it is worth examining the remarks of Eliyahu Golomb, the unofficial commander of the Haganah organization. Golomb enumerated a long list of difficulties and possible courses of action, described logistical and various other problems, and stressed that, notwithstanding the difficulties, everything possible should be done because "there might be some substance to these propositions." He stressed the importance of waging a relentless battle against the clock and attempted to quantify the dimensions of the operation: 1.2 million Palestinian pounds (4.8 million U.S. dollars) would have to be raised in order to rescue thirty thousand people from Europe, based on an estimated 40 Palestinian pounds to transport each person aboard Turkish ships. Even if the JAE managed to raise such a sum from contributions by America's Jews, it would be difficult to transfer the funds on account of the ban on the transfer of monies to occupied Europe. Would America's Jews donate such a sum? Golomb answered in the affirmative, as did Ben-Gurion, who interjected his comments in the same positive spirit.

According to Golomb, the need to raise money from the Yishuv made it essential to create a sense of obligation among the public, to stress the opportunity of rescue, and to remove the unnecessary cloak of secrecy. It was permissible and imperative to print "daily on every page of the newspaper: a possibility exists to save Jews. Money is needed for this purpose—it will have an effect." Every possible avenue for the transfer of funds was to be explored, in order to prevent the possibility of rescue plans being thwarted by of a temporary lack of cash.[32]

Among Mapai members there was a common assumption that the leadership refused to risk large amounts of money for plans that were destined to fail. This was erroneous. The consistent attitude of the JAE and the practical policy it adopted at the end of 1942 were expressed in Ben-Gurion's apt formulation in connection with Eichmann's proposal: "If there is a one-in-a-million chance, we should grab it." The leadership was involved in a series of complex activities. In general, it was not possible to discuss them in public forums without running the risk of dooming them to failure.

The embattled members of the JAE were beset by a furious wave of criticism at a time when they had to prepare the relatively inexperienced branches of the agency for operations of extraordinary complexity. It was a painful polemic. All of those involved were convinced that they were doing the right thing on behalf of the Jews of Europe. One of the speakers expressed the nature of the argument as follows: "The most difficult argument is with friends whom you feel share the same attitude toward the issue as you yourself."

KAPLAN DEFENDS HIMSELF

Members of Kaplan's and Ben-Gurion's party actually denounced them, claiming it was they who were preventing the allocation from the agency funds for rescue. Kaplan vigorously rejected the criticism. He absolutely denied any "division of duties" between "plaintiff and defendants" and rejected the claim that "someone interfered." He himself attempted to manage the JAE's two means for collecting money—the PFF and, to a certain extent, the Mobilization Fund—but the experts rejected his suggestions for professional reasons.[33]

Kaplan explained why the JAE could not fund the rescue plans from its own resources, stressing that this did not mean the JAE was washing its hands of the necessity to produce interim funding or guarantees for the financing of rescue plans until the required amount was collected. In his own words, he acted thus "yesterday and today," and when he heard from Bader about the possibility of rescuing five thousand children and bringing them to Palestine, he gave instructions to allocate forty thousand Palestinian pounds for the operation "without much argument and without embittering the life of each of us." It now "only" remained to find the financial backing for this measure. Tens of thousands of Palestinian pounds were allocated for the purchase of ships for the illegal immigration operation. The JAE's participation was approved to create a monetary reserve to be made available to the Yishuv's emissaries in Geneva, contingent on partners being found.

Kaplan also made an apparent reference to the Transnistria and Slovakia plans when he said that he had given instructions not to jeopardize the possibility of rescuing Jews because of financial constraints. Consequently, talk of opposition and an inappropriate rate of progress were demagoguery, Kaplan declared, and in response to demagogic remarks one did not alter one's rate of progress. The gist of his position was that no rescue operation would be thwarted by lack of money, and that the JAE would obligate itself financially and seek funding afterward. From Kaplan's remarks it emerged that he had already allocated forty thousand Palestinian pounds and an extra ten thousand. It seems that at that stage he had even allocated larger sums than those his critics demanded of him.

Ben-Gurion spoke up a number of times at that session, but he totally ignored the criticism directed at him and his colleagues. He contented himself with the "exoneration" Kaplan bestowed on him: "Who interfered? [They] accuse the Jewish Agency. Ben-Gurion is not to be blamed in this instance. He did not deal with it. So then Kaplan should be blamed." Ben-Gurion supposedly left it to Kaplan to deal with such matters and did not involve himself in them.

This description was quite chivalrous but not at all accurate. Ben-Gurion was most decidedly involved in determining the funding policy of the rescue operations and in the decisions concerning its offshoots. As we have seen, he participated in the activities of the central bodies dealing with the rescue of children and its funding. Up to this point, he had taken part in one gathering of the Mobilization Fund for the purpose of collecting money and received regular updates on various fund-raising activities or on activities that required the allocation of funds.[34] It should therefore not be assumed that Ben-Gurion relied on such a factually dubious "exoneration." Furthermore, it is hard to imagine that a man like him, aware of his responsibility as leader, would take cover behind such a smokescreen.

Nevertheless, Ben-Gurion paid no attention to criticism leveled against him and adopted a businesslike approach. He told the gathering that rescuing the forty-five hundred children and five hundred adult escorts would require the purchase of ships at a cost of fifty thousand Palestinian pounds. They already had thirty thousand Palestinian pounds, said Ben-Gurion, and the completion of the sum was a "burning issue" being handled by "three people—one of whom represents the treasury of the Jewish Agency, another the treasury of the Executive Committee [of the Histadrut], and a third the Mobilization levy or the National Council—all of whom are here." From Ben-Gurion's remarks it is clear that the JAE had already transferred more money than the critics knew about and that Ben-Gurion was not in need of the "exoneration" that Kaplan had bestowed on him.

In all of his remarks Ben-Gurion referred to the rescue of Jews from Europe. On the other hand, he adopted a different attitude toward what was termed "the small rescue" concerning the question of aid to the remaining Jews in Europe: "I don't know anything about money for this. I think that this question is not apposite at this moment." The astonishment elicited by this statement has already been discussed (see chapter 5). Had Ben-Gurion not some time earlier urged the JAE to implement the Transnistria Plan, one of whose main points was the transfer of Jews trapped inside Romania from the horrors of Transnistria to Romania proper? Was it his intention to circumscribe the functions of the JAE, to clarify what it would not deal with and what the area of responsibility of the other Jewish bodies was? Was he perhaps inferring that at this stage the Transnistria Plan was not practical, and that consequently there was no point in discussing its funding?

According to Ben-Gurion's and Kaplan's subsequent actions, it appears that now, too, Ben-Gurion tried to prevent other bodies in the Yishuv and the Jewish people from hiding behind the limited financial resources of the Zionist movement and the Yishuv institutions in Palestine. Apparently he wished to force them into participating in funding the rescue effort to the largest extent possible, stressing that the financial sponsorship coverage extended by the JAE to the various rescue initiatives did not "exempt" them from the general financial burden. This was not a question of shrewd diplomacy or pure bargaining: public pressure and the natural inclination to want to help led the JAE to exceed its means, to a large extent, making the maneuvers of Kaplan and Ben-Gurion to attract contributors essential from their point of view.

In the course of the meeting, Ben-Gurion elaborated on his comments concerning limits to the activity of the JAE in the rescue effort. With regard to "rescue [meaning] the bringing out of Jews and their transfer to Palestine," there can be no argument "that the Jewish Agency takes upon itself the transportation costs of the children." By contrast, Ben-Gurion distinguished between two types of "assistance to Jews in the place of their residence": the JAE would support veteran Zionists and would send them passports, but "for bribes to prevent decrees"—meaning the Transnistria Plan and apparently the Slovakia Plan, too—"the JA cannot give money."

At the start of the meeting Ben-Gurion had stated that there was no actual plan of this kind, whereas afterward he simply stated that the JAE was unable to meet the cost of bribe payments to prevent killing. The JAE was dealing with the rescue of the first five thousand children, which "will require large investments and great efforts from the Yishuv, from the Jewish people, and the Zionist movement"—according to Golomb 4.8 million U.S. dollars for twenty-nine thousand children. Ben-Gurion acknowledged the difficulty of raising such a large sum of money in a such a short space of time, but he again exuded the same optimism he had expressed in his interjection to Golomb, repeating that he believed it was possible to do so. This, therefore, was the JAE's narrow space for maneuvering and Ben-Gurion staunchly stood by it. The bag was riddled with holes.

WORD VERSUS DEED

Ben-Gurion hinted at another difficulty: the need to look after the Jews in Palestine. The background to his comments included, among other things, public pressure exerted on the leadership to also deal with the families of the mobilized men. This was a trenchant statement, not polished from a political or public relations point of view. In due course such statements would be used to prove that Ben-Gurion turned a cold shoulder to the fate of Europe's Jews during the holocaust. The truth of the matter is that the JAE simply was unable to meet its financial obligations. Despite this powerlessness—and this verbal dissociation—the JAE did transfer a great deal of money to Europe and allocated bribe money to prevent killings.

Every statement that was interpreted then— or is interpreted today—as comparing two types of concerns and "obligations" was an incorrect and even unreasonable interpretation. These two concerns existed on two very different planes, and Ben-Gurion was not alone in realizing this. There was no practical significance to this comparison made by Ben-Gurion. It was simply another example of his not inconsiderable talent for slipping up from time to time, allowing stinging and cruel utterances to distort the true meaning of his own actions.[35]

In early February 1943 Ben-Gurion had maintained that it would be preferable for the JAE to concentrate on financing the rescue of children and aid to veteran Zionists and several other operations of the "small rescue" type rather than to allocate sums for ransom. Ben-Gurion's reason was the JAE's inability to meet the huge payments required. His intention was apparently to force every Yishuv or non-Yishuv group to participate in financing ransom demands.

It took all of February for the JAE to establish its financing policy for the rescue projects, and it was subjected to severe criticism. It was one of the topics that preoccupied the Mapai Center in a debate on 24 February 1943 after hearing a report by

Zvi Schechter (Yehieli), who had returned from Istanbul. A few days earlier the JAE had decided that Kaplan would leave for Istanbul and, while there, would examine the financial requirements of the rescue, among other things.[36] Schechter, one of the leaders of the illegal immigration operation and the Agricultural Workers' Federation, was an important member of the Yishuv's secret service team. From the middle of 1943 he liaised with the British on the Parachutists' Scheme.

After analyzing the financial significance of the Transnistria Plan, Schechter tried to minimize the audience's concerns and concluded that "the matter of the ransom is incorrect," since what was involved was "a huge migration tax," common in Germany and Romania before the war. The Yishuv should not act like "the JDC, afraid to deal with any matter involving a prohibition," but it should be wary of becoming enmeshed in unnecessary complications.[37] Most of the other topics Schechter mentioned touched on matters of financing, including the high cost of purchasing ships and the ban on transferring funds to enemy territories. He stressed the importance of bribes as a means of rescuing Jews and improving their ability to survive in Europe. He described how to transfer monies to the Axis countries through various couriers and raised the possibility of expanding the scope of this activity if funding were increased.

This meeting is important not only in understanding the needs and difficulties involved in funds allocation but also in understanding the development of Ben-Gurion's attitudes toward financing rescue operations. At the end of Schechter's remarks, Ben-Gurion dealt at length with all aspects of the rescue issue, both the "small rescue" and the "big rescue." He recalled a meeting held "ten to fourteen days ago" that included Mapai members of the JAE, but he mentioned no names. "Members dealing with immigration" had also participated (apparently a reference to Golomb, Meirov-Avigur, and others

who dealt with Aliyah Bet), as had members of the Agricultural Workers' Federation (who, like Schechter, did not deal solely with agriculture), and members of the Histadrut's Executive Committee. Two central issues were discussed: aid to Jews in Nazi-occupied lands and emigration from those countries. For the benefit of his colleagues, Ben-Gurion reviewed the various problems involved and examined what had already been implemented based on the decisions of that meeting of activists.

In a detailed survey, one that reflected considerable knowledge of the various aspects of the rescue, Ben-Gurion described the difficulties, the possible courses of action, and what was required from the Yishuv for their implementation. Hunger was a common concern, but he estimated that it was more essential to save Jews by transferring them from dangerous countries to a country like Hungary, in which there was less of a danger. Ben-Gurion also described the necessity of bringing the Jews close to the borders of neutral countries, which, of course, was a reference to the "Tiyulim" (walkabout) system, whereby Jews were smuggled out of occupied territory or into areas where they had a better chance of survival.

"There are places where rescue is possible," said Ben-Gurion, " but money is required; there are countries where gentiles are willing to help, and there are places where this is possible only with money. . . . Simply put, officials must be bribed in order to prevent massacres, slaughters, deportations." Aid and rescue operations of this kind were also possible because of communications available to the emissaries in Geneva and Istanbul. Contact had been established with almost all the occupied countries, with the exception of Poland, through regular post or special couriers. Some of the couriers—particularly priests—did their work "for the sake of heaven," while others demanded payment. This enabled emissaries to know "more or less what is going on in those countries." There are unmistakable echoes here of briefings Ben-Gurion received from Zaslani-Shiloah, Epstein-Ealth, and others regarding the initial system, established and operated from Istanbul and Geneva. Beginning in mid-1943 this system was expanded and during the summer of 1944 the intelligence failure associated with it subsequently became clear.

Ben-Gurion stated that the Yishuv leadership and its emissaries were also involved in immigration. They were striving to bring over forty-five hundred children and five hundred adults and had plans to use up the entire quota of permits. "The difficulties are enormous," he noted, with the stupid and cruel Turks placing obstacles in the children's way. "Ships are at a special premium, now that they are being used in the war effort," so "we shall need our own vessels. No easy task even in ordinary times."

All of this was, in one way or another, connected with money—a great deal of money. Ben-Gurion told the members of the Agricultural Workers' Federation that the cost of bringing over a child in a foreign ship was about forty Palestinian pounds, and the purchase of ships, which necessitated large sums even in peacetime, was even more expensive in wartime.[38] An additional big expenditure was bribery, which was indispensable.

Ben-Gurion described the funding decisions thus far approved. He included all that had been decided until then in the Mapai secretariat and the JAE—including the period of his resignation from the JAE—in coordination with the Rescue Committee, the Mobilization Fund, the National Council, and the Histadrut. Ben-Gurion also mentioned the decision to hold a secret fund-raising campaign among the wealthy people in the Yishuv, the first function having been held the day before with his participation. The plan was to make a concentrated effort to raise at least 125,000 Palestinian pounds to be placed "at the disposal of our friends in Istanbul and Switzerland."

It was decided to hold a secret fund-raising campaign on account of things "that you heard and things you didn't hear, and it is perhaps advisable that you should not hear," said Ben-Gurion, thereby clearly hinting at a series of actions conducted far from the public eye and even from the eyes of his representatives in most of the decision-making bodies. The reasons for the secrecy are also clear: the ban on the transfer of monies and the fear of having information leaked, which would harm rescue efforts. Ben-Gurion reiterated that the JAE would be responsible for financing the rescue of children, claiming that funds had been allocated for this purpose: forty thousand Palestinian pounds for the first thousand children (according to Kaplan in the Mapai secretariat). He reported on attempts to find ships to transport the children and explained that Kaplan had been sent to Istanbul to decide on "spending larger sums." Ben-Gurion summed up his remarks by stating that the challenge of the rescue required the Yishuv to prepare itself logistically and mentally for "urgent, large-scale aid. One cannot know how much time remains and how long people will need help."[39]

Ben-Gurion had come a long way since uttering his remarks at the Mapai secretariat on 10 February 1943 that it wasn't the JAE's job to pay for bribery; now, only two weeks later, he was agreeing that money had to be allocated for bribes. The difference reflects a maturation process and a change of attitude. It appears that Ben-Gurion was influenced by the cumulative effect of the reports of the various emissaries, which also led to the decision to send Kaplan to Istanbul. I am unaware of any significant change in the JAE's finances that occurred in the interim. Nevertheless, Ben-Gurion was now prepared to increase the financial stakes and even to risk paying bribes.

Although the extent of the risk had changed, Ben-Gurion's basic premise had not: the JAE would continue to demand that every possible source of revenue be tapped in funding rescue operations and would increase the scope of its interim funding. At the same time, the JAE would strive to reduce, as far as possible, the harm to the Yishuv's security and establish an infrastructure for mass immigration. The financing policy was based on borrowed time: providing interim funding from Yishuv sources and extending financial coverage by the JAE until external sources could be located. The problem, of course, was that even borrowed time lapses in the end, and that the JAE's ability to extend interim funding was finite.

Against this background, one can discern a number of actions: Ben-Gurion's plan to embark on a fund-raising campaign in South Africa during March, which never materialized;[40] the appeal to the governments of the United States and Britain for assistance in securing a ship;[41] and Kaplan's trip to Istanbul. Kaplan's journey was altogether "a commander's visit" to the front, involving study, encouragement, organizing the operation, making decisions, and so forth. This journey also contributed to a change in Ben-Gurion and Kaplan, which began crystallizing during February, since Kaplan was now persuaded that something could be done, that there was a point in firing an arrow in the dark, leading him to approve the allocation of seventy-five thousand Palestinian pounds in Istanbul and Geneva for special projects. This sum, which was put at his disposal before he left for Turkey, came from three sources: the JAE, the Histadrut, and the Mobilization Fund. This amount was in addition to the ten thousand Palestinian pounds that reached the emissaries each month for funding their ongoing activities.[42]

Upon his return, Kaplan presented reports to the JAE, the Rescue Committee, and his Mapai party. Ben-Gurion heard two reports and was able to read the minutes of the third. Furthermore, it is also known that he and Kaplan had a long conversation in which the latter summed up his mission to Istanbul.

Kaplan expanded on the three sources of funding for rescue operations and on aid to Europe's Jews, which included the following: previous Yishuv allocations in the possession of the emissaries in Istanbul and Geneva prior to his arrival; JDC monies, which served to pay "deportation tax" or "sitting tax" in Slovakia; and funds obtained by the local communities in the Axis countries.[43] According to Kaplan's calculations, in addition to the 75,000 Palestinian pounds he had allocated in Istanbul, another 75,000 to 100,000 Palestinian pounds to finance the transport of five thousand children from Transnistria to Romania were required immediately. Kaplan said he had already instructed the emissaries to undertake any action necessary and had committed the JAE to obtain the required sum. He told Mapai it was "imperative to continue" this action and commented, with regard to its scope, "life will tell."[44]

Reports on Kaplan's journey reveal that the overall policy delineated within Mapai by Ben-Gurion at the end of February was indeed implemented. The interim funding proved insufficient, especially as the rescue activities grew in scope. As a result, some operations were frozen, resulting in loud complaints by the emissaries. There simply wasn't enough money.

THE EMERGENCE OF NEW POSSIBILITIES

The period between spring and early summer 1943 was characterized by expectations that accompanied the convening of the Bermuda Conference. Attempts to carry out the other rescue plans—the rescue of children,[45] the ransom plan, and the secret cooperation plans—continued but resulted in no significant change in the dimensions of the rescue.[46]

The paucity of results aroused contrasting reactions: criticism of the behavior of the Yishuv leadership,[47] on the one hand, and harsh resignation at the hopelessness of the rescue attempts, the feeling that the money was being thrown away for nothing, on the other. The most striking example of this type of resignation is found in the previously cited memorandum by Apollinary

Hartglas, where he states that "despite the vast sums required for this operation, its results—at best—would be extremely limited."[48]

At that time discussions of the financing policy were influenced by the agreement signed between the Rescue Committee and the Mobilization Fund, which stated that the Mobilization Fund would also be responsible for raising funds for rescue activity.[49] Efforts to raise contributions from abroad were redoubled, while the internal criticism of the JAE's handling of the financing was renewed.

The Zionist Actions Committee meeting held on 18 May 1943 was the scene of sharp criticism. Bader, in Palestine to alert the leadership and to mobilize the support of various institutions, described the rescue activities and their chances of success, thereby fanning the flames of criticism and calling on the JAE to adopt a different way of thinking in order "to break the mood . . . that it is impossible to act, that it is impossible to help."[50] The gap was thus revealed yet again between the Yishuv leadership's feeling that everything was being done to achieve a breakthrough and the opinion of the Zionist Actions Committee or the Yishuv's delegation in Istanbul that this was not enough.

David Remez called on the JAE "to appoint a Minister for Rescue Affairs." Ya'akov Zerubavel, a member of the Po'alei Zion Left, praised a speech by Ben-Gurion entitled "Reply to the Ruler" (apparently delivered at a gathering of the Elected Assembly on 24 March 1943) that expressed the feeling of the people, but he maintained that it was not followed by action and called for the establishment of a twenty-five million Palestinian Pound fund. Anshel Reiss, a member of Mapai and one of the heads of the Polish community in Palestine, while sensitive to the JAE's difficulties in maneuvering between conflicting needs—mobilization as well as settlement—both of which were important, called for more fundraising activity by world Jewry in order to avoid the situation where "a telegram arrives from Slo-

vakia demanding many thousands of 'Pfunds'" and one cannot comply because of insufficient cash.[51]

Yitzhak Gruenbaum rejected the criticism and explained the emissaries' pressure not as reflecting failings by the JAE but rather as the result of a feeling that opportunities for rescue had increased, that "there is . . . a certain collapse in the Nazi camp. . . . Cracks have opened that were previously not visible or nonexistent." He explained that the JAE and the Rescue Committee were increasing the funds allocated for rescue.[52] Bader and other emissaries did indeed feel that the network of couriers they established now made it possible to penetrate almost anywhere in the occupied areas, and that one should capitalize on this.

The criticism and appeals for help were aimed directly at Ben-Gurion. (In chapter 5 I discussed at length the appeal of Schind and Pomeranz to Ben-Gurion on 25 May 1943.[53]) The emissaries asked him to demand an increase in the monthly allocations for rescue in view of the newly expanded operational opportunities, the latter referring primarily to the Europa Plan and the establishment of contact with the Jews in Polish ghettoes through Rudi Scholz. Scholz's return had made them extremely happy (they were unaware that he was a leading Nazi agent). They asked that the monthly allocations be increased from ten to twenty-five thousand Palestinian pounds for each of the next two months. This increase was intended to support activity in Poland. The Europa Plan would require separate and far greater allocations.[54]

Pomeranz and Schind called on Ben-Gurion to mobilize "the Diaspora in the free countries, starting with the U.S.," the political difficulty involved in transferring funds to the occupied countries notwithstanding. They were experts in illegal action and knew it was possible to circumvent prohibitions. They also recommended that Golda Meir go on a U.S. fundraising mission. In the meantime all was ready for an operation—only funds were lacking—and they asked for these to be made available from the Yishuv's resources. Pomeranz and Schind were therefore requesting a big increase in the interim funding.

The important letter from Pomeranz and Schind reached Palestine in late May or early June. Ben-Gurion was out of the office due to illness.[55] The main response to their appeal was made by Bader on his way back from Palestine to Istanbul. He had been arrested on the border between Syria and Turkey for having invalid documents. His letters provide a comprehensive picture of his contacts in Palestine, his authorizations and instructions, working methods in Palestine and Istanbul, and something of the resources he brought with him. Here I shall focus on funding.

First, Bader carried with him explicit authorizations from Kaplan, Sharett, and Ben-Gurion to use bribes. Other partners in the Yishuv's rescue operations also gave their approval, including Rescue Committee chairman Gruenbaum and Histadrut leaders: "The idea was that if they want a bribe—pay it," wrote Bader.[56] He also carried with him a similarly explicit authorization concerning the Slovakia Plan: "Aside from this, 25,000 Palestinian pounds were approved for the rabbis' offer, if only it would be relevant."[57]

Second, Bader carried not only money but apparently also diamonds.

Third, from documents containing calculations sent by Bader to Istanbul, it appears that Schind saved some of the money sent to the emissaries there in order to deposit it in the hands of the courier Popescu, who was due to return from a mission in Poland and Theresienstadt and to embark on a new mission. The emissaries reported with great excitement about these developments and anticipated Popescu's imminent arrival. Not wishing this sum to be used to fund other operations, they decided to tell Palestine that the money had already been transferred to Poland and Theresienstadt. In the end, the money was not sent because Popescu was late in arriving, and treasurer Bader "adapted" the reports and accounts in his hands to the situation prevailing there. This minor affair also testifies to the high degree of freedom of action and flexibility the emissaries permitted themselves even toward their superiors. It also reveals that the emissaries at times tended to be inexact in their reports on account of what seemed to them to be operational constraints.[58]

Fourth, according to Bader's reports, it appears that the Histadrut also had no clear understanding regarding its participation in the funding of operations. Some of the JAE's sharpest critics came from that quarter, including David Remez, Golda Meir, and Meir Ya'ari. Nonetheless, the Histadrut also was beset by internal friction that disrupted the allocation of funds.[59]

Fifth, Bader discovered that the convoluted nature of financial sources, the differing ways of transferring funds, and their allocation among various initiatives and enterprises resulted in the treasurers losing the ability to keep track of the movement of funds. Six months after operations began in full swing, there were already two accounting "versions." According to the first, 84,000 Palestinian pounds remained from what the Yishuv had allocated for rescue until the end of the fiscal year. According to the second, only 59,000 Palestinian pounds remained. This discrepancy made Kaplan unwilling to increase monthly allocations.

Sixth, among the operations for which funds had been allocated, there were bribe payments destined to advance the Slovakia Plan, money for various expenditures by the operation centers in Istanbul and Geneva, the dispatch of food parcels to the occupied areas and Russia, and the purchase of ships for transporting immigrants. What clearly emerges from all this is that in June 1943 the JAE allocated funds both for the "big" and "small" rescues.[60]

RITUALS OF BLAME

Despite the commitment Bader carried with him, there was insufficient coverage even for the required interim funding. Nor did Kaplan see any reason to retreat from the usual policy of not "exempting" potential partners from their responsibility to fund rescue operations. Consequently, in the face of every conceivable financial demand, his initial response was always: "I haven't any." This continued to arouse anger and amazement among several of the second- and third-rank members in the Yishuv leadership and often among the emissaries as well.

In a tense session of the Zionist Actions Committee held on 24 June 1943, the pattern of attack and defense recurred. Ben-Gurion listened without comment, apart from a plea not to attack Gruenbaum in his absence. Again Anshel Reiss led the attack. He complained that the emissaries had been sent away empty-handed and pointed to the leadership's failure to respond to Bader's requests on his last visit, as well as to letters by other emissaries. He described lost opportunities regarding the "large" and "small" rescue plans[61] and referred to the repeated rejection of an advance payment on account of the ransom demanded by Wisliceny. It is doubtful whether Reiss had any knowledge of the replies received by Bader or knew about the resources at his disposal.

In time this criticism became a kind of purification rite needed by the critics, whereas those who were criticized learned to live with it. Even Reiss, who at that time had already gained the standing of "professional critic," testified that he knew "that money is not only a question of goodwill. I know that fund-raising is no easy thing . . . and does not depend solely on the feelings . . . of public officials." The critics' suggestions that the Yishuv increase its efforts "to appeal to those sections of Jewry that are still untapped, who can do something, to the Jews of America, of England, of South Africa . . . that funds should come from there" sounded increasingly like hollow statements.

Despite the difficulty of finding new ways of responding to criticism, Gruenbaum and others tried to confront it. For example, Gruenbaum, who had arrived late at the meeting, claimed that despite the real fear of losing money allocated for the Europa Plan, he had nevertheless decided to take the risk and try to save Jews. The problem was not a reluctance to take risks by allocating funds for a dubious plan but rather the simple fact that there wasn't sufficient money. Gruenbaum explained that efforts to obtain additional monies by expanding the circle of those bearing the financial burden was no simple matter. Attempts at roping in the JDC "were faltering a little," and it appeared that at best the JDC would be prepared to contribute one Palestinian pound for every pound put up by the Zionist movement and the Yishuv.[62] Nor were efforts by the JAE to raise contributions from among Egyptian Jews and those of South Africa meeting with success.[63] Difficulties also arose regarding fund-raising in Palestine.[64] Notwithstanding these setbacks, the JAE transferred limited funds to Istanbul but could not transfer more because "we have none." It was suggested that Reiss and Neustadt remember that they were not alone in their pain, that "others also feel the same pain and remember . . . the same things and do all in their power"[65] to help the Jews of Europe.

Dobkin and Kaplan were also roped in to rebuff the criticism. Dobkin called on the Zionist Actions Committee to institutionalize fund-raising and avoid ineffectual discussions, since nobody denied that they had a duty to assist the Jews of Europe. To gain the ear of the critics, he surveyed the allocation of funds up to that point. The first decision in early 1943 was to raise 250,000 Palestinian pounds. Five months later 113,000 Palestinian pounds had already been expended on aid and rescue. The income until that stage amounted to 45,000 Palestinian pounds from the Mobilization Fund and 25,000 Palestinian pounds from a special allocation by the Histadrut. The Jewish Agency had spent 43,000

Palestinian pounds, representing the remainder of the money from its fund. Now another 45,000 Palestinian pounds had been allocated, and of this sum 25,000 Palestinian pounds was an advance that apparently would not be returned to the JAE's kitty. An additional 25,000 Palestinian pounds had been earmarked for July and August.

Dobkin also stressed that "there has not yet been a financial request with which we have not complied," apart from "the Slovakia matter, which is pending," and that "there was money in Istanbul and Geneva that they were unable to retrieve." The situation had now changed. New opportunities had arisen that surprised even those with guarded expectations. Consequently special resources had to be raised. It was agreed that it was essential to raise this money, but "it would be one of the easiest things to decide that the Jewish Agency must provide the money"—a statement echoing Kaplan's and Ben-Gurion's resolve to prevent various parties from evading responsibility.[66]

KAPLAN'S FATIGUE

Kaplan was exhausted by futile discussion, predictable criticism, and endless debate. He reiterated that the problem was not one of lack of will or even of action: "[W]e knock on every door . . . but this does not depend on us."[67] Kaplan proffered what was apparently an administrative reason. The approval of the Jewish Agency's budget and changes in its goals, among other things, begin in the Zionist Actions Committee's budget committees, not in its plenum. Consequently if the Zionist Actions Committee did indeed desire a new appraisal of the budget structure, it had to go to the Budget Committee. Kaplan thus tossed the ball back in the Zionist Actions Committee's court and expressed a preference for a "businesslike" discussion with a committee that was practical in its approach.[68]

It could be that a sense of weariness resulting from the purposeless debates explained Ben-Gurion's silence at that meeting, apart from the fact that Kaplan, Dobkin, and Gruenbaum fielded the criticism extremely creditably. Kaplan wanted to prevent a limited budgetary debate in a wide but binding arena like the Zionist Actions Committee. He asked the presidium at the meeting to "erase from the protocol all the numbers . . . they should not be entered in the internal protocol of the Zionist Actions Committee, but I would point out that we are talking about very important matters. And Dobkin threw out a figure of 50,000 Palestinian pounds, the other 40,000 not remaining in any coffer."[69]

Kaplan suggested that the Zionist Actions Committee content itself with a general public announcement that lack of funding would not affect rescue operations and another to the emissaries that they could continue "with fairly wide-range activity." Changes in the fund-raising arrangements and fund activities would be discussed in a reduced committee of the Zionist Actions Committee "together with the appropriate institutions" far removed from the public eye. (One can surmise that he was also referring to British as well as other "eyes.") The Zionist Actions Committee adopted Kaplan's proposal to transfer the discussion to a reduced committee.[70] From the critics' standpoint, too, this round of talks occurring at the end of June 1943 ended with a feeble outcry, followed by adoption of the JAE's position. The most scathing attacks against the JAE achieved nothing because the main problem was that there wasn't enough money, period.[71]

"SOME TRAGIC MISUNDERSTANDING"

There were not many supporters in the Yishuv for the JAE's declared funding policy. Public criticism continued unabated throughout the summer of 1943 up to the end of the year. Golda Meir was one of the leading critics on behalf of Mapai and the Histadrut. At a discussion in the Histadrut secretariat she claimed the JAE suffered from "some tragic misunderstanding" that manifested itself in an unwillingness to allocate monies in the requisite amount for rescue. Her remarks were certainly aimed at Ben-Gurion, Kaplan, and Sharett. Others at that discussion went still further and maintained that the JAE was exploiting money earmarked for rescue to advance other objectives.

Besides internal criticism, there was also general recognition that the JAE members were pained by the killing of Jews in Europe, and manifest care was taken not to undermine the Jewish Agency's standing as the central authority for the Jewish people. Even the severest critics understood that the JAE needed help to bear such an immense financial burden. In the background there lurked the fear that too severe a criticism or flagrant an action against the JAE would erode its standing in the Yishuv and in the eyes of the outside world. The critics did not wish to weaken the JAE's position with respect to the British, nor did they wish to play into the hands of the Revisionists or the ultra-Orthodox factions.[72]

The Zionist Actions Committee continued to be an arena for the expression of sharp criticism. Yehoshua Suprasky, a right-wing member of the General Zionists and a member of the presidium of the Rescue Committee, was particularly sarcastic, choosing "Polish Jewry Day" to attack. The Zionist Actions Committee convened to mark the event on 1 September 1943. After Sharett's report on his journey to Istanbul and Cairo, Suprasky commented: "I am very pleased that after almost four years our friend Shertok [Sharett] traveled to Istanbul, and that a few months before that Kaplan traveled to Istanbul, and they began to take a serious interest in the matter, to look for ways to save the Jews of Europe." As a member of the presidium of the Rescue Committee he knew that the JAE had done a little "in matters of rescue," but on the whole all the "meager" means that had been devoted to rescue was equivalent to "nothing" compared to the monies required. In early spring he and other members of the Zionist Actions Committee's budget committee had demanded an allocation of 250,000 Palestinian pounds, but their demands had been rejected. The emissaries from Istanbul had reported that it was possible to rescue, and it was therefore up to the Yishuv leadership "to approach this problem with somewhat greater largesse than it had done heretofore."[73]

In Suprasky's evaluation of the previous four years, there was a great deal of wise hindsight, for until the end of November 1942 he, like his colleagues, did not know for certain what was taking place in Europe. Furthermore, even when Suprasky was making his remarks, he already knew that until the summer of 1941 mass extermination had not taken place. Suprasky was surely unaware of the scope of the covert and overt action taken until September 1943, but he knew enough to rid himself of the sarcastic tone that pervaded his remarks, for he himself was a member of the Rescue Committee, whose development into a body lacking operational ability was, in large measure, due to the functioning and the nature of the considerations of his fellow members and of the social systems they represented. These words of criticism were not devoid of political tendencies and appeals, nor of the constant frustration that cast its shadow over rescue activities.

The emissaries also leveled criticism. Although they represented organizations, parties, and movements that were part of the mainstream Yishuv establishment, they were nevertheless unable to overcome their frustration. Pomeranz, Bader, and Schind warned against lost opportunities to save Jews and described the despairing cries emanating from Gizi Fleischmann and the working group in Slovakia and elsewhere. The emissaries announced that what had been transferred to them covered only about a third of the advance payment Fleischmann had agreed to hand over. They requested "a limited, telegraphic power of attorney to act with Moshe [Sharett, who was visiting Istanbul] on everything we consider right."[74]

When it became clear what had, in fact, been known from the outset, namely, that the Yishuv could not cover the ransom sums on its own, Ben-Gurion and Kaplan turned to the Jewish community in South Africa. Sharett had also been authorized to make decisions on the spot, and he did intervene, issuing directives on all the problematic items on the agenda. However, Sharett's presence in Turkey could not alter the fact that the requirements outweighed the JAE's funding capabilities.

BEN-GURION FACES HIS CRITICS

Ben-Gurion broke his relative silence and boldly confronted the criticism at the Mapai Center on 24 August 1943. He vigorously rejected the claim that the JAE was not doing its job with respect to the rescue issue. Once again his tendency was not to allow other groups in the Yishuv and the Jewish people to evade their responsibility and to salve their consciences by pointing an accusing finger at the JAE, which, without their help, would not have been capable of even beginning to confront the horror of the extermination. Ben-Gurion reiterated that responsibility for the rescue of the Jews of Europe lay with all the Jewish people in the free world.

Earlier Venja Pomeranz had presented to Mapai a report detailing the activity of the emissaries in Istanbul, including the possibilities for rescue and their needs, as well as the expectations of Europe's Jews for help from the Yishuv and world Jewry. Pomeranz reported on successful attempts to infiltrate into Poland and to send money and parcels. According to him, the Jewish community in Slovakia was the focus of assistance to Poland, but Slovakia itself stood at the edge of the abyss and was only saved by "golden blood" preventing the spilling of "red blood." Pomeranz stressed the importance of bribes as a means of saving Jews and reiterated his demand to increase the interim funding from the Yishuv's finances.

It is quite feasible that most of his listeners at that Mapai meeting had not been exposed to information of the sort included in one of the let-

ters written by Shaul Meirov-Avigur from Istanbul in May 1943: "I cannot detail here the procedural techniques—arrangements, guarantees, etc.—but in spite of all the arrangements that can be made and that I made, they are obviously tied to the losses that could be incurred. Here there is no wise counsel." They did not know to what extent the Jewish Agency's financial risk in Europe had been increased. At the same time, it is possible that most activists in groups like the Mapai Center were already aware of the kinds of action undertaken there, and that the policy was to examine every possibility of rescue. They apparently did not know that Ben-Gurion and Kaplan had allowed the emissaries to invest money in rather overambitious attempts.[75]

At that discussion the same sharp criticism of the JAE's financing policy was again voiced. Haft and Reiss were once more among the chief critics. This time Ben-Gurion confronted them with trenchant remarks, as did Kaplan. Ben-Gurion distinguished between the overall responsibility of the Jews in the free world for the Jews of Europe and what was, in his eyes, the dual responsibility of the Yishuv: responsibility for the fate of the Jews of Europe and responsibility for the consolidation and establishment of what would ensure that such an anomalous situation would not recur. The nonpopulist essence of his remarks was to define the room for compromise that existed between these two functions. It should be stressed that, according to his conception, they were liable to come at the expense of each other in the short term. In the long term they were two sides of the same historic endeavor. Some of Ben-Gurion's forceful remarks were reminiscent of the earlier discussion held in February 1943. Here, too, the principle that reality was stronger than any declared policy was manifest, and the declaration would have to be judged in the light of events. Here is how Ben-Gurion defined his policy in the summer of 1943: the JAE would participate in the funding of any plan having to do with the immigration of Jews; monies for this would be found in the JAE budget. Other rescue operations, ransom plans, or "small rescue" and its spin-offs were not included in the JAE's direct sphere of responsibility. Consequently the JAE would try to raise money for their funding from extrabudgetary sources inside and outside the Yishuv.

Ben-Gurion emphasized that it was morally incumbent on the Yishuv to inspire the Jews in Europe and to give them hope. He said that the Yishuv emissaries were giving tangible expression to the saying "All Israelis provide for one another." Moreover, their moral mission had a dual import: it was their duty both to encourage the Jews in Europe and to rouse the Yishuv public from its indifference. There was additional moral value in the very fact of "being a fighting Jew," an important symbol both to the Jews of the Yishuv and those in Europe, which "redeems the sense of insignificance" and "incompetence." On the practical side, the Yishuv had to increase the mobilization of soldiers to the British army as well as its contribution to the general struggle against the Nazis, which meant bringing victory and rescue closer.

The Yishuv had taken and was taking additional measures. The day before there had been "a meeting of the secretariat where they discussed with greater practicality the questions on the agenda in light of the report of Moshe [Sharett, who had returned from Istanbul]." Within a week an additional meeting would be held with the aim of "examining aid and counseling we are able to give." The Yishuv leadership must "consider this agenda a second and third time, clarify to what extent we may intensify—and we can undoubtedly intensify—the material and moral aid to those who are there." The Yishuv and its leadership have to "wake up" and "examine anew the efforts of aid and rescue," how to increase "popular participation" and awaken "humane Jewish solidarity."

The demand that the JAE allocate all the monies from its budget was futile. This is obvious

from a simple calculation of the cost of the two ransom plans and the plan to rescue children. There was practical logic behind the demand that the JAE direct its efforts to raising money from Jews in other countries, or from rich Jews in the Yishuv. Ben-Gurion maintained that the JAE was, in fact, doing this even though it did not have "overall Israeli authority over the Israeli wallet, or over all Jewish affairs." Organizations such as the World Jewish Congress, the American Jewish Congress, the JDC, and other organizations were not subject to JAE control. Ben-Gurion and his colleagues were, in fact, soon compelled to abandon the expectation of being able to dictate their policy to these organizations.

It is worth quoting the penetrating remarks Ben-Gurion chose during such a tense period. The Jewish Agency was "the all-Jewish organization for the building up of Eretz Israel." The mingling of concepts and functions would not be effective in terms of the activities to which it was assigned, according to its definition, nor for rescue: "I do not wish to say what is more important, to build Eretz Israel or to rescue a single Jew from Zagreb. And it may be that at times it is more important to save one child from Zagreb, but they are two different things, and this jumbling . . . to whom is this beneficial [and] why this confusion of concepts?" The JA must do "all that is required to rescue Jews through immigration to Palestine." This is what it must be concerned with; this is its function and this is what it is doing. . . . [T]o save one more Jew, to do something to prevent deportation, this is very important— perhaps even more important than running a school in Palestine or other things that are done—but . . . for this there must be other organizations and other funds."[76]

Is Ben-Gurion speaking here in all innocence? Are we to understand his words according to their plain meaning? It seems to me that Ben-Gurion was trying to break the vicious circle of accusations and self-recrimination of Haft and Reiss through the use of provocation, whose objective was to force other organizations into financing rescue operations, for only by this means would it have been possible to allocate large sums to these operations.

In the summer of 1943 Ben-Gurion was well aware that the decisive issues were the possibility of rescue and the availability of funding, not debates about what kind of rescue operation would win funding or who and where the money would come from. Even when announcing, during that tense meeting, what the JAE would not fund, Ben-Gurion abandoned his reservations and almost in the same breath said that "material aid" to Europe's Jews had to be increased. Ben-Gurion knew very well that the emissaries, the next link in the Yishuv's chain of action, did not distinguish between different forms of rescue and did not prefer one kind over another. When the opportunity presented itself, they unhesitatingly provided assistance.

Moreover, the entire system did not function solely in accordance with resolutions adopted by the JAE, Mapai, or any other body. It was a very complex system that reacted to a myriad of smaller units and responded to deeper motivations, not always being guided by declarations or decisions. Neither Kaplan nor Sharett observed these restrictions when they reached Istanbul.[77] At the end of 1944, when Ben-Gurion made a dramatic visit to Bulgaria, he ignored all the restrictions he had so heatedly advocated at that meeting.

Latter-day researchers tended to interpret these remarks in two different ways. Some saw in them an expression of introversion, alienation, a sign of Ben-Gurion's opaqueness and that of those who shared his outlook, which in the researchers' opinion narrowly focused on the needs of Palestine and the Zionist movement. Others were impressed by Ben-Gurion's, Kaplan's, and at times even Gruenbaum's capacity for endurance in the face of criticism and pressure, the conscious and unconscious demands "to be exempt" from responsibility by pointing an accusing finger at the leadership.

It appears that what guided Ben-Gurion and Kaplan and fed their readiness to stand firm against inimical public opinion was the desire—the necessity—to do everything possible to harness all available resources for immediate rescue operations, on the one hand, and to build the infrastructure for the rehabilitation of the Jewish people after the holocaust, on the other. Ben-Gurion and his colleagues believed that the two goals were inextricably intertwined. The hands of the Yishuv leadership were, to a large extent, tied, with no power to enforce. Consequently the main weapon of a leader like Ben-Gurion was the creation of an artificial vacuum in the funding and a firm announcement that the only way to fill that vacuum was through external funding and not from Jewish Agency resources. It might thus be possible to exert pressure on Jewish circles inside and outside of Palestine, who preferred to evade personal responsibility by laying the latter at the feet of the Zionist movement and various Yishuv institutions, which did not have the ability to supply the required amounts of money.

If one takes into account the sums involved, one could say that Ben-Gurion and Kaplan were indeed tight-fisted, but only in order to exert public pressure on the wealthy Jews with private capital and on other Jewish organizations. Their "stinginess" was therefore carefully considered and required great spiritual strength. One tends to scrutinize self-justifying utterances of leaders by pointing out discrepancies between these and their actions, yet here we have the cruel statements of a leader that do not correspond to his actions, which were not at all cruel. And what does this discrepancy reveal? It appears that this leadership took a moral stand, namely, absolute concentration on the ultimate goal rescuing Jews regardless of how that leadership might be viewed.[78]

Thus, a number of actions were undertaken overseas and especially at home. These peaked in "the month of solidarity with the Diaspora" (from late September to early October 1943), during which the intention was to collect 250,000 Palestinian pounds. After considerable organizational effort, the goal was not attained and it was necessary to continue to apply pressure until the sum was obtained. Among these efforts was Gruenbaum's trip to South Africa and Ben-Gurion's appeal for aid from South Africa's Jews, in which he asked them to contribute their share in funding the ransom that Wisliceny was extorting in Slovakia.[79]

At the end of October Ben-Gurion resigned from his post on the JAE, precipitating a crisis that continued until the beginning of 1944.[80] Relations with the British had become strained, the result of searches for weapons and the confrontation at Ramat Hakovesh.[81] The emissaries' hope that a concerted effort would result in a large fund to finance rescue operations, thereby sparing them the necessity of constantly pointing to wasted opportunities, were dashed. They were again compelled to call for increased allocations, and in October 1943 Barlas came to Palestine and demanded "at least" forty thousand Palestinian pounds per month.[82]

Before absenting himself from the JAE sessions, Ben-Gurion participated in a debate on Barlas's demand. The extent of the Yishuv's aid was discussed, together with a description of the "interim funding" system, whereby advance payments were made that would probably never be reimbursed to the JAE. There were differences of opinion over the extent to which aid could be increased. Ben-Gurion suggested that Kaplan and Gruenbaum work out an agreed-upon proposal and bring it before the JAE for approval. Barlas's pressure resulted in an increase in the monthly allocation by the Mobilization Fund of from ten to fifteen thousand Palestinian pounds for a three-month period.[83]

This was a third of what Barlas had hoped to obtain, particularly at a time when a feverish fund-raising campaign was taking place in the Yishuv. His failure filled Barlas with doubts and led him to make a gloomy prediction: "In January or February allocations will probably dry up completely." Bader, the emissaries' treasurer in Istanbul, was again sent to Palestine "to prevent disaster and disgrace." He requested that the budget for rescue operations be institutionalized and wished to partake in the fund-raising activities.[84] He organized at-home fund-raising drives, with Ben-Gurion present at the most important of these,[85] but this campaign did not bring about a tangible change in the scope of the funding.

At the end of 1943, earlier tendencies resurfaced. First, the argument over fund-raising methods was renewed: Should there be a separate fund for rescue or a continuation of the joint fund? The controversy intensified after experts of the fund estimated that its monthly income during 1944 would not exceed fifty thousand Palestinian pounds.[86]

Second, the question of the desired format for distributing funds between the JDC and the JAE was again debated. In the end the immediate needs proved decisive. Ben-Gurion tried but failed to establish guidelines for the delegation of tasks between the two organizations. He himself adopted a more flexible pattern of action. For example, toward the end of 1943 the issue of aid to Jewish refugees in Italy surfaced. Several members of the JAE suggested leaving the care of the refugees to the JDC "because our financial resources are limited," but Ben-Gurion maintained that "Jews are suffering and we must extend aid immediately. Obviously we shall approach the JDC, but until they respond we must supply help of some kind."[87]

Third, it is patently clear that the JAE supported all types of rescue according to its ability and available opportunities. Its decision to fund only rescue operations whose ultimate purpose was immigration to Palestine remained so only on paper. The only practical purpose was to attract donors from different circles and organizations, and to motivate them to contribute to the types of rescue the JAE had announced it would not support. Final proof of this may be found in the reports of the emissaries issued toward the end of 1943. Barlas and Bader reported on a series of far-reaching activities, and no one within the JAE, including Ben-Gurion, blocked them or de-manded an explanation as to why they were not following JAE guidelines. Ben-Gurion's only question concerned not the actual violation of JAE decisions but whether the recipients of the aid knew that it came from Palestine.[88]

11

Financing Aid and Rescue Activity in Liberated Europe

By 1944 Ben-Gurion, Kaplan, Gruenbaum, and, to a lesser extent, others in the JAE were highly experienced. They had long faced an almost constant barrage of criticism over the funding of aid and rescue missions for Europe's Jews. In response to public pressure, they adopted a position designed to meet two pressing needs simultaneously: (1) to ensure that rescue and aid opportunities should not be missed through lack of funding, and (2) to frustrate the tendency of Jews in Palestine to sidestep their obligations by saddling the Jewish Agency with full responsibility for funding.

This maneuver drew fire and was frequently interpreted as reluctance on the part of the JAE to provide funding. Both Ben-Gurion and Kaplan did not hesitate to perform a thankless task and adhered—at least verbally—to the principle that JAE funds would only be used for interim funding would be allocated only after all other sources had been tapped unsuccessfully. Not only did Ben-Gurion maneuver between the two poles, he also actively sought to enlarge the circle of partners in financing rescue activity and attempted, both overtly and covertly, to mobilize partners in Palestine and abroad.

"INSTRUCTIONS ARE CLEAR: DO NOT HESITATE"

Ben-Gurion was absent from the JAE for two of the first three months of 1944, when the progress discerned in 1943 continued. The 1944 budget followed the regular pattern of proposal, debate, criticism, and approval, and once again the rescue was not funded from the current budget. The emissaries reiterated their demand that the JAE should increase the allocations for aid and rescue. They were not satisfied with the sum allocated (100,000 Palestinian pounds and an addi-

tional 50,000 for special occasions), nor were they appeased by Kaplan's commitment that the JAE would find interim funding when the need arose. Public pressure in Palestine continued and was even fanned by testimonies from refugees. Criticism also raged following the occupation of Hungary and the raising of the slaughterer's knife over a big Jewish community that until then had been spared the fate of Jewish communities in neighboring countries.

Nor did the solutions suggested reflect significant innovations. It was proposed to increase the monthly allocation of the Mobilization Fund, or to hold a onetime fund-raising campaign to raise large sums placed at the disposal of rescue activists.[1] Tense debates, crises, and even the resignation of Gruenbaum (not solely because of the funding issue) resulted in an additional project to raise funds for rescue.[2]

While the Yishuv was still preparing the new project, which was named "Yishuv to the Rescue," the German army invaded Hungary (19 March 1944). It was now necessary to start thinking of rescuing Jews from "the great center of Jewry," which is how Ben-Gurion described Hungary a few days after the invasion, as well as from the Balkan states.[3]

How did the new situation affect Ben-Gurion and Kaplan's financing policy? Ben-Gurion saw in the Nazi invasion of Hungary the portent of a new disaster, and asserted that action would have to be taken on three planes: political,[4] organizational,[5] and financial. He did not enter into detail as to what needed to be done to finance the requisite operations, contenting himself with stating that "financial aid must be increased."[6]

What he said very briefly at the JAE meeting he had expanded upon several days earlier at a meeting with representatives of Hungarian Jewry: more money had to be sent to Hungary "because the nation is not totally poisoned, and sometimes things can be done with money." This expressed Ben-Gurion's own departure from his and Kaplan's "rules," one of which stated that there would be no funding for bribes. He had reaffirmed those "rules" in August 1943 at the Mapai Center,[7] which illustrates how Ben-Gurion and Kaplan sidestepped their own "prohibitions" and "permissions" and applied them whenever it suited their current operational needs.

Two weeks later the JAE held a debate in which Ben-Gurion issued a vague directive on the need to increase allocations for aid and rescue due the deteriorating situation in central Europe. The participants were undecided as to whether to wait for donations to be collected from the special "Yishuv to the Rescue" fund-raising drive or to once again allocate interim funding from the JAE budget pending the arrival of pledged cash. Gruenbaum and others wanted to proceed and proposed authorizing Kaplan to allocate an advance of 100,000 Palestinian pounds for rescue operations, in particular for the purchase or leasing of ships. People from the Mobilization Fund anticipated receiving large sums of money, which would cover the new advance as well as the previous ones. The JAE adopted Gruenbaum's proposal in the spirit of Ben-Gurion's stance two weeks earlier.[8]

The fund-raisers' hopes were dashed. Once again it became apparent that even comprehensive and concentrated fund-raising did not meet the massive requirements, and interim funding from the JAE budget was turned into "bad debts." The fund-raisers had hoped to raise 250,000 to 300,000 Palestinian pounds, but by late May the "Yishuv to the Rescue" coffers contained only 130,000. After extending the fund-raising drive into the summer months, the sum approached the 200,000 mark.[9] Donations did not cover all needs and the JAE continued to make "advance

payments," which, for all intents and purposes, were allocations and not interim funding. Thus, the JAE allocated 200,000 Palestinian pounds by the end of June, knowing that 70,000 would not be reimbursed from any source.[10]

The centralized fund-raising effort in the spring and summer of 1944 did not substantially ease the financial burden, which still weighed unbearably on the JAE. Nevertheless, the policy remained the same: interim funding with the proviso that only a portion would be returned. The Palestinian emissaries knew that the JAE would do all in its power to ensure that rescue projects were not foiled by funding constraints. Some of them could not take the public pressure and even "leaked" this directive, which was typical of those emanating from Jerusalem. For example, in April 1944 the normally very discreet Shaul Meirov-Avigur told members of the Histadrut Executive Committee: "Instructions are clear: do not hesitate. This is not official . . . but you are not to hesitate to undertake financial commitments where there exists a chance for rescue. I hope they are encouraged by successful attempts. . . . We may be facing a large financial commitment."[11] To remove any lingering doubts, Meirov emphasized that "our friends in Istanbul must know that the Yishuv stands behind them, as does the Mobilization and Rescue Fund, and that there should be no hesitation over fresh commitments, where there are real chances at rescue. Clearly, considerations are difficult, and there are reasonable chances of losing a great deal of money, but as we have learned, we can hope for reward."[12]

If the Yishuv possessed "reliable couriers abroad"—here Meirov hinted at the untrustworthiness of the couriers the Palestinians were compelled to use—"our results could have been more significant." Meirov also revealed that the Yishuv was unreserved in offering money for the purchase of ships, "which seemed to others to be outrageous."[13] All the while Ben-Gurion and Kaplan maintained a facade of tightfistedness.

CHANGES RESULTING FROM BRAND'S ARRIVAL

Eichmann's ransom offer brought about a complete change in the budgetary debates on deployment for the rescue of Hungary's Jews. [14] It was clear that the rescue of hundreds of thousands of people also entailed money for food, transport, escorts, travel passes, and so forth.

The first JAE debate on the proposal brought by Brand from Eichmann made no mention of where the ransom money would come from. The funding question was clearly not the first obstacle to be overcome. It was also common knowledge that the Yishuv would be unable to bear such a burden, either in goods or in cash. Nor was mention made of the role assigned by the Nazis to the Yishuv, namely, mobilizing the financial forces of the entire Jewish nation to produce ransom payments. Only Sharett made an indirect reference to the issue of funding when he raised the question the superpowers would surely ask: What was to be done with so many Jews and how were they to be fed?[15] Nor did the issue of funding arise during the JAE's discussion after Ben-Gurion's and Sharett's meeting with the high commissioner[16]—ostensibly for the same reason.[17]

Evidence of discussions about budgeting the rescue in Hungary emerge from Gruenbaum's remarks at a meeting of the JAE on 4 June 1944. It may be that the dispatch of the first interim agreement was what impelled Gruenbaum to address the issue of funding. The agreement sent by the Yishuv emissaries in Turkey explicitly mentioned "tariffs." It was agreed that the Nazis would receive four hundred dollars (they had demanded five hundred) for every Jew permitted to immigrate to Palestine, or one hundred dollars for every Jew permitted to immigrate to a neutral country. In return for immediate cessation of deportations, the Nazis would receive one million Swiss francs and an additional million every month for not renewing deportations. Another item in the draft agreement promised the Nazis a wagonload of goods in return for every wagonload of medicine, clothing, and food sent to the ghettos and camps.[18]

The agreement was dispatched mainly to prevent a break in communications with Eichmann as a result of tardiness in replying to his proposal. Nevertheless, the emissaries tried to confine themselves to commitments within their reach. For example, they did not promise trucks and gave sums in Swiss francs, the currency most convenient for them at the time. It is almost certain that they took into consideration the possibility that the draft of the agreement would deviate from its intended purpose—to prevent a break in communications—and would form the basis for practical discussions. They apparently assumed that interim funding from Palestine would enable them to meet their financial commitments.

At the June 1944 session, Gruenbaum mentioned for the first time the sum Barlas was requesting for the rescue of Hungary's Jews, namely, half a million Palestinian pounds (about two million dollars). This indicates that the emissaries did, in fact, ask Jerusalem for financial backing for their commitments. The sum Gruenbaum mentioned could not have been considered adequate to cover the huge ransom payments demanded by Eichmann, and it is possible that Barlas was requesting funding in the event that the Nazis approved the first interim agreement, in which case there would be an immediate need for money for initial operations.

The JAE listened to Gruenbaum's remarks but did not discuss them. The discussion quickly shifted to another subject, one connected to fundraising: the confrontation with the Revisionists, which resulted in reduced contributions to the Mobilization Fund. There are no indications in the meeting's protocol that the JAE addressed Barlas's request. It seems abundantly clear that his request was far in excess of the JAE's limited budgetary capacity. It may also be the case that such issues were not discussed in the JAE plenum.[19]

In the minutes of JAE meetings prior to the end of the Brand affair, no mention is made of any discussion devoted to funding the ransom demanded by Eichmann. Nor is there any trace of summations by Moshe Sharett, Joe Schwartz (the JDC representative), and Ira Hirschmann (the War Refugee Board representative) on setting up a large fund to pay ransom money to the Nazis. Eichmann's proposal was presented to Kaplan in Palestine and subsequently discussed in Istanbul, but it is completely absent from the protocol entries of JAE meetings in Jerusalem.[20]

The proposal Brand brought did not lead to a comprehensive rescue operation for Hungary's Jews or other Jews surviving in Europe. It is possible that the vast monetary expense, coupled with the ransom plan itself and its various offshoots, would have doomed the effort to failure. The matter was not looked into at all because political, military, and logistical obstacles took precedence over the financial hurdle and prevented any real discussion of it. It was not the problem of funding that put an end to the suggestion to absorb the Jews of Hungary in camps under the protection of the International Red Cross or the Swiss government by means of international funding or funding from American Jewry. The efforts of the Yishuv, the Zionist movement, and the other Jewish bodies in the free world were focused on first overcoming political and logistical difficulties. This fact is clearly reflected in Yishuv documentation.[21]

Thus, until the summer of 1944 the policy of Ben-Gurion and Kaplan for funding rescue activity remained unchanged: the Yishuv would allocate money to the best of its ability, would try to find other contributors among the Jewish people, and would conserve the meager budget of the Jewish Agency as the last "iron ration" to finance the discrepancy between monies raised and protection against possible harm resulting from these shortfalls.

AID POLICY IN THE LIBERATED AREAS

Things changed toward the end of 1944 and the war's end. As Europe was gradually being liberated and it became possible to reach these areas with relative ease, the immediate danger to the lives of the surviving Jews seemed to dissipate somewhat. Consequently, the question arose as to whether it would not be more appropriate for the Zionist movement to concentrate solely on funding immigration. In the final analysis, this danger, which perhaps was lessening to some degree, is what had dissuaded Ben-Gurion and his colleagues from implementing their declared policy and had caused them to allocate "Zionist" monies for "non-Zionist" goals (although it should be stressed that almost from its inception the Zionist movement had been involved in the lives of Jewish communities, which was then termed "present work").

Nevertheless, the Zionist movement and the Yishuv could not restrict themselves solely to activities on behalf of immigration for various reasons. First, following liberation the distress of Europe's Jews was great. Certainly there were no longer any forced labor camps, systematic extermination, and death marches, but the scars of the war were very marked among the few survivors, and the danger of death from cold, hunger, and disease had still not passed. After the Kielce pogroms and similar incidents in other parts of Europe,[22] it became clear that even the danger of murder had not entirely disappeared. The Jewish Agency and the Zionist movement could not remain indifferent to these phenomena or assign responsibility to local authorities or non-Zionist Jewish organizations.

Second, the situation became confused because of competition among the various organizations over the few survivors. Everyone realized that this struggle would decide the future image of Yishuv society—including the leaders of that society—when refugees from Europe were integrated, as many hoped they would be. It was a vital struggle for political supremacy. The general assumption was that an immigration certificate, a food parcel, shoes, or medicine were items of great "ideological significance" in view of the miserable state of the survivors.

It was clear that if the Jewish Agency did not assume responsibility in Europe as the largest official, centralized organization of the national Jewish movement, non-Zionist organizations and movements that had other plans for the survivors would fill the power vacuum. There was also another discouraging scenario in the form of Zionist splinter groups that functioned independently of the national umbrella organization. The precedent of a splintered Jewish representation at the Evian Conference (July 1938), experiences from the previous three years with the Rescue Committee, tension surrounding relations in the Palestine office in Istanbul—all these signaled the pressing need for the Jewish Agency to establish a strong central presence in Europe.

Ben-Gurion's visits to the survivors after the war; Bulgaria (November–December 1944); the DP camps and Germany (October 1945, January–February 1946); his attempts to unify the youth groups within the framework of Nocham (United Pioneering Youth)—all expressed his fear of fragmentation and his desire to meld the conflicting forces into one central source of strength under his leadership and under the umbrella organization of Mapai.

Third, active concern about the concept of repatriation became rife toward the end of 1944. This involved a tendency to distinguish between a humanitarian solution to the Jewish refugee problem and the Zionist movement's struggle to establish a Jewish state in Palestine. It was clear that Britain would encourage such a distinction. It did not require a particularly keen political sense in order to notice this and to understand that the Zionist movement had to increase the presence of its emissaries in the liberated areas.

This necessity was eventually translated into allocations of money.

Many Jews clung to the idea of emancipation even after the holocaust, wishing to perpetuate Jewish life among the gentiles. Support for the idea of rehabilitating Jewish life in Europe was widespread among Jews as well as non-Jews. Members of the various underground movements—and even ministers in exiled governments— wanted Jews to return to their homes, which would project a more humane image of their society's actions. Several European statesmen and economists were interested in the special contributions of Jews to economic activity during postwar reconstruction.

The fourth, very important reason that prompted the Jewish Agency to organize Europe's surviving Jews and to place itself at their head was what Ben-Gurion termed the "Red Paper," namely, the danger of Jews being imprisoned in Europe under Communist rule. This fear of the Communist version of western emancipation prompted a race against time that impelled the Zionist leadership to organize the Jews to flee while it was still possible, before the fate of the Jews in countries that Stalin was about to swallow up would become that of the Jews of Russia: isolation, the uprooting of all Jewish life, and the constant shadow of official anti-Semitism.

The liberation of many Jews from the horrors of nazism did not reduce the heavy financial burden of the JAE. It is possible to assert that even now there was a discernible gap between the JAE's declared funding policy and the policy actually implemented. Decisions did not always stand the test of reality, and reality repeatedly raised problems that had not been discussed. Ben-Gurion reserved a degree of operational freedom for himself and used political and humanitarian reasons, either consciously or unconsciously, to explain his divergence from the funding rules he and his chief colleagues had laid down.

ROMANIA

Throughout 1943 attempts were made to rescue Jews from Transnistria and to bring them back to safer places in Romania proper. The Yishuv emissaries also worked to bring to Palestine those Jews who were already in Romania proper, particularly after the Transnistria Plan had been leaked to the press. The Romanian government had to agree to such a plan and the Nazis had to turn a blind eye; also, "safe conduct" had to be guaranteed by the Soviets before the very prosaic matters of ships, transport within Turkey, transit permits, and money could even be considered. The financial burden this operation placed on the Yishuv was heavy, especially the cost of transport, and here, too, the pattern was repeated: the JAE sent to its people advance payment in the hope of retrieving a small part of it. This was after it had forced every other possible body to participate in funding. Natural partners in this enterprise were the political parties, movements, and organizations in Palestine; Jews in various communities throughout the free world; and especially the JDC.

The JAE took charge of this operation and was required to allocate money from the Yishuv budget, and not when "it arrived" or when "we have it" but forthwith. Simultaneously, throughout 1944 it continued to fend off criticism that it was working too slowly and inefficiently and for the impression it gave of being averse to funding vital rescue operations not of direct concern to Palestine—thereby forcing others to supply funds in its stead.

As more and more countries were liberated, the number of Jews who could be reached, taken care of, and possibly brought to Palestine grew. Thus, in early summer 1944 the Palestine office in Istanbul wrote to the JAE, the Rescue Committee, and heads of the illegal immigration operation. While describing confusion surrounding the Brand affair, it also pointed to some success regarding Jewish immigration from Romania: The *Kazbek* had arrived in Constanţa, with the *Bulbul*

and *Smyrna* arriving shortly thereafter, and perhaps within a few days they would set out with immigrants. Among other things, they stressed that "the lack of money was beginning to make itself felt" and noted that they urgently required five hundred thousand Swiss francs.[23]

Venja Pomeranz, who was visiting Palestine at that time, and Shaul Meirov-Avigur savagely attacked the JAE. They described the numerous possibilities of immigration, noting that four thousand Jews who were waiting in Romania could be brought over if money were found. Pomeranz and Meirov talked about wasting "Zionist credit" and ignoring "the shining Zionist role," which would "diminish the Jewish Agency's Zionist role in this world and the next," among other topics.

Intense debates were held in various branches of the Histadrut. Some of the speakers threatened the JAE by announcing their intention to circumvent it. In the end it was decided that the Histadrut would help the Mobilization Fund finish its fund-raising drive from the previous spring and would use its contacts to involve Jews abroad.[24] A Histadrut delegation conferred with Kaplan and categorically demanded that he immediately allocate 250,000 Palestinian pounds to transport four thousand people and a similar sum for another four thousand.[25] The Histadrut was an important factor in the rescue debate, both on account of its great ideological commitment to the fate of the Jews and because of its conspicuous readiness to allocate monies for funding the rescue.

The Rescue Committee, with Gruenbaum at its head, also veered between criticism and admission that the JAE was playing its part. Its members knew that the JAE had recently allocated 180,000 Palestinian pounds, and a week later they even acknowledged that the Rescue Committee already owed the JAE about 300,000 Palestinian pounds. Still, members of the Rescue Committee continued to level criticism at the JAE and even threatened to borrow money from the Anglo-Palestine Bank (APB). And because the committee depended on the JAE, it would thereby increase the latter's debts.[26]

Among those leveling criticism now was Shaul Meirov-Avigur. Having only a few months earlier explained to the members of the secretariat at the Histadrut Executive Committee the rationale behind the Jewish Agency's behavior, he now joined the fray. His earlier remarks about not letting lack of funds prevent them from carrying out rescue operations, to which the Jewish Agency gave its full backing, now haunted him as he, too, succumbed to despair.

Ben-Gurion and Kaplan were united in facing the onslaught of criticism, both adopting the same stance: to give as good as they got; to hurl blame back at those who were not doing their fair share. Only after realizing that its provocative position had run its course and was no longer effective in raising money was the JAE prepared to allocate money from its budget.

Nevertheless, by the middle of June 1944 certain differences between Ben-Gurion and Kaplan became apparent, perhaps for the first time. At a JAE session Kaplan described the various types of pressure applied by the Histadrut, the Rescue Committee, and the emissaries. These demands totaled 500,000 Palestinian pounds in two equal amounts, designed to finance the immigration of eight thousand people. Kaplan said that the JAE had allocated an advance of over 200,000 Palestinian pounds over the past three months and, according to accounts, about half that amount had not been used. Schind had reported on the allocation of funds that had, in fact, not been used, fearing that the treasury was not transferring to him other allocated funds and mistakenly believing that the postponed use of the funds was only temporary. In June 1943 Bader corrected his accounts and supplied Schind with a defense. The correction prompted Kaplan and his people to examine more closely the utilization of the budget. They discovered that the nonutilization of allocated funds was a recurring phenomenon,

the funds apparently not having been utilized because of routine upheavals in the aid and rescue processes.

At the conclusion of the meeting it was decided that the JAE would make its usual announcement, namely, that in the interim it would assume responsibility for funding the first part involving the transport of four thousand people. The difference between Ben-Gurion and Kaplan became evident at the decision stage. Ben-Gurion said that "we must cable our friends in Istanbul that we are underwriting the necessary funds, up to a ceiling of 250,000 Palestinian pounds for bringing 4,000 people." Kaplan interrupted Ben-Gurion to propose a more cautious formulation that did not mention sums. "The JAE authorizes Gruenbaum and Kaplan to commit to the sums required for the immigration of 4,000 people." Ben-Gurion agreed to Kaplan's wording with one proviso: "If this is not sufficient, we shall hold an emergency session to rediscuss the matter."[27]

The JAE decisions guided Kaplan during his visit to Istanbul, and he conferred with people in the Palestine office and local JDC representatives to determine the extent of funding. He also worked out a basic agreement with the JDC, requiring approval from Jerusalem and New York. It mainly centered upon funding for the first wave of immigrants in the plan to transport Romania's Jews (about three thousand people). The JDC agreed to bear the brunt of the burden. One of the paragraphs in the agreement saved the JAE a lot of money: the JDC would transfer its part in Swiss francs (from the United States or directly from Switzerland), whereas the JAE would pay its share in Palestinian pounds according to the relatively low rate of exchange instead of the black market rate.

Kaplan maintained that the agreement proved that the JAE's funding policy was justified. Despite all the criticism, "the immigration of even a single person had not been delayed through lack or absence of money when it was needed."[28] Until Kaplan managed to obtain JDC backing, the JAE supplied its usual "safety net" for the various aid and rescue operations by assuring their funding. While still in Istanbul Kaplan announced that there was an allocation of at least 35,000 Palestinian pounds for July to safeguard rescue operations until outside funding was obtained. This was the usual pattern.[29]

Immediately upon his return, Kaplan first reported to Ben-Gurion and Gruenbaum on his activity in Istanbul, and then to the JAE and the Rescue Committee. The wealth of details and their complexity necessitated an in-depth discussion, as did the complicated relations between the Jewish Agency and the JDC. The JAE consequently appointed a four members subcommittee consisting of Ben-Gurion, Gruenbaum, Shapira, and Kaplan, and entrusted it with the task of examining Kaplan's decisions in Istanbul one by one.[30]

POLAND

The aid provided to the Jews of Poland in the summer months of 1944 even more strikingly illustrates Ben-Gurion's tendency to depart from his and Kaplan's funding policy. The Polish National Liberation Committee called on the Yishuv for help, and Ben-Gurion and his colleagues understood the humanitarian and political repercussions implicit in this appeal: establishing contact with an organization subject to Soviet control and, through it, with the Soviet authorities themselves; dispatching emissaries to areas that heretofore had been impossible to enter on account of the Nazi presence and were now off limits because of a Soviet prohibition.

In one particular JAE debate, Ben-Gurion deviated from many of his own constraints regarding aid to refugees and rejected every proposal whose ultimate effect was to procrastinate, make conditions, or jeopardize opportunities for rescuing Jews. He rejected suggestions to wait for a more favorable atmosphere to contact the Russians: "We don't have the time, we must extend the aid immediately and must appeal to whichever side can help us right now. . . . We must appeal directly to the Russian government and the Polish [National] Liberation Committee, which today controls . . . the liberated areas," to permit a JAE emissary entry into Poland to help the surviving Jews. Ben-Gurion also sought material aid from the United States and Britain for Poland's Jews, who were to be transferred along routes to be opened by the JAE as a result of its contacts with the Soviet government. He suggested asking the Soviet representatives in Cairo and London to support the agency's appeal. The JAE adopted Ben-Gurion's plan.

In August and September 1944 the Jewish Agency followed Ben-Gurion's lead. Dr. Emil Sommerstein, a member of the Polish National Liberation Committee, contacted the JAE and asked for emergency aid in the form of food, clothing, medicine, and welfare workers. He received a prompt reply from the JAE, which requested details of the aid required. Kaplan stressed that "everything must be done to provide assistance as soon as possible." Sommerstein cabled Palestine the kinds of aid needed for tens of thousands of refugees (in actual fact there weren't that many refugees). The JAE adopted Ben-Gurion's proposal of putting Kaplan and Gruenbaum in charge of organizing an aid program.[31]

BULGARIA

Ben-Gurion's visit to Bulgaria provides an excellent example of his and Kaplan's flexible funding policies as the war was drawing to a close. Ben-Gurion visited Bulgaria during late November and early December 1944. He had hoped to make it to Romania, where the greatest number of Jewish survivors were concentrated, but Britain influenced the Russians to forbid such a visit and he had to be content with a weeklong visit to Bulgaria.[32]

Ben-Gurion arrived in Bulgaria during a transition between a monarchical and a Communist regime, which was just beginning to establish itself. He saw the sorry state of the local Jews and sensed their tremendous thirst for contact with other Jews in the free world, the Yishuv, and the Zionist movement, with Ben-Gurion himself regarded as "the king of the Jews." Ben-Gurion became aware of the ideological vacuum and the desperate need for leadership. He also noticed how the Jewish Communists dominated the community, its institutions, and migration trends. Although there was much suffering in evidence, Ben-Gurion knew that the Bulgarian Jews were actually much better off than other Jews in Europe. He therefore regarded the suffering of Jews in other parts of Europe proportionately.

Emotionally it was an extremely intense visit. One of the most memorable incidents was Ben-Gurion's visit to the slum district of Yotch-Bonar in Sofia. His diary entries and his reports upon returning home were especially powerful:

I was in four rooms. In the first I found only one family; the father was in the army, the wife receives 500 leva per month, from which rent is deducted—in our money that is less than 20 grush— two naked, barefoot children, she also barefoot, she cannot go outside, the children cannot go to school. I entered the second room: two families, a healthy woman, her husband is a butcher, she also apparently from a butcher's stock; a second woman, pale, suckling a child, pregnant, with two more pale children, terrible to look at, thin. I am sure those children will not survive more than a month, six weeks, barefoot, all of them barefoot, dressed in rags, nothing in the room besides two beds, and two families live in it. In the third room: four families, lots of children, all of them pale, the mark of death on their foreheads; two men among them, one old and paralyzed and a young crazy one, all in the same room. In the fourth room: three or four families,

the same picture, children about to die, a terrible thing. I tried to speak to them, but I was ashamed. Those who were with me spoke Bulgarian. We were all dressed. I saw they were insulted—why have you come to see us?—people on the verge of total despair, such a terrible thing.[33]

Ben-Gurion summed up his description with the words "atrocity, shame, abyss . . . horror."[34] In the restrained emotional world surrounding Ben-Gurion, such expressions testify to a profound shock. The visits to Yotch-Bonar and other places gave Ben-Gurion a concentrated overview of the situation of the surviving Jews in Europe. The need for aid from Palestine was brought home to him directly and sharply. Upon his return, he told the JAE:

What I witnessed in Bulgaria applies equally to all the Jews of Europe, but I shall confine my remarks to those 45 thousand. We must extend immediate aid, particularly to the children. I am sure that the great majority of the children will die from cold, disease, lack of food, and medicine. There is no medicine in Bulgaria; we have to provide assistance. There is tremendous danger in the matter of aid. There are the Jewish Communist authorities, who can cause us to lose those Jews who survived physically.[35]

Ben-Gurion wasted no time. He demanded immediate aid and made sure it was supplied. The best type of assistance, in Ben-Gurion's view, was to organize the Jews of Bulgaria for immediate immigration to Palestine. Yet he knew that mass immigration was not practical; not all Jews wished to immigrate and, in any case, even if all the permits were obtained, there were only some ten thousand immigration certificates on record and the number of valid certificates was even smaller.

These obstacles prompted Ben-Gurion to differentiate between short-term and long-term aid. While still in Bulgaria, he had set about arranging for emergency aid and continued this effort upon his return to Palestine. Immediately after the visit to Yotch-Bonar, the JDC complied with Ben-Gurion's request and supplied clothing and footwear.[36] He instructed the Zionist leaders in Bulgaria and the local Yishuv emissaries to obtain the appropriate permits in order to receive assistance from the Yishuv. While still on his way home, Ben-Gurion received news in Istanbul that Bulgaria's trade and finance ministers had agreed to permit the entry of shipments containing clothes, shoes, and medicine for the Jews of Bulgaria. In response, Ben-Gurion made the following note to himself: "To announce quantities and expedite delivery."[37] Upon his arrival in Palestine, he gave instructions to arrange for the shipment of five thousand pairs of children's shoes, medicine, and soap. A few days later he requested confirmation that this had been done, and in a letter to Ehud Avriel, one of his escorts in Bulgaria, he asked if his instructions had been carried out and if the shipment of shoes had arrived. More aid was sent later.[38]

From Ben-Gurion's point of view, accelerated immigration to Palestine, especially of children, was included in the emergency aid. In a meeting summing up his visit to the Yotch-Bonar neighborhood, Ben-Gurion instructed emissaries Avriel and Pomeranz to "organize groups of youngsters for immigration, include in the groups large numbers of the poor children—organize a study of the children, including photographs, descriptions of their condition—so they can be brought to Palestine *ex gratia*." Three days later, in Bulgaria, Ben-Gurion decided to allocate to children 450 of the 1,000 remaining immigration certificates from previous allocations and place them at the disposal of Bulgaria's Zionist Federation. The permits had not yet been taken advantage of because of restrictions imposed by the Bulgarian authorities plus transportation problems. Of the total permits allocated, 200 were designated for children from poor neighborhoods, 150 for children already on the waiting list whose certificates had arrived, and 100 for children from provincial towns. In instructions to members of the Bulgarian Zionist Federation he reiterated the urgency of caring for the children:

> The Zionist and Hechalutz centers will pay very special attention to the poverty-stricken children of Sofia and elsewhere, will take care of them, will look after their health, their affinity with the Jewish people, their Hebrew education, and, above all, their immigration to Palestine, because bringing over Jewish youth from infancy to army age as soon as possible to Palestine is the vital and urgent duty of Bulgaria's Jews and the world Zionist movement.[39]

Upon his return, Ben-Gurion tried to impress upon his colleagues the enormity of the distress. His instructions touched not only upon the alleviation of physical suffering but also on reinforcing Jewish and Hebrew education in Bulgaria. On his way back, he instructed Israel Goldin, a member of the Palestine Office in Istanbul, to send out school textbooks.[40]

Once back home, Ben-Gurion issued instructions to allocate a certain sum for the expansion of the Hebrew education system and for aid to teachers of Hebrew and Jewish subjects.[41] He repeated instructions to send textbooks, Hebrew journals, and newspapers "to generate energy and resources for teaching Hebrew to Jewish youngsters, and to fend off schemes of assimilation that were being forced upon Bulgaria's Jews, particularly on the younger generation."[42]

The funding requirements dictated by reality were insurmountable. The Jewish Agency was not content with funding the rescue of Jews from Europe and did not leave the funding of other essential activities to Jewish and international charity organizations. Ben-Gurion himself was one of the first to override the rules he himself had been primarily responsible for laying down. In Bulgaria, as in Poland, Greece, and other places, the JAE financed essential operations as long as its leaders were convinced of the impossibility of awaiting funding from another source. There was a combination here of humanitarian concern coupled with external political considerations and internal governmental considerations.

12

The Jewish Agency Budget and Fund-raising Appeals in Palestine

THE JEWISH AGENCY BUDGET

Three budgets (1943, 1944, and 1945) were debated and approved in the JAE and the Zionist Actions Committee between news of the extermination in Europe and the end of the war. Ben-Gurion and Kaplan did their best to ensure that aid and rescue operations of all kinds were funded by the JAE only when no other alternative was available; they approved direct monetary allocations from the agency budget only when it became clear that all the other possibilities had been exhausted, and that there was a real danger that rescue or aid would be thwarted through lack of funds. This policy exposed them to criticism from various quarters.

The JAE was a coalition organization that reflected the delicate and complex social and political composition of the Zionist movement and the Yishuv. Its activity was voluntary. Consequently, Ben-Gurion and Kaplan were extremely vulnerable to criticism, and it might be assumed that the result would have been a change in policy, a change in the order of the JAE's priorities. The de facto split in Mapai in 1942 severely undermined Ben-Gurion's political base, and in the spring of 1944 it even ended with the official splitting up of the party. Ben-Gurion was therefore very vulnerable from a political standpoint and, as a result, ostensibly open to compromises. Under the circumstances, one might have assumed that he would not have adhered to a "tough" policy, nor try to draw fire upon himself, and would also have "retreated" on the funding policy. On examining the political situation of the JAE under Ben-Gurion and Mapai, one might have expected those who leveled criticism at the funding policy to have succeeded in changing it.

THE 1943 BUDGET

The need to finance wide-ranging rescue operations descended on the leadership when the budget proposal for 1943 was already prepared. Like every budget proposal, it was the result of pressure exerted by various interest groups within the Yishuv, which naturally represented specific economic and social strata, as well as political and ideological concepts.

How did the public outcry and emotional upheaval affect the budget? How was the latter shaped by the political input of pressure groups, interested parties, and sealed commitments? Was the budget framework altered? At the time it was a question of immense sums in comparison to the size of the Jewish Agency budget. Did the critics suggest reducing or abolishing ministries or activities in their own backyards? To what extent did Ben-Gurion and Kaplan manage to control the Jewish Agency budgetary discussions? Let me state categorically that the harsh criticism barely affected the order of priorities. The critics did not volunteer to trim their own domains.

On 13 December 1942, following news of the extermination, the first JAE discussion on the 1943 budget was held. There was no manifest tendency to introduce a basic change in the proposed budget, which had already been drawn up. For example, at the time the JAE members were deliberating how to fund the rescue of children, but this did not affect the budgetary discussions themselves. Ben-Gurion felt it was necessary to allocate money to the Planning Committee in charge of coordinating Zionist activities after the war. Others raised routine requirements of one sort or another. Only Dobkin remarked that it was necessary to add twenty thousand Palestinian pounds for immigration; he may have been hinting at the budgetary repercussions following the sad tidings from Europe, although the sum he mentioned was far from what was required. Ben-Gurion proposed that any reservations about the budgetary structure should be addressed to the Budget Committee of the Zionist Actions Committee.[1]

The Budget Committee was a controlling and supervisory body. It examined and approved Kaplan's budget proposal. It also noted having "heard the [Jewish] Agency treasurer's announcement concerning its willingness to finance the immigration of children from the Diaspora and to fund this activity with necessary resources, in addition to sums raised from other sources." The Budget Committee demanded a change in the budget's structure to underscore this commitment.

There were two possibilities: set aside 250,000 Palestinian pounds for immigrant youngsters in the 1943 budget, or leave a fifth of the budget in reserve for this goal, inasmuch as it was needed. The proposal to set aside a quarter of a million Palestinian pounds was retracted after Kaplan explained that the numbers of children and actual costs of the rescue were still unknown. It was therefore decided to assign 20 percent of the budget to the rescue of children, which was to serve as a reserve for interim funding, to be drawn from various Jewish Agency departments as the need arose. There was a danger of outside funding not being available and the allocation not returning to the agency coffers. Reluctant to have its freedom of action restricted, the JAE was consequently unwilling to assign a fifth of its departmental budgets to another cause. Kaplan was quick to explain that this would involve only "a number of departments."

Ben-Gurion was well informed regarding the proposal to designate a fifth of the JAE budget as interim funding for aid and rescue, and it appears that he and Kaplan had discussed it before the meeting. He defended the decision against its critics. Although no mention was made in the summary of the meeting of the amount of reserves to be devoted to aid and rescue, the budgetary priority of rescuing children was stressed.[2]

From Ben-Gurion's and Kaplan's point of view, pressure from the Budget Committee was desirable. If the current budget had to be used, they preferred that the request be made by a "parliamentary" committee of the Zionist Actions Committee, consisting of representatives of all the parties, rather than a directive from the two leaders. They would thereby not be a party to potential budgetary conflicts, or would at least be supported by the Budget Committee in forcing the JAE to relinquish some of its own budget. Ben-Gurion or Kaplan many also have been called in to mediate between the critics' demands, the committee's guidelines, and the JAE's stipulations on behalf of its departments.

The JAE did not vote on the Budget Committee's proposals. In the end, both bodies announced that the JAE would assume financial responsibility for rescuing children from Europe. The budget itself, which did not reflect this commitment, was a compromise based on the fact that the plan was not yet in operation (for the most part it remained on paper for some time afterward); it acknowledged the JAE's commitment without mentioning specific sums, until such time that it became clear whether the plan was practicable.[3]

The Budget Committee held further discussions when the budget was being shaped, and here again the criticism proved sterile. Several committee members wished to examine the possibility of tailoring the structure of the budget to the new situation. They suggested assigning special clauses to rescue, or at least reducing expenditure in other areas and increasing aid to the Diaspora. In addition, some members felt it was worth trying to implement rescue plans even if "there is no assurance of money reaching its destination." However, it was also acknowledged that the JAE could not shoulder the entire burden, and that other partners must be found. It was also claimed that it would be difficult to reopen budgetary debates at such a late stage because irreversible commitments were involved. The JAE insisted that it could allocate only twenty-five thousand Palestinian pounds to aid and rescue activity from its 1943 budget.[4]

Nor did the criticism leveled by the Zionist Actions Committee on 18 January 1943 lead to any change in the budget. Apparently the committee realized that the JAE was not allocating large sums because it was still not certain that lack of funding was the main obstacle to carrying out planned operations. The Zionist Actions Committee almost certainly understood that funding the plans would greatly exceed the Jewish Agency's financial capacity. The criticism was therefore only a manifestation of frustration and pain rather than representing real pressure for change.[5] In the end, a budget of 1,150,000 Palestinian pounds was approved, based on the previously determined framework.[6]

THE 1944 BUDGET

The JAE's debates concerning its 1944 budget, beginning in late 1943 and ending with the budget's approval in March 1944, were characterized by an almost unanimous agreement that the budget would follow the same pattern as its predecessor and would not allocate large sums to aid and rescue. There was the usual struggle over departmental budgets and the interests of the various groups represented by the JAE. Here, too, there was a noticeable disparity between remarks made in the JAE and other bodies at the beginning of the year and what was said at the time of the budget's approval in March. Several of the budgetary clauses remained vague despite repeated requests for clarification. These could have constituted a budgetary reserve held by Kaplan and Ben-Gurion for maneuvering between various requirements, especially aid and rescue activity in Europe. In any event, Ben-Gurion did not participate in the 1944 budgetary discussions.

Kaplan's original proposal for the "regular" 1944 budget resembled the regular 1943 budget in scope, totaling 1 million Palestinian pounds. Following pressure to increase the allocation in a number of areas, the regular budget was slightly increased and stood at 1.1 million Palestinian pounds. Together with the additional "special" budget, which depended upon future income, the Jewish Agency's budget for that year totaled some 2.1 million Palestinian pounds. The budget's inner division also reflected continued support for standard items like housing, settlement, defense, immigrant integration, and religious affairs.[7]

It took about five months to examine and approve the budget. As always, the JAE tried to preserve—and perhaps even increase—the budgets of its own divisions. There were the usual demands for settlement, industry and finance, agricultural and maritime enterprises, and the merchant fleet. Funding had to be found for soldiers as well as for various religious and educational organizations.[8] Kaplan and Ben-Gurion were evidently not the only ones who believed in the necessity of developing an economic and social infrastructure for statehood.

Many of those demanding an increase in the aid and rescue allocation in the Jewish Agency's budget were inconsistent, veering between "the Yishuv's needs" and those of the "Diaspora." For example, Rabbi Leib Yehuda Fishman-Maimon, head of the Department of Commerce, Industry, and Labor, claimed that the "JAE budget for 1944 could not feasibly exclude a rescue clause," while hastening to pin his hopes on the Budget Committee of the Zionist Actions Committee pressuring the JAE into correcting the omission.[9]

Rescue Committee chairman and JAE member Yitzhak Gruenbaum also tended to veer between the two poles. After asserting that additional aid and rescue funding had to come from the budget itself,[10] he later adopted Kaplan's approach, welcomed his support, and accepted his promises that rescue operations would be unaffected even if no obvious funding was set aside for it in the budget.[11] Gruenbaum linked his January 1944 resignation from the Rescue Committee to the issue of funding. But the resignation did not influence the distribution of funds and Gruenbaum did not repeat his demand to increase rescue funding from the Jewish Agency's budget.[12]

Eliyahu Dobkin, the most consistent of the JAE's faultfinders, was also unsuccessful. He called to avoid making any differentiation between "the needs of Palestine and the Diaspora," because the rescue of Jews was a prime Zionist objective. He proposed adapting the budget "to the immense change in immigration trends over previous months," immigration that far exceeded expectations (only two thousand); deterioration in the employment and housing situation as a result of the need to integrate Jewish deserters from General Wladyslaw Anders's army; poverty of the immigrants from Europe or those coming from Teheran or Yemen. Dobkin pointed out that "immigration offices are involved in rescue" and demanded an increase of forty-five thousand Palestinian pounds for immigration.[13] He also demanded the establishment of a fund totaling one million Palestinian pounds for any potential rescue opportunities.[14]

The Jewish Agency budget for 1943 totaled 1,150,000 Palestinian pounds, and the proposed regular budget proposed for 1944 amounted to 1,100,000 Palestinian pounds. An additional million Palestinian pounds budgeted for 1943 was dependent on income. Dobkin's request, therefore, was for twice the already substantial increase, which in practical terms meant an increase of about 200 percent in direct and indirect public fund-raising within the Yishuv and, in part, from world Jewry. This demand was rather unreasonable given the Yishuv's size at the time.

Dobkin succeeded in increasing the Immigration Department's budget by twenty-five thousand Palestinian pounds. A further ten thousand (in addition to the fifteen thousand) was approved for housing, and a smaller increase

was also approved for miscellaneous items. All these were substantial additions from the standpoint of the JAE budget itself, but they fell far short of meeting rescue needs.[15] Melekh Neustadt, Moshe Kolodny, and other critics of the JAE not bound by positions in the Jewish Agency also failed to enlist public pressure to alter the budgetary structure.[16]

Public criticism was thus not productive during 1943 either, once the public had been exposed, in one way or another, to information on the murders and the possibility of rescuing Jews. This could simply be explained by the fact that the JAE's budget was mostly earmarked for nonrescindable actions. Only minor alterations to the budget were possible. Ben-Gurion and Kaplan sought to obtain the rest of the money from extrabudgetary sources in Palestine and outside it. Far-reaching structural changes in the budget might lead to the cancellation of plans for settlement, security, the economy and industry, social welfare and education. Even if there was some logic in taking such a drastic step—highly doubtful in view of the nonfinancial obstacles that foiled aid and rescue—it would have necessitated a comprehensive and systematic reorganization of the Yishuv's fragile structure. This could not happen when the leadership lacked the power of enforcement. In any event, such a process would clearly have taken considerable time in a voluntary society that had committed itself to democratic and representative forms of action. It also required a solid party base and all that this entailed. The Yishuv leadership lacked the power of enforcement and the political clout required for such a fundamental change.

Was there any logic in a radical structural and budgetary move at this time? Was such a step even possible? Not necessarily. Such a move could not significantly alter the Yishuv's ability to save the Jews of Europe. Such a mission far exceeded its financial capacity. Moreover, the major problems involved in the rescue were not financial but logistical, military, and political.

FUNDING AND DELIBERATE OBSCURITY

Several of the budgetary items were left intentionally vague, and Kaplan presented them in the most general manner. Even after being questioned repeatedly, he did not divulge their full significance. For example, Kaplan allotted 120,000 Palestinian pounds for "repaying debts," and 160,000 Palestinian pounds for "political activity."[17] Werner Senator, who questioned several of the components in the budget proposal, estimated the allocation to the Political Department at 250,000 Palestinian pounds, assuming one included the budgets of the London and Washington offices. He also voiced a general complaint that the JAE knew very little about the Political Department's work and even less about defense matters; the latter's budget allocations already totaled 400,000 Palestinian pounds.[18] At a budgetary meeting held a week later, Senator pointed to irregularities, since "the expenditures budget of 1943 includes 423,000 Palestinian pounds for political matters," and expressed astonishment at the absence of detail. Dov Joseph, a member of the Political Department, tried to help but may have "spoiled things" in clearing up the mystery: "I must reassure Senator and say that 60,000 Palestinian pounds is all that is allocated to the department's actual activity."[19] Indeed, if only 60,000 Palestinian pounds had been designated for the department's activity, what was the purpose of the remaining 393,000 Palestinian pounds?

Kaplan's explanations were very general. One "reply" consisted of the following counter-complaint: "The JAE does not find the time to listen to surveys on economic and financial matters ... having more urgent things to attend to.... When a discussion does get going, it is short-tempered, the members being occupied elsewhere altogether."[20] He explained to Senator that there was no deviation from the Political Department's original allocation, since, "apart from this, we also had specific income for specific goals." It was only "an accounting arrangement for obvious reasons." He may have felt uneasy, for in principle Kaplan preferred that checking budgets be done by a public representative: "It must not be to assumed that one man has control over large sums." Yet he still made do with mentioning incomes and specific "goals" and "obvious" reasons.[21]

It appears that the budget gave Kaplan and Ben-Gurion some leeway to shift allocations to the Political Department for defense and paying off debts. Kaplan even remarked that "we receive monies for special purposes from various sources, and as an example I entered an item of 50 thousand Palestinian pounds for this in the expenditure of the nonregular budget"[22] It may be assumed that such patterns of action were not a Zionist invention, and even today they serve different governments and organizations.

A second category of funds supplied another means of maneuvering. These consisted of special funds at the disposal of Yishuv heads and leaders of the Zionist movement, enabling them to undertake secret operations. Regulations and common practice allowed them to undertake certain activities without reporting them to the official institutions of the Zionist movement. In the twenties Chaim Weizmann had a similar fund at his disposal, thanks to which he financed a secret tour of the Ha Shomer people in the Negev. The activities of the Intelligence Office, an early intelligence service used by Weizmann, were also funded secretly from this fund, as were intelligence operations, rescue, the purchase of ships for illegal immigration, and the acquisition of arms during the thirties and forties.[23]

The B funds and the obscure nature of some budgetary items were what enabled the JAE to provide interim funding for the rescue operations. The secret undercover operations of what was termed the "Special Tasks Section in the Political Department," which mostly related to rescue, were funded from some type of budget "basket." It would appear that this funding originated in part in the B funds and in blocked budgetary items.[24]

Only one budgetary clause was explicitly defined as a rescue expenditure: twenty-five thousand Palestinian pounds were designated for the immigration of children.[25] A complete copy of the Jewish Agency budget appears to have fallen into the hands of the American and British intelligence services; a fact the Yishuv leaders were apparently aware of. This is probably the reason why it was precisely the plan for rescuing children that was mentioned in the budget, whereas other rescue plans were omitted; for it was the only plan the British adopted and even discussed in Parliament. All the other plans obviously demanded caution and secrecy.

Ben-Gurion was absent from JAE budget discussions because he was in a state of semi-resignation at the time. This, however, does not signify that he was not involved in drawing up the budget and setting priorities. It would appear that he did assist in its preparation. First, preliminary discussions on such a subject were generally held far in advance, and he did take part in the first discussion. Second, organizations and parties generally reach the essential decisions on budgetary matters after extensive preparatory work, most of which takes place beyond the reach of protocol writers' pens. Third—and perhaps most decisive for my argument—it must not be assumed that Ben-Gurion did not know that he would ultimately return to the JAE and have to "live" with the approved budget.

Furthermore, Ben-Gurion was consulted during his absence and received regular reports of JAE meetings. This was established practice, and there is no reason to assume that budgetary matters, which were of decisive importance, were excluded.[26] At the time Ben-Gurion was deeply involved in the activities of the Planning Committee, which had direct repercussions on the development of the budget, and he wrote a letter to the JAE on behalf of the committee that was read aloud during the budgetary debate.[27]

Whether or not I am correct in assuming that Ben-Gurion participated in shaping the budget, it can be asserted that he adhered to the policy adopted by himself and Kaplan during 1943, namely, to raise money for funding rescue operations from extrabudgetary sources, and to use funds from the budget only when there was no other alternative. Ben-Gurion participated in the Zionist Actions Committee session that discussed the budget at length and approved it. In this debate Ben-Gurion covered a wide range of political matters[28] yet made no reference to the budget. If he had harbored any misgivings about the budget, he would hardly have missed such an opportunity to modify it.

FUND-RAISING WITHIN THE YISHUV

The decision to greatly increase fund-raising efforts both within and outside the Yishuv derived from Kaplan's and Ben-Gurion's stated as well as unstated policy of minimizing, as far as possible, the use of Jewish Agency funds. They were afraid that without contributions the Jewish Agency's budget would totally collapse beneath the immense burden of funding aid and rescue in Europe.

The Jewish Agency held fund-raising drives in Palestine and overseas. It utilized the regular appeals system, whose role was enlarged to include fund-raising for rescue activity, and it established special rescue funds. The Mobilization Fund was the main instrument operating in Palestine from July 1942. It was originally designed primarily to support the families of volunteers to the British army, as well as to fund various defense expenditures and training of the Haganah. During 1943 its goals were enlarged and its name was changed to Mobilization and Rescue Fund. Additional funding operations existed in the United States, South Africa, Britain, and Egypt. A portion of the monies was transferred to Palestine, disguised either as contributions to the development of Palestine or financial "investments." Rescue operations were also funded, in part, through "straw companies" and by means of money transfers from one company to another.

THE MOBILIZATION FUND

The first fund-raising debates were held when the plan to rescue children was initially broached. Spontaneous contributions started flowing in, and there was a fear within the Yishuv that one-upmanship or unorganized, uncoordinated activity would ultimately diminish the size of contributions. Discussions took place in the Budget Committee of the Zionist Actions Committee and the JAE. According to Gruenbaum, various fund-raisers had been hampered by the Mobilization Fund's professional staff. He asked the JAE to dictate fund-raising policy and to announce the creation of a "Child Rescue Fund."

Ben-Gurion channeled the discussion to a special subcommittee and rejected Gruenbaum's repeated calls for a Jewish Agency debate on the establishment of a special child rescue fund. He was afraid that hasty decisions might lead to uncontrolled competition among the various funds, which would adversely affect overall fund-raising both from the public sector and private organizations within the Yishuv, ultimately harming the Mobilization Fund.

Anyone with even a superficial knowledge of fund-raising matters inside and outside the Yishuv knew all about competition among the various organizations and the damage it caused. Thus, Gruenbaum understood Ben-Gurion's aversion to his proposal and reconsidered it. He then suggested that he and Kaplan discuss and formulate a proposal with the Mobilization Fund, to be presented to the JAE. Others supported the need for coordination and centralized fund-raising efforts. Ben-Gurion insisted on leaving the issue with the subcommittee, and the JAE decided to adopt his position.[29]

Aside from his desire to protect the Mobilization Fund, Ben-Gurion was also afraid of the Mandatory government's reaction. The JAE's decision to assume responsibility for funding aid and rescue operations included the words "when the time comes we shall announce this publicly," hinting at the complication associated with transferring money into occupied Europe. The fear was twofold: first, such transfers were prohibited in wartime; second, it was expected that Britain would attempt to thwart the mass rescue of Jews to Palestine. A financial deployment that worried the British was liable to jeopardize contributions, as well as actual cooperation with the British, which was essential for the success of the rescue plans. This led to the idea of a secret fund-raising appeal among the wealthy in the Yishuv. They would be invited to intimate secret soirees, where the Yishuv heads would coax them into contributing money.[30]

The JAE and National Council promised the Mobilization Fund that this secret fund-raising drive would not affect its activities, and that no proposal would be implemented without its approval. As reassurance, the JAE allocated an advance payment of 15,000 Palestinian pounds, as did the Histadrut. Similar sums were demanded by other bodies. The fund organizers hoped to raise between 100,000 and 120,000 Palestinian pounds.

Nevertheless, a month later the JAE retracted its support for the organizers of the secret appeal, who came from the Rescue Committee, and, bowing under pressure from the Mobilization Fund, decided "to prohibit any kind of fund-raising activity until it became clear whether there was any chance of saving the Jews of the Diaspora." If it emerged that there was a chance, the function of the Mobilization Fund would be amplified to include fund-raising for rescue operations, contingent on there being a possibility of increasing the sums contributed.[31]

Two days after the Rescue Committee was apprised of the JAE's plans to relieve it of the secret fund, Kaplan proposed setting up a new committee consisting of representatives of

Mapai, the Histadrut, and the Mobilization Fund, which would be charged with establishing the secret fund.[32] Apparently the JAE changed its mind because the Rescue Committee was gradually developing into a cumbersome body, and was probably too pluralistic for the JAE and Mapai, which aspired to be the primary factor in this body.

In late January the JAE held a comprehensive discussion on funding that included a debate on the character of the Yishuv's rescue fund. Ben-Gurion remained silent throughout the debate, leaving Kaplan to raise the issue. He only chaired the debate and summed it up. In the course of the debate, he rejected Gruenbaum's complaint that the JAE were not acting in accordance with the spirit of urgency that emerged from the Zionist Actions Committee on 18 January 1943. Ben-Gurion kept to himself the fact that on 26 November 1942 he had instructed his secretary, Zvi Maimon, to receive from Dr. Aharon Bart, chairman of the Mobilization Fund, a financial statement detailing "total income, where it came from, which people participated . . . and distribution of expenditures." Presumably he asked for data at this early stage, having already begun to examine the best ways of funding rescue activity.

The main thrust of the debate revolved around the question of who would manage the fund and what its function would be: Would it be part of the Palestinian Foundation Fund or would it be a new and special fund? Would it be used solely for the rescue of children, for refugees in general, only for Zionists, or for all types of Jews? There was also the fear that Agudat Israel or other bodies might establish separate funds if no solution proved acceptable to them.

There was also the formal difficulty of rerouting funds donated to the Jewish Agency for building the Yishuv, and legal repercussions involved in proclaiming a fund for an illegal purpose, namely, transferring money to enemy countries. While pointing to the danger inherent in changing the fund's goals, the PFF stressed that

it was prepared to exclude the rescue of children. It was finally decided to accept the PFF's proposal to organize—as part of its 1943 fund-raising—a special, separate fund to aid the Diaspora and the refugees.[33]

"MAYBE BEN-GURION WILL AGREE TO DEVOTE A MONTH OR TWO"

February 1943 was an intensive month for wrestling with fund-raising issues since several operations and rescue plans were up for discussion. Ben-Gurion was absent from most of the JAE meetings in February. He and Kaplan had received harsh criticism from the Mapai secretariat on 10 February, when Kaplan's funding policy was attacked and Ben-Gurion's nonintervention in fund-raising activities also drew criticism.

In rejecting hints that someone had interfered with fund-raising efforts, Kaplan apparently also touched on the inconsistency ascribed to the JAE on the matter of the secret fund. Kaplan rejected the criticism out of hand, maintaining that he had been working to institutionalize all fund-raising drives and was trying to rope in the PFF and, to a certain extent, the Mobilization Fund. He insisted that his suggestion that the PFF hold a special drive for funding rescue activity had been ruled out. He had also suggested that the Mobilization Fund do this, and this, too, was rejected.[34]

Kaplan refused to allow the JAE to take charge of fund-raising, which would have been impossible both organizationally and administratively. Fund-raising is not a spontaneous, amateurish affair, confined to speeches at gatherings, Kaplan declared. It needed experienced personnel, special people, solely devoted to the matter. The JAE's "triumvirate," Ben-Gurion, Sharett and himself were not "unemployed."

Kaplan told his fellow party members about his proposal to set up a limited committee—consisting of Mapai, the Histadrut, and the Mobilization Fund—whose main job would be to raise funds for aid and rescue in Europe. He pointed to a difficulty raised by the Mobilization Fund, namely, the need to provide positive results from rescue operations. So far there had been no real achievements. In the meantime, Kaplan followed Ben-Gurion's suggestion and asked the Mobilization Fund for an undertaking to give—or at least lend—twenty thousand Palestinian pounds to cover the fifty thousand needed to purchase ships. The matter would require JAE approval, Kaplan said, since transferring money from the fund was liable to cause it to violate the ban on sending money to Axis countries.

Various questions were raised regarding fund-raising: Which fund-raiser should be entrusted with collecting money for rescue activity? Should the various funds be lumped together?[35] What would Ben-Gurion's role be? (It was a given that Ben-Gurion's contribution to the effort was crucial.)

Ben-Gurion stressed the importance of an immediate allocation of fifty thousand Palestinian pounds to purchase ships to transport children and other refugees, adding that the JAE, the Histadrut, and the Mobilization Fund would be responsible for fund-raising. He favored establishing a single fund and suggested that the functions of the Mobilization Fund be enlarged.

Ben-Gurion refused to join the committee of three called for by Avraham Haft in addition to the Mobilization Fund. Only Haft and Golda Meir were elected. Instead, Ben-Gurion agreed to place himself at the disposal of the secret fund as a "soldier," intervening when necessary to communicate with the Yishuv's affluent Jews. Notwithstanding the sharp criticism directed at Ben-Gurion and Kaplan, in practice the Mapai Secretariat adopted their stand: the Mobilization Fund would also be put in charge of fund-raising for rescue, and quotas imposed upon different sectors would be increased, as Eliyahu Golomb had suggested. The Mobilization Fund would immediately transfer twenty-five thousand Palestinian pounds for rescue operations, and the Histadrut and Jewish Agency would transfer

similar sums. The estimation was that these contributions, together with those from wealthy people in the Yishuv, would amount to a hundred thousand Palestinian pounds.[36]

After formulating its position, Mapai raised the subject for debate in the JAE (in Ben-Gurion's absence). Representatives of the National Council, the Mobilization Fund, and the Histadrut were also present. Relations between the fund-raising bodies were clarified,[37] and the difficulties of the Mobilization Fund and its predictions were presented. Competition remained fierce among the various organizations. The monthly sum of 40,000 Palestinian pounds could not be raised, nor did this amount meet all the present needs. A onetime secret project to raise between 100,000 and 150,000 Palestinian pounds or a similar fund-raising appeal aimed at the Yishuv's wealthy would destroy the Mobilization Fund. Such contributions would come at the expense of regular contributions. Only a month had elapsed since the regular quotas imposed on the workers and the employers had been adjusted, and it was impossible to increase them now.

Dr. Aharon Bart, chairman of the appeal's presidium, was the main speaker on behalf of the appeal at the meeting. He announced that, despite the difficulties, the appeal was prepared to put at the disposal of the rescue operations fifteen thousand Palestinian pounds and to consider what the JAE had already expended—eight thousand and a further fifteen thousand—as a loan on account of the future fund-raising appeal. Moreover, if rescue operations were successful and extra funding was required, the appeal could adopt them, either directly or indirectly.

Bart presented two further conditions: first, the sums placed at the JAE's disposal by the various organizations would be considered loans. If the fund-raising appeals succeeded and it was possible to repay "loans" allocated to the various institutions that had rallied to the cause, there would be equality of "debtors" and the loans would be repaid to them all in equal portions.

(This clearly hinted at the JAE's wish to give priority to institutions close to it, especially the Histadrut.) Also, this proposal required the agreement of the "defense committee" responsible for the matter, which the Mobilization Fund was designed to serve.

Gruenbaum rejected Bart's proposals. He did not wish to precipitate in the Rescue Committee "an argument over what took precedence over what—the needs of the Yishuv or the needs of the Diaspora." One way or another, the Rescue Committee needed between 100,000 and 120,000 Palestinian pounds to be spent as the necessity arose. The committee had to be able to act, knowing that it had such a sum at its disposal. The Rescue Committee would not hold independent fund-raising appeals, which harmed the operations of the Mobilization Fund, unless the committee had 200,000 Palestinian pounds, which had to be raised throughout the Yishuv. Gruenbaum doubted the possibility of Agudat Israel or the Revisionists contributing money.

Kaplan insisted that fund-raising efforts must be increased, that it was important "to give those people who wanted action the opportunity to act." In order to avoid damage caused by noncoordination, it was desirable to establish a limited committee of the appeal's presidium with the addition of partners. The JAE and the fund's executive would announce their willingness to provide an advance payment at the appeal's expense and, like the Histadrut, would not lay down conditions for allocation. The JAE was uncertain as to the fate of the money being allocated to rescue. Although the JAE "was shouldering a very heavy burden," instructions had been sent to Barlas a few days earlier, together with a power of attorney "to lease a ship, speed up the transport of children from Bulgaria, waste no time, even if it costs 40 Palestinian pounds per child."

Kaplan suggested that the basis of participation should be twenty-five thousand Palestinian pounds from each party, the JAE and the Mobilization Fund. As for the Rescue Committee, Ka-

plan's response sounded determined, with a hint of sarcasm: "And one last word to Gruenbaum. If we reach this conclusion, I suggest you inform the Rescue Committee that this is the position of the responsible institutions, responsible in deeds and not in words: if they [the people from the Rescue Committee] can add their money, let them, not merely being content with giving an opinion."[38] There is a clear hint in his words of the state of mind that prompted the decision to restore responsibility for managing the secret fund to the Mobilization Fund and of the influence of Mapai.

It is worth lingering over the four days that elapsed between the meeting of the Mapai Secretariat (Wednesday, 10 February) and that of the JAE (Sunday, 14 February). Kaplan remarked at the JAE meeting that instructions and a financial power of attorney had been sent to Barlas the previous Thursday (the day after the Mapai Secretariat debate). This is important in that it reflects a set pattern of decision making in the Yishuv leadership. A few days before the convening of the JAE meeting, the operations that were slated for discussionhad already been carried out. If so, who approved them? The JAE had not convened between Wednesday and Thursday. Did Kaplan decide on his own? Did Ben-Gurion and Kaplan decide to act following pressure within Mapai, and after consulting with Golomb and Meirov-Avigur? It would seem that the decision was made in a restricted circle outside the meetings of the JAE, following that same "parallel system" discussed in previous chapters. Although Ben-Gurion had suspended himself from JAE discussions at that time, in doing so he did not surrender his real authority, and his central standing in that same "parallel system" proved this to be the case.

Kaplan was very determined. Apparently he was relying on the support of Ben-Gurion, who was absent from the JAE meeting. He clung to his demand that all organizations participate in funding, insisting that the JAE was only a "go-between" where money from the PFF (one of the JAE's main sources of funding) was concerned. The PFF took good care of the money, but because the latter did not belong to the JAE, it could not alter the money's designated destination. The JAE did not have permission to divert money to aid and rescue operations in Europe. The Zionist Actions Committee had already discussed the budget and had not found a way to allocate funds for such missions. Consequently, aid and rescue had to be financed from sources outside the agency budget. Kaplan laid this obligation at the foot of his critics—everyone was required to chip in.

The Mobilization Fund presidium understood that Kaplan was unyielding and that a more accommodating proposal would not be forthcoming. It agreed to establish a coordinating committee consisting of three to six members drawn from the Mobilization Fund, the Rescue Committee, and the Histadrut. The committee would try to map out new avenues of fundraising that did not compete with the existing fund. The Mobilization Fund also agreed to allocate twenty-five thousand Palestinian pounds to rescue operations.

It was decided that the JAE, the Mobilization Fund and the Histadrut would each contribute twenty-five thousand Palestinian pounds, and that the total of seventy-five thousand would be allocated immediately. It was defined as a loan, and negotiations would subsequently be conducted concerning repayment terms. Furthermore, the coordinating committee was charged with determining a fund-raising format for obtaining money from of the Yishuv's wealthy Jews.

Kaplan asked for clarification as to "who controlled the money and who was auditing." Rescue Committee chairman Gruenbaum would have signatory power, but the agency treasury would hold the money and the JAE would decide on each expenditure as it saw fit until the Rescue Committee had reached a decision. The agreement was approved the same day both by the Mobilization Fund and the Rescue Committee.[39]

THE SECRET FUND

On 23 February 1943 several wealthy members of the Yishuv gathered in the home of Eliezer Hoofien, manager of the Anglo-Palestine Bank. Ben-Gurion was often called upon by Mapai to involve himself in such activities, and he was indeed the main speaker at the first gathering, whose organizers wished to invest it with a very special character. Also invited was Menahem Bader, who was visiting Palestine. Bader was a key Yishuv rescue activist in Istanbul, and apparently he was to explain to the donors exactly what was being done with their contributions.

Ben-Gurion and Bader gave lengthy descriptions of the Jewish situation in Europe, specifically what could be done to help its Jews and how much it would cost. They asked for contributions from those present and for help in raising money from those unable to attend. The following day Ben-Gurion informed his colleagues of the previous evening's success: "Several made on-the-spot contributions of a thousand Palestinian pounds," while others promised to raise similar sums from among their friends. He wasn't sure they could secure the 100,000 Palestinian pounds they expected from this quarter, but he asserted that "a large portion of it will be raised in the near future if only those who took it upon themselves to work will do so."[40] Six months later Ben-Gurion repeated the same approach.

Ben-Gurion heard things in Hoofien's home that made him doubt the fund-raisers' ability to reach the financial target they had set themselves. People complained about their tax burden and were worried that the authorities would raise the income tax even higher. On 18 February 1943 the *Palestine Post* published a report on the Mandatory government's intentions to raise the income tax and impose new taxes.

The day after the meeting Isaac Arditi explained the concerns of the merchants and industrialists in a letter to Ben-Gurion. The message was clear: regular, long-term commitments from this public would have to be part and parcel of the economic planning of their businesses. Every ill-considered decision of the Mandatory government or the Jewish Agency to collect more money from them was liable to damage the fabric of their businesses, adversely affect their stability, and, in the final analysis, limit their ability to contribute.[41]

Whether Arditi's letter accurately reflected the true position of the Yishuv's wealthy remains uncertain. In any event, it confirms the very important fact that substantial and frequent donations were generally contingent on the overall planning of the businesses. Donors could not be expected to abort operations or impede development for the sake of a donation to even the most worthy of causes. There was a certain logic in all this: by strengthening the business, donations would also increase. A contribution that caused a business to go under or damaged it extensively might perhaps be larger, but it would probably be a onetime and restricted affair.

Several weeks before the secret meeting in Hoofien's home, Ben-Gurion participated as a "soldier" and fund-raising activist at a more public event. He gave the main speech at a gathering organized by the Mobilization Fund on 11 January 1943 in the Ohel Shem Hall in Tel Aviv.[42]

BETWEEN MOBILIZATION AND RESCUE

In spring 1943, following negotiations between the JAE, the Rescue Committee, and the Mobilization Fund, an agreement was reached for enlarging the appeal's operations and entrusting it with raising funds for rescue operations. Its name was subsequently changed to Mobilization and Rescue Appeal. The agreement detailed the division of the money among the various bodies and how it would be collected. The hesitation accompanying the negotiations found expression in the agreement itself. In order to provide an escape hatch, it was decided that the agreement remain in force for one year and, if necessary, undergo reevaluation in three months.[43]

Toward the end of the third month, pressure grew to change the agreement and obligate the Mobilization Fund to increase its rate of allocation to rescue operations. Gruenbaum complained that the Rescue Committee was dependent on the Mobilization Fund. He also mentioned misunderstandings between his committee, the Histadrut, and the fund. The Histadrut held a special fund-raising day at the beginning of May. Gruenbaum hoped the income would be applied to the rescue cause. The fund and the Histadrut thought otherwise, and in the end Dr. Bart informed him that only between fifty and fifty-five thousand Palestinian pounds would be allocated instead of the promised seventy-five thousand.

The incident left bad feelings between the Histadrut, the Rescue Committee, and the Mobilization Fund.[44] The distress of the mobilized soldiers' families was marked, as was the pressure they placed upon the Yishuv offices. A letter sent to Ben-Gurion and his colleagues by a member of the Committee for the Care of Soldiers and Guards illustrates this. The committee's finances were dwindling, it had an accumulated deficit of over four thousand Palestinian pounds, and it was unable to balance its budget. The need to give equal support to the families of soldiers and guards, to supply aid to the parents of mobilized soldiers who had previously been the main breadwinners, and the high cost of living and mounting expenses—not to mention the suspension of the Mobilization Fund's allocation—forced the committee to adopt three tough decisions: "(1) To accept no new cases unless as a substitute for cases that were no longer receiving aid. (2) To undertake no new operations or establish new institutions for children. (3) To avoid raising any item on the expenditure budget except for the cost-of-living increment, which, unfortunately, was not regulated by the committee but rather in accordance with general policy in the Yishuv." This meant that "several thoroughly deserving cases" were deprived of "even the minimum" degree of assistance. The committee called for a special session of the JAE and the fund's presidium to discuss the matter.[45] The Mobilization and Rescue Appeal continued to exert similar pressure throughout the period in which it raised funds for the two charities.

CONFLICTING PRESSURES AND LIMITED RESOURCES

Efforts to stretch resources in opposing directions came both from within and without the JAE. Even Dobkin, of the Immigration Department, called for changes in the agreement during the first three months of its experimental phase. He demanded an increase in money quotas for rescue operations at the expense of quotas to the Haganah and to the families of mobilized soldiers.[46] Dobkin pointed out that new rescue options in Poland meant that financial needs had multiplied; he was almost certainly alluding to what appeared to be a direct link with Poland through the couriers Schulz or Popescu. Dobkin demanded parity between the sums allocated for aid rescue and those allocated for the families of soldiers. Although he preferred this, as an alternative he suggested separating the two objectives and establishing a separate rescue fund.[47]

Kaplan vigorously rejected suggestions to alter the agreement with the Mobilization Fund, arguing that Dobkin did not understand the Jewish Agency's complex financial maneuvering. The facts were plain: the fund failed to meet its fund-raising goals.[48] Throughout this debate Ben-Gurion remained silent, Kaplan appearing to express his own view and sparing him having to participate in this argument. Ultimately the JAE did not adopt Dobkin's suggestion.[49]

Two months later another major fund-raising appeal, to be known as "Solidarity with the Diaspora Month," was proposed for the Yishuv. Ben-Gurion supported the proposal and was involved in the details of its planning and operation. The Mobilization Fund demanded active participation by the JAE in organizing the new drive and pointed out the possibility of British objections, on the pretext that any money collected was destined for the Axis countries. Relations between the Yishuv and the British authorities were at a low point and there was even a fear of the latter trying to harm the Haganah organization by striking at an important source of funding.[50]

The "Solidarity with the Diaspora Month" drive also took place on account of the Mobilization Fund's reduced income. The fund hoped to take advantage of the public outcry over the situation in Europe to replenish its coffers. This tendency reawakened the controversy over keeping fund-raising for rescue operations separate from fund-raising for all other objectives, specifically the fact that by answering the national call to help Diaspora Jews, the Yishuv soldiers serving in the British army were part of rescue efforts and that therefore no separation should be made between the dual objectives of the Mobilization and Rescue Fund.

The debate centered on the distribution of donations between the soldiers and their families, on the one hand, and rescue operations, on the other. The Mobilization Fund collected occasional donations and regular pledges from all sectors of the Yishuv economy. At that time monthly income was about fifty thousand Palestinian pounds, forty thousand of which were allocated for "mobilization" and ten thousand for "rescue." The question remained as to what would be done with income from the "Solidarity with the Diaspora Month" drive.

The two schools of thought went as follows: (1) Every Palestinian pound above the regular total (fifty thousand Palestinian pounds), regardless of its source, should be allocated for rescue operations. (2) All funds collected for rescue operations should be used for this purpose; in addition to the regular allocation of ten thousand Palestinian pounds, money collected as a result of increased revenues from pledged income should be used to fund the needs of mobilized soldiers. Obviously the hope was that pledged income would increase as a result of the planned public fund-raising campaign.

Kaplan and Sharett favored the second school of thought, while Dobkin preferred the first. No agreement was reached in discussions between the Mobilization Fund, the National Council, and the JAE.[51] Kaplan and Sharett were afraid that the families representing the Committee for the Care of Soldiers and Guards would carry out their threat to organize mass demonstrations on behalf of the recruits. An agreement was eventually reached and Kaplan asked the JAE to approve it. The idea was to hold a month-long fund-raising drive, whose objective would be to collect between one and two hundred thousand Palestinian pounds and get all those who should and could to pay their fair share based on their ability.

Kaplan hinted that there were people and organizations within the Yishuv who were evading taxes; it will be recalled that the Yishuv lacked the power of enforcement. The choice of this particular "month"—from September 15 until after the Day of Atonement—was no accident. As Bart explained to the fund, the JAE, and the National Council, the plan was for the drive to peak just as the population "was facing 'judgment day,' when they would do their utmost to clear their consciences."

The date was already "taken." Other fund-raisers made a habit of holding their annual drives at that time. Kaplan asked the PFF and the Jewish National Fund (JNF) to postpone their drives, but they refused. Undismayed, Kaplan asked for JAE intervention. Ben-Gurion said that the JAE agreed with the designated date and promised all possible assistance. Also, although he agreed that the date might be awkward to the other fund-raisers, "the issue of rescuing the Jews of Europe was not only a financial but also a moral one. It is now one of the central issues." There was another aspect to the Yishuv taking the lead in the rescue venture. As Ben-Gurion said, "It is not only aid to the Jews of Europe—it also raises the prestige of the Yishuv and thus of the

[Yishuv's] charity foundations. The fact that the Jews of the Yishuv were heading the rescue effort is an important Zionist asset, and any Zionist asset is also an asset to the charity funds.[52]

This was a further indication of Ben-Gurion's basic belief that the Zionist enterprise did not contradict rescue efforts and reinforced the hypothesis that when he did distinguish between the two, it was mainly for tactical purposes, namely, to force other to participate in fund-raising. This was really the main objective of the "Solidarity with the Diaspora Month" drive. The JAE did not have to pass judgment on the needs of soldiers or rescue operations. The question was most likely settled behind the scenes before the JAE meeting.[53] The "month" would include the Jewish New Year and its attendant celebrations and holy days, and the JAE would participate in all scheduled events.[54]

MOBILIZING THE YISHUV'S WEALTHY POPULACE: ROUND TWO

On 23 September 1943 Ben-Gurion again met several of the Yishuv's capitalists in Jerusalem in order to induce them to donate money for rescue operations. Also at the meeting were Kaplan, Rabbi Isaac Herzog, Mobilization Fund chairman Dr. Aharon Bart, and Dr. Emil Schmorak, who represented the General Zionists in the JAE and had recently returned from Istanbul. Schmorak was also a leader of the ex-Polish community in Palestine and was a member of the Committee of Four and the Committee of Five, representing the nucleus of the Rescue Committee.

The meeting was meticulously planned in close coordination with Ben-Gurion. The organizers, who viewed it as a touchstone for the whole "Solidarity with the Diaspora Month" drive, requested that Ben-Gurion sign the invitations. They also conferred with him about wording and format. Kaplan was asked to persuade one of the wealthy participants to be the first to announce his contribution and thereby to set the bar at an obligatory high level.[55]

Ben-Gurion opened the meeting by voicing the widespread opinion that victory was near, although there was no telling exactly when. He also described the political state of the Zionist movement and the Yishuv, claiming that he detected a note of "repentance" and possible regret in Britain's attitude. But he also warned against being overly optimistic. Hitler was still powerful, and even though the Germans had been forced to retreat, there was still one victim left upon whom to vent their hatred and revenge: the Jews. The danger was not yet over, and the one thing that was at a premium was time. It had to be bought in order to defer the calamity for another "day or two," and could spell the "difference between life and death for many thousands [of Jews]." Ben-Gurion provided up-to-date information on the situation in Europe supplied by "friends who had recently spent time in the vicinity of the Holocaust," referring mainly to Schmorak but also to reports reaching Istanbul and sent on to Palestine.[56]

One of Ben-Gurion's most important utterances on the rescue issue was the following: "If in some town, some region in Palestine, in some tiny way . . . we can stand guard, if in some minute way we are able to stand guard . . . if the horror can be postponed for some time, the significance of this could be rescue." He went on to stress the ongoing fight against time and the importance of funding:

> Saving the lives of Jews waiting to be executed . . . tells us one thing only: [We must] do whatever is humanly possible . . . to extend material aid to those working on rescue operations in order to save what can still be saved, to delay the calamity as far as it can be delayed. [And we must] do it immediately, to the very best of our ability. I hesitate to say—since the matter is so serious—that we shall do our utmost; we are flesh and blood and cannot do the maximum, but we shall do what we can.

He went on to say that they had to do "more than had been done so far. We wanted those people congregated here to give the signal to the whole of the Yishuv, to the Jewish communities overseas, that they also give more aid, do a little more than they have done up 'til now. Because the danger is great."

Schmorak explained that the aim of the meeting was for "each of you to contribute ten times more than he had thought to contribute when he came here." He described the rescue operations in vivid detail.[57] His visit to Istanbul had taught him the following simple truth: if more money were available, more Jews could be saved.

Schmorak, who was head of the Trade and Industry section within the Jewish Agency, tried to speak as one bourgeois to another. He reminded his audience that their recent tax benefits were due to the intercession of the JAE, the British authorities having responded to pressure and reduced the new tax brackets. One of the JAE's arguments had been that "the Jews pay a special tax . . . to take care of the Yishuv . . . and also to look out for the Jews of the Diaspora because of their tragedy." The British had seen the logic of the argument and it was now fitting to make good on the debt.

Schmorak reminded his audience of the fear-filled days before El Alamein and the threat of invasion from Syria. Many had been willing at the time to donate large sums to avert the danger. Now was the time to regain that sense of urgency and to contribute generously. He made them think of their brethren, their families, and asked them to contribute even if this meant less wealth for themselves. When the time came, he wanted them to answer the following question in all sincerity: What did you do to save us from death, slaughter, and deportation?

"We have no government, no police force, and we cannot impose taxes," said Schmorak. If no example is set by this meeting to the rest of the Yishuv, "our enterprise will fail and we shall lose the option of saving those that are still alive."

Following Schmorak, Dr. Bart said that solidarity month was designed to awaken the conscience of the Yishuv, which perhaps tended to distance itself from the horrors of Europe "as spiritual balm against insanity." Bart asked his listeners to do their utmost so that in times of emotional stock-taking "we can face our conscience."[58]

The words of Ben-Gurion, Schmorak, and Barratt did not fall on deaf ears. Erich Mohalier turned to his colleagues (he may have been secretly asked by Kaplan to do so) and announced that he was pledging 5,000 Palestinian pounds on behalf of his company. Dr. Bart explained that all monies collected were earmarked for rescue efforts. Most of those who had been invited had turned up. Some sent their excuses, while others said they would consider making contributions. Ben-Gurion summed up the results. "The total sum gathered at that meeting was 30,330 Palestinian pounds [U.S. $121,000]. The Yishuv can be proud of this gathering. I hope each one here will do his utmost to foster the spirit of this meeting."

Chief Rabbi Herzog mentioned the rule that "if anyone who saves a single soul in Israel, it is as if he had saved the entire world," stressing the religious significance of contributing money to the rescue effort. After explaining how the donations would be transferred, Kaplan pointed out the need to keep the affair out of the press.[59] Between fifty and seventy thousand Palestinian pounds were collected, which was not bad given the target of a hundred thousand for the entire fund-raising drive.

That meeting illustrated the fact that no distinction existed between "Zionism" and "rescue" or between the "big rescue" and the "small rescue," as Ben-Gurion had always insisted. Schmorak, Bart, and especially Ben-Gurion regarded rescue as a single unit. In the past the JAE had been accused of diverting contributions originally meant to fund rescue operations for other ends. Bart found himself having to emphasize that all donations from this meeting would be used solely to fund rescue operations. He was not

referring to all the money collected during the solidarity month.

The organizers of the solidarity month may also have wished to breathe new life into the Mobilization Fund. The decision to keep secret the fact that funds collected during this month would also be used for mobilization and defense could have reflected the leadership's fear of a direct public polemic on this issue, which is quite understandable. On the one hand, most people in the Yishuv were relatively young at that time and were mostly of European origin, having more relatives in Europe than they had soldiers fighting on the British side. On the other hand, the Yishuv leadership felt obliged to support families of soldiers who had answered the call to help the Allies crush Hitler and thus to save the Jews of Europe. Forsaking these families was not a viable option in a voluntary community like the Yishuv, which was based on the trust of those who were sent as well as on those who did the sending. A leadership capable of betraying this trust would have been of no use to anyone, least of all to the Jews of Europe.[60]

FAILURE OF THE "SOLIDARITY WITH THE DIASPORA MONTH" CAMPAIGN

The campaign was preceded by intensive publicity, which took the form of meetings, advertisements, and press releases. Its objectives were clear: to make the Yishuv aware of new rescue possibilities and to help finance them.[61] The targeted goal was 250,000 Palestinian pounds. It was reported that the Histadrut Executive Committee was prepared to allocate 50,000 Palestinian pounds for rescue if other bodies in the Yishuv agreed to contribute a total of 200,000 Palestinian pounds. The JAE announced that it had allocated considerable sums from its current budget.[62] The private sector and the general public were therefore called upon to contribute 200,000 Palestinian pounds.

Progress reports on the fund-raising campaign were published periodically in *Davar* and other daily newspapers.[63] The points that were given prominence in the press touched on the heart of the problem. For example, Golda Meir asked: "Are we going to say that we shall rescue such and such a number and no more because we have no money?" In order to stress the importance of the "small rescue" and how important the Yishuv's contribution was, Sharett quoted a letter writer from the Diaspora: "For the Yishuv it is a time of self-fulfillment. . . . Jews [in Europe] can be reached and helped through Istanbul. Money is needed. Someone wrote: 'There are a number of circles in hell; if we can bring one Jew from the ninth to the sixth, then we shall have done something great.'"

Absolute salvation meant bringing Jews to Palestine, and great effort is being expended to this end, but "on no account must we see this as the only possibility. Even within this valley of death, flowing with blood, . . . there are islands of relative safety, and we can bring people to these islands—even if only a few. We shall have to face our consciences, if we don't. We succeeded in bringing hundreds, and with intensified efforts we might even reach thousands."

Kaplan tried to explain the difficulty in appealing to the public by saying: "Some people are quite happy to translate their feelings into money, but they don't really like having their peace of mind disturbed, and by going to fund-raising meetings, they are reminded of the enormity of the disaster." According to Kaplan, the Yishuv was willing to fund all kinds of rescue operations, making no distinction between "large" or "small," or between immigration to Palestine or any other country willing to take Jews.[64]

In the end, the fund-raising drive failed to achieve its hoped-for objectives. Despite all the publicity and the moral and social pressure, avoiding making contributions was a clear trend.[65] The targeted 250,000 Palestinian pounds was not obtained even after the month was extended beyond the drive's closing date.

According to data, only 90,000 Palestinian pounds were collected.[66] The Histadrut contributed 50,000 Palestinian pounds conditionally, but the latter was not fulfilled and it only contributed 20,000.[67] After deducting the Mobilization Fund's share and the loans, only 32,000 Palestinian pounds—a far cry from the hoped-for sum—remained for rescue operations.[68]

Researchers have offered a number of explanations for this failure. First, the Yishuv was weary from constant exposure to reports from the Diaspora. This wearing down could be explained in terms borrowed from social psychology. Kaplan and the Histadrut leadership noted that the Yishuv was suffering a kind of dulling of the senses.[69] This explanation appears rather far-fetched, since the Yishuv was tied to events in Europe through familial, emotional, and personal connections.

Second, the drive may have failed because too moderate a position was adopted, under the influence of Ben-Gurion and several of his colleagues in the leadership, who were not in favor of fueling an already charged atmosphere, preventing more strident manifestations of protest and outrage. It may be that less restrained and more shocking propaganda would have created a more favorable atmosphere for fund-raising. Be that as it may, it is clear that this explanation contradicts the first explanation, since any emphasis on the terrible plight of Europe's Jews would have increased the sense of weariness and reluctance to make contributions to ensure their salvation.[70]

Third, it may be possible to relate the failure to inappropriate preparation despite all the organizers' efforts. The fund-raising campaign was moved up to coincide with the "terrible days" that form part of the religious period preceding the Jewish New Year. This created an impossible schedule and led to hasty preparations.[71]

Fourth, the organizers may have erred in their estimation of the public's economic power. Several special fund-raising campaigns had been held since the end of 1942, in addition to regular

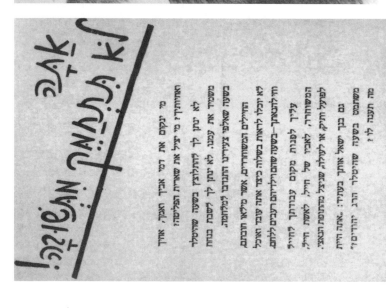

Poster calling to enlist to save Jews
(*CZA, poster collection*).

Poster calling to enlist to save Jews
(*CZA, poster collection*).

taxes paid to the Mandatory authorities as well as the other Zionist movement voluntary funds and Yishuv institutions. A detailed economic study would answer the question of how realistic the organizers' objectives were.

Another possible explanation for the failure of the drive was the public's suspicions that the funds collected were not arriving at their intended destination. Finally, the inability to discuss rescue activity and some of the operation's successes almost certainly had a negative effect on fund-raising efforts. People probably thought that if the money raised thus far had proved so ineffective, any additional money was hardly going to change the situation.[72]

The soldiers and their families continued to exert strong pressure on the leadership. For example, in July 1944 Schmorak described to Ben-Gurion the "great dissatisfaction" among the representatives of the wives of soldiers, who had met with him and complained about "the difficult situation of the soldiers' families." They demanded double the monthly allowance and the establishment of more institutions for the children of soldiers. They claimed that in Jerusalem alone there were about five hundred children of soldiers who were not being adequately cared for. Many families of soldiers were in arrears with their rent and some landlords had obtained court eviction notices. The women demanded that Schmorak and his colleagues make "special arrangements with the courts not to issue eviction orders on the apartments of soldiers' families." Schmorak wanted to avert the possibility of unpleasant outbreaks "If we do not take steps that prove to those interested parties that the leadership is doing all in its power to deal with the matter in the best possible manner."[73]

Appeals reached Ben-Gurion from the soldiers themselves. One, from a company sergeant-major, informed Ben-Gurion that he was

Poster calling to enlist to save Jews
(*CZA, poster collection*).

voicing the distress of many of the soldiers - in his company. Although it had increased considerably, the army's financial support to the families was still insufficient. Palestinian (Yishuv) soldiers did not benefit from the increase. Unlike British soldiers, who could apply to their local MP, the Palestinian soldiers had only Ben-Gurion and his colleagues in the Yishuv leadership to write to. The soldier's letter continued:

> Obviously, no one could be expected to be a good soldier if he has to worry day and night about his wife and children. I am not asking for increased support from the Yishuv—I am aware of the situation—but I have no doubt that we Hebrew soldiers supply a service in this war which is in no way less worthy than that of others in the British army, and knowing that our families are starving, that they are deteriorating physically . . . this is the worst kind of deprivation."[74]

THE MOBILIZATION AND RESCUE FUND IN 1944

Notwithstanding the failure of the "Solidarity with the Diaspora Month" drive, attempts were made throughout 1944 to increase the fund-raising activities of the Mobilization and Rescue Fund.[75] Organizers of the new drive remained true to the agreements preceding the earlier drive regarding the division between rescue, mobilization, and defense.

At the end of March 1944, arrangements surrounding the fund-raising campaign were widely publicized. The National Council issued a declaration (its wording was submitted to Ben-Gurion for approval) on "the special rescue project" that could "determine the fate of the few survivors: it is an obligation from which there is no exemption." The Mobilization and Rescue Fund would carry out fund-raising, and all the money collected "would be devoted to rescue." The Na-

tional Council announced that there would be rallies in the three main cities, and Ben-Gurion would be the main speaker at the event to be held on Saturday, 1 April, at Tel Aviv's Esther Cinema.[76] Ben-Gurion did indeed deliver a speech on that date in the Tel Aviv movie theater, and the newspapers reported that there was a great throng at the entrance.

Great effort went into organizing and publicizing the fund-raising campaign. It received wide press coverage and this time it encompassed a large section of the local society. Still, it also ended with disappointing results even after the deadline was postponed. The organizers accused the Yishuv leadership, the JAE representatives in the National Council, and Histadrut affiliates of insufficient support to ensure the drive's success.[77] There are a number of possible explanations for the failure, the main reason probably being economic uncertainty. First of all, the campaign was hampered by the Mandatory government's intention to increase direct or indirect taxes. Discussions of this issue created a sense of uncertainty as to the burden that would be shouldered by people of means, as well as by the general public.[78] Second, there was a widespread feeling that economic recession was lurking around the corner. Third, although in 1944 there were clear signs that the war would end in victory, no one knew for certain how long it would take and how much in the way of "emergency rations" one had to reserve. This uncertain atmosphere provided an excuse for those opting out of contributing to the rescue fund, both among the Yishuv's self-employed and well-to-do as well as among the wage earners. In some cases the opting out was mutual, with plant management and workers jointly agreeing not to pay the quotas.

Rabbi Binyamin, one of the leaders of the Al-Domi group, told Ben-Gurion about one such case in the Dead Sea area. He asked Ben-Gurion to exert pressure on the company manager, Moshe Novomeysky, and to force him to stop this disgusting behavior. Together with Rabbi Binyamin, Ben-Gurion invited Novomeyesky to atone for his sins by becoming a fund-raiser.[79] Although typical of the pressure brought to bear by Ben-Gurion himself on the "dodgers," it also exposes the basic weakness of the fund-raisers and the leadership, for whom moral pressure was the main instrument.

A concentrated fund-raising effort in the spring and summer of 1944 did not substantially alter the sources of funding. It showed that such fund-raising campaigns, which obliged the Yishuv to stretch its limbs, were able to reduce somewhat the burden on the Jewish Agency's budget, but they did not exempt it from direct allocations. The Mobilization Fund did not abide by its commitments, and it is worth remembering that the JAE relied on it when transferring interim funding to the emissaries in Istanbul. In fact, beginning in September 1944 the fund transferred no money whatsoever to the JAE.[80]

In discussions in late 1944 and early 1945 on the Mobilization and Rescue Fund, several of the contributors explained that they would "support a fund that provided only for rescue operations. Only for a specific operation, at a specific time . . . only for operations in countries under Nazi control." It was suggested that a six-month agreement be signed; according to estimates at the time, this would take them to the end of the war.[81] Once again there was obvious tension over the various functions of the Mobilization and Rescue Fund. Many people in the Yishuv were not happy

that their money was not earmarked from the start for a clear objective concerning direct aid or rescue for the Jews of Europe.

Was it a serious mistake to combine fund-raising on behalf of soldiers' families and aid and rescue to the Jews of Europe (as opposed to the aid they would receive from the men of the Jewish Brigade in Europe)? This joining of forces actually prevented harmful competition between the two objectives. It also widened the circle of those shouldering the financial burden without affecting support for the soldiers' families and the Haganah. Did funding for rescue operations have to suffer in order not to thwart these objectives? Possibly. It is also possible that separate fund-raising would have meant more money for rescue and less for what was termed "self-defense." Would separate fund-raising drives have resulted in a larger total contribution? It is difficult to say. Further research, especially in the economic area, might provide a more definitive answer.

The results of the fund-raising appeal might have been better had Ben-Gurion exerted pressure on the wealthy of the Yishuv, had he made more speeches or even manned the fund-raising barricades himself, but this probably would not have affected the size of the donations. It is more likely that contributions to the Mobilization and Rescue Fund accurately reflected the desire of the Yishuv's Jews to help and, in particular, their ability to contribute.

13

Fund-raising Campaigns Abroad

Overseas fund-raising focused on the United States, Britain, and South Africa. The JAE also raised funds in Egypt, Australia, and Sweden.[1] Ben-Gurion's parameters for fund-raising efforts were geographically widespread, with the emphasis on specific countries based on previous experience in raising funds to aid persecuted Jewish communities.

COOPERATION WITH THE AMERICAN JEWISH JOINT DISTRIBUTION COMMITTEE

The American Jewish Joint Distribution Committee (JDC) was the main U.S. organization involved in raising funds for Jewish aid and rescue in Europe. A philanthropic body in which assimilated Jewish circles had a considerable influence and with an essentially different in outlook from the JAE, which was Zionist and nationalistic in nature. During the Second World War, however, the JDC was not at all anti-Zionist; despite their differences, there was close cooperation between the two organizations during the second half of the war. The public's impression at the time was that the JDC was conservative and cautious, an organization enmeshed in a "double loyalty" to the United States and Palestine and the Zionist movement and bound by the prohibitions imposed by the Allies on the transfer of funds to Axis countries. These assumptions are not supported by my research into the cooperation that existed between the JDC and the Yishuv leadership.

Ben-Gurion's first meeting with JDC leaders took place during his second wartime visit to the United States. With Rommel's forces approaching El Alamein, Ben-Gurion wanted to mobilize the JDC to help families of the people who would be recruiting during the emergency situation. The JDC responded speedily and allotted fifty thousand Palestinian pounds (two hundred thousand U.S. dollars). Ben-Gurion was very pleased with his success, thanked Paul Baerwald, the JDC president, and instructed Miriam Cohen, his secretary, to make sure the money arrived safely.[2]

Although the JDC did not renege on its promise, Ben-Gurion had reason to be skeptical. A letter from Baerwald to Ben-Gurion detailed the problems involved in cooperation between the JDC and the Yishuv. Baerwald thanked Ben-Gurion for his warm words and asked that the allocation be kept secret.[3] It is not altogether clear what worried Baerwald, since his agreement with Ben-Gurion did not contravene currency regulations and was simply a monetary transfer from a dollar area to a pound sterling area, both of them in Allied territory. He knew that the British and American intelligence services were keeping track of the Yishuv's and Zionist movement's activities and thus may have wished to reassure them that the JDC would not involve itself in illegal activities. Furthermore, Baerwald may have wished to demonstrate what the JDC was risking by agreeing to such a transaction and thus to gain glory for his organization; considerations of prestige were not alien to any organization at the time.

Kaplan, the first to learn of the JDC's promise from Ben-Gurion, was full of praise for his colleague and wrote that he was the only one whose work had "borne fruit, 'which would make it possible to fund recruitment over here,' without having to wait for the results of the [United Jewish Appeal] fund-raising drive." Kaplan informed Ben-Gurion that the JDC's Jerusalem branch was upsetting cooperation with the parent organization. On more than one occasion the Jerusalem branch professed a holier-than-thou attitude, reminding the JDC's New York leaders of things they preferred to forget.

THE JDC AND THE EXTERMINATION REPORT

The possibility of mobilizing the JDC for the cause was broached immediately upon receiving news of the situation in Europe.[4] At JAE sessions and at meetings of the special five-member committee established by Ben-Gurion to deal with child immigration, debates were held on ways to get the JDC involved in aid and rescue activity. Ben-Gurion suggested a pragmatic cooperation, based on the relative advantages of the two organizations—to transfer JDC funds to Europe through the JAE and the Yishuv. Clearly, this was a convenient model for the JAE to work with.

Ben-Gurion acknowledged that the JDC was a valuable source of funding in that it was well endowed and had great logistic potential. He wanted the JDC involved in aid and rescue in Europe through the JAE. Working from a position of strength, Ben-Gurion was able to offer the JDC the services of the JAE because "the JDC has millions that it doesn't know what to do with . . . [and] there is almost no field of activity left to the JDC." These remarks referred to the JDC's limitations as an American Jewish philanthropic organization subject to accusations of a "double loyalty" and bound by the severe regulations prohibiting the transfer of money to Axis countries.

Ben-Gurion tested the bonds of cooperation with the JDC against the JAE's relations with other American Jewish organizations, particularly Zionist organizations. Too much cooperation with the JDC posed an "internal and external risk . . . a big obstacle in our political dispute, and was also [likely] to harm the Zionist movement in America." American Zionists had supported Ben-Gurion's political line at the time of the 1942 Biltmore Conference and he probably did not wish to jeopardize this support. He also wished to avoid direct contact with the JDC branch in Jerusalem.

The feeling of power that motivated Ben-Gurion into outlining this modus operandi was based on the assumption that, if refugee children did indeed arrive from Europe, and if the Yishuv proved it was allocating funds from its own resources for their housing and social integration, a direct appeal could be made to American Jews, who would certainly come round and contribute their fair share. Since this would pose a serious threat to the JDC's financial sources, the JDC could be "blackmailed" into cooperating with the Yishuv. This was part of the ongoing relationship between American Zionists and non-Zionists, whose cooperation was imposed on them by the fact that they all were appealing to the same community of contributors. Kaplan's great satisfaction over the pledged allocation, which implied freedom from dependence on the UJA, was based on the Zionist movement's relative role in the UJA.

From Ben-Gurion's standpoint, the model also involved some risk, in that various American Jewish organizations might infer from the JAE's arrangement with the JDC that it was reconciled to participating in direct activity in Palestine by means of delegates from various organizations and by bypassing the JAE. For Ben-Gurion this was a very real fear, not least because at the time he was engaged in creating tools for action and operational discipline within a fundamentally voluntary society that was also very fragmented politically. He was also aware of the activities of Dr. Judah L. Magnes, . Ben-Gurion believed that some of Magnes's activity had serious political repercussions affecting the JAE. A strengthening of the JDC's Jerusalem branch would have enhanced Magnes's political career in Palestine and his standing in the United States.[5]

The committee responsible for this issue accepted Ben-Gurion's suggestion that an attempt be made to subject the JDC to JAE conditions and to postpone the decision on cooperation until after Kaplan's meeting with JDC representatives in Palestine, so as to clarify the JAE's position.[6] It soon became clear that the JDC held a different view of cooperation with the Jewish Agency.

The JAE's attempt to follow Ben-Gurion's model did not last long. Given the political reality of the time, several of his assumptions were unfounded—in particular, Ben-Gurion's assumption that the JDC would be apprehensive, wishing to avoid any action that might involve a deviation from currency regulations, and would therefore require the Jewish Agency's operational channels proved wrong. It soon emerged that the JDC had already violated the currency regulations by independently transferring aid to occupied Europe from Geneva and Lisbon. Kaplan learned this during his journey to Istanbul. The JDC funded the "settlement tax" and the "deportation tax."[7]

Consequently, at their official meeting on 11 May 1943 with the JDC's Jerusalem branch (consisting of Magnes, Harry Vitals, Julius Simon, and others), the JAE did not propose a model that stressed its superiority. Instead, it proposed setting up a parity committee to discuss all items of aid and rescue concerning the two bodies.[8] Ben-Gurion and Kaplan agreed to forgo the hegemony of the JAE in organizing aid and rescue, provided that money required for transport and ransom plans was transferred. This was more important to them than the hegemony of the Zionist movement, which was a cornerstone of Ben-Gurion's political thinking and action at the time.

RIVALRY WITH MAGNES

In April and May 1943 a number of sessions were held between JAE representatives and the JDC to work out the terms of their cooperation. The JAE's proposal to set up a parity committee boxed the Jerusalem branch into a corner. Its people could no longer claim that the JAE was ready for cooperation solely on its own terms and only from a position of superiority.

In his distress, Magnes penned a long letter to Paul Baerwald in New York asking for instructions. In Magnes's opinion, the JAE's proposal would be beneficial in helping to define the areas of cooperation between the JDC and the JAE. However, he also believed that its realization was likely to adversely affect the JDC's nonpolitical and neutral status. The funding for immigrant refugees was not problematic, in his opinion, since the JAE had always dealt with immigration and the JDC had always been willing to assist it in this endeavor. Here the JDC could continue to be a "willing contributor" if sufficient information was provided. Magnes believed that the plans for rescuing Jews from enemy countries was an altogether more complex issue. He wished to know the JDC's official position concerning these plans and wondered if it was appropriate to participate in discussions about them.

Magnes recommended that the JDC remain firm on one point in any discussions by the parity committee: exclusivity of the JDC's role in supplying regular aid to the Jews still trapped in Europe, or at the very least a clear leadership role. He suggested that Viteles should be the JDC's permanent representative in Istanbul, the locus of aid to Jews in Nazi Europe.[9]

Magnes's letter illustrates a characteristic noticeable in all the activities of the Jerusalem branch of the JDC until the end of the war: the attitude of the JDC's representatives in Palestine was more rigid than that of its regional executive in Europe, and even more so than that of the presidium in New York. Political differences between the JAE and Magnes and his circle apparently exerted a pernicious influence here. For example, even before receiving instructions from New York, Viteles and Magnes responded negatively to the JAE's proposal. They did not wish the JAE to receive undeserved distinction. It would appear that impassioned power struggles are not alien even to confirmed pursuers of peace.[10]

Sometime later, instructions arrived from New York that obliged the Jerusalem branch to act with greater moderation, to look for ways to cooperate with the JAE and to await the arrival of Joseph Schwartz, the head of the JDC in Europe, who was given responsibility for working out the final agreement. The Jerusalem branch announced that in the interim it had agreed to match one Palestinian pound for every pound from the Yishuv. It would appear that it was not only instructions from New York that softened Magnes and his friends but also their fear that the Yishuv was getting organized and conducting fund-raising drives, and that if they did not cooperate they would find themselves outside the circle of activity. The end result was this somewhat "stilted" cooperation, as Gruenbaum termed it.[11]

During his visit to Palestine in June 1943, Menachem Bader learned of the positive signals from the presidium in New York. Detained on the Syrian border while en route to Turkey, he reported on monies that had been approved for payment of bribes in connection with the Europe Plan, mentioned the Egyptian Jewish community's readiness to participate in funding, and recounted positive developments in relations with the JDC: "Item number 7 shows that even the JDC wants to be involved in aid."[12]

THE FIRST AGREEMENT BETWEEN THE JAE AND THE JDC

Schwartz arrived in Palestine in August 1943. An agreement was reached after two rounds of talks with JAE representative Dobkin. The first item concerned aid to the Yemenite Jewish refugees in Aden. It was further agreed that the JDC would allocate thirty-five thousand Palestinian pounds to transport a thousand Jews from Bulgaria once the JAE provided information about the plan and set a departure date. In one section it was agreed that the JDC would allocate "the entire amount required" for leasing a ship to transport six hundred refugees from Spain directly to Palestine, with the JAE arranging immigration certificates for them. Based on an appeal by the Jewish Agency's Immigration Department, the JDC would continue to cover the travel expenses of impoverished Jews from various countries, with the operation conducted out of Schwartz's Lisbon office.

The problematic items were obviously the transfer of funds to occupied Europe and the funding of ransom plans. Schwartz demanded that the ban on money transfers to occupied Europe should be mentioned. However, he and Dobkin figured out how to circumvent it: "The JDC is prepared to place a sum of money, to be repaid in America at the end of the war, at the disposal of people willing to contribute to aid for Jews in occupied Europe." The sum mentioned was between twenty and twenty-five thousand Palestinian pounds a month, and he provided the names of "JDC trustees, based on whose instructions these sums would be deposited in America: [Joseph Joe] Blum in Hungary, Gizi Fleischmann in Slovakia, Vittorio Valobra in Italy, and [Wilhelm] Fildermann's deputy in Romania." Schwartz announced that he would go to Turkey to make arrangements with the local Yishuv emissaries.[13]

A system was set up for transferring funds. The JDC emissaries would borrow money in local currencies from Jews—and occasionally from wealthy non-Jews—inside occupied Europe. They were prepared to undertake repayment of the loans after the war (hence the name "after" [*après* in French] given to the system). Alternatively, they could deposit a sum equal to the value of the loan in Swiss or American banks. The lenders could withdraw their money from these banks after being rescued from the occupied territories (an incentive for lending the money to the JDC in local currency). The loans also helped them to preserve all or part of their capital in the midst of wartime uncertainty.

The JDC thereby avoided the need to smuggle money and did not violate currency laws. The dependence on intermediaries was the system's main flaw. Some of the intermediaries involved in these exchange deals demanded advance payment for their "labor" in foreign currency, often vanishing with the loan itself in addition to their payment. In any event, they were secret partners in operations about which the less that was said the better.[14]

The agreement between Schwartz and the JAE included paragraphs that the JAE had previously suggested back in late April and early May, which the JDC adopted only during Schwartz's visit. It expressed the JAE's repudiation of its intention to dictate conditions to the JDC as well as the JDC's agreement to the compromise it was offered. Schwartz permitted the JAE to go over the heads of the JDC's Jerusalem representatives.[15]

After signing the agreement, Schwartz met with the National Council, the Histadrut Executive Secretariat, and the Rescue Committee. The difference here was obvious: in dealing with these bodies Schwartz mainly fended off criticism and provided information, whereas the JAE was his true partner.[16] In his meetings Schwartz gave a general picture of the JDC's activities and future trends and referred to rescue operations being carried out by the Yishuv at that time. He rejected the severe criticism leveled at the JDC and asserted that his organization was acting in the face of mounting anti-Semitism in the United States, insisting that he had to remain loyal to the U.S. government and to consider American public opinion. If the JDC did not abide by the strict rules of the game, it might jeopardize its relations with authorities and institutions that enabled it to operate in different parts of Europe and outside it. He said that the JDC had participated—and would continue to participate—in funding the transport of Jewish refugees from Europe to Palestine and elsewhere, and in supporting Jews in different temporary locations.

According to data supplied by Yehuda Bauer on the extent of JDC aid at that stage of the war—covering what reached and was channeled through its Geneva branch—it emerges that Saly Mayer received $235,000 in 1942. During 1943 he received $1,588,000. In 1944 the amount sent by the JDC to its Swiss branch was $6,467,000, and during the first months of 1945 an additional $4,600,000 was allocated. The bulk of these sums was meant to fund the upkeep of the twenty-five thousand Jewish refugees who had managed to flee to Switzerland. Another segment was designated for funding undercover rescue operations in the occupied areas and setting the ransom plans in motion. In 1944 $1 million was transferred to support undercover operations in France. An additional $850,000 was sent to Romania, with other sums forwarded to Slovakia, Croatia, and Shanghai. Roughly $6.5 million passed through Switzerland, representing about 41.5 percent of the JDC's funds.[17]

According to figures pertaining to 1942 and 1943, the JDC transferred almost $1,800,000 through Switzerland in aid to Jews in Europe. Although well informed about these amounts as well as other JDC funding channels, Schwartz was nevertheless obliged to listen to a lecture on aid and rescue from Golda Meir, Yosef Sprinzak, and Zalman Rubashow-Shazar, among others. Maintaining his composure and acting with restraint, he did not reveal the fact that just a few days earlier the JDC's areas of activity had been expanded and that he had agreed with the JAE that it's the JDC's funds would be transferred through the JAE into occupied Europe. In his talks with representatives of nonoperational factors, was careful to repeat the JDC's stated position—it would assist every Jew who managed to flee from occupied Europe—and did not so much as hint at his involvement in the funding of semilegal operations behind enemy lines. Like Ben-Gurion and Kaplan, in fending off criticism Schwartz was adept at maneuvering through a complex situation; like them he did not disclose the existence of a sensitive clause in the agreement he had signed with the JAE even though it could have helped him deflect criticism.[18]

Available documentation does not indicate whether Ben-Gurion and Schwartz met, but the former was the first designee of the letter summarizing the meeting between Schwartz and Dobkin on 4 August 1943. It is inconceivable that Ben-Gurion and Kaplan did not have any input in such an important step. It would appear that they were involved in every stage of the discussion, formulated (with Dobkin) the draft of the agreement, and then approved it. The agreement was not presented for discussion either at the JAE meeting on 8 August 1943 (the day after it was signed) or afterward. The matter was finalized in utmost secrecy, with the only persons guiding and approving it being Kaplan and Ben-Gurion, plus a handful of others who may have been in on the secret.[19]

It was assumed in the Yishuv that Schwartz was conducting an independent policy and that he was more courageous and freer than his New York colleagues. Sharett tried to help him dispel the reservations of the JDC's senior officials in New York by instructing Nahum Goldmann to explain that, although several British and American officials in Istanbul knew all about the illegal operation being conducted there and in Geneva, they had done nothing to thwart it[20] and indeed had even assisted in the illegal transfer of funds. The Yishuv suggested to the JDC different methods of camouflaging money transfers.[21]

In October 1943 the JDC began sending to Palestine twenty thousand Palestinian pounds per month, allocations that were to be transferred to occupied Europe. This was substantial assistance to the Istanbul aid operation, constituting about half the Yishuv's monthly allocation for rescue activities.[22]

That month the JAE charged a subcommittee with examining the overall relationship with the JDC. It is not known if the increase in support was contingent upon setting up the committee. It is possible that the agreement was contingent upon agreeing to part of the JDC's repeated demand to be given responsibility for the care of distressed Jews. In his letter to Baerwald, Magnes proposed that fulfillment of this demand be a condition of the agreement with the JAE.

Amendments by the U.S. Treasury Department to regulations facilitating the transfer of funds outside the United States were an additional factor influencing the rules of the game between the JDC and the JAE. The amendments enabled the JDC to act legally and with greater freedom, and gave added weight to its demand to return to the traditional division of responsibility: the JDC would be active in occupied countries, while the JAE would restrict itself to helping Jews who reached Palestine. The JDC's demand

was debated in the Yishuv and by Zionist movement members, reflecting a definite power struggle between the JDC and the JAE.

Nevertheless, cooperation between the two remained unaffected. Good working relationships continued to exist between the two organizations, as did efforts to camouflage the objectives of the JDC allocations. Thus, Schwartz cabled Kaplan that as of December the JDC had approved a monthly allocation of twenty thousand Palestinian pounds (eighty thousand U.S. dollars) for "special aid operations in Palestine."[23]

Ben-Gurion resigned from the JAE at the end of October. He still chaired the meeting that decided to appoint a subcommittee to examine relations with the JDC, but most of the discussion took place after his resignation. Nevertheless he received regular reports, inspected protocols, and was involved in the matter by virtue of the fact that Sharett, Kaplan, and others asked for his opinion and instructions.[24]

At the beginning of 1944, after an easing of American currency regulations went into effect, the JDC again demanded that it be put in charge of activity in occupied countries. A further possibility for cooperation—sending food parcels, medicine, and clothing to Europe—was examined. The JDC had considerable experience in this sphere, and several JAE members feared that this might sideline them.

A proposal that the JAE establish a world Jewish umbrella aid organization was examined. Also considered was the question of whether it was appropriate for the JAE to include the JDC in discussions concerning the demand for future reparations from Germany and its dependent states,[25] and on aid to Jewish refugees in Aden, whose condition had deteriorated as a result of a typhus epidemic. The political and legal sensitiveness of the JDC's activity prompted the two sides to keep JDC-affiliated activities secret, in accordance with Baerwald's request to Ben-Gurion in August 1942.[26] This may have given the false impression that ties had been severed between the two organizations.

A CRISIS IN THE RELATIONSHIP
WITH THE JDC

Both sides wanted to help Jews and, to this end, they needed each other, but their working relations were accompanied by attempts to block each other's access to positions of influence whenever one of the sides felt sufficiently confident of its ability to shake off cooperation.

Thus, once the currency regulations had eased up by the end of 1943 and the War Refugee Board had been established in early 1944, the JDC felt it could do without the services of the JAE.[27] The administration's three most senior ministers were included on the board, which was authorized to establish branches in all the neutral countries and was permitted to transfer money and aid to the occupied areas. For a time it appeared that the War Refugee Board would do a better job in the role assigned to the JAE, making it unnecessary to go through the latter for the transfer of money and aid. It also gave certain legitimacy to the independent activities of the JDC.

By June–July 1944 it became clear that the American administration had experienced no substantial change in attitude. In the end, the Brand affair revealed the ineffectiveness of the War Refugee Board. But until this fact became widely known and its significance was understood by the JDC, it was easy to discern a deep crisis between it and the JAE in Jerusalem and Istanbul.

In May 1944 Kaplan met with the JDC heads in Palestine. He asked them to fund a special project to rescue twenty-six hundred Jews who were candidates for immigration on the *Milca* and the *Maritza*. He mentioned that it had been agreed with Schwartz that in August and September the JDC would transfer to the JAE a monthly sum of twenty thousand Palestinian pounds for aid and rescue and would bear the full cost of sea transportation from the ports of occupied countries to Turkish ports, the upkeep of the Jewish refugees in Turkey, and their transfer to Palestine. The Yishuv emissaries had already transported more than a thousand people by sea, said Kaplan, and now they were waiting for authorization to transport another twenty-six hundred. The cost was estimated at two hundred thousand Palestinian pounds. There was already a feeling in the air that the JDC planned to act independently out of Istanbul. Kaplan issued an overt threat, warning that if the JDC did not respond positively to the JAE's proposal, he would turn to the American Zionists.

Kaplan "went over the edge," and it is worth dwelling on the meaning of his threat. Most of the JAE's current budget consisted of financial contributions collected by the UJA in the United States. They were also the source of the JDC's budget. This appeal was the result of the agreement between American Jewish fund-raising organizations, including Zionist ones. In fact, Kaplan was warning the JDC that the Zionists would violate the fund agreement and raise funds independently in the United States. The fact that the JAE and the JDC shared the same financial source sheds a particular light on their disagreements; in one sense each wanted their fair share of the budgetary pie.

After Kaplan left the meeting, the JDC's Jerusalem representatives formulated their recommendations and cabled them to Schwartz in Lisbon. They adopted the principle that no connection should be made between the tendency to alter the agreement and the immediate need to fund the immigration of twenty-six hundred Jews on the *Milca*, the *Maritza*, or other ships. The Jerusalem branch recommended that the JDC participate in funding the immigration of all those unable to pay their own way. They did not specify the desirable level of participation, stressing that money would only be transferred following a careful examination of the operation's details.

However, the JDC's representatives rejected Kaplan's threat to bypass them and appeal directly to the American Zionists. They suggested that the JDC dissociate itself from the JAE and establish an independent system to aid the Jews in Europe and those who had reached Turkey. They also proposed that the JDC fund and arrange independently the immigration of Jews from

Turkey to Palestine. The proposal would receive the help of the U.S. administration's War Refugee Board. Once it was established, the agreement between the JDC and the JAE would be canceled and the twenty-thousand-pound monthly allocation would cease. These recommendations were signed by Judah L. Magnes and Reuven Reznick, the JDC representative in Istanbul, who was visiting Palestine at the time. They were made known to Kaplan and probably also to others in the Yishuv leadership.[28]

At the beginning of June emissaries in Istanbul reported that the JDC was planning an independent operation there, which caused a furor. The Histadrut secretariat was considering a proposal to conduct a campaign against the JDC in the United States. It decided to pressure Magnes into returning to the previous modus operandi.[29] Kaplan raised the subject with the JAE, describing the "bitter argument" between the JAE and the JDC, and told of the JAE's effort to bypass the JDC's Jerusalem branch and to contact Schwartz in Lisbon directly.

Kaplan also described efforts to reduce the tension. The JDC's Jerusalem representatives suggested that Magnes leave for Istanbul and formulate his opinion once there. They tried to minimize the significance of their original intention to disassociate themselves from the JAE and expressed surprise at the virulence of the reaction their efforts aroused. Despite Magnes's declaration to the Histadrut delegation that he was actually "in complete accord with them," this is not reflected in the recommendations he and his colleagues sent to Schwartz.

The Yishuv leadership was preoccupied at the time with the Brand affair. In June Sharett returned from his meeting with Brand in Aleppo and transmitted information about Grosz's part in the mission. While Magnes and his colleagues had reached the breaking point in their dealings with the Palestine leadership, Schwartz (their section head) together with Sharett and Hirschmann (of the War Refugee Board) were preparing for a

semi-independent operation to rescue the Jews of Hungary and the remaining Jews of Europe. That operation in Cairo was diametrically opposed to the policies of the Jerusalem branch.

To briefly review the main points of the proposal, Sharett, Schwartz, and Hirschmann examined a plan to establish a large fund to cover the cost of bribes. These funds would be paid to Nazi leaders if it transpired that Britain and the United States ultimately rejected the Brand mission. They raised the proposal with Lord Moyne, Britain's colonial minister, and Pinkney Tuck, who was responsible for U.S. interests in Cairo, in order to determine whether their governments would agree to turn a blind eye to such an initiative.

American intelligence records reveal that this possibility was discussed in Cairo. According to these records, Schwartz and Hirschmann included Magnes in this move. On 22 June 1944 Hirschmann informed Magnes (through Tuck) of the Cairo talks. On June 24 Schwartz set out for Jerusalem on his way to Turkey, met Magnes there, and apparently told him what was then being discussed by the JDC, the War Refugee Board, and the Jewish Agency.[30] This step obviously greatly embarrassed Magnes and his colleagues in Jerusalem.

When the JAE considered the suggestion that Magnes should travel to Istanbul, Ben-Gurion, Kaplan, and Sharett knew that Magnes was not the one who ultimately decided and that his superior, Joe Schwartz, called the shots. In order to help Magnes climb down from his tree, the JAE decided to support his Istanbul trip, which would also scotch rumors that it was being thwarted "for political reasons." There was a fear that the JAE might be accused of attempting to hinder JDC procedures, even at the risk of damaging rescue operations, because of political and ideological differences. The JAE also decided that Kaplan and Gruenbaum, who were about to depart for Istanbul, would review cooperation with the JDC there. In the meantime, the JAE would bear the responsibility for funding the immigration of four thousand Jews.

Thus, through its contacts with Schwartz and Magnes's invitation to Istanbul, the JAE drove the JDC Jerusalem branch into a corner. Ben-Gurion even suggested placing more pressure on the JDC leaders in New York through the local JAE branch.[31] There was also the lingering feeling that the JAE leaders found Baerwald and Schwartz easier to get along with.[32]

Kaplan and Magnes traveled to Istanbul, where their meetings were colored by the difficulties surrounding the Brand affair and the ongoing deportations from Hungary. The JDC, including Magnes, were privy to the affair and its developments. Magnes even brought back updates on the German offer to meet with Bader and reported to Ben-Gurion on negotiations between the JDC and the JAE in Istanbul, estimating that it would end in an agreement.[33]

The atmosphere in Istanbul—the hope that some of Hungary's Jews might be smuggled to Black Sea ports; the presence of Schwartz and Hirschmann; and the fateful matters to be resolved—discouraged intensification of the struggle between the two bodies. If Magnes had gone to Istanbul to gather data and impressions prior to severing relations, he returned with insufficient "ammunition." He saw that the local emissaries were carrying out their mission in accordance with the highest moral standards and with relative efficiency. The visit revealed that in certain areas the JDC was still dependent on the JAE. The limitations imposed on Hirschmann from Washington were by then an open secret among the rescue emissaries in Turkey. It weakened attempts by the JDC's Jerusalem branch to dissolve the partnership with the JAE for rescuing Europe's Jews.[34]

THE SECOND AGREEMENT BETWEEN THE JDC AND THE JAE

An agreement was worked out during Kaplan's Istanbul meetings with Schwartz and other JDC representatives (Magnes, Viteles, and Reznik) that extended the cooperation between the two groups. Under the terms of the agreement, the total cost of funding sea transport for seven thousand Jews was split between the JDC and the Jewish Agency according to a 70–75/25–30 ratio.[35] The Jewish Agency welcomed increases in aid by the JDC, and a regional division was to be implemented by taking into account the relative advantages of the two bodies. The JAE would be dominant in Istanbul, while the JDC would oversee operations in Geneva and Lisbon. (Saly Mayer acted on behalf of the JDC in Geneva for the entire period and Schwartz was based in Lisbon.) The JDC announced its willingness to fund *tiyulim* ("excursion"; Hebrew for "smuggling Jews from place to place") and, where possible, to also pay to have Jews taken from occupied Europe. The JAE would continue to fund self-defense in all countries. Efforts were in progress at the time to establish a base camp and headquarters at a meeting point along the Yugoslav-Hungarian border. Lastly, this agreement would remain in force for three to four months, after which it would be reevaluated based on events. During this time the JDC would continue to allocate twenty thousand Palestinian pounds for rescue through the Yishuv.[36] The possibility of establishing a body to coordinate the activities of the War Refugee Board, the JDC, and the JAE was also discussed. This body would convene at regular intervals to exchange views on what had been done and what still needed be done, but it could not decide on operations.[37]

All the clauses required the approval of the parent offices. Kaplan raised them with the JAE, and they were also discussed in part by the Rescue Committee. The JDC representatives required the approval from New York. Schwartz came to Palestine and ironed out the final details with Kaplan.[38] The JAE approved in principal the proposals Kaplan presented, and Ben-Gurion asked for them in writing. It was also decided to establish a JAE subcommittee consisting of Ben-Gurion, Kaplan, Gruenbaum, and Shapira. Such a lineup reflected the importance of the subject and its complexity.[39]

Schwartz was also in Palestine to sort out his relations with the JDC branch in Jerusalem. To them he was "too Zionist," and for him they staffed a subsidiary branch with advisers whose opinions could be accepted or rejected. He felt they were too involved in local politics, which colored their judgment with respect to relations with the JAE. Schwartz presented them with the Istanbul agreement and clarified their position and role as he viewed them. He told the *Davar* reporter about "a ratified agreement" between the JDC and the JAE, mentioned "complete harmony with the JAE," and denied "all so-called ill feeling."[40]

At that time combined rescue efforts were being made by the JAE, the JDC, and the World Jewish Congress in Switzerland, Sweden, Spain, and Portugal.[41] In addition, the JDC and the JAE's Immigration Department, headed by Eliyahu Dobkin, had reached a compromise with respect to immigration: the JDC would deal with legal immigration and the JAE would handle illegal immigration.[42]

In Lisbon Dobkin tried to establish a joint committee to deal with refugees from enemy countries. On 13 July 1944 he succeeded in getting representatives of the World Jewish Congress and the JDC to agree to the establishment of a joint committee.[43] The agreement, however, did not last long. Another development proved more important. About two weeks earlier Dobkin had managed to persuade the JDC representatives to allocate two hundred thousand Palestinian pounds to the JAE and an additional half million Swiss francs for financing the transportation of refugees. He met with them in Lisbon, together with representatives of the World Jewish Congress, who were helpful in doing the persuading.[44] Given the tense relations with the JDC, it was a big achievement.

Nonetheless, suspicions and the desire to shove the other parties aside had not dissipated. The JDC's Jerusalem branch continued to be re-served over cooperation with the JAE. Indeed, on 11 October 1944 the JDC head office in New York announced to its Jerusalem branch that it would no longer support immigration operations from Romania and Bulgaria, since the JAE had violated the Schwartz/Kaplan agreement by not including the JDC in its preparations and failing to consult with it on issues of shipping security. The decision came after the Jerusalem branch had notified New York that "small Turkish and Bulgarian ships would continue to sail without safe passage."[45]

Magnes rushed to inform the JAE of the JDC's decision and told New York that he had indications that the JAE was not acting sincerely, and that it had never intended to abide by the conditions of the agreement; even before the announcement from the New York branch, the JAE had discussed the possibility of transporting the refugees without help from the JDC or anyone else. The JAE continued to ask the JDC for a monthly allocation of 20,000 Palestinian pounds (eighty thousand U.S. dollars), as agreed, but was also looking into the possibility of participating in rescue operations in Europe, which was not in the spirit of the agreement.[46]

Indeed, in late October the JAE began to examine preparations for the end of the war. All the organizations involved in aid and rescue, including the JDC, were discussed.[47] The trend was obvious: it was natural for the JAE to want to increase its involvement in immigration activity, its primary area of interest. At the same time, it was stipulated that the JAE must not begin a "war with the JDC" nor allow itself to be dragged into such a war. The reference was to a struggle whose "natural" field of operation would be the activity among Jewish survivors in the liberated territories. Everyone who read the data on the size of aid extended by the JDC understood why it was imperative that the JAE avoid such a confrontation or at least postpone it as long as possible. The figures presented the following picture:

Expenses in Palestinian Pounds for Transportation of Immigrants and JDC Participation
(to end of September 1944)

	Total Expenses	JDC Payment	Participation
Total expenditure on immigrants minus 1943 expense	293,447 24,800	89,364	
1944 expenses	268,647	89,364	
Additional: transfer of immigrants from Turkey (to end of June)	81,739	74,210	
	350,386	163,574	46.6%
Additional: transfer of immigrants (July–September)	9,476		
	359,862	163,574	45.4%
Additional: JDC payments in October on account of 1944 expenses	975		
	359,862	203,549	56.5%
Additional: JDC payments in Switzerland	52,125	52,125	
	411,987	255,674	62.0%
Additional: cost of transfer and upkeep of Yemenite Aden Jews	28,723	3,006	
	440,710	258,680	58.6%

Until the end of September 1944, the JDC funded over half the cost of transporting immigrants. Any confrontation between the JAE and the JDC would have had serious negative repercussion on the aid and rescue enterprise. There was no point in trying to convert the JDC members into enthusiastic Zionists. There was also the danger of Jewish communities being dragged into the struggle and ending or drastically reducing their support for the JAE.

It was decided to step up JAE involvement in aid operations in order to minimize the JDC's influence in the liberated territories. There was also a proposal to establish a Jewish umbrella organization to handle issues of aid and rescue, the assumption being that this would eliminate the JDC's exclusivity and reduce its influence.[48]

The JAE was aware that positions of leadership, organizations, and movements in liberated Europe were in a state of collapse, leaving a vacuum that it didn't want the JDC to fill or even dominate. It understood the connection between rescue and economic or other types of support, on the one hand, and the emotional state of people being helped, on the other. It therefore strove to increase its material aid as well. Although the JAE did not want a confrontation with the JDC, it hinted that, if it were coerced, it would not retreat. At the end of 1944, when much of Europe had been liberated, the JAE decided to alter its primary objective from physical rescue to rescuing "the Zionist soul." It sought to redefine the division of functions between it and the JDC, while realizing that such a procedure could lead to confrontation.

Contacts between the JDC and the JAE remained tense. The JDC claimed that the JAE was overstepping the mark by sending aid to Jewish refugees through the Polish National Council. The JDC also complained that one of the arguments voiced at meetings of the Mobilization and Rescue Fund was that the JDC was not assisting in aid and rescue operations.[49] Even when funds were transferred, the JDC did not conceal its fear that the JAE was submitting false reports with respect to expenses incurred in operating the *Smyrna*. The JDC even threatened to deduct the current sum from future payments if its suspicions were confirmed.[50]

In late October the JDC informed the Yishuv that it was canceling the Istanbul agreement. Kaplan instructed Ehud Avriel not to undertake any new commitments regarding transportation without consulting with him; since 1 November the JDC was not transferring its share for funding the ships and he was not about to fund the *Salah-a-din*, which was in action at the time.[51]

Despite all this, the JDC and the JAE continued to cooperate in a limited fashion. For example, during his visit to Bulgaria, Ben-Gurion initiated an aid program with the local Jews. He made similar gestures during his stopover in Istanbul on his way home, as well as during his visits to DP (displaced persons) camps after the war. In all three cases, compromise was dictated by reality.[52]

THE THIRD AGREEMENT BETWEEN THE JAE AND THE JDC

By the beginning of 1945 relations had improved, thanks in part to the realization that the ultimate objective of both organizations was caring for Jews, the good relationship between Schwartz and the JAE, and Nahum Goldmann's conciliatory overtures in the United States. These also affected the atmosphere in Palestine.

Following a series of meetings between representatives from the JAE (Kaplan, Dobkin, and Shapira) and the JDC (Magnes, Passman, and Simon), a new memorandum was signed in mid-February 1945 reaffirming cooperation between the two institutions. It was decided to establish a six-member parity committee that would convene twice a month to discuss urgent cases. Moreover, JDC aid to different countries would now be conducted through local committees consisting of representatives from all the various groups, including Zionists. The new parity committee in Jerusalem could express its reservations concerning the composition of the committees, and there would be no discrimination in the distribution of aid based on ideological grounds.

Both sides agreed to enlist international help in funding physical assistance to the refugees, with the JDC's and the JAE's own funds promoting a Jewish lifestyle based on education, vocational training, and so forth. The JDC would support schools operating "in the spirit of Judaism and the Hebrew language," and the JAE would supply books and teachers. The JAE would bear the organizational costs of training refugees to adapt to life in Palestine. The JDC agreed to include people from the Yishuv among its first emissaries to the liberated regions.[53]

The agreement was achieved partly in the wake of Ben-Gurion's visit to Bulgaria. First, the two bodies had cooperated in supplying emergency aid. Second, it was obvious that they shared a common enemy in Communism. Ben-Gurion confirmed his fear of the Communists' tendency to eradicate Jewish life. They were a menace both to the Zionists and the JDC. Ben-Gurion was keenly aware of the danger that any laxity or infighting on the part of Jewish organizations would permit the Communists to take control of the Jewish community. The new agreement was again marked by a broad spectrum of opinion, from calls for confrontation with the JDC to appeals against jeopardizing the aid program.[54] The wording of the agreement shows that a pragmatic desire for cooperation won the day.

Throughout this period both sides sought ways to enhance their positions. Ben-Gurion was forced to retreat very quickly and quietly from his original intention of dictating the format of the relations after it transpired that such an approach could jeopardize JDC funding. He and his colleagues were also compelled to "swallow" Magnes as JDC representative in Palestine despite his other political activities, which were perceived as dangerous and inimical. They did not even insist that the JDC operate in Palestine through the JAE

and not its own branch, where the agency's bitter rival, Magnes, was in charge. As far as Ben-Gurion and his colleagues were concerned, this meant relinquishing the crucial principle of authority. Such a concession illustrates the JAE's and Ben-Gurion's limited powers and how little space they had for maneuvering around the other players in the field. The JDC went through a similar process. It also gradually realized that it had no alternative but to cooperate with the JAE. In the end, the realization by the two organizations that neither could achieve anything without the help of the other is what forced them to cooperate.

THE MISTRUST OF SOUTH AFRICAN JEWRY

Before and during the Second World War the Jewish community in South Africa was second, after the United States, in its contributions to Zionist funds. According to Dina Porat and Gideon Shimoni, this community contributed a total of some 2.8 million U.S. dollars (700,000 Palestinian pounds) during the Second World War. I will attempt to resolve the question as to whether it contributed as generously to rescue, since such activity might have required that donors violate the prohibition against money transfers to Axis countries and territories under their control.[55] I shall also try to assess the impact of Ben-Gurion and his colleagues in mobilizing this community to fund rescue operations.

In February 1943 the Yishuv discussed the need to get South Africa's Jews involved in rescue funding, and it was even suggested that Ben-Gurion go to South Africa to launch fund-raising drives. It was a time when Ben-Gurion and Kaplan were subject to heavy pressure to increase Yishuv and Zionist movement allocations for rescue activity.[56]

Ben-Gurion did not travel to South Africa, but an appeal was made to the Jewish community to contribute to rescue expenditures. South Africa agreed to allocate forty thousand Palestinian pounds to bring children from Europe to

Palestine.[57] An additional appeal was made in May 1943—immediately following the Histadrut's fund-raising campaign, in which workers were asked to contribute one day's pay to demonstrate the Yishuv's volunteer spirit—asking the Jews of South Africa to act in a similar fashion. The appeal was sent to Louis Arye Pincus, a member of South Africa's Zionist Socialist party (who in the sixties became chairman of the JAE). Pincus submitted it as a memorandum to the South African Jewish War Appeal, an emergency committee established in South Africa to aid the Jews of Europe.

It was already clear that South Africa's Jews were very distrustful. The South African Jewish War Appeal hastened to cable Ben-Gurion that it had indeed decided to allocate twenty-five hundred Palestinian pounds on condition that Ben-Gurion or Kaplan personally guarantee that this allocation would only fund rescue and would not be distributed along party lines. It even set conditions for modest sums. Zvi Maimon, Ben-Gurion's secretary, handed the cable to Kaplan in Ben-Gurion's absence. The next day Kaplan's secretary replied to Zvi Maimon that Kaplan was prepared to sign a guarantee, but that Ben-Gurion would have to be consulted.[58]

In June 1943 the Yishuv already knew that the South African Jewish community had collected forty thousand Palestinian pounds (eight per person) earmarked for transporting rescued Jews. It is not certain if the allocation was made after the JAE had stated the conditions. Based on the following undated letter in Ben-Gurion's files, it would appear that he asked the JAE whether it was interested in the Revisionists participating in fund-raising and whether the JAE would also handle the rescue of Revisionists:

We made no formal decision at our last meeting regarding our reply to the Revisionists. I'm afraid I'm to blame for this because I forgot to bring the matter to a vote. However, I feel it is undesirable to leave the Revisionists without an answer and plan to ask each member [of the JAE] to let me have written confirmation of his affirmative response, namely, that we are willing to include the Revisionists in fund-raising operations and to share funds with them.[59]

Ben-Gurion's appeal to the JAE conforms to South African Jewry's wish to prevent discrimination arising from party affiliation. It can be assumed that the JAE complied with the South African and Revisionist request in order to facilitate the June allocation.

Around this time the JAE decided that it was necessary to send one of its leaders to allay the suspicions of the South African Jews and to encourage them to contribute to rescue operations. Since it was not possible—for fear of leaks—to send a written report of all the aid and rescue operations, a personal visit was needed. Yitzhak Gruenbaum was selected because Ben-Gurion and Kaplan were unable to absent themselves from the Yishuv and Sharett was engaged in other missions. Gruenbaum held fourth place in the undeclared hierarchy. He may have been selected because of his many ex-Polish acquaintances and admirers in South Africa, as well as his position as chairman of the Rescue Committee, some of whose members were not represented in the Zionist coalition of the JAE.

At the JAE meeting held three days before his departure, Gruenbaum announced his intention to consult with Ben-Gurion, Kaplan, and others. Ben-Gurion, in turn, said that he wanted "to speak with Gruenbaum about the rescue issue and the kind of money he could ask for it."[60] It not inconceivable that Ben-Gurion suggested to Gruenbaum that he try to extract from the South Africans a promise that they would take part in efforts to raise the large sums required for the ransom plans.

Gruenbaum arrived in South Africa in early August and met the community's Zionist and non-Zionist leaders, from Field Marshal Smuts to "the Jewish man in the street." Gruenbaum Jewish counterparts usually made a point of interrogating him at length. Some of them did not like the JAE's central role in the rescue operations. Gruenbaum tried to assuage their suspicions by explaining that the Rescue Committee consisted of Yishuv representatives from all walks of life. He described ongoing efforts to institutionalize cooperation with the JDC and the rescue emissaries in Istanbul and Geneva, stressing that for the time being the Yishuv held overall responsibility for rescue operations. He promised his listeners that any monies they contributed would not be used for purposes other than rescue.

Gruenbaum cabled regular reports on his activities, which were inevitably passed along to Ben-Gurion. Gruenbaum had succeeded in persuading the local emergency committee and the South African Zionist Federation's Executive Committee to allocate a monthly sum for rescue, an achievement that filled him with hope. In his reports he stressed that support would increase if the Yishuv leadership could demonstrate that it could actually save Jews.[61] This was around the time of the Europa Plan, and the optimistic prognosis prompted the Yishuv leadership to send Gruenbaum a series of cables with suggestions and requests. As mentioned above, Ben-Gurion asked him to try and get the Jews of South Africa to raise the ransom money for the Europe Plan.

Gruenbaum discussed all the proposals and requests with "a number of members" of South Africa's Jewish leadership. He again reported that the South Africans had decided to allocate thirty thousand Palestinian pounds for rescue operations until January 1944, stressing that this was not at the expense of money promised for the transportation of children. It may have been intended to cover a portion of the ransom.[62]

Nevertheless, Nicolai Kirchner, chairman of the South African Zionist Federation, advised Gruenbaum against making a definitive allusion to the sums required for rescue. It would seem that the Jews of South Africa were not inclined to take upon themselves the main brunt of funding questionable and very costly operations, such as the ransom plans. They were prepared to contribute "their fair share" in the form of a monthly allocation.[63]

Gruenbaum felt that he had accomplished his objective only after signing the agreement with South African Jewry's emergency committee. From clauses in the agreement one learns that the South Africans' suspicions had not disappeared. According to the agreement, no discrimination would be exercised in distributing funds and the JAE would continue to allocate money for rescue from its own resources. It would announce that the Jews of South Africa were also participating in the funding and would open the books for audit to any of their representatives. The South Africans promised to send an immediate allocation of thirty thousand Palestinian pounds in addition to the forty thousand they had already promised for the children's transport.[64] The agreement was approved and the promised money began to arrive shortly after Gruenbaum's return.[65]

Gruenbaum had not succeeded in breaking down the barrier of mistrust. The Jews of South Africa could have contributed more money. He insulted the local community's pro-Soviet circles, and it appears that the ensuing controversy did not make for a sympathetic atmosphere.[66] In various discussions following his return, there was outspoken criticism over the discrepancy between the South African community's financial capacity and its contributions. There was also resentment at the South Africans' demand for guarantees of success and receipts to prove that funds really did reach their objective. The demands showed that they had failed to grasp the intricacies of the rescue operations; clearly, Winninger, Popescu, Bandi Grosz, and their colleagues did not keep account books. The secrecy of the rescue operations was a stumbling block to Gruenbaum's efforts to placate his counterparts in South Africa.[67]

SOFTENING UP THE SOUTH AFRICAN POSITION

Kirchner visited Palestine at the end of 1943 and the start of 1944, having been invited in August 1943. It was suggested that he also travel to Istanbul to take a close look at the emissaries and the enormity of their task. During his visit the Yishuv tried to persuade him of the need for increased contributions from the South African Jewish community. Kaplan and Gruenbaum did most of the persuading, their efforts directed mainly at increasing the monthly allocation and unfreezing the funds that were being withheld because no children had as yet been rescued. Kirchner promised to cable Kaplan immediately following his return to South Africa and to determine the likelihood of the South African community continuing its allocations for at least another six months. A positive answer would enable Kaplan to allocate interim funding from JAE resources.[68]

Kirchner was criticized for presenting the fate of the Europe's Jews as being the concern of the solely of the Yishuv, not of all Jewry in the free world, but all efforts at persuasion produced nothing beyond promises.[69] There is no direct evidence of a meeting between Kirchner and Ben-Gurion, who, having resigned from the JAE, was not in a position of leadership at the time. They could have met, since they did share a working relationship.[70] An indication of this can be found in the cables of support Ben-Gurion received from South African Zionist groups, attesting to the fact that Kirchner had acquainted them with Ben-Gurion's position.[71]

Kirchner's attempts at getting the agreement changed and expanded were not easy. In April the South African Zionist Federation's leaders announced to the JAE that the local Revisionist leaders were spreading rumors that their people were being discriminated against in rescue operations. The Revisionists said that they were being forced to purchase and fund their own ships to rescue their people. The JAE was alarmed. Such rumors could hinder efforts at getting the Jews of South Africa to fund rescue plans. It immediately sent out detailed cables in an attempt to refute the accusations of the Revisionists. A typical cable ran: "[Wolfgang] von Weisel's statement is completely distorted. Our Palestine offices organized transportation and we covered the cost."[72] The South African Zionist Federation's Executive Council felt that cables were not sufficient. They demanded that a senior member of the JAE—either Ben-Gurion or Sharett—visit South Africa. Peace would not be restored otherwise, and it would also adversely affect the 1944 Keren Hayesod (PFF) appeal.[73]

In Ben-Gurion's office, the leaders discussed who should go. Sharett was not in Palestine. Ben-Gurion did not feel good about going himself. Two other candidates were David Horowitz of the Finance and Planning Department or Dov Joseph of the Political Department. In mid-June they again discussed the matter in the JAE, but a suitable candidate had still not been found.[74] It became clear that the South Africans were determined not to renew their support. Further efforts at persuasion by Gruenbaum proved fruitless.[75]

Some time later the South African Zionist Federation belatedly began to examine information it had received at the end of May. At the time Sharett had informed Kirchner that Ira Hirschmann and the War Refugee Board were preparing to persuade the Allies to assist in obtaining transportation for Jews out of Turkey. This information was designed to show the federation that it was possible to rescue many Jews as a result of its financial contributions.[76]

The South African Zionist Federation wanted more details and simultaneously renewed its invitation to Ben-Gurion to visit South Africa in order "to describe and analyze the situation and to establish contact." Ben-Gurion immediately replied that "on account of the situation I shall not be able to leave Palestine for the next four months," but he promised that Joseph would leave immediately for South Africa.[77] These cables were exchanged at a time when the convoluted Brand affair was reaching its climax. Within a few days the appropriate permits were obtained and Joseph set out for South Africa.

Joseph's journey was designed to coax Smuts into renewing his support for the JAE's political program, to halt erosion within the local Jewish community as a result of the Revisionists' activities and, naturally, to prompt the community to renew its financial support, especially for funding emigration from Turkey. Dr. Joseph held a regular round of meetings, including one with Smuts. The Emergency Committee and the South African Zionist Federation cabled reports to Palestine Joseph's efforts at calming the situation and clarifying the JAE's positions.[78]

On the contributions front, there were positive results thanks to Joseph's visit. The greatest impact was his the news of his strengthening of relations between the JAE and the JDC as the main players in the rescue operations, with the Emergency Committee basically powerless. It had erred in predicting that the war would end by the beginning of 1944, and this error led it to assume that it was capable of helping the Jews of Europe on its own. The emergency committee was now afraid to make another mistake and thereby find itself outside the rescue loop for reasons that might appear petty. It had collected five hundred thousand Palestinian pounds to aid the Jews of Europe, yet it could do nothing without the JAE's input.

The emergency committee contacted the JAE and announced that it had been decided at a meeting with Dr. Joseph that it would renew cooperation with the JAE in the area of refugee aid. The committee asked the JAE to consult with it "whenever it consulted with the JDC,"[79] to which the JAE immediately cabled its agreement. The South Africans announced that they would participate in funding the transport of twenty-three hundred refugees from Turkey to Palestine and agreed to send thirty-five thousand Palestinian pounds for this purpose immediately. There were some conditions, however, reflecting the lingering distrust that had not been completely allayed: the JAE would provide the committee with receipts for its expenditure and official confirmation that the refugees were ready to sail and that all official arrangements had been made. The committee also demanded a declaration that it was a third partner in the operation, together with the JDC and the JAE. It announced that its part in the funding would be 10 percent of the sum allocated by the JDC, and stated that it was prepared to allocate five thousand Palestinian pounds for the rescue of rabbis and yeshiva students.

The JAE immediately cabled its agreement to these conditions, announcing that according to its calculations "35,000 Palestinian pounds were the equivalent of a third of the estimated costs for October–December," and asked for the money to be sent promptly. The JAE added that some changes were possible in the operation, and asked to know the extent of the committee's possible future participation. Sometime later Kaplan sent the emergency committee a long letter surveying the issues of immigration and funding. He wrote that the JAE was adhering to the agreement and was not practicing a double standard in the choice of immigrants. He also wrote that there were many requests being made to the Palestine offices in Balkan countries, where Ben-Gurion was currently visiting and encouraging immigration.[80]

The renewed support of South Africa's Jews for JAE aid and rescue operations did not eradicate their mistrust. This can be explained by the structure of South Africa's Jewish community and the relations between the various Zionist parties there. It can be stated that the South African community denied money collected for the Jews of Europe to people involved in rescue activity. This affair clearly illustrates the extent to which the Yishuv and the Zionist movement did not "lord it over" the Jewish expense budget.

FEEBLE ASSISTANCE
FROM BRITAIN'S JEWS

According to available documentation, the financial support of the Jewish community in Britain for aid and rescue totaled about forty thousand Palestinian pounds. This was minute given the size of the community and the fact that an important branch of the JAE and a prestigious branch of the Zionist movement were headquartered in England. Britain's Jewish community was far more effective in areas other than fundraising, such as loans obtained from very wealthy and influential Jews. It would seem that Britain's Jews were reluctant to donate for fear of contravening currency regulations, and possibly from an unwillingness to act against their government in wartime. The paltriness of the contributions aroused anger in the JAE.[81]

The JAE leaders tried to persuade the British Jewish community leaders to let the Yishuv have some of the money collected in Britain as part of the "United Palestine Appeal for Aid to the Diaspora." Ben-Gurion wanted to minimize the damage to Zionist fund-raising activities in England done by ultra-Orthodox Jews. In the summer of 1943 London's devout Jews issued a ban against participation in the appeal and demanded religious education for the "Teheran Children," refugees from Europe, most of whom were parentless, and to the children due to arrive from the Balkan states. It was a controversy that raged around growing hopes of saving tens of thousands of Jewish children. The various religious factions rejected the idea of refugee children being integrated into educational institutions in the secular left wing agricultural settlements in Palestine. It was a stormy and bitter polemic that led to the establishment of a committee of inquiry. The Yishuv leaders and the chief rabbis expended time and energy over an issue that ultimately proved unnecessary since the children never reached Palestine.

On 24 June 1943 complaints were voiced at the Zionist Actions Committee over interruptions in fund-raising. That day Ben-Gurion, Kaplan, and Gruenbaum conferred with the two chief rabbis, Isaac Herzog and Meir Uziel, in order to iron out the differences and quell the storm that was also harming fund-raising efforts through Zionist appeals.[82] Ultra-Orthodox circles in Palestine exerted pressure on people in the United States and England to boycott the appeals.[83] There was a consensus in the JAE that the ultra-Orthodox boycott and propaganda would harm fund-raising efforts, which were not very successful to begin with. The JAE feared the boycott might spread to the United States and South Africa. As mild-mannered Sharett told Rabbi Herzog:

> I have to say that children must first be rescued and only afterward must their education be discussed, and any rabbi who says that their education must be discussed before they have even been rescued is no rabbi. The English rabbis' boycott against Keren Hayesod [PFF] means annihilation for the children, because any chance of rescuing is funded by Keren Hayesod. . . . And if there is any hope left of rescuing children from the Balkan states, this too will be funded by Keren Hayesod, and anyone who dares boycott Keren Hayesod is forsaking the children of Israel.[84]

Ultra-Orthodox circles must remove all boycotts immediately, said Sharett, and a way must be found to satisfy everyone.[85]

The matter of the "Teheran Children" served as a good excuse in various quarters, such as the Polish government-in-exile, which transferred money for the children's upkeep in Teheran, among other things. It now announced that these transfers would be discontinued until the quarrel with the ultra-Orthodox Jews was settled. The latter contacted the Polish government-in-exile over this issue in January 1943, by which time the Poles were already reconsidering their participation in the funding of children's camps in Tehran. Early indications showed that further appeals in May and June would indeed erode Polish support.

In May 1943 Jan Stanchik, Poland's minister of labor, met with Gruenbaum and Schmorak and told them that the ultra-Orthodox faction was exerting pressure on his government in Britain and the United States to halt monthly payments. Gruenbaum proposed that the Polish government express its recognition of the ultra-Orthodox claims but avoid adversely affecting financial support. He suggested the Poles simply announce that for unspecified reasons they had decided to stop monthly payments while in fact handing over, without announcing it, the full amount in one lump sum. Stanchik was sympathetic and agreed to forward Gruenbaum's proposal and the JAE's position to his government.[86]

The ultra-Orthodox boycott was painful because it could also be used to mask fears and suspicions. Britain's Jewish community was faced with a complex situation. The British government had issued the Balfour Declaration and was now leading the fight against Nazism, but it was simultaneously implementing the White Paper policy in Palestine, with all its attendant repercussions affecting the rescue of Jews. It was also afraid of a Jewish refugee problem, which would complicate matters in Palestine, and consequently sought to thwart large-scale rescue operations. In an attempt to minimize the damage, Ben-Gurion met with the rabbis and sought to arrive at a compromise that would satisfy all parties. In the end, his efforts succeeded, and an arrangement was reached that permitted the boycott to be lifted.

This provides further proof of the very tangible connection between Zionist fund-raising efforts (for PFF and the JNF) to promote settlement and training and fund-raising efforts whose objective was the rescue of Jews. It also explains why Sharett was so agitated when he said that the rescue of children was being funded by

PFF. In effect, there was but a single funding pool into which funds from different sources were channeled and from which money for various causes was drawn.[87]

APPEALING TO EGYPT'S JEWISH COMMUNITY

In late January 1943 the JAE was informed that Egypt's Jewish community had decided to set up a special fund to help refugees. Many emissaries were also trying to raise money from the community, including some from the Histadrut, Revisionists, Rabbi Herzog, the Hebrew University, and the National Council. The competition had an adverse effect on the willingness of the community to contribute.

Still, Egyptian Jewish leaders set themselves a target of two hundred thousand Palestinian pounds, "believing that large numbers of refugees needing assistance would pass through Egypt." Dr. Joseph, who was visiting Egypt in January 1943, was aware of the dangers involved in uncoordinated fund-raising. Damage had already been done: twelve thousand Palestinian pounds that had been collected for Europe's Jews were handed over to the British to help finance the war effort and were thus not distributed to the JAE or any other group to fund rescue efforts. He tried to persuade Egyptian Jewish fundraisers to turn to the JAE as the main channel for allocating funds. The Jewish Egyptians were willing to give the JAE 70 percent of all contributions, with the rest being withheld for other purposes. Joseph neither complied with nor rejected their proposal, simply agreeing that an Egyptian representative would visit Palestine to discuss arrangements with the Jewish Agency.[88]

Kaplan and Gruenbaum decided to send Ruth Klieger-Eliav, a leading immigration activist, to Egypt and entrusted her with the task of establishing a framework for local fund-raising efforts. Her efforts proved unsuccessful,[89] and in April 1943 Ben-Gurion and the JAE were again informed of disorderly and haphazard fund-raising in Egypt.

This time funds were being raised on behalf of the National Council. Ben-Gurion demanded that the National Council cease its independent fund-raising, which deviated from "their authority in the framework of Knesset Israel, the only organization of the Jews of Palestine."[90] Kaplan also visited Egypt at the end of May 1943 with the aim of getting fund-raising under control. He found that the local Jews and other activists were opposed to placing fund-raising for refugees under the auspices of the JAE. Kaplan tried to persuade the community leaders to transfer their funds through JAE "channels," thus neutralizing somewhat the damage done by the independent emissaries.[91]

Following his return, Kaplan sincerely believed that the Egyptian community had adopted his proposals. His impression was that they would cooperate with the JAE and prevent other Yishuv fund-raisers from operating there. He felt they would participate in ransom payments to the tune of forty or even a hundred thousand Palestinian pounds and would be part of the Europa Plan. At the end of May Ben-Gurion and Kaplan gave the emissaries in Istanbul permission to announce that monies had been obtained and would be transferred. Egypt's Jews agreed to share in funding ransom payments, but only after it was evident that the bribes had indeed saved Jews, or after the fact. It was not the agreement Kaplan had wanted, but it was important nonetheless.[92]

It soon became obvious that Egypt's Jewish leaders had little faith in the Yishuv and its institutions. They reiterated their refusal to transfer funds directly to the JAE or elsewhere until proof was provided that funds were being used solely for rescue operations. Their attitude was similar to that of the emergency committee in South Africa. Their pledges to double and triple contributions remained unfulfilled.[93]

SPECIAL AID TO THE JEWS OF GREECE

Throughout 1944 the JAE was concerned with problems of fund-raising in Egypt. Kaplan had

planned another visit at the beginning of the year, but he was prevented by Ben-Gurion's absence from the JAE. In March 1944 the JAE considered giving no further recommendations to fund-raisers from other Yishuv bodies. Werner Senator, of the Hebrew University administration in Jerusalem and a JAE member, was deeply concerned about the fate of the university appeal, and Ben-Gurion and Kaplan acceded to his request that the university emissaries be exempted from their ruling. Senator represented the non-Zionists in the JAE, primarily Jewish capitalists whose contributions were vitally important. Ben-Gurion and Kaplan therefore directed the brunt of the JAE ruling at the National Council.[94]

The JAE attempted to influence the Jewish community in Egypt by sending Gruenbaum, utilizing Zaslani-Shiloah's many connections there, as well as through other means of persuasion. The Egyptian Jews continued to demand proof from the JAE that refugees were indeed on their way to Palestine, compelling Kaplan to send them a detailed and accurate accounting.[95] They, in turn, transferred between fifty-five and eighty thousand Palestinian pounds to the Yishuv that year to fund rescue projects.[96]

Most of the money was given to the Rescue Committee and funded the transportation of refugees or was used in direct aid to Europe. A portion of the money was set aside to aid the Jews of Greece, as demanded by relatives who had migrated to Egypt. The rescue of Greek Jews by ships sailing across the Aegean Sea to Turkey was conducted from Izmir (Smyrna) beginning in the autumn of 1943 and throughout 1944. It required payments to sailors and other persons in Greece and Turkey; funds were also required for refugees in Turkey pending their transport to Palestine.

The issue of fund-raising in Egypt serves as a good example of the entire picture. The JAE was unable to impose its authority on the local community. There was a general mistrust of the

Yishuv among Jewish communities in the Diaspora. Money transfers were careful and controlled, mainly in small amounts and for clearly defined goals, and they were contingent on the provision of proof that they were indeed being used for rescue. The general mistrust proved very damaging. Funds that had been raised for rescue did not flow at the required rate to the JAE. In the final analysis, these fund-raising efforts only partially achieved their objective.

14

Money Transfers

Providing aid to the Jews of Europe and efforts to rescue them required complex monetary transfers. The Yishuv and the Zionist movement had to find ways to pool donated funds and transfer them into the occupied territories. Regular and uninterrupted money transfers were also essential for the smooth functioning of "interim funding," the method that enabled the Yishuv to conduct operations beyond its financial capacity at any given time.

The transfer of money is always a sensitive issue. Even during times of peace and internal security, large sums of money are moved by means of armed guards and armored vehicles, elaborate security systems, escape routes, and so forth. These precautions are even more in evidence during wartime. The side doing the money transfers can find itself accused of treason or other grave security violations. Jews or their representatives had to contend with accusations, from outside as well as inside the Jewish community, of a "double loyalty," which was especially hard to bear in times of war.

Couriers were the main means of transferring money to deployed areas and from there into the occupied regions. The Yishuv parachutists also carried cash, diamonds, and gold into enemy territory in order to fund their aid and rescue operations. Other methods consisted of bank transfers from Allied countries to banks in neutral countries, straw companies and personnel, and international organizations. On occasion the Yishuv emissaries in Istanbul also transferred cash, diamonds, or gold in the course of their travels.

Reconstructing these methods is a complex endeavor. They were intricate and ultrasecret.[1] Recently opened American and Yishuv archives make it possible to sketch a more reliable picture.

Further research in this area will add another layer to the discussion of how the Yishuv went about funding the rescue of Europe's Jews during this extremely trying period.

Available documentation reveals the following: attempts were made to obtain a number of loans from Lloyds Bank;[2] Kaplan tried to mobilize Jewish capital in Britain for what were described as investments but were, in fact, loans for interim funding;[3] attempts were made to expand the operation of the Histadrut's American investment company AMPAL;[4] contacts were made with Poland's government-in-exile regarding financial aid;[5] Polish underground channels were used to transfer money and information to Poland; an attempt was made to transfer money from wealthy British Jews and banks to the accounts of Greek and Turkish shipowners or to British and American espionage services that assisted the Yishuv. Two Turkish Jews, Shimon (Simon) Brod and Goldberg, played an important part in the Yishuv-sponsored money transfer system, as did Istanbul branches of the Deutsches Bank and a Dutch bank in Istanbul, the Turkish Bank Anatalia, Swiss banks, a certain mysterious Arthur MacRogers, and even the Socialist International network of activists in Europe.

Most of the methods used by the Yishuv to transfer money were common to the undercover world and had been used by Jews and their organizations since the early thirties, when there was a frequent need to rescue Jews and Jewish property from Europe. The Yishuv made use of them in arms purchases for the Haganah and in establishing the Yishuv's Middle East intelligence network, as well as for illegal immigration operations.[6] In time these methods would be adopted by the "Sonborn Institute" (established in the

United States in 1945, shortly after the Second World War, in order to centralize donations and conduct arms deals), the Mossad's rescue operations, the "Communications Office" and the JDC on behalf of the Jews of Eastern Europe and the USSR. Under the circumstances, not only dollars, gold, and diamonds but also vodka, whiskey, cigarettes, nylon stockings, and jeans were used as payment.

The main objective behind these transfers from country to country was to increase the amount of money for rescue and to establish a secret fund that could pool money from various sources. The fund afforded Kaplan financial flexibility and enabled him to operate the interim funding system.[7] Kaplan was able to establish such a secret fund without encountering any significant opposition because the Yishuv was not noted for its administrative and financial orderliness. As Kaplan said, in the matter of rescue issues they would act "according to what we learn from life." This *modus operandi* suited wartime conditions and the restrictive regulations that had to be circumvented. The flow of money into a secret fund also illustrated Ben-Gurion's and Kaplan's acknowledgment that, in the final analysis, there was no distinction between "Zionism" and "rescue."

The Yishuv activists were aided by various organizations, movements, merchants, banks, and smugglers who were interested—each for their own reasons—in injecting money from the free world into occupied Europe. They were also helped by a number of British and American intelligence officers. The transfer of money took place under the watchful eyes of intelligence services belonging to the Nazis, their dependent states, the neutral countries, Britain, and the United States. These secret services turned a characteristic blind eye so they could preserve their ability to supervise money transfers. For example, it appears the Nazis were quite well informed about money transfers. The British and the Americans displayed a marked duality: some branches of their intelligence services foiled money transfers, whereas others provided essential support for this illegal activity.

MONEY TRANSFERS BY MEANS OF THE PARACHUTISTS

The help given by British and American agents to the Yishuv in transferring money to occupied countries was the outcome of both written and unwritten agreements. Typical was the agreement or understanding between Yishuv rescue emissaries and British intelligence officer Harold Gibson (spring 1943) and U.S. colonel Valerian Lada-Mocarski of the OSS (August 1943).

This agreement served the needs of all the cooperating parties. Among the American and British intelligence circles, those who supported cooperation gave various reasons for doing so, one political-moral reason being the conviction that in due course this aid would serve as proof that Britain and the United States had indeed helped the Yishuv to save Jews. Another more pragmatic and far less altruistic reason was that the party providing the aid, acting as a partner, could obtain classified information on the size of the transfers, their destinations, and so forth. This information sometimes proved more important than blocking money transfers. The partnership also made it possible to regulate, control, and recruit agents. Nonetheless, it should be noted that the intelligence community extended its support out of a sincere desire to rescue Jews. Some of these people were conflicted by their government's policies toward the Jews.

The infiltration plans proposed by the Yishuv to Britain and the United States were very broad. In the end only a handful of parachutists saw action, most of them during 1944. They were charged with serving Allied interests as well as those of the Jews. The transfer of money and valuables was an important task entrusted to them by the Yishuv and the Zionist movement.

Most of the parachutists carried money and valuables to be handed over to contact people.

The money was for funding aid, purchasing weapons, and organizing rescue operations. Often the parachutists were given larger sums than those agreed upon with the British and American partners. Rehavam Zevalovsky (Amir) took a thousand British pounds to Salerno for Jewish refugees.[8] Yitzhak Makarscu-Shoham, who parachuted into Romania under the alias John Marcus, and "Milo" (Uriel Kanner), who parachuted into Romania as Louis Robbins, each carried twenty-four thousand Romanian lei, sixty-five British pounds in gold coin, twenty-five U.S. dollars, and diamonds worth one hundred British pounds. They concealed some of the money in their clothing, and Zaslani (Shiloah), who accompanied them, reported that "arrangements were executed with great expertise and would arouse no suspicion even if the money were found, since pilots always took money along on their operations—if necessary to pay a bribe for their release."[9]

When she set out on "Operation Challock," Marta Martinovitz (alias Haviva Reik or agent Stickler) carried one thousand dollars. Abba Berdichev (agent Willis), who parachuted in March 1944, was co-opted in August to another operation and carried three thousand dollars when he again parachuted into Slovakia after Reik.[10] Arye Fichman (Orni), who parachuted as Lieutenant Gideon Jacobson, and Lyova Gukovsky (Yehuda Achishar), who parachuted as Second Lieutenant Joseph Kahana, carried money for missions in Romania. Following their capture, the Romanian press reported that the two carried large sums in Romanian currency, American dollars, Swiss francs, British pounds sterling, as well as food parcels and medicine.[11] So it was with other parachutists who ultimately managed to go on missions.

British and American intelligence knew of the money carried by the Yishuv parachutists. Occasionally they even promised to transfer the money themselves if the parachutists were unsuccessful. Reports of money given to the parachutists by British operators routinely reached Zaslani in Jerusalem.[12] The arrangement was simple: the British colleagues transferred money to the parachutists' points of dispatch and allocated part of it for the Yishuv parachutists; with Kaplan's approval, Zaslani or Kollek would then ensure that the money was reimbursed to their British friends, either in Palestine or elsewhere.[13]

For example, Zaslani reported to his colleagues in the infiltration project that various parachutists had received "considerable sums of money" through their American and British contacts. He reported that Taylor ("the tailor"), the British officer in charge in Bari, had been instructed "to meet all their financial demands," and they had given him five thousand Palestinian pounds to this end. Zaslani also reported that "whenever they send them [parachutists operating in occupied territories] food and equipment, they also add supplies for Jewish refugees."[14]

Enzo Sereni was also prepared to supply Jews in occupied regions with money. He tried to equip himself with as much money as possible before setting out, and knew that Colonel Harold Gibson's men had placed an additional two thousand British pounds at the disposal of the Yishuv delegation in Bari. Sereni asked Kaplan for the two thousand pounds "from heaven" and advised him "not to be miserly," adding that if he was refused he would take the money with him anyway and ask "his mother" (i.e., his kibbutz, his political movement) in Palestine to "return it to the Jewish Agency." This proved unnecessary. Kaplan and his colleagues were not miserly with money they sent with the parachutists, as is amply supported by available documentation.[15]

Among the people who helped the Jewish Agency transfer money to the parachutists were the following: Colonel Harold Gibson, SIS commander in Istanbul; Reed, his squadron leader; Colonel Tony Simmonds, A Force commander; SOE officers George Francis Taylor, who operated out of Bari; Captain Hooker, Allied forces Jewish chaplain in Beri; Lowell Pinkerton,

American consul in Jerusalem; and Rodney S. Young, head of the Greek division in the Middle East OSS command in Cairo. For example, Reed worked with Zaslani on money transfers to Bari in accordance with the agreement that British agents would send money to Yishuv activists in takeoff areas, which would be reimbursed by the Jewish Agency in London.[16]

Arrangements of this kind were typical of preparations for sending parachutists into Romania, Hungary, and Slovakia in March 1944. Their missions centered on Jewish matters, as agreed upon between the British and Zaslani, and a crucial one involved carrying cash, diamonds, and gold.[17] In May 1944 the Yishuv reimbursed Simmonds's people, transferring to Budapest and Bucharest a sum equivalent to two thousand Egyptian pounds in various currencies. The equivalent amount was handed to Zaslani in Cairo by Simmonds's people.[18]

American intelligence documentation on the underground in Slovakia provides a partial clue to the destinations of the money transfers from Palestine. According to one memorandum, the underground connected with the Edvard Benes government-in-exile were suitably equipped, the Communists being supplied with weapons parachuted to them by Soviet planes, while the Jewish groups "have funds available for the purchase of arms."[19] It is quite possible that this is a reference to the money brought by Haviva Reik, Abba Berdichev, and other Yishuv agents—"injections" or "blood transfusions," as the emissaries referred to them.[20]

Funds transferred through close cooperation between the emissaries and British and American intelligence also served combined and joint operational objectives. For example, the Zionist underground and British intelligence jointly raised funds in Romania for an attempt to rescue Lyova Gukovsky and Arye Fichman and U.S. aircrews from the same POW camp. Gukovsky and Fichman were captured in Romania on 1 October 1943, immediately after parachuting.[21]

While still in the hospital, Gukovsky established contact with the Zionist underground through a Romanian nurse, Maria Tzika. The contact continued even after his transfer to the POW camp, from which he tried to escape several times between October 1943 and July 1944. Such escape attempts required funding. In the spring of 1944 Gukovsky appealed for funds (through Maria Tzika) to Shmuel Enzer, head of the Palestine office in Romania. He asked for a million lei and whatever else Enzer could provide in pounds sterling and gold coins. With this money Gukovsky wished to speed up his escape to the Carpathian mountains. Time was at a premium, not least because the Nazis were preparing to overrun Romania and deport all Western prisoners to Germany. Enzer sent whatever he could to Gukovsky (through Maria Tzika) and gave an additional sum (two hundred gold coins) to Zvi Basse, of the Dror leadership, who was to conceal it on his body until such time that aid could be safely transferred to Gukosvsky.[22]

Gukovsky tried to get money from another source to fund his and his colleagues' mission. Through Maria Tzika he made contact with Moshe Moskowitz, a Jewish underground activist in Romania, from whom he requested four thousand pounds. Moskowitz obtained the sum from a local source (whose identity was not disclosed) and awaited a suitable opportunity to give the money to Gukovsky.[23] All these activities were known to British intelligence and were conducted under the auspices of staff and agents in Istanbul, Romania, and Jerusalem.[24]

Milo (Uriel Kanner), who was sent into Romania, was also supposed to transfer money for funding aid and rescue operations. He was entrusted with thirty pieces of gold. At the last moment Kanner decided not to take the gold, which annoyed Zaslani, who saw this as a serious breach of operational discipline. Zaslani knew how much this gold was needed in Europe.[25] These incidents, though typical, require further research into the manner in which money was transferred by Yishuv agents and how their operations were funded behind enemy lines.

From 1943 to the end of the war in May 1945, emissaries in Istanbul transferred money to Hungary, Romania, and Poland[26] through a courier web. At some point confirmation of money transfers also arrived from Poland, the hardest country to penetrate. Money was routinely transferred from Istanbul and Geneva to other countries, including Romania, Slovakia, Bulgaria, Austria, and Hungary.[27]

The question remains as to the total amount funding brought by the parachutists and couriers into Europe. It is known that the parachutists usually carried what they had received from their British and American operators for their military requirements, plus what they had received from their Yishuv operators for the Jews. Obviously, the amounts provided were not recorded in such a way as to enable us to reconstruct and analyze the financial scope of their activity.

Further clues may be gleaned from reports and accounting practices dating from the end of the war. One such report by Teddy Kollek detailed contacts he had with Yitzhak Gruenbaum, Rescue Committee chairman, in order to persuade him to participate in covering the Political Department's budget deficit, the result of expenses incurred by infiltration operations. Kollek described the operations and their costs. About 120 people were ultimately prepared to infiltrate, of whom only about 40 were sent. Preparations and sorties cost Kollek's department 14,000 Palestinian pounds. The Rescue Committee contributed 9,000 pounds, leaving a gap of 5,000 pounds. The emissaries spent an additional 4,405 pounds on "actual rescue activities," which made the deficit Kollek placed at Gruenbaum's doorstep over 9,000 Palestinian pounds.[28] Even if these figures do not reflect the total picture, they do shed some light on the financial aspect of the parachutists' operations.

TRANSFERRING MONEY TO RESCUE THE JEWS OF GREECE

The Yishuv cooperated with Britain and the United States in attempting to rescue Jews from occupied Greece by smuggling them across the Aegean. Obviously this operation required funding, thereby providing an outstanding example of secret cooperation in the transfer of money. The funding for rescue activity derived in part from the wealthy members of the Greek Jewish community. The Jewish underground obliged each affluent Jew to assume responsibility for the rescue of a few more Jews.[29] The Jewish community in Izmir was another source of aid, supplying mainly food, clothing, and shelter until the refugees' papers were in order and they could continue on to Palestine.[30] A third source was the War Refugee Board.

The balance of the funding came through two channels, namely, from the Jewish Agency (through Gibson's people) or through the transfer of gold. Gibson's people gave the Yishuv emissaries cash in the field and Zaslani reimbursed them in Jerusalem. For example, the British supplied a thousand pounds in January 1944, and a few days later they were reimbursed in Jerusalem.[31]

Egypt's Jewish community was involved in the second method of transferring money. The JAE bought or obtained gold in Palestine and sent it to Egypt. (It also purchased or obtained gold in Egypt itself.) Zvi Yehieli collected all the gold and transferred it directly to British intelligence services in Cairo, which passed it on to Istanbul. From there it was transferred to the area of operations by Commander Ṣandres Walfson, Tony Simmonds's representative in Istanbul. Walfson also transferred gold to his unit, which was engaged in smuggling escapees out of captivity in the Aegean. He brought the gold sent by the JAE to Moshe Averbuch (Agami), who coordinated the operation in Greece from his headquarters in Izmir.

Though an important conduit, this network was subject to crises with the British. For example, aid ceased when relations broke down between Averbuch and Tony Simmonds's people in Came, and when there were other political and operational tensions.[32] Averbuch possessed a large stockpile of gold that enabled him to keep his commitments to partisans and providers of other services in the region.[33] There was a crisis when Simmonds stopped transferring gold from Palestine and Egypt to Turkey. With Kaplan's approval, Zaslani and Kollek appealed to the Americans, who did, in fact, send money to Averbuch. Repayment was then arranged in installments from the JAE in Jerusalem or through money transfers via the OSS courier system in Cairo. Rodney S. Young, head of the Greek Department at OSS headquarters in Cairo, took part in this operation.[34]

Earl Taylor, commercial attaché at the American consulate in Istanbul, was apparently a further link in the attempt to obtain credit in the form of foreign currency, gold, and diamonds. He was known among various circles of the intelligence community in Istanbul as having good relations with the Istanbul black market. It is not inconceivable that the Yishuv also benefited from his contacts.[35]

BANK TRANSFERS

In many cases the complex processes of transferring or smuggling cash or its equivalent were remedied through bank transfers. For example, a bank located at one end of the world (Bank A) could put money at the disposal of a client whose account was managed by a bank at the other end (Bank B). It was sufficient for Bank A to receive notification from a colleague in Bank B that this person was indeed Bank B's client for Bank A to give him money in local currency or in any other currency possessed by the bank in sufficient quantity. Bank A could profit from this transaction in different ways: it could earn commissions; it could pocket the difference between the selling and buying currency rates; it could increase its volume of activity; and it could offer its clients a unique service. Money transfers were an essential

activity for any bank dealing in international commerce.

Such transfers can be conducted among several banks, often blurring the identity of the individual who began the transfer of the money or the one receiving it at the other end. This is accomplished through the utilization of straw companies or individuals in the chain of transfers. Such a process serves the needs of secret organizations engaged in illegal activities, especially in wartime. Frequently these methods are used for the purchase of weapons or contraband (components that are now used to create weapons of mass destruction).

Such methods were also used by various organizations during the Second World War. Although Yishuv activists did not invent them, they were quick to make use of banks and various other organizations, secret services, and couriers. The "transfer agreement" signed with the Nazis in 1933, as well as the "clearing" agreements discussed with the Polish government at the end of the thirties, were, in fact, expressions of these methods of transferring property between countries. Both domestic and foreign documentation indicates that the Yishuv was already using such methods at the beginning of the war, when the need first arose to rescue Jews and Jewish property from occupied areas. This was the purpose of Teddy Kollek's first mission to central Europe.[36] Not long afterward it became necessary to transfer money in the opposite direction—from Palestine and other locations in the free world into Nazi-occupied Europe—for the funding of aid and rescue. These were always complex and intricate operations, becoming even more daunting after the Allies imposed restrictions on money transfers to enemy countries. Banks were then obligated to report every deposit or interbank transfer that exceeded a certain amount. Allied intelligence services monitored the activities of moneychangers, diamond dealers, and black market traders in order to prevent the transfer of currency likely to assist the Nazis and to strengthen their faltering economy.

Various methods were devised to bypass such restrictions, including multiple transfers of smaller sums, which did not have to be reported, and the use of a third or fourth party. Usually the latter transferred money from a bank in the West to a bank in a neutral country near the final destination. In some cases the money was transferred from one neutral country to another one closer to the final destination. In other cases the bank in a neutral country would transfer funds to one of its branches, or to other banks connected with it, in the occupied areas themselves.

Another method devised to bypass restrictions utilized Western companies that conducted routine business dealings in neutral states or even in occupied countries. Such transfers were camouflaged as routine monetary transactions. The companies that agreed to cooperate had their own reasons for doing so. Some owners wished to help for ideological reasons or as a result of personal relationships, while others agreed to participate in exchange for a commission paid to the company itself or to its officials.

Profits resulting from differences in currency rates were occasionally an important motive. U.S.-owned international companies or those based in the United States or Britain that had branches in neutral countries were able to receive payments to their branches through accounts kept in the United States or Britain. The branch in the neutral country would provide an equivalent sum in local currency in the neutral country or in the occupied country based on the black market exchange rate. The difference between the official rate, which was obligatory for the deposit, and the black market rate could amount to more than 10 percent. For example, the official rate of exchange for deals conducted through the National Bank of Switzerland was 4 francs, 30 centimes to the dollar, whereas on the black market this same dollar changed hands for only 2 francs, 70 centimes. Clearly, when such companies were suffering from the effects of the war, this "gray" branch could provide the revenues necessary for survival.

Another strategy depended on private individuals. People in the United States or Britain would permit to have deposited in their accounts a certain sum of money from the Jewish Agency or its branches for a relative or friend in a neutral country, who would hand it over to the Jewish Agency emissaries. The main disadvantage of this arrangement was its dependence on people who were not always trustworthy and who might even be tempted to resort to blackmail.[37]

PAYING BACK JONAS'S DEBT

A striking example of how bank transfers worked is provided by the purchase or leasing of a ship from a man who was called by the emissaries only "Jonas." It will be described in great detail in order to illustrate the many complications encountered in the transfer of money for funding rescue and aid to Europe's Jews.

The affair began in the spring and early summer of 1943. Jonas was residing in Istanbul at the time. Ze'ev Schind, Ehud Avriel, Teddy Kollek, Reuven Zaslani-Shiloah, and (later) Eliezer Kaplan were all involved in the affair, together with the JAE London branch and several bankers in London, Tel Aviv, Switzerland, and Istanbul. Representing the secret services were British intelligence officer Arthur Whittall and American diplomat and intelligence man Cedric Seager. The now familiar figures of Bandi Grosz and Alfred Schwartz, head of the Dogwood network, were also involved.

Despite holes in the documentation and the unknown identity of the man called Jonas, the affair still provides us with insight into how these "deals" were conducted. The Palestinians wanted to pay Jonas back for an important service. To this end, they carried out a round of bank transfers among a number of banks in London and Istanbul, all the while bypassing the foreign currency inspectors in the various countries. Hints of this enterprise are sprinkled throughout the documentation for October 1943, when the money transfers began to encounter obstacles.

Schind urgently contacted Kollek, who had recently returned from Istanbul and was running the headquarters in Jerusalem, and asked him to ensure that Jonas received his due, minus the payment for "Tamar" (whose identity remains unknown). Schind's request was conveyed by his friends in the British and American intelligence services.[38] Because his requests were not answered, on 22 October he appealed to Zaslani to inform Kaplan about his urgent need.[39]

While Schind was pressing Zaslani, Kollek's reply reached him and Avriel. It appears that Kollek answered them in two separate letters. The letters had been delayed on account of the difficulty of passing information through protected channels. "The situation regarding Jonas is very complex and I don't know how to untangle it," wrote Kollek. Those responsible for payments issued three instructions, one for a payment of two thousand dollars and two others for payments of fifteen hundred dollars each. The first payment to a Glyn-Mills was executed and reached its destination. The instruction to pay fifteen hundred dollars to a certain Aleksan Horasanoi [Horansci] was not honored, ostensibly because the name was not properly spelled and the account could not be located. There was also a foul-up in the third payment, which is referred to as "6101" in the correspondence. The bank announced that it could not honor the instruction, because it was issued on behalf of a Turkish citizen. This was "very surprising," wrote Kollek, since the previous payment into the same account, a transfer of five thousand dollars, "had been executed without any problem." Another payment in the same amount to Jonas himself had, for the same reasons, also not been executed, and attempts were made to settle it. Kollek concluded, "Caspi, alias Kaplan, did not find an appropriate solution to the problem of foreign currency accounts ... and the matter is very complicated." He recommended "checking with Weiss, alias Arthur Whittall, to see if he could pay the bills, and we shall reimburse his organiza-

tion."[40] Arthur Whittall, an SIS officer operating in Istanbul under the cover of a passport control officer, was one of the British friends close to the Yishuv emissaries in Turkey.

Schind—and apparently also Avriel—discussed the problem with Jonas and with Whittall. They looked into the possibility that monies owed by the Yishuv to Jonas could be deposited in his name elsewhere. This was actually a variation of the "Après" system operated by the JDC. Jonas agreed conditionally, the terms of which were sent to Jerusalem.[41]

Kollek was now required to determine whether it was possible to meet Jonas's terms and to execute a complicated process. The JAE London branch would obtain the requisite sum from Britain's Jewish community. The money would be deposited in Barclays Bank in Tel Aviv in the name of a man living in Istanbul; his name and personal details would be conveyed to the bank before the execution of the transfer. This individual would be authorized to withdraw the money in pound notes from the account that had been opened for him in Tel Aviv and in London. Schind also requested from Istanbul that Kollek check to see if the JAE London branch would be able to deposit monies in three types of accounts: pounds sterling; European currency; and Palestinian currency. If the answers to these questions were affirmative, it would be possible to carry out additional operations in Istanbul and to pay for them in other areas, or to transfer payment to Turkey from other areas.[42]

Schind and Avriel added further details in another letter to Kollek that was transmitted by "Segal" (Cedric Seager).[43] Several days later Kollek sent to Istanbul photocopies of the bank authorizations for the transfer of three payments out of five. Repeated attempts to get the remaining two payments to Jonas were unsuccessful. The money was sent to private accounts, the details about which were furnished from Istanbul, but some of the accounts were closed on the banks' instructions. It appears that the inspector in charge of foreign currency transfers had gotten wind of the system.

Kollek promised that further attempts to overcome these obstacles would be made and new methods sought. He gave instructions for the money to be paid back to Jonas from the emissaries' fund in Istanbul even if these efforts also proved unsuccessful.[44] The reason was simple: it was essential to preserve the emissaries' good name. The rules of the game were rigid, and whoever did not abide by them lost creditworthiness in the black market. The interim funding system was also built on such credit, and any blow to the trustworthiness of the Yishuv was liable to destroy it.

It also emerged from Kollek's letter that the courier and double agent Bandi Grosz and Alfred Schwartz (Dogwood) also played a part in the complexities surrounding the payment of the debt to Jonas, although I have been unable to clarify their precise role in this affair. It is known that they were involved in the transfer of money, the operation of straw companies, and various black market activities.[45]

New efforts to transfer money to repay Jonas's debt of five thousand British pounds proved unsuccessful, as did and another instruction to transfer three thousand pounds, because the accounts were blocked in Turkey. The idea of depositing money in an account in Barclays Bank in Tel Aviv was found to be impractical, as were other, similar notions. Kollek wrote to his friends that this time he was completely "at a loss," although London-based Joseph Linton continued to look for ways to transfer money.

THE "FRIENDS" ARE CALLED IN TO HELP

In his distress, Kollek contacted Seager, who had been his partner in various operations during his Istanbul service. Seager had come to Palestine on business in October 1943, around the time the difficulties surrounding the payment to Jonas were surfacing. Earlier, Whittall, the British SIS officer, had also been informed of the problem,

and Kollek made sure Seager was made aware of the cooperation that existed with the British, in order to win his trust.

Kollek told Seager that the Yishuv emissaries had received money in Turkey—and even in occupied territories—from the British intelligence people, and had repaid it in Palestine, London, or elsewhere. He asked him for similar American aid, and Seager promised to discuss the matter with his colleagues. In fact, Americans did provide such aid during the rescue of Jews from Greece at the end of 1943 and 1944, as well as in other operations.[46]

Despite his being "at a loss" as to what to do, Kollek and his colleagues in Jerusalem sought other ways to get the money to Jonas. They found a Turkish Jew who agreed to raise twenty-seven hundred British pounds from among his friends and to give the money to Schind and Avriel in Turkey, thereby enabling the emissaries to repay some of the debt to Jonas. The Jewish Agency would pay interest and a 20 percent commission on this loan, but the payment would be made in Palestine.[47]

During November 1943 they tried a bigger round through a third and fourth party. The emissaries opened bank accounts in the name of Ze'ev Schind in Istanbul. Afterward they requested that a bank transfer be executed from London through Zurich to Istanbul. According to documentation, the transfer was arranged in advance with the Union Swiss Bank branch in Zurich and the Union Holland Bank branch in Istanbul.[48] However, once again hopes were dashed. At the end of November Kollek again referred to the obstacles and instructed Schind and Avriel not to accept more loans on the basis of a commitment to repay them through such bank transfers.[49]

Another method designed to increase funds available to emissaries in Istanbul sought to utilize money that Jews who had managed to flee from occupied Europe had carried with them. There weren't many such cases, but when they were traced they tried to borrow their money. In September 1943 an expenditure of 500 British pounds that had been received in this manner was recorded. In November an expenditure of 2,682 British pounds was recorded from a similar source. Schind and Avriel took the money and furnished the Jews who provided the loan with a receipt, which they could cash in upon arrival in Palestine.[50]

Another method Kollek considered involved money that Yishuv emissaries held for Bandi Grosz. Kollek suggested that, when Grosz visited Istanbul the next time, the emissaries ask if he would be willing to invest his money in shares of plants and properties in Palestine. This way they could use the money they held in safekeeping to repay their debts in Turkey. It appears that the emissaries also paid Grosz for his services by keeping money and valuables that he had smuggled out of Nazi Europe for himself. Grosz believed the emissaries were the most secure "bank" for him and assumed that they would not make life difficult for him in due course by asking too many questions. After the war Grosz's wife did, in fact, ask Kollek to return his money and valuables.[51]

During this entire period the British and American friends continued to help Schind and Avriel deal with their financial problems. Both emissaries sent frequent appeals to Palestine for help, explaining that their colleagues in the secret services were endangering themselves for them, and now the emissaries could not repay their debts.[52]

The documentation for December sheds a little more light on the affair. Jonas was still waiting for his money. In the meantime the emissaries obtained interim funding from the British totaling five thousand British pounds from "Weiss" (Whittall). It was agreed that the money would be repaid in Britain. The JAE London branch would deposit funds in a specific account in one of the Manchester banks, which was apparently a hidden SIS account. The emissaries thus managed to obtain a little more breathing space and to partially reimburse Jonas in a roundabout way: Whittall gave Jonas five thousand pounds from British intelligence funds, and the Jewish Agency repaid the loan in Britain without needing to transfer the money in the Middle East.[53]

These efforts continued throughout 1944. Documentation from the end of 1944 shows that Jonas continued to lend a great deal of money to Palestinians: twenty thousand dollars. This is a clear indication that in the end the emissaries kept their commitment to Jonas. Nevertheless, the difficulty of transferring money by means of banks remained unresolved. Also, at the end of 1944 Avriel once more urged his superiors to ensure a continuous flow of money because of the hectic schedule of the planned operations.[54]

The Palestinian emissaries could not wait for the money to arrive in Istanbul, so they borrowed it there. The repayment of the loans was due to arrive from Palestine without delay in order to preserve the Yishuv's good name. However, the Jewish Agency treasury was not always capable of sending the repayment. It sent money in the hope of recouping some of it from the JDC, as well as from Jewish communities in South Africa, Britain, and elsewhere. Each link in the chain was therefore dependent on the next, with the hope that in the end the commitments would be met—and on time. In May 1943 Schind and Pomeranz requested that Ben-Gurion announce "to our friends [i.e., colleagues in the JAE] that we cannot miss this opportunity, and it is possible that we shall have to make a commitment here for monies from the above quota—even before we receive your permission."[55]

LOCAL JEWISH SUPPORT

Shimon (Simon) Brod and his colleague Goldberg were a central link in the movement of loans, aside from Moslem and Christian moneychangers and members of the British and American secret services in Turkey. Brod was a wealthy cloth merchant, the son of a tailor who had immigrated to Turkey from the Austro-Hungarian empire. Although he was affected by the *Varlik* (a tax imposed on "foreigners" during the Second World War by the Turkish government), he was still affluent enough to help Jewish refugees arriving in Turkey. For purposes of aid and rescue, he acted as a liaison between the emissaries, on the one hand, and Turkish officials and money-changers in the local-currency market, on the other. Brod was also a friend of Whittall and lived in the same apartment block.

According to Kollek's description, he was "a good-hearted and likable man, with a freckled face, a sense of humor, and a perpetual cigarette hanging from the corner of his mouth." He was then in his mid-fifties and in poor health. Kollek asserted that Brod devoted himself "with all his heart and soul to the rescue operations." Avriel described Brod as a small man with a plump red face, crowned by silvery hair, who worked energetically and voluntarily for the rescue of Jews. The cartons of cigarettes he chain-smoked were the only reward he consented to receive from Avriel and his people. Judah Magnes, who encountered him in Istanbul in the summer of 1944, described him as a "demon," a man with a fiendish capacity for work and a devilish power of expression, in short, an unpleasant man who was nevertheless a great asset for the rescue effort.

The Palestinians borrowed money from Brod whenever they ran into financial difficulties. Brod knew when it was worthwhile to convert money, where to buy gold sovereigns, and where to convert diamonds or pounds sterling into dollars. Kollek described Brod as "an asset worth his weight in gold," a man without whom they could not conceivably have managed. According to Avriel, Brod was the chief liaison between the Palestinian delegation and the Turkish authorities. Only thanks to him, and to others like him, was it possible to implement the interim funding method. The emissaries were extremely grateful to Brod for his valuable assistance and

maintained a warm relationship with him even after the war.[56]

Goldberg, another valuable link in the financial system in Istanbul, was a banker who had managed the Deutsche Bank branch in Istanbul until the Nazis came to power. Kollek pointed out that he wasn't as active as Brod, "but he had some extremely important contacts" that the emissaries reserved for special occasions. At such times they were of "immense importance." Goldberg was close to government circles in Turkey, thanks in no small part to his beautiful wife, who, Kollek testified, had been the mistress of Mustafa Kemal (Atatürk), the father of modern Turkey.[57]

The financial assistance provided by certain elements in the British and American secret services was not confined to the operating expenses of the parachutists or occasions like Whittall's and Seagers's attempt to supply Schind and Avriel with a safety net in the Jonas affair. It is also reflected in the activity of the Yishuv, such as the Histadrut-owned Solel Boneh company. The latter built fortifications and bridges, among other structures, for the British while simultaneously serving as a central location for diverse intelligence activity, including overt and covert money transfers.

Abba Eban, then a British intelligence officer who liaised with various Yishuv institutions, testified that David Hacohen, director of Solel Boneh and treasurer of the Haganah, used to transfer as much British money as possible to the coffers of the Palmah, the Haganah's elite strike force from 1941 to 1947.[58] Documentation from 1943 reveals that money was transferred, with the full knowledge of the British, from the fund of the Political Department to Solel Boneh and back again. This phenomenon can be explained, for example, by the payment arrangements for funding the operations of the Haifa Interrogations Bureau and the lively intelligence activities of the Solel Boneh people in Iraq.[59]

During the spring and late summer of 1944, there was some very notable financial assistance from friendly elements in the British and American secret services. Attempts to rescue the Jews of Hungary and the remnants of the Jewish communities of Europe had reached a climax with respect to the Brand affair and its aftermath. Emissaries in Istanbul needed funds to fuel the "interim agreement," to send aid to occupied Europe, and to arrange rescues and transfers. Attempts to purchase or lease the *Milca, Maritza, Vita, Smyrna, Kazbek, Bulbul,* and *Salah-a-Din* took place more or less during this period and required large sums of money. Yishuv institutions and the Zionist movement, the JDC, the War Refugee Board, and British and American friends went out of their way to obtain the money and to transfer it to Turkey or to repay loans that had been made in Turkey.[60]

The transmission of financial information through Pinkerton, the American consul in Jerusalem, became so "in the family" that Pinkerton conveyed all information to Istanbul together with code names: "Ben-Yehuda" for Shaul Meirov-Avigur, "Meir" for the Palestine Office in Istanbul, and so on. Pinkerton knew the names of those traveling to Cairo and when they would return; those on vacation and the names of their replacements; and, of course, how much money was required, its purpose, how it would be transferred, and the form of reimbursement.[61]

Amid all this optimism, there were also moments of disappointment—for example, when it was learned that Joel Brand would not return and that the reply to the proposal to open negotiations with the Nazis, which had been held up, ultimately proved negative. It should not be forgotten that a section of the British secret services was in charge of enforcing the limitations set out in the White Paper. There is no better way to learn about the plans of one's "enemy" than to enter his offices, share his problems and hopes and even help him from time to time while monitoring his activity

Nevertheless, it is hard to ignore the comradely atmosphere and the considerable efforts of

the Americans and British to assist in the transfer of money. For example, their help was noteworthy when the opportunity arose to rescue Jews from the Balkans. The Yishuv emissaries requested large sums of money to fund the new plans, far in excess of what the Yishuv was able to transfer to Istanbul. At the beginning of May they urgently requested two hundred thousand British pounds, plus an additional half million Swiss francs that the JDC would transfer through a Swiss bank to an account in Turkey. Meirov hastened to instruct them to go ahead with the operations at full speed, announcing that Kaplan had asked the JDC to transfer the half million Swiss francs to Switzerland and from there to Turkey.[62]

Three days later the emissaries told Zaslani that they had begun to borrow money from their British friends in Turkey. They would receive from "Shimon" (Tony Simmonds) the equivalent of three thousand British pounds in gold in three consecutive weekly payments. They were to repay Simmonds as soon as possible in Palestine. This was a small sum compared with what was demanded of them then, and they asked to receive the remainder of the money in bank transfers. The money would be deposited in the Union Swiss Bank branch in Zurich. From there it would be sent to the Union Holland Bank branch in Istanbul care of Ze'ev Schind-Wulf Ze'ev Szynd Istanbul, Istiklal caddesi four-eight. For safety's sake replies were sent from Palestine utilizing channels established by Pinkerton and Reed.[63]

In an additional letter sent by the emissaries to Palestine—which was not forwarded through the British or the Americans—the emissaries went into greater detail: "The gravest question facing us, upon which the continuation of the work in the coming days depends, concerns the money that is available at our disposal in Switzerland. We have nothing to add to what we already wrote and cabled you. *You have to do everything in your power to comply with our request* [underscored in original]." The emissaries intimated that cash was required immediately, not merely commitments from the JAE to repay the loans.

"VIRTUAL" MONEY TRANSFERS BETWEEN SWITZERLAND AND TURKEY

The emissaries also expanded a little on the arrangements agreed upon with the Union Holland Bank branch in Turkey: they would be able to use the money inside Turkey after the branch received a cable confirming that money had been deposited in Switzerland in the name of Schind, or that the money had been sent in the form of a bank transfer from Switzerland to Turkey in his name. The emissaries pointed out that they had asked Barlas to bring the information to Palestine and to receive confirmations there. In this matter Barlas referred directly to Joe Schwartz, head of the JDC in Europe.[64]

At that time (May 1944) negotiations were being conducted between the JDC and the JAE against a background of tension between the two organizations. The JDC refused to send half a million francs without first checking, as Schind and Avriel had requested. One by one the JDC's people (Reuben Resnik, Judah L. Magnes, and finally Joe Schwartz) set out for Turkey.

The speed with which Schind and Avriel acted did not suit the JDC. It needed a lot of money immediately. The relationship with the JDC and its inclination to increase its independence did not concern them. They again asked pointedly why the JAE did not convince the JDC to deposit the required amounts in Switzerland and transfer them from there to Turkey.

In Jerusalem the JAE understood the distress of Schind and Avriel, but they also knew that the JDC would ultimately decide what to do with its money. Kaplan and his colleagues tried to speed up negotiations with the JDC. In order to encourage Schind and Avriel, and to give an objective picture of the situation, Kaplan and his colleagues informed Istanbul from Jerusalem that Resnik would shortly be coming to Turkey. Be-

fore setting out, he promised to recommend that his superiors approve the request. Avriel was asked to meet with him in Ankara, apparently to begin the process of "proper conversion" by establishing a "Zionist seminar" for him.

In order not to be left empty-handed, they informed Istanbul that Kaplan was putting at their disposal "fifty thousand [British pounds] which we are sending," ten thousand of which was to be transferred through "Shimon" (Simmonds), and that they were trying to obtain Swiss francs. They also asked that "Ehud [Avriel] cable whether there were Swiss francs available in Istanbul to replace the francs in Switzerland." In this way it would perhaps be possible to escape the necessity of transferring funds from Switzerland and thereby avoid dependence on the JDC.[65]

Concurrent with the announcement that fifty thousand British pounds were being sent, they also informed them that Simmonds was prepared to transfer gold to them as well.[66] This important announcement mitigated the feeling that time was running out and that nothing was being done. On 28 June 1944 the emissaries announced that "nothing new has happened between Resnik and ourselves" and that no answer had been received from the JDC.[67]

A day later it was as if the heavens had opened. On 29 June they informed Kaplan from London that they had cabled five thousand British pounds "to the Anglo-Palestine Bank." On 1 July an even more important announcement came from Lisbon: representatives of the JDC had promised Dobkin to put two hundred thousand British pounds and half a million Swiss francs at the Jewish Agency's disposal. Dobkin immediately phoned this information to Switzerland. Such an announcement could be considered an authorization to begin the money transfer process.

Information on important developments in Lisbon was conveyed to Jerusalem through American channels. Kaplan was visiting Istanbul at the time and was informed about them in a roundabout manner (Pinkerton to Seager, Seager to Schind, Schind to Kaplan), proving that the Americans were also aware of this development.[68]

TRANSPARENCY OF TRANSFERS TO THE GESTAPO

Evidence of money transfers from the United States to Nazi-occupied Europe using this method may also be gleaned from Gestapo documentation, which fell into the hands of American agents in Romania at the end of 1944. For example, in October 1944 an American agent in Bucharest reported that, according to Gestapo documents that had come into his possession, Romanian Jews received more than half a million dollars from an American source. Based on lists obtained by the Gestapo, it appears that most of the money was in the form of personal donations, "which were sent to Switzerland for aid to Palestine, but there is reason to believe that they were rerouted to Romania."[69] This is further testimony to money being transferred from the United States to Romania through Switzerland.

These examples prove the existence of a money transfer system that encompassed Lisbon, London, Switzerland, Istanbul, and Jerusalem, one that involved emissaries in Istanbul, Jewish Agency heads, the JDC, the World Jewish Congress, officers in the British and American secret services, and a number of banks. This is probably only a fraction of the whole operation.

Efforts to transfer money by these methods continued until the end of the war. Among the individuals involved in the chain of transfers was the anonymous "Arthur MacRogers," which might have been the name of a straw company, a bank in Anatolia, or perhaps the code name for financial contacts with Alfred Schwartz ("the Black"), who headed the Dogwood network. According to one document, the Yishuv had financial dealings with him that were halted in October–November 1944.

Teddy Kollek was a central figure in the transfer and smuggling of money. The following reconstruction of his activity is based both on Palestinian and foreign documentation. Additional information is contained in his memoirs, where he described the smuggling of funds to the Working Group in Slovakia as well as many other places in Europe, writing that "a surprisingly high percentage of enemy agents worked with us with absolute integrity." As we have seen, these agents required this "integrity" as a professional tool and a means of building trust. Kollek recalled one incident from August 1944: "The sum of $150,000 was sent to Gizi Fleischmann through one of the double agents. Several weeks later we heard that she had been executed. We heard nothing further about the agent and we didn't discover what happened to the money, but it is possible that the agent was also caught and killed."

In the course of his work in Istanbul, Kollek came to Palestine five or six times—roughly once a month—and thus was able to report and be updated properly, for "in letters the whole story cannot be told, and we certainly were unable to send money, gold, and diamonds through the British diplomatic pouch." He also wrote that the Yishuv felt duty bound to transfer money to the occupied areas (including concentration camps) in order to make it possible to bribe key figures and to purchase weapons, medicine, food, and even liberty.[70]

Kollek wrote that the Yishuv emissaries smuggled money and diamonds with the full knowledge that they were violating the law and were even likely to be helping the German war effort. "This did not give us a pleasant feeling, but the highest priority was given to saving Jews," and this was no time to be concerned with "hairsplitting." According to Kollek, the preferred means of payment in Europe was gold or diamonds. It was therefore necessary to convert dollars or pounds sterling into gold or diamonds and afterward to try and smuggle them from Palestine into Turkey and from Turkey into Nazi-occupied Europe.

In his memoirs Kollek recalled that smuggling was carried out through couriers, who could have "reaped great profits through the clever exchange of currency for gold, or by trading optical instruments for cash." Whoever was able to travel freely in Europe under Nazi patronage "could have made a huge fortune by transferring money, diamonds, optical instruments, gold, and even just tea and coffee." Bandi Grosz was just one among several main couriers; there were others, including visiting Gestapo agents in Istanbul. "We paid them for their services, but they had more important reasons for coming to Istanbul. They sensed that the end of the war was imminent and wanted to buy themselves insurance in case of an Allied victory." Through these people, medicine, letters, and money were sent to Hungary, Slovakia, and Poland.[71]

According to Kollek, it was most fortunate that diamonds were available in Palestine thanks to Jewish refugees who had arrived from Antwerp at the start of the war and had established a diamond industry. He did not know the extent to which the Palestine diamond industry was subjected to surveillance by American intelligence.[72] The British forbid diamonds to be taken out of Palestine and sent to neutral countries—and certainly not to enemy countries—so they had to be smuggled out by the emissaries. The real control point was at the Syria-Turkey border crossing, not far from Aleppo. Menahem Bader was stopped there on his way to Istanbul with money and diamonds. Fortunately, the diamonds and the money he was carrying were not discovered.[73]

According to Ira Hirschmann, the War Refugee Board representative based in Turkey, elements in the British and American intelligence services cooperated with "the lads," as he affectionately called the Yishuv emissaries, despite the knowledge that their governments did not look kindly on their activity. British and American intelligence officers helped the Palestinians because they valued their operational skills and wanted to make use of them for their own purposes. Hirschmann wrote that the Yishuv emissaries es-

tablished good contacts with Germans, Hungarians, Bulgarians, and Poles on the Nazis' payroll. These individuals demanded payment in gold or hard currency, so the emissaries went to the black market for this purpose.[74]

We now know how self-serving the couriers were. Some were double agents, while others were full-fledged members of the Abwehr and the Gestapo. Some of the damage caused by these agents was immediately apparent. For example, Hans Welti, a Swiss journalist who served as a courier between the Geneva and Zionist movement headquarters in Romania, was actually a double agent who showed his Nazi masters every letter or task he received in Romania or Geneva. The Nazis consequently read part of the correspondence between Istanbul, Bucharest, and Geneva. The arrest of Zionist activists in Romania at the beginning of 1944 was directly related to this betrayal.[75]

THE SOCIALIST INTERNATIONAL AS A CHANNEL FOR THE TRANSFER OF FUNDS

The Socialist International actually consisted of a network of Socialist activists extending across most of Europe—a big organizational asset in wartime. The Socialist International and its cells were instrumental in passing classified information from Europe, and they possessed a great intelligence potential. The question remains as to whether the notion of using the Socialist International for money transfers as well had already arisen in the first years of the war?

The relations of the Yishuv's labor movement with the Socialist International and, in particular, with its first secretary, the Belgian Walter Schevenels, are already reflected in documentation from the early thirties. They developed steadily against a background of the growth of Fascist movements worldwide.

Quite a few "security people" who held senior positions in the fields of arms dealing, illegal immigration, and rescue, such as Eliyahu Golomb and Dov Hos, maintained close ties with the Socialist International center. Immediately after the Nazis took control in Germany, the Histadrut and Mapai, the local Socialist party, were mobilized for the anti-Fascist struggle. There was even a fundraising campaign in Palestine for Socialist parties in countries suffering from Fascism, including the Austrian party, and money was transferred to the Socialist International secretariat.[76] There was therefore a strong link between Mapai and the Socialist International. The Histadrut also sent money to Schevenels intended for the anti-Fascist struggle.[77]

From the standpoint of Mapai, whose heads led the JAE, the Socialist International was an arena for the recruitment of allies throughout the world and for the establishment of intelligence networks in different locales. For example, through the Socialist International contact was established with a prominent young leader of the worker movement in India, who was invited to visit Palestine. Zaslani arranged meetings for him with Moshe Sharett and Gershon Agronski, who were already engaged in intelligence matters in the thirties.

The Socialist International sought to impose a boycott against the Nazi regime in Germany. On this point it clashed with Mapai, since the Zionist movement was in the process of discussing the "transfer agreement" with Germany. Dov Hos was asked to explain to Schevenels the importance of this agreement. According to Hos, he "accepted these things with complete agreement."[78]

Ben-Gurion and the heads of the foreign relations departments in Mapai and the Histadrut were also associated with John Brown and the Bulgarian Georgi Dimitrov, both high-ranking members of the Socialist International. Brown and Dimitrov even visited Palestine and met with Ben-Gurion. Members of the Socialist parties in Europe who were affiliated with the Socialist International could have extended organized aid to

the Jews in Nazi-occupied Europe. Available documentation reflects the efforts of Ben-Gurion and his associates to employ their services; the subject warrants further research.

According to entries in Ben-Gurion's diary dating from the beginning of 1941, combined with correspondence with Israel Mereminsky, the Histadrut emissary based in the United States, it seems that members of the Socialist International, including Schevenels, helped to transfer money to Jews in the occupied areas. In short, the topic was providing support for the activities of the Hechalutz office in Warsaw, which was headed by Zivia Lubetkin. Mereminsky complained to Ben-Gurion that his Histadrut emissaries were disrupting the dispatch of money. He reported on a complex system of transferring money from the United States to occupied Europe involving, among others, Histadrut emissaries in the United States, ex-Polish Jews in Palestine, Jewish Agency representatives in Geneva, and the Jewish Agency's London branch.[79] This correspondence mentioned the Histadrut appeal fund in the United States as well as other companies, apparently including AMPAL (American Palestine Trading Corporation), which had been established in the United States at the beginning of 1942.

This correspondence might be a key factor in pointing to a system of money transfers and aid to the Jews in the occupied regions through the Histadrut appeal fund, AMPAL, and the Socialist International. One of the possibilities emerging from a study of the documentation (which is enigmatic and full of code names) is that a rotating system of money transfers, which had been frozen in countries like Romania, was carried out in order to fund the immigration and rescue of Jews from Europe, especially Poland. In any case, painstaking research in the archives of various countries is still necessary to shed additional light on this topic.

15
Funding Aid and Rescue Operations
A Summary

The figures presented on the JAE budget allocations for aid and rescue operations show that these constituted at least a quarter of the JAE's expenditures, representing one of four major expenditure items, the others being settlement, labor, and housing— the traditional "Zionist" items of the JAE expenditure.

Nevertheless, this is not the total picture. In actual fact, much more Yishuv money was transferred for aid and rescue from Jewish Agency funds and those of other Yishuv organizations. It also seems worthwhile not only to specify the extent of these allocations but also to evaluate them, that is, to view what was allocated and provided for aid and rescue in terms of several essential economic variables:

- the balance of the budget after deducting its "mortgaged" components
- the extent of flexibility permissible for an organizational system like the Yishuv and the Zionist movement in those years, once the leadership recognized the emergency situation and reorganized accordingly
- the relationship between the annual increase in aid and rescue and other economic variables in the Yishuv economy at that time, such as growth rate and improved economic situation of individuals and organizations

This last aspect, involving a balancing of contributions to aid and rescue after specific calculations, requires additional economic research.

I believe that what I have presented is sufficient to show that the question of how much the Yishuv allocated for rescue should not be examined exclusively from the perspective of the annual Jewish Agency budget during the relevant years,[1] nor should it be viewed in light of the severe criticism leveled against the JAE. This issue should not be examined solely by citing the public declarations of Kaplan and Ben-Gurion. As one has seen, these pronouncements were often contradicted by their actions.

How can one explain the gap between the overt and covert dimensions of the funding for aid and rescue and the fierce criticism that accompanied the debate over this issue? One explanation would require economic-historical research that approaches these "loaded" issues from an unemotional, empirical viewpoint. For example, one should not examine these questions primarily based on a criterion of "will," which is difficult to evaluate and quantify, but rather according to the Jewish Agency's and the Yishuv's economic potential. Only after such research has delimited the boundaries of the latter can any evaluation of public will or the will of the leadership be made.

A second explanation for the harsh criticism leveled at Ben-Gurion and Kaplan arises from the fact that the Jewish Agency's declared "budget"— the source of the criticism—did not reflect all the actions undertaken by the JAE. This was due to the fear that budgetary figures would reveal political and defense plans, settlement plans, and so forth. It is worth remembering that all these activities were conducted at a time when there were many internal and external reasons for the Jewish Agency not to reveal its hand. These details were of great interest to the Arab population of Palestine, the Arab states, the British, and the Americans. Domestic opposition on the Left and the Right presented a different but no less tangible threat to the Yishuv leadership.

In short, the Jewish Agency budget does not accurately reflect the entire scope of operations, which also included the purchase of weapons and defense and illegal immigration in addition to aid and rescue. The budget did not reflect these activities in their entirety, and Ben-Gurion and Kaplan were unable to defend themselves by revealing their secret operations. Their silence, coupled with a budget that contained only meager allocations for aid and rescue, greatly exacerbated the situation and increased the criticism.

Furthermore, it is uncertain whether the Yishuv economy in those days was subject to a united leadership, making it doubtful that any analysis can provide a full and accurate picture of its economic potential. Just as the Yishuv had several "armies" and leaderships—the JAE and the Haganah being the dominant organizations—from a certain point of view it also had several "economies." This phenomenon also resulted from the fact that the Yishuv was under foreign rule and functioned on a voluntary basis. Two opposing tendencies were engaged in a struggle that had no clear outcome, namely, crystallization around a single political authority versus protests from disparate groups. The Yishuv was a politically immature society that lacked operational discipline.

All of the following were typically debated during this period: the political structure of the Haganah's national headquarters; dismissal of the Palmach central command in the midst of the War of Independence; what was known as the "Season," that is, the season of hunting—a code name for an operation in which the Zionist movement cooperated with the Mandatory government in its effort to capture IZL leaders; the struggle over certificates and immigrant quotas; distribution of the long-awaited orphan children from Poland and the structure of the Infiltration Advisory Committee; the Altalena affair, in which twenty-one immigrants to Palestine were killed in a confrontation with the IDF; the refusal of certain parties in all quarters in the Yishuv to hand over their weapons to the central command during the War of Independence. This argumentative mood also characterized debate over the al-

location of economic resources and influenced the funding policy for aid and rescue. It should also be remembered that at this time there was a pervasive feeling of political and economic uncertainty that derived, among other things, from disturbances during the Arab revolt, the memory of economic and political crises between the two world wars, and the Second World War itself.

Given this uneasy atmosphere, there was a reasonable fear that the "central authority"—principally the Jewish Agency, which was a problematic coalitionary body—might collapse. Amid a social existence marked by a degree of fragmentation characteristic of a voluntary society, it was natural for certain groups to wish to preserve their organizational and economic autonomy. They sought to secure their diverse interests and would not rely solely on any central authority. In response to the question "Who will look after us, our children, and our dear ones?," the tendency was to give priority to the private individual by preserving independent "funds" and personal resources and connections.

A rending inner contradiction was experienced between the trend of isolation and the dejection, to mounting tension caused by frequent reports of fellow Jews being murdered in Europe. Occasionally this tension found an outlet in communal gatherings, where those present went through the ritual of heaping accusations on the shoulders of the leadership. This pattern of assembly and simultaneous accusation was a "solution," as it were. Nevertheless, the atmosphere in the Yishuv was not altogether grim and it may be supposed that pressure from the Yishuv leadership acted as a counterweight to this pattern of seclusion and accusations. These were the forces that Kaplan and Ben-Gurion had to confront. They met the tendency of "to each his own" head on in a constant struggle to compel all the elements in the Yishuv to participate in the overall rescue effort.

In this connection, Menahem Bader's letter to the Kibbutz Ha'artzi is enlightening:

Concerning our special aid account—please take note that to date I have transferred 748 Palestinian pounds. I have therefore almost reached the sum you agreed to—and I ask you for your further decision. The overall amounts are insufficient—and the little that falls to the credit of the youth movements—and a little of this little that our friends receive does not meet the needs. Do make an extra effort. . . .[2]

From Bader's point of view, in addition to the general economy there existed a type of separate "aid and rescue economy" of his movement, Hashomer Hatza'ir. It may be supposed that this was characteristic not only of Hashomer Hatza'ir but also of the Revisionists, the United Kibbutz Movement, Mapai, and various religious groups.

The Jewish Agency's open budget concealed more than it revealed about undercover activity on behalf of Europe's Jews. A very considerable part of the rescue funding was "buried" in "reserves" and B Funds managed by Kaplan, Ben-Gurion, and their aides. Based on Bader's last remarks, it may be supposed that other bodies in the Yishuv also managed similar B Funds; Weizmann and Ben-Gurion occasionally used these funds. Further striking evidence of the management of such a fund is found in JAE discussions of the 1945 budget. Moshe Shapira, a member of the Immigration Department, praised Kaplan for making sure to keep "reserves" on hand since they funded a number of vital operations that had not been budgeted for beforehand. The mystery surrounding these categories in the JAE budget enabled Kaplan to increase the budget of the Immigration Department fourfold.[3]

Parallel to a certain degree of fragmentation in the Yishuv society and economy, there was also a blurring of borders and mutual incursions among various organizations. The Histadrut economy also funded missions by the Haganah. The Agricultural Workers' Federation, of which Zvi Yehieli was a chief activist, was engaged in more than just growing lettuce. Solel Boneh and David Hacohen did more than just produce support beams for the ceiling in the Histadrut Executive Committee building. *Davar,* as well as AMPAL and *Paltours,* a company owned by the Anglo-Palestinian Bank, were apparently involved in undercover activity. Any economic research into the funding of rescue operations will require differentiating among the different kinds of activity.

Another possible, quite simple explanation for how the Yishuv institutions and the Zionist movement finally funded rescue and aid operations in Europe to an extent not at all in keeping with the fierce criticism they were subjected to may be the failure—or the rather limited success—of the rigid tactic adopted by Ben-Gurion and Kaplan to compel external organizations to extend aid. In the final analysis, the JAE had to allocate more than it had intended for the aid and rescue of European Jewry because many other organizations hid in its shadow, primarily because they preferred to keep their independent funds to themselves.

There is presently no objective research based on economic statistics. Early investigators of the funding issue tended mainly to rely on discussions of rescue funding, that is, they mainly examined "what they said" about rescue funding and not "what they did." Some of these critics were unaware of other operations that were being conducted but were not reflected in the budget. The severity of their criticism was greatly influenced by the frustrating paucity of means in the face of the atrocity, irrespective of the Yishuv's contribution to the rescue effort. In other words, to a large extent this harsh criticism was an expression of internalized, helpless indignation. Later students of the protocols of the Yishuv institutions saw mainly the rigid tactics employed by Ben-Gurion and Kaplan—including a number of stinging, somewhat regrettable statements by both—and the severe criticism leveled at rescue funding.

Such a distorted view is based on the following analogy: if scathing criticism is voiced with regard to rescue funding, there must be some basis to it, so the leadership must have neglected European Jewry. I have already demonstrated that the critics at that time were either not aware of the true dimension of the funding or preferred to ignore its scope and to vent their anger through harsh criticism. I have also shown that Ben-Gurion's and Kaplan's apparent neglect of rescue funding was only verbal and tactical; in truth they allocated a great deal of money for rescue. It thus emerges that a lack of knowledge and utter frustration at the time has a tendency to repeat itself. The only way to avoid such a trap is through empirically based economic research.

Such research will necessarily involve a long list of activities not based on "receipts" or "bills," since most of them were not legal and involved individuals of dubious character. In many instances the interim funding from the budget became "bad debts," which are very difficult to trace. The prohibition against transferring funds to Nazi-occupied Europe led Jewish donors, including the Yishuv, to cover up contributions and to transfer them by roundabout means. For example, the Gestapo cable from Romania on the transfer of over half a million dollars to Romania illustrates our incomplete knowledge of the money trail and the extent of the contributions that the Jewish people injected into Europe.

Did Ben-Gurion's and Kaplan's inflexible declarations concerning the rescue funding policy produce positive results? The answer is best expressed in the form of questions: What would have happened to the Jewish Agency's other goals had Ben-Gurion and Kaplan announced beforehand that the JAE was taking upon itself full financial responsibility for rescue and aid? How much would other organizations in the Yishuv and the Jewish communities in the free world have contributed? To what extent would the Zionist movement have succeeded in funding preliminary plans to rescue the Jewish people

from their plight and achieve independent statehood only a few years after the destruction that occurred in Europe?

At any rate, Ben-Gurion's and Kaplan's budgetary policy was dictated by their belief that, given this impossible reality both internally and externally, no one should consider himself exempt from responsibility. They believed that it was their duty to exhibit an inflexible and aggressive front and to "concede" only when there was no alternative. The harsh criticism mainly involved the shaping and splitting of the budget. After it had been signed, the critics—second- and third-ranking members of the leadership—were silent, indicating that deep down they, too, adopted Ben-Gurion's and Kaplan's reasoning.[4]

It emerges that Ben-Gurion was involved in determining the rescue funding policy in the form of interim funding allocations until funding could be obtained from extrabudgetary sources. When it became clear that such funding would not be forthcoming, Ben-Gurion and Kaplan authorized the allocation of funds that would clearly not be reimbursed, including interim funding for plans involving mass rescue of Jews from Europe. There is clear evidence that Ben-Gurion was also involved in efforts to obtain funding for such rescue plans, whose overall cost far exceeded the financial capacity of the Yishuv and the Zionist movement.

Ben-Gurion was personally involved in various fund-raising efforts, including campaigns and appeals to wealthy Jews in the Yishuv community to increase their contributions, as well as in mass fund-raising gatherings. He used his public stature to reduce the number of those wishing to evade responsibility. Ben-Gurion was involved in efforts to recruit the JDC for rescue operations mounted by the Yishuv and the Zionist movement; in this case he even departed from the inflexible model of cooperation he had originally proposed. His hand could be detected in efforts to get the various Jewish communities to contribute.

"Your Country calls you to enlist"
(*CZA, poster collection*).

Eliezer Kaplan was his partner and confidant. The two adopted various unorthodox measures in order to overcome a lack of coordination resulting from an inability of the Yishuv institutions to enforce their authority. They accomplished this by stretching democratic rules governing public supervision: decisions were arrived at in a restricted forum; money for aid and rescue was allocated based on vague, nonspecific budgetary clauses.

Ben-Gurion revealed something of his innermost thoughts, and indicated the difficulties of leadership in remarks he made at the beginning of 1944 to those attending the third students' convention. He and his colleagues had no choice but to depend on the public's goodwill. The inability to enforce authority also manifested itself in evasion of army service and increased difficulty in collecting money for essential aims. Ben-Gurion stressed that many young people from all walks of life were volunteering to serve in the British army, but he also remarked that the phenomenon of evasion encompassed many levels of society and cut across all political boundaries. Ben-Gurion noted a parallel manifestation in the context of contributions to fund the mobilization and rescue effort. Stating that "the Yishuv has contributed a million Palestinian pounds a year," he nevertheless carefully distinguished between contributors and evaders.

In order to placate his listeners, Ben-Gurion drew a comparison with this type of activity in the United States. He explained that the phenomenon of evasion also existed in other societies where individuals were compelled to live and function in the nonsovereign state that characterized the life of the Jewish community in Palestine. The United States is "a great country, not merely in terms of size." It created a "great culture" and "prevailed in the last war, and will prevail in this one." But even the United States could not have achieved what it had were it not for its administration, congressional houses, president, treasury, and enforcement system. Had the United States been confronted with a test such as the Japanese attack against Pearl Harbor, but without the means to govern and enforce, it would not have been able to raise millions of dollars, industry would not have been able to mobilize for the war effort, workers would not have redoubled their efforts, and millions of American citizens would not have voluntarily joined the armed services. In his view, there had been a real danger of a crisis developing in the United States over whether or not it should enter the war, which could have developed into a civil war. His conclusion was clear: "We have no Congress, . . . we have no government, we have no taxes. If a Jew wishes to deny the hope of Israel and the tribulations of Israel, nothing can be done to him. There is a government here that protects him, there is a government here that encourages evaders and protects them.[5]

In fact, what lies behind Ben-Gurion's words is the belief that it is not enough merely to enumerate the contributions for rescue efforts. Rather, their value has to be considered in the light of the inability of the Yishuv leadership and the Zionist movement to control the "overall Jewish coffers," the great dependence of the leadership on the goodwill of the public, and the deterrent effect of the prohibition against transferring money to enemy countries.

Conclusion

The Yishuv in Eretz Israel and its leadership did act in accordance with Kaplan's recommendation "to shoot an arrow in the dark," but it was very murky indeed. Despite their fierce determination, the arrows had very little effect. The failed attempts to save Europe's Jews was yet another aspect of the bitter fate of the Jewish people in those days.

My research has demonstrated that Ben-Gurion was an important and central partner in receiving information on what was happening, including rescue plans and operations, and that he was involved in weighing issues and making decisions. The main information concerning rescue and aid operations first arrived on his desk, and he decided on the direction to be taken. At crucial junctures in the big rescue plans, he insisted that everything possible had to be attempted, however unlikely were the chances of success. In this respect he, too, shot arrows in the dark.

Ben-Gurion participated in discussions on rescue funding and, together with Kaplan, developed the policy of allocating interim funding. The two laid down the rule that no plan would be rejected due to a lack of money. Ben-Gurion was prepared to pay the price for adopting the tactic of brinkmanship and upholding tough positions aimed at forcing the public, the Jews in the free world, and their organizations to bear the cost of funding. He did, in fact, pay for this tactic. It did much to shape his past and present public image.

Ben-Gurion took part in fund-raising campaigns and was involved in their planning, even drafting the text of invitations to closed appeals. He participated in a variety of protest activities, though he did not believe in their effectiveness beyond satisfying the Yishuv's and his own psychological needs. He was personally involved in negotiations for the establishment of the Rescue Committee, took part in various controversies within the Yishuv over issues of aid and rescue, and supervised cooperation efforts with British and American intelligence services.

Having established, beyond any doubt, Ben-Gurion's deep involvement in such matters, one must still ask if he was up to the special challenge demanded of a Jewish leader during the Holocaust. Was Ben-Gurion able to accurately interpret the major events? Did he offer real solutions in the long and short term? Did he succeed in forging the necessary tools to accomplish this?

THE INTEGRATIVE CONCEPT

Perhaps more than any other Jewish leader, Ben-Gurion formulated for himself and conveyed to the public his sense of approaching calamity. He dreaded it intuitively and rationally analyzed its conditions and causes. However, Ben-Gurion neither foresaw the Holocaust nor was quicker than others in interpreting the testimonies of wholesale slaughter in Europe. A great many people failed to correctly interpret the information that arrived from Europe, because what was taking place was atrocity on a scale previously unknown to human experience, and for a time the Nazis even succeeded in camouflaging it.

Nevertheless, Ben-Gurion sensed that a great calamity was approaching and suggested a comprehensive, basic solution. In his view, the root of the Jewish people's problems lay in the political anomaly of being stateless, lacking an army, and being unable to determine its destiny. The fundamental solution was therefore Zionist-political in nature, and based on this Ben-Gurion initiated a series of actions. First, he took it upon himself to inculcate in everyone the recognition that the solution proposed at the start of the modern era for this anomalous state of affairs—

emancipation and assimilation in the non-Jewish world—would end in disaster. Although he did not foresee the nature of the disaster, he pointed to its source: traditionally distressed countries like Poland and "enlightened" countries like Germany and Austria.

Ben-Gurion sought to raise awareness within diverse groups: the Jewish Diaspora, the Yishuv and its leadership, and British and American political circles. He constantly reiterated his belief that a political solution for the Jews of Europe was urgently required, as was a state that would restore to the Jews control over their destiny. This is the underlying conception behind the various tactical approaches adopted by Ben-Gurion during the thirties and forties: control over mass immigration; the achievement of a Jewish majority in Palestine; and the establishment of a "commonwealth" or a "national home" in Palestine.

Naturally, he was not alone in holding such views, nor was he the only one to insist on the establishment of a state for the Jewish masses. Weizmann and Jabotinsky held similar views and underscored their urgency. However, such views were not held by the majority, nor even by all Zionists. Already at the beginning of the thirties Ben-Gurion endeavored to inculcate his conception among the Yishuv workers' movement and Zionism as a whole.

Many did not realize that mass immigration required much advance preparation. They continued to favor the immigration of a select few in order to foster the pioneer spirit of the Yishuv under the leadership of a Zionist workers' movement. They relegated mass immigration to a more distant future, when "the model Zionist-Socialist society" in Palestine would be strong enough to absorb them without losing its character.

Another no less forceful source of opposition came from the Right, which wished to create "a free economy" in Palestine, not one mobilized in response to such a speedy mass immigration. The demands of this historic enterprise—at the

very least involving the transfer of several thousand people—generally deterred the liberal-minded capitalists as well as the nonideological elements within Palestinian Jewish society.

Consequently, Ben-Gurion's conception aroused opposition on both sides and was greeted with indifference or opposition by the general population. Yitzhak Tabenkin and other prominent leaders in his movement viewed it as an ideological digression. There are those who maintain that this difference led to the split in Mapai in 1942–1944. Many respected people in Mapai and Hashomer Hatza'ir saw in Ben-Gurion's call for mass immigration from Eastern Europe a recipe for the destruction of the Zionist enterprise in Palestine. A similar pattern of opposition was characteristic of those belonging to such diverse forms as the Ahad Ha'am [Asher Zvi Ginzburg] Zionism on the "civilian Right." Ben-Gurion termed this approach "Yishuvism," which he used to describe both those holding capitalist-liberal views as well as those nonideological types in the Yishuv who wished to live their lives undisturbed by historic and revolutionary enterprises. This was also meant as a well-aimed barb at his opponents in the workers' movement, who considered themselves revolutionary Zionists.

In contrast to the rightist "Yishuvists" and the leftist "elitists," Ben-Gurion believed that mass immigration was Zionism's main objective. Beginning in the thirties, it became increasingly urgent. In his view, the Yishuv in Palestine was a means of realizing that historic goal, an extremely valuable tool, a broad elite worthy of leading and educating the entire Jewish people, but nevertheless a serving elite that was not in and of itself a goal. In this sense Ben-Gurion was not at all "Palestinocentric" or a "Canaanite of sorts." He persisted in his efforts to propound his conception within Mapai, and to a considerable extent he succeeded until the Ahdut Haavoda movement broke off from Mapai. His inclination to transform Mapai from a "class" to a "people's" party,[1] the signing of the "transfer agreement" with Germany (1933), and attempts to reach a similar agreement with Poland shortly thereafter have to be viewed against this background.

In 1935 Ben-Gurion presented his party with "the million plan," which involved transporting a million Jews from Poland and Germany to Palestine within five to ten years. The notion of a "militant Zionism" had already surfaced in May 1938, and the slogan "Jews will fight" was well within the realm of a clear declaration of intent on Ben-Gurion's part to lead the Yishuv in a determined struggle to permit the mass immigration of Jews who wished to escape the mounting distress in Europe.[2]

Ben-Gurion realized that there was no other solution for European Jewry, a fact borne out by the Evian Conference, which took place less than two months after he announced his intent to fight for the right of immigration. The conference ended without results. Britain refused to sanction the mass integration of European Jews either in Palestine or in Britain itself. The United States and other Western countries refused to open their doors to Jews, giving Hitler an opportunity to comment cynically on their self-righteousness.[3] Consequently, Ben-Gurion saw no hope for the Jewish people other than challenging Britain for the right of Jews to escape from Nazi-occupied Europe to Palestine.

In the end, Ben-Gurion and those who shared his views proved victorious; they succeeded in imparting their outlook to the whole of Mapai.[4] After the mass slaughter in Europe became known, Ben-Gurion intensified his rhetoric and demanded immediate immigration. He insisted that Zionist ideology adapt to harsh reality, for Zionism was no "metaphysical theology," as he put it, but a veritable freedom movement. He led the struggle against the White Paper in the first half of the war and placed himself at the head of the Planning Committee, which drew up a program for the accelerated integration of a million Jews in Palestine. The practical application of this policy occurred during the second half of the war.

Ben-Gurion did not content himself simply with implementing the outmoded tendencies within the Yishuv or the Zionist movement. He realized that it was up to him to also make known to foreign statesmen and army commanders, to intelligence people and diplomats, the urgent need to rescue large numbers of Jews from Europe. In April 1936 he informed Sir Arthur Wauchope, the British high commissioner for Palestine, that the accelerated evacuation of Jews from Poland and Germany was vital.[5] This was also the gist of his statements to prominent figures in Britain and the United States during his visits there in subsequent years. Explaining the need for mass immigration following the war and for a political solution to the plight of the Jews in Palestine was a major reason for his frequent travels in the course of the war. It is worth noting that, despite his efforts, Ben-Gurion never succeeded in meeting with either Churchill or Roosevelt.

A few years earlier, this same outlook had motivated Ben-Gurion to support the Peel Commission's proposal to divide Palestine into a small Jewish state and an Arab state covering most of the area of Palestine.[6] The opportunity for free mass immigration was so important to him at the time that he agreed to the establishment of a small Jewish state as long as the Jews were granted control of the entrance to Palestine. The urgent need to absorb Jews from Europe into Palestine was preeminent in his view. The sinister trap that was emerging in Europe—no one at the time knew to what extent it was a death trap—is what determined Ben-Gurion's stance regarding the political status of Palestine and relations with Palestinian Arabs, not vice versa. To say the least, this was not the stance of a "Palestinocentrist" or "Canaanite of sorts," as some would call Ben-Gurion in later years.

Although Berl Katznelson, Ben-Gurion's partner in the Mapai leadership, and Yitzhak Tabenkin, head of the Kibbutz Hameuhad movement, held opposing political views, both rejected

Ben-Gurion's acceptance of the reduced geographical territory for the future Jewish state that the Peel Commission had proposed. Faced with fierce internal party opposition, here is how Ben-Gurion expressed his views to the Mapai Council in March 1944:

> Had a Jewish state been established [in the thirties] . . . we might have brought millions to the state . . . and they would be here. We shall not bring them . . . because those Jews are no more. . . . I did not relinquish [the idea] of the greater land of Israel; rather, I believed that bringing two million Jews is worth more than all the highfalutin phrases about the greater land of Israel.[7]

Ben-Gurion's overtures favoring a compromise with Palestinian Arab leaders in the thirties were also impelled, among other things, by that same sense of urgency. He wished to reach a compromise with Palestinian Arabs in order to ensure that the Jewish people had something agreed-upon and acknowledged to hold on to, thereby removing the major political stumbling block to the resettlement of European Jewry in Palestine.

The Biltmore Program, which was called the Jerusalem Plan after being approved in Palestine by the Zionist Executive Council, was an important component of Ben-Gurion's policy framework of the thirties and forties. "Control over immigration" to facilitate the rescue of the Jewish masses from Europe was one of the central goals of that program. Ben-Gurion sought to muster the broadest possible agreement around this goal among American Jews, including those that clung to a belief in the continuation of Jewish existence in the Diaspora. He supported the demand for the restoration of Jewish rights in every part of the world.

In an altogether different context involving the Balfour Declaration, representatives of the Zionist movement adopted a similar approach in their contacts with non-Zionists. This was even given expression in Lord Balfour's letter to Lionel Rothschild, which became known as the Balfour Declaration. As a matter of fact the Zionist movement included in its political platform a demand for equal civil and national rights for Jews in their countries of residence, although it affirmed among its principles "the negation of the Diaspora." In any case, Ben-Gurion did not distinguish between a "Zionist" interest and "Jewish" interest. For him "the negation of the Diaspora" was not a slogan of the blinds meaning "deserting the Diaspora" during the Holocaust.

Ben-Gurion's words and actions throughout the war were carried out in this spirit, even when the Yishuv itself was faced with the real danger of conquest by the Nazis in a pincer-like movement from Egypt in the south and Syria in the north. Despite the danger, Ben-Gurion stressed the Zionist character and role of the Yishuv, insisting on what he deemed the proper relationship between the Yishuv and the Diaspora. At the Forty-third Histadrut Council and at a meeting with General Zionists in Tel Aviv—in remarks directed at both the Right and the Left—Ben-Gurion warned against the possibility of the Yishuv retreating into self-imposed seclusion in the face of danger. Repeating a previously mentioned term, he warned against "the danger of Yishuvism."

> We see the Yishuv as a goal in and of itself [and there is a real danger that] we shall act and conduct ourselves only on our own account, of the "here" and "now." Besides a "here" there has to be a "there," a place where the communities of Israel are being destroyed. Instead of "now" there [must] also [be] "in the future"; efforts have to be directed to the days to come, not the days of the Messiah or the distant future, but to the end of the war.[8]

He also spoke in this vein to Sir Stephan Elliot Luke, a Colonial Office official, during his visit to London at the end of 1941: "The concern for the

Jews of Palestine is not the only thing, nor even the main thing, that preoccupies us."[9]

Here one should recall Ben-Gurion's dramatic words at the Elected Assembly convention held a week after news of the extermination was revealed. He called on the free world and the neutral nations to open their doors and to integrate Jewish refugees. He pointed to Palestine as being only a third alternative for the refugees. He also spoke in a similar fashion a few days later at a gathering of his party's activists.[10] After it transpired that both Britain and the United States as well as Palestine would be closed to Jewish children from Europe, the activists searched farther afield for a place for refugees—in South Africa, in the Iberian Peninsula, and even in Afghanistan.[11] When the Jewish Agency attempted to transport Jewish children to Sweden, it was not unaware of the geographical distance separating Scandinavia and Palestine. Eichmann's demand that Jews redeemed as a result of the ransom plan should not be brought to Palestine but rather to the Iberian Peninsula or to any other place did not deter Sharett when he heard about it in Aleppo. It did not dissuade Ben-Gurion and his JAE colleagues from their intense efforts to advance the ransom plan brought by Brand from Hungary.

In Ben-Gurion's view, immigration was a major instrument in materialization of the Zionist ideology but not the only means for rescuing Jews during the Holocaust. On the eve of the war and after the nature of the cataclysm in Europe had become clear, Ben-Gurion developed a plan of action that combined rescuing Jews from Europe and transporting them to anywhere in the world while stressing that Palestine was the main land capable of absorbing the Jewish refugees on a permanent basis. Under his leadership, the Yishuv and the Zionist movement first drew up practical plans and subsequently initiated and carried out operations to rescue and transport Jews beyond the reach of the Nazis, while at the same time deploying them politically for mass absorption in Palestine as the main target for

settlement of Jews. Ben-Gurion's "dual formula" was designed to cope with the crisis of the Jewish people by means of short-term emergency measures as well as deployment for a fundamental, long-term solution. This was Ben-Gurion's complete answer to the catastrophe, developed while the events were taking place, when all the knowledge and experience vouchsafed later observers of the history of that period were not at his disposal.

I have categorically refuted the claim that Ben-Gurion adopted a Palestinocentric stance during the Holocaust and sacrificed the needs of "the Jewish people" for those of "the land of Israel" or "political Zionism." As I have demonstrated, the needs of the Jews were what tilted the scales. Ben-Gurion repeatedly stated that although for the first time in history there was the real possibility of a state for the Jewish people in the Diaspora, there was less of a chance of there being a people for this state. In remarks made in 1943 at a youth gathering held at the grave of Joseph Trumpeldor on Tel Hai Day, he expressed this view, which does not lend itself to simplistic formulas:

> For us this earth is holier than for previous of generations of Jews—who believed in its historic and religious holiness—because it has been consecrated by our sweat, our toil, and our blood. But we possess a greater holiness: the holiness of the Jewish people, the holiness of its life, its genius, and its honor. What good is this land, with its mountains and valleys, if the Jewish people do not find redemption there? The Jewish people will not find redemption and will not experience rebirth unless the Nazi foe that has risen over us is crushed and destroyed to its very foundations.[12]

Even those who attempt to prove that Ben-Gurion betrayed the Jews of Europe do not believe he was a fool, for only a fool or a wicked person would strive for a state without a nation and ignore the extinction of the people who form the state's human pillar. Ben-Gurion was neither foolish nor wicked. The slaughter of European Jewry affected him profoundly. Hypothetically assuming that he didn't feel this way—one knows to what extent the image of a cruel Ben-Gurion has struck deep roots—even from a narrow "Zionist" standpoint Ben-Gurion and his colleagues could not have viewed with equanimity their people going up in the smoke of the crematoria. Assuming a contrast in Ben-Gurion's view between "a narrow Zionist outlook" and "a broad Jewish outlook" in the thirties and forties is distorted and untenable. I have repeatedly demonstrated that this distinction was totally alien to Ben-Gurion's spirit and that of his comrades. I have presented it here for the sake of argument and in order to put things in their proper perspective.

I have found support for this assertion in many of Ben-Gurion's actions. I have relied not merely on tactical statements at events like Tel Hai Day but also on his remarks during rather prosaic occasions, such as a debate on the fund-raising campaign called "Solidarity with the Diaspora Month." Ben-Gurion said the following to the representative of the Keren Hayesod fund [PFF] appeal:

> I am ready to accept your opinion that this fund [Mobilization and Rescue Fund] is liable to prove harmful to some degree to [Zionist] funds, but we must not accept the principle that nothing must be done that might harm the funds, although it is not clear to me why it should. The rescue of European Jewry has not only a financial aspect but also a moral one. This is one of the central issues.[13]

According to Ben-Gurion's conception, volunteering for the British army was also an important element of the Yishuv's contribution to the Diaspora during the Holocaust. Some thirty thousand young men and women answered the call of Ben-Gurion, Sharett, and their colleagues and volunteered for service. The Jewish Brigade Group (Jewish Fighting Brigade) was established not before the summer of 1944 only because of Britain's obstinate refusal to permit its establishment earlier. The Yishuv leadership and the Zionist movement had sought its establishment long before then.

This issue provides an important illustration of Ben-Gurion's integrative conception. Volunteers were recruited in order to defend the Yishuv against a Nazi attack and to aid the Jews of Europe. They were sent to fight Hitler and, at the same time, to lead the Jewish people step by step out of the circle of helplessness. Thousands of young men and women who answered the call did indeed contribute to the elimination of Hitler. They established contact with the Jews who remained in Europe and formed the nucleus of the army of the future Jewish state.

The non-Palestinocentric conception of the Yishuv leadership and of the Zionist movement was expressed succinctly by Moshe Sharett in an interview he gave to *The Observer:*

> When one's house is burning, its inhabitants must be evacuated even in the pouring rain. But if it is possible to place people in another house, to give them a glass of milk and a warm bed, why lead them into the darkness and the pouring rain? I wish to say one more thing: when the house is burning, its inhabitants must be evacuated, after which the fire has to be extinguished and inquiries must be made as to why the house burned. Why was it that this house went up in flames? Why didn't fire-fighting equipment work?[14]

In a certain sense Ben-Gurion actually was a Palestinocentrist—even enthusiastically so—but in a way quite different from that attributed to him. Ben-Gurion vigorously maintained that the Jewish people could emerge from their anomalous situation only through a process of coalescing and shaping society into a state that they would establish for themselves in Palestine. In his opinion, only through the establishment of a state in Palestine would the ingathering of minorities from all over the world eventually constitute a nation in control of its destiny and able to shape its life. Ben-Gurion never tired of repeating that the task of leading the Jewish people to their own land lay, first and foremost, with the tiny and rather sparse society of Palestinian Jews, who were required to prepare themselves ideologically, logistically, and operationally.

Ben-Gurion did not believe that the Holocaust fundamentally altered his basic opinion of the ultimate solution required to save the Jewish people. On the contrary, it merely confirmed it in the most shocking manner, revealing the Jewish people to be dependent on weak emancipatory solutions and exposing the hopelessness of their plight. In the final analysis, the small and poor Palestinian Yishuv was the single force most able to spring to the defense of the Jewish people, even though it was threatened with Nazi occupation and was subject to a foreign and not always sympathetic rule. The bitter truth was that, although relatively free, its strength was of little avail when confronted by the Nazi extermination machine.

Consequently, the assumption by the Yishuv of the role of guiding the Jewish people to a state of sovereignty—and in this respect Ben-Gurion was indeed a Palestinocentrist—did not influence the Yishuv leadership to abandon the Diaspora in its time of need, a fact abundantly confirmed by available documentation. Ben-Gurion and his comrades led a society totaling some half million individuals to assume three tasks simultaneously: self-defense, saving the Diaspora, and laying the groundwork for the absorption of hundreds of thousands of Jews after the war.

Perhaps Palestinocentrism can be attributed to Ben-Gurion from another vantage point. After the war it gradually became apparent that a large segment of Jews residing in the free world—plus a handful of those Jews who had survived the Holocaust in Nazi-occupied Europe—chose to remain in the Diaspora, that is to say, they rejected the analysis and plans of political Zionism insofar as this touched upon their private lives. In the face of this reality, Ben-Gurion asserted that the Yishuv had to offer practical and ideological assistance for organizing the Jewish people in the Diaspora. Among other things, Ben-Gurion called on the Yishuv to uphold the honor and right of those Jews who preferred to remain in the Diaspora.[15]

Although not a completely new approach in the history of the Zionist movement, what was new in Ben-Gurion's appeal was its Palestinocentric character. In the past, the political platforms of Zionist organizations in the Diaspora had also included the struggle for equal rights and national autonomy for Jews. What was termed "the work of the present" was a central element in the actual political life of Diaspora Zionism.[16] Now Ben-Gurion was charging the Palestinian Yishuv itself with this task, which was definitely a Palestinocentric move, but in a direction contrary to that attributed to him by his later critics.

In his orchestration of the aid and rescue operations in Europe, did Ben-Gurion possess those attributes—acute political sense; trenchant realism; flexibility of mind; profound awareness of the importance of organization—that scholars assign to him?[17] Ben-Gurion was quick to master "the rules of the game" and to grasp the complicated situation faced by the Yishuv and its leadership during the war. In this he was perhaps more prescient than his colleagues. He even willingly suffered isolation when forced to choose between difficult alternatives in the face of extremely harsh criticism. There are many examples where his leadership qualities were manifest. I suspect that the enormity of the challenge, the fact that his hands were tied, and limited internal authority partially explain his resignations, or threats to resign, and account for those periods when he fell ill.[18]

Ben-Gurion divined the nature of the trap that prevented the mass protest of Jews in the free world from having a tangible effect. He knew that the British "friend" was also an "enemy" who viewed the exodus of Jewish refugees from Europe as a serious political threat. He also knew that the Americans were insensitive friends for whom the fear of anti-Semitism at home, economic considerations, and plain indifference led them to close their gates to Jews fleeing for their lives. The tragic voyage of the *Saint Louis* was not an isolated instance. The Americans were almost as fearful as the British of a wave of Jewish refugees. Ben-Gurion realized that, given such circumstances, protest would lead nowhere. It remained a gesture that invited counterreactions bereft of practical significance.

Furthermore, Ben-Gurion understood that the weakness of the Jews during the Second World War prevented them from openly confronting Britain and the United States. The British held the key to the success or failure of most of the big rescue operations. There can also be no doubt that without the goodwill of the United States it would not have been possible to do anything for European Jewry. This was a political and operational dependence dictated by reality. I have already described how Palestinian and American Jews sought to escape from this dependence. In fact, that attempt actually demonstrated their great and unavoidable dependence; they were only capable of a semi-independent effort ultimately designed to maneuver Britain and the United States into accepting the rescue of large numbers of Jews through the payment of a ransom.

On the other hand, it was clear to Ben-Gurion that pain and frustration could be harnessed to counter those opposing Mapai, the JAE, or the Zionist movement in general. Consequently, he favored protest and even participated in it, although he tried to keep it within bounds. Ben-Gurion feared that unchecked attacks by Yishuv elements would adversely affect rescue attempts and would turn the public in the free world against the Jewish cause. Public opinion in

Britain and the United States was most affected by the loss of soldiers' lives in the course of the war; for example, it would not forgive attacks against British soldiers stationed in Palestine.

Ben-Gurion immediately grasped that the Rescue Committee and the committee he had suggested setting up to supervise the rescue and integration of children would mainly become nonoperational bodies. His political acumen also served him during debates over the Jewish Agency's budget. These debates, which took place three times in the course of the war, proved that even the most outspoken critics of the funding policy for rescue were not quick to abandon their own budgetary interests.

Ben-Gurion's ability to maneuver was not unlimited. In fact, this strategy revealed his weakness: he was compelled to maneuver because he bore responsibility without the ability to enforce and depended upon a rather unstable party and coalitionary foundation. Yishuv institutions were rather chaotic, as was only to be expected of a quasi-governmental system predicated on volunteerism. Even when basic agreements were reached, differences over details would occasionally surface. There is no truth whatever to the image of Ben-Gurion as an all-powerful leader.

Conducting the affairs of the Yishuv was extremely complicated because of the disparate bodies: the Elected Assembly; the Histadrut; the various political parties; the rabbinate; the old and new immigrant organizations; Ashkenazic and Sephardic sects; religious and secular groups; the political Left and Right.[19] The split between the Haganah, IZL, and Lehi (the radical anti-British paramilitary organization that sought the removal of the Mandatory government from Palestine), and the diverse implications of that split, constituted perhaps the gravest limitation on the Yishuv leadership's control. To this must be added the adversarial relationship between Ben-Gurion and Weizmann and the latter's supporters in Britain and the United States.

Ben-Gurion's quest for effective democratic authority in a society of volunteers subject to foreign rule was revolutionary. The Yishuv was a young migrant society. Many of its residents had left nondemocratic societies in Eastern Europe or in Islamic countries, where relations between Jews and the local government did not prepare them for citizenship in a democratic society. The process of shedding behavioral patterns acquired in countries of origin was a slow one. (One could even argue that this process is still continuing in the State of Israel.) The Jewish Yishuv in Palestine was a young, inexperienced society lacking political maturity and discipline. The ideological devotion and fervor that characterized many groups within it imbued the Yishuv with a special magic, but it also made governing such a society a very complicated task.

Ben-Gurion's attempts to impose authority were aimed at extricating the nation from its helplessness and restoring its ability to act as a collective. Disciplined action guided by a democratic leadership was a most important goal. Ben-Gurion often connected these issues to the rescue of Jews. For example, on 1 September 1943 he chose as the subject of his address to members of the Zionist Actions Committee "the authority of the nation, the authority of the cataclysm, the authority of the great hope":

> When one sees what is being done to us in Europe, on one side Hitler and on the other those who are against Hitler, how they spill our blood, when we see what is being done to us here . . . there has to be among us a minimum of internal solidarity, of responsibility, some modicum of restraint in [our] actions, arguments, and appearance, for whether we wish it or not, we are now all—all the Jews— caught in a trap. . . . [A] camp must have a minimum of unity and a minimum of authority in order to prevail in war.[20]

Even before Ben-Gurion had news of the exterminations, even before he understood the full significance of what was taking place in Europe, he had said that "rescue, if it is still possible to rescue—and I believe that it is possible—requires government."[21] This is the context for a proper understanding of his endless preoccupation with the issue of schism and unity in the Yishuv during the war—for example, his preoccupation with the grass roots of minor politics in the Tel Aviv Workers' Council. He believed that in such places he would find the key to the proper course of action on very important matters.

BETWEEN THE OVERT AND THE COVERT: THE DEVELOPMENT OF THE "PARALLEL SYSTEM"

Dina Porat prefaces her study with the following quotation:

> At the end of 1942 the Polish minister for Middle Eastern affairs, Professor Stanislaw Kot, visited Palestine and met the members of the JAE and representatives of the Polish Jewish community in Jerusalem. At the beginning of the 1980s a prominent historian discovered in a Jerusalem archive a report written in Palestine in 1942 during that same visit, which disclosed that the participants discussed various subjects, including—and featured prominently—the condition and the rights of the Jews of Poland after the war. "I ask you," said the historian resentfully to some of his colleagues, "is this what was in their minds then—the rights after the war? Didn't they realize what was going on? Even Ben-Gurion?"

> Shortly thereafter the same historian returned from a visit to the archive of the Polish government-in-exile in London, where he informed those same interlocutors that he had discovered the report given by Kot to his government after the said visit to Palestine. Kot had written

that following the meeting Ben-Gurion took him on a night tour of Jerusalem, where he told him in more or less these words:

> What was said at the banquet held in your honor is one thing. And what I shall tell you now is another, and the essence of it is this: I do not sleep nights from worrying about the fate of Polish Jewry. You must help the Jews of Poland, who are increasingly being slaughtered! This is the most burning issue at the moment, and we shall never forget it if you do not extend a hand to help them![22]

The tale picturesquely depicts the duality that existed between overt and covert activity, particularly Ben-Gurion's oscillation between these two planes. It also demonstrates that scholarship cannot avoid decoding the "story behind the story" in the majority of rescue operations, which, by their very nature, were covert. This secrecy was a necessary feature of the way of life of the Palestinian Yishuv, both in its dealings with domestic and foreign groups. Ben-Gurion tended toward secrecy, which he adhered to from the outset of the war, especially with respect to rescue operations, most of which would have been thwarted had they been revealed.[23]

It was difficult to talk about rescue operations then, and it remained so even afterward (before the Grünwald-Kasztner trial, for example). At any rate, some are not even mentioned in the documentation because of their classified nature.[24] The paucity of documentation has fueled claims that during the Holocaust the Yishuv community was still capable of sponsoring a dance festival at Kibbutz Dalia, going to the beach, and filling restaurants in Tel Aviv. Further research is needed to reconstruct and analyze more of these rescue operations.

The Yishuv's social and political structure also obliged Ben-Gurion to maintain a secret system that enabled him to enforce disciplined action. It would appear that Ben-Gurion coped with the organizational runaround in the Yishuv by compartmentalizing rescue operations, concealing them under the cloak of secrecy, and bypassing some groups that had been pressed into service to deal with rescue. To this end, he worked both overtly and covertly, as illustrated in his night tour with Kot.

The overt arena included Mapai, the JAE, and public gatherings of one kind or another. Ben-Gurion also vigorously demanded that his Mapai and JAE colleagues keep secrets. On a number of occasions he hinted at secrets he had confided to his colleagues, and at times he even explicitly mentioned these.[25]

The covert arena was what I have termed the "parallel system," which Ben-Gurion established and maintained. This system was subject to his authority and was one in which he trusted. It enjoyed operational freedom, escaping public pressure and that of its elective institutions, and could be activated when needed to advance rescue operations.

It consisted of a three-pronged leadership and an executive arm. The administrative triumvirate included Eliezer Kaplan (treasurer of the JAE) Moshe Sharett (head of the Political Department), and Ben-Gurion. They were, of course, the three most prominent representatives of Mapai in the JAE.[26] Kaplan was then Ben-Gurion's right-hand man. In my estimation he was second in importance under the parallel system. He undertook a long list of political—notably secret—missions.[27] Nonetheless, Sharett figured more prominently in a number of spheres. He was a central figure in the establishment of the undercover systems and was in charge of most political tasks involving the rescue of European Jewry.

This triumvirate played a major role in primary rescue operations. Important decisions fell to Ben-Gurion, Kaplan, and Sharett, and they received full reports regularly. (This was demonstrated in my discussion of the mysterious invitations issued to Bader.)[28] Depending on the circumstances, the circle of covert control was occasionally widened to include, among others, Yitzhak Gruenbaum, head of the Rescue Committee and member of the JAE, and Berl Katznelson, Ben-Gurion's Mapai colleague. Katznelson's inclusion in decision-making should not to be viewed solely in a quantitative sense, that is, based on the number of times his opinion was requested. Until his death in August 1944, Katznelson's moral and political support for Ben-Gurion and the leadership triumvirate was deeply appreciated.

Reuven Zaslani-Shiloah, Teddy Kollek, and Ehud Avriel were in charge of the executive arm of the parallel system and reported to the administrative triumvirate or to Ben-Gurion himself.[29] Also working with them—the exact nature of the relationship remains unclear—were Eliyahu Golomb and Shaul Meirov-Avigur, who had a politically independent status. Golomb was one of the heads of Mapai and commanded the Haganah organization until his death in 1945. Meirov was the head of the illegal immigration operation, a Haganah leader, and a central figure in Mapai and the Kibbutz Hameuhad movement.[30]

Within the Zaslani-Kollek-Avriel trio, Zaslani was at the time the veteran, possessing the most experience and closest to Ben-Gurion. Kollek gradually increased his standing, but he was still second to Zaslani. Avriel was then just starting his career. Working alongside or under the trio were Eliahu Epstein (Ealth), Ze'ev Schind, Zvi Schechter (Yehieli), Venja Pomeranz (Ze'ev Hadari), and Menahem Bader. As we have seen, they often also had direct contact with Ben-Gurion to a greater or lesser extent.

Many members of this latter group belonged to the JAE's Political Department, specifically the Special Tasks Section, while others belonged to the Illegal Immigration Operation. The group also included emissaries from other branches of the labor movement. Although I have been unable to determine the exact chain of command—

apparently it was not clear-cut—one fact stands out: with few exceptions, all were subordinate to Ben-Gurion, Kaplan, and Sharett. A number of them silently reported to their party or movement secretariats.

An interesting duality manifested itself in the parallel system. On the one hand, it was considered part of the formal hierarchical structure of Yishuv institutions. On the other hand, it bypassed this system. The parallel system was a part of the formal system since it was run by no less than the chairman of the JAE, the JAE treasurer, and the head of the Political Department; they instructed senior people in the Political Department. The JAE heads simply developed a system of subordination and of action not subject in any way to the supervision of the JAE plenum. It appears that its activities were funded based on vague budgetary clauses (generally termed B funds) as well as from sources outside the current budget. Budgeting for the parallel system was well concealed and consequently is very difficult to investigate today.

The parallel system was not devised solely for rescue purposes. It also served the Haganah, illegal immigration, and the purchase of arms. It is possible that it also operated during the early years of the State of Israel, until more orderly apparatuses were developed. At any rate, in the thirties and forties this was the arena for dealing with undercover matters. It was not coordinated and "tied up" in all respects, remaining vague to a certain extent. Although it was characterized by relative discipline, it occasionally experienced disruptions and conflicted loyalties.

Differences in temperament played a part, as did natural competition for status and prestige in the magnetic field surrounding Ben-Gurion. Vertical affinities linking various parts of the parallel system to the triumvirate (particularly to Ben-Gurion) were at times stronger than the horizontal ones between, say, Kollek and Zaslani or Zaslani and Pomeranz. Occasionally a different pattern of relations emerged, with the mutual affinity between the people in the sphere of activity being the strongest.

The parallel system emerged from a minority opposed to an inimical majority and subject to foreign rule, a reality of ideological and structural pluralism, a lack of operational experience, and the absence of a tradition of public administration. It was forced to operate at a time when it was necessary to cope with a world war and the Holocaust, and to counter foreign intelligence services that kept track of the leadership and weighed the extent to which the Yishuv was affecting its own regional interests. At the same time, it had to cooperate with those same services. The result was that improvisatory and "bypassing" strategies, as well as operations in gray areas, were required. At times the parallel system engaged in operations that the majority of JAE members opposed.

This pattern of covert operation stretched the limits of the Yishuv's democratic framework. Ben-Gurion, in fact, was a firm believer in authority based on formal democratic practices. It would appear that he and his two senior colleagues justified these violations on three counts. First, they were afraid of leaks and surveillance by foreign intelligence services; prime examples were the Transnistria Affair, the missions of Agronsky and Brand, and the offers Bader received.[31]

Second, they felt that the type of democracy prevailing in the Yishuv was still a "limited liability" form in which only some of its rules were observed by various elements. The terminology used at the time bears this out. Important groups in the Yishuv set up independent undergrounds and were called "dissidents," whereas those who withdrew from the "dissidents" were called "aberrants," to indicate that it was possible to ignore the rules of the game so long as the decision was not made by the party withdrawing. Such phenomena existed on the Right and the Left, among religious and nonreligious groups. The heads of the JAE could not ignore them and simply follow the democratic rules. They adopted a middle path, operating under both a democratic, volunteer-based system of leadership, control, and mobilization as well as a system of control and execution that directly enforced their authority. A similar and even more complex pattern was followed by the Haganah organization.

Third, Ben-Gurion, Kaplan, and Sharett were well aware of the powerful feelings surrounding the issue of rescue. For example, there was little chance that the representatives of a movement, a party, or a particular immigrant organization would react with equanimity to any decision that gave preference to another segment of the public in rescue operations even if there were clear-cut operational reasons behind such a decision. They were in no doubt that open debate would doom all such operations.[32]

Although Ben-Gurion, Kaplan, and Sharett generally preferred to violate democratic rules rather than risk losing an opportunity to rescue Jews, they found it difficult to justify these violations, since so few Jews were saved in the end. In the face of contemporary and later attacks on its ostensible failure, the leadership could not defend itself by pointing to its secret operations, since these were not considered legitimate according to the rules of the Yishuv and Zionist democracy. Such covert activities were linked to partners with dubious credentials, about whom it was difficult to "boast," and involved strategies too complex to be grasped by the general public and that at least superficially appeared "cruel." In the end, even those undercover operations did not succeed in rescuing many Jews. It might have been possible to use them to prove that the leadership was trying to act, but, in view of their failure in such a horrifying context, it was very difficult to prove that success was not possible. The task of presenting such proof clashed with very profound spiritual tendencies. Consequently, from the end of the Second World War to the early fifties and beyond, Ben-Gurion and his people had already given up trying to explain the nature of their undercover operations, since such an attempt was sure to fail.

METHODOLOGICAL LULL

Some of the information I have uncovered remains vague, and I have not been able to embroider from it a context that succeeds in explaining all of the events relating to my subject. I have not managed to get to the bottom of certain events, even though I have clarified some aspects. Have I exhausted their logic? Certainly not. Do my findings enable us to uncover causal relations and inner regularities that differ from those that characterize the existing paradigm?[33] I believe they do. Does what I have discovered lead to new questions and additional assumptions requiring further research? Here, too, the answer seems to be in the affirmative.

In which organization of the Yishuv leadership was the important decisions on rescue made? Was it the JAE, the Rescue Committee, the Zionist Actions Committee, or one of Mapai's units? It is my belief that Ben-Gurion, Kaplan, and Sharett made the decisions regarding rescue and conducted a parallel system based on personnel in the JAE's Political Department, the Illegal Immigration Operation, Haganah, and, to a certain extent, Histadrut institutions.

This assertion can also be tested through a process of elimination. The Rescue Committee was definitely not a decision-making body. Furthermore, it was frequently not involved in the major events and received only partial reports afterward. A typical example of this is provided by discussions of the offer Brand brought back from Eichmann. On 4 June—ten days after Venja Pomeranz had arrived in Palestine with information about the offer—Gruenbaum asked Ben-Gurion if he could pass the information along to the Rescue Committee. From Ben-Gurion's reply one gathers that he was uncomfortable with the very question itself. Although Gruenbaum headed the Rescue Committee, it appears that in Ben-Gurion's eyes Gruenbaum's membership in the JAE was more important, and he was to represent the JAE on the committee and not the reverse.[34]

Nor was the JAE a decision-making body or the main recipient of information concerning rescue. It was a coalition, with all the advantages and disadvantages that that implies. A wide organization where secrets could easily be leaked, the JAE did not receive a report on the August 1943 agreement with the JDC. It was not in the know concerning discussions in Cairo on independent Jewish action. Nor was the matter involving the secret courier arrested in Turkey and released following the intervention of what surely were prominent members of the Yishuv discussed in the JAE. To this day we still do not know which group made the decision, early in 1943, that determined the outcome of the Slovakia Plan. We know that the decision "to make contact with the devil" was not debated in the JAE but was arrived at by Ben-Gurion, Kaplan, Sharett, and perhaps two or three other individuals.[35]

One could cite numerous other examples, usually involving highly sensitive issues, that do not appear in JAE discussions: the agreement with Gibson at the beginning of 1943; the names and duties of the heads of British and American intelligence services who were in close contact with the Yishuv; the establishment of relations with the American intelligence service; the functioning of couriers, the hitch in their operations, and its repercussions. Nor is it known where the decision was reached to adopt Gruenbaum's suggestion that Jews should demand the bombing of concentration camps and rail or other approaches to them.

This being the case, it is worth repeating that the Yishuv had no clear-cut agreement as to where decisions were to be reached and who was subordinate to whom. The more delicate and complex the subject—rescue issues being extremely sensitive—the vaguer the documentation.[36] Even the special committee established to supervise the parachutists' and other infiltration operations was bypassed; its status had become problematical as a result of mutual suspicions within the labor movement concerning secret cooperation with the Americans.

This elimination process also supports my assertion that the parallel system headed by Ben-Gurion, Kaplan, and Sharett made the decisions on rescue matters and directed operations in the area of operation itself. This conclusion sheds light on the type of documentation required to uncover the rescue operations involving European Jewry. The documentation of groups at the summit of the official hierarchy—such as the protocols of the JAE or the Rescue Committee— is not significant, nor, for that matter, is any other kind of documentation from these two institutions. The same may be said of documents from the major political parties at the time (such as the records in Mapai units) reflecting discussions of rescue operations. I can assert with confidence that these were not the decision-making arenas.

In fact, what is absent from the documentation of these organizations is more important than what is included. The Rescue Committee provides an outstanding example of this. A study of the discussions held by this group reveals a wide gap between its name and its actual accomplishments. Any researcher basing conclusions on documentation mainly restricted to this and similar bodies cannot reconstruct the Yishuv's activity concerning the rescue of Jews, nor can it be analyzed or evaluated correctly. Furthermore, there were many who wished to thwart the rescue operations; hence the tendency to conceal them. Zaslani, Meirov, and their colleagues were by nature extremely reticent and wrote very little. Keeping a secret was of the highest importance in their eyes. The Yishuv's documentation on these issues is therefore limited, fragmented, and encoded. The Yishuv emissaries verbally debated among themselves and did so secretly in Istanbul. They wrote home only on matters that could not be conveyed orally through an emissary.

Such message-bearing emissaries included Venja Pomeranz (who orally transmitted Eichmann's offer), Agronsky (who reported on his contacts with Sharett in London), Magnes, Viteles, Kaplan, Meirov, and Mordechai Eliash. One can assume that many other messages about which one remains unaware passed between various countries. Things expressed through word of mouth will never be known to scholars, apart from the little revealed in memoirs and testimonies. All of this largely undermines the study of undercover operations, particularly since they involved many operational, political, and ideological variables. Without proper documentation it becomes very difficult to track such activities.

In view of the fact that most of the operations proved unsuccessful, with little or no tangible results, it is impossible to select a clear end point and undertake an analysis of the processes in reverse. Furthermore, those engaging in rescue activities were essentially men of action who tended to evaluate things in terms of results. In their eyes an operation was measured not by the planning, imagination, daring, dedication, resources, and effort invested in it but by the level of success in the execution of the mission. Given the lack of results, everything was considered by people like Zaslani or Meirov as "tales," "words," "verbiage," among other contemptuous labels aimed at the world of the talkers and nondoers. They were not the least bit interested in the significance of abortive actions in order to better understand the motives behind them or the reflections of those who had failed.

One can find a fascinating example of such a phenomenon from recent times in Venja Pomeranz's (the late Professor Ze'ev Hadari) book *Tsomet Kushta* (Kushta Junction*)*, In it he describes his and his colleagues' intensive efforts in Istanbul, and almost in the same breath he concludes by stating that in actual fact they did nothing. In the eyes of a man like Venja Pomeranz, he and his friends did nothing, since most of the operations failed and the successes were very minor compared to the size of the task and its importance.

Because of the political sensitivity surrounding rescue operations, which involved both friendly and hostile foreign influences, one can find documentation concerning these operations among those who kept track of them. In the documentation of foreign intelligence services one occasionally comes across information that the Yishuv concealed. It can be found in British and American archives, and it may be assumed that after the opening up of the Russian and former Soviet archives, such documentation will also be found among those of Poles, Czechs, Yugoslavs, Romanians, and others.

In British or American archives may be found two kinds of sources: (1) summaries and correspondence of intelligence people on secret cooperation with the Yishuv leadership and its emissaries, including aid extended for rescue operations; (2) documentation written by those intelligence agents who rejected cooperation with the Yishuv, considered its activities suspect, kept surveillance tabs on its leaders, and attempted to thwart rescue operations. We are therefore dealing with documentation that is hard to obtain and to understand, not simply with the account of an operation that did not take place or an experience that never occurred.

Moreover, built into the kind of intelligence documentation I utilized, there lies the additional difficulty unique to the world of intelligence and espionage. Lies and deceit, deception and camouflage—these are the "tools of the trade" in this closed world. That being the case, when do intelligence people report the truth? What is the level of reliability of intelligence documentation? It should be obvious that this documentation requires extremely careful handling and that the conclusions to be drawn from it have to be weighed with the utmost care.

All of these obstacles present a difficult challenge to researchers, one frequently impossible to overcome. The scholar's composite picture will always be fragmented and the blank spaces will require interpolations far in excess of what is needed for the analysis of standard historical sources. The incompleteness of the documentation also demands a considerable amount of extrapolation to fill in the gaps. These hypotheses will necessarily obfuscate the validity of the researcher's descriptions and generalizations.

On the other hand, one cannot avoid making such conjectures to complete the picture. To try to avoid them is to risk paralyzing the will and rendering the available information virtually worthless. Such self-paralysis would not result in the suspension of critical judgment but would open the door to less well-founded hypotheses than those withheld due to excessive caution.

Consequently, researchers must tread a narrow path. They must retain such conjectures only for certain special cases. One can err both in hesitating to fill in the gaps or by not restraining oneself enough. I hope I have used this vital analytical procedure evenhandedly. Obviously, I have not presumed to evade the relative nature of historical research.

It is the reality of the life of the Jewish people and the Yishuv that generated those mysterious and complex adventures, although one can easily believe them to have been spun from the febrile imagination of a John Le Carré. This is obviously a pitfall for the writer dealing with such matters, for there will always remain in the heart of the reader—and the author—the suspicion that the imagining here outweighs the reality. In view of the paucity of sources, on the one hand, and the intricacy and daring quality of the plot, on the other, the boundary between historical writing and fiction is liable to become blurred. Thus, historians may find themselves corroborating Hayden White's definition of his writing, and willy-nilly become spinners of tales.[37] The historical research is liable to turn into an historical novel. The avoidance of this temptation demands a high degree of restraint.

DEHUMANIZATION AS A TOOL IN THE DEBATE CULTURE

The image of Ben-Gurion as a cold, pedantic, even cruel revolutionary dedicated to a single goal was associated with his attitude toward

European Jewry during the Holocaust. In particular, critics have used this association to prove their claim that the heads of the Yishuv ignored the Holocaust and that Ben-Gurion insulated himself from what was happening in Europe and even remained emotionally indifferent to the fate of its Jews.

There are two components to this claim. First, it relies on a pair of rather redundant and unfortunate statements by Ben-Gurion that were uncalled for at the time. Second, the claim tries to quantitatively assess the pain expressed by Ben-Gurion during those years. Ben-Gurion uttered a harsh and painful statement shortly after Kristallnacht. He spoke of the ten thousand German and Austrian Jewish children whose parents had been killed or deported. The British did not permit them to enter Palestine and the suggestion was made to send them to Britain, to which Ben-Gurion replied: "If I knew that it would be possible to save all the German children by bringing them to England, and only half by bringing them to Palestine, I would choose the second option—because we have to take into account not only these children but the historical considerations of the Jewish people."[38] Although these words were uttered before the outbreak of the Second World War, that is, before the atrocity became known, they were nevertheless harsh and cruel.

The second statement was made during the Sixth Histadrut Conference (late January 1945). According to some accounts, Ben-Gurion commented that Yiddish was "a foreign and discordant tongue." His remark was aimed at Rozka Korczak, who used Yiddish to describe the horrors of the Holocaust to those present. This remark aroused great anger given the atmosphere surrounding Korczak's shocking report. There are those who maintain that Ben-Gurion did not say what was attributed to him, that his comments were grossly distorted. The important point remains the use made of the sentence, whatever its true meaning at the time of its utterance.[39]

The first component of the claim under investigation is therefore the explicit or presumed belief that these two harsh statements reflect the thinking and, in particular, the actions of Ben-Gurion from the end of 1938 to the beginning of 1945. My findings have largely refuted this belief.

The second component of this claim—the attempt to quantify Ben-Gurion's pain, to examine the number of statements he made concerning the killing of European Jews and compare this to his remarks on other subjects—assumes that a research method of this kind has the ability to reflect Ben-Gurion's attitudes. A qualitative interpretation of such a quantitative measurement is a very problematic matter. At times a single-word cable either to "permit" or "prohibit," "attack" or "wait" is of greater historic value than a hundred speeches. Furthermore, those espousing this system failed to encompass the entirety of the existing documentation, as their system requires.

Whoever counts statements and attempts to weigh the level of feelings contained in them—according to which indicator?—risks excluding those who are restrained and reticent. Such people are at times exposed to high-powered emotional experiences coupled with intense moral fervor. Restraint or reticence does not necessarily reflect insensitivity. At times they are actually the result of an abnormally violent emotional storm requiring restraint. "Normal" people may be able to express their feelings more easily than those individuals whose emotional excess demands restraint.

Moreover, as I have hinted elsewhere, a profound moral commitment—profound also in its emotional aspect—is liable to lead such reticent people to attribute decisive weight to actions, and what is derived from the logic of actions, at the expense of the verbal modeling of reality. For others priorities are sometimes the reverse. Focusing on the appearance of things may actually shed light on the nature of their own moral commitment. Rather than essentially reflecting an attempt to delve into the historical reality, it may well be that this focusing is nothing more than a decadent retreat from reality. It seems to me that this is a clear indication of a cognitive and ethical crisis.

Nevertheless, I decided to follow in the path of these writers and evaluators in order to test the validity of their conclusions according to their method. There is a tendency among many of them to miss quite a number of Ben-Gurion's statements concerning the slaughter of European Jewry and the surviving remnants. Their examination is not at all comprehensive. Moreover, a certain degree of methodology is discernible in the omissions: frequently precisely those statements that had a particularly emotional and fiercely expressive aspect were not mentioned. Although this aspect was not a prominent feature of Ben-Gurion's personality and style of leadership, and although such a process of enumerating and quantifying statements raises difficult questions, perhaps it should still be mentioned because it has served, among other things, as a kind of "scientific" groundwork for the dehumanizing of Ben-Gurion and several of his colleagues.[40]

Ben-Gurion was accustomed to including essentially political messages in his personal and more intimate statements. For example, he alluded to "the bear rearing up on the banks of the Rhine" in a poetic description of his plane flight in early summer 1936, which appeared at the beginning of his diary. In a letter dated September 1938 to Renana, his thirteen-year-old daughter, he expressed his loneliness in London following the departure of Paula, his wife, and his longing for his children, feelings commingled with a dread of the sinking world following the Munich Pact agreement.

This combination of the political and the personal was a common practice in the letters Ben-Gurion wrote to his family. Some were intended to be seen by colleagues like Berl Katznelson or Moshe Sharett and were passed on to them at his behest. This was just one of the ways of circumventing British censorship and evading the surveillance of the intelligence services, which kept track of his preparations and his plans.

At any rate, these two examples present the other, more personal side of Ben-Gurion. At times he was a man racked with pain, agitated and filled with dread. This clearly emerges from the aforementioned letter, which he wrote to his close friend Miriam Cohen-Taub after his meeting with Helinka, a member of the exchange group from Poland. Helinka's description of this same meeting also sheds light on this facet of his personality.

The emotional side hidden beneath Ben-Gurion's outwardly businesslike and dry manner is revealed in things he wrote or said both during and following the Holocaust. For example, it appears in his diary entries written during an emotional visit to Bulgaria and during visits to DP camps in Germany. Among other things, he copied into his diary the "Song of the Partisans" and Mordechai Gebirtig's "The Town Is Burning." In another place Ben-Gurion inserted a list of inscriptions copied from headstones at the mass graves at Bergen-Belsen. When responding to appeals from ordinary people, he sometimes deviated from a formal reply to reveal his personal feelings.[41]

Such comments were generally reserved for more intimate settings like a diary or personal correspondence. Nevertheless, they do contribute to the overall picture of Ben-Gurion during the Holocaust. Ben-Gurion's diary was, among other things, a working tool. The data he amassed there facilitated communication with his colleagues. Some claim that Ben-Gurion was calculating in everything he wrote and always wrote "for posterity," but an examination of his diary reveals numerous entries free of any calculation and without any practical aim. Often a short entry consisting of one or two lines and occurring in an extremely dramatic moment and amid a "dry" sequence of data succeeds in encapsulating the complexity of the moment, expressing either a tempestuous feeling or an intimate thought.

Ben-Gurion uttered similar feelings in very public arenas, but the rhetorical tools he employed make it more difficult to gauge his sincerity. Given the nature of such public speeches and their declamatory requirements, these guidelines also applied to Ben-Gurion, particularly when issuing a call to the nations of the free world or demanding that Britain open the gates of Palestine to Jewish refugees. By the same token, words uttered on such public occasions generally attracted publicity and were subject to wide dissemination. It is therefore particularly odd that most of these public utterances were not included in the enumeration and consideration of things Ben-Gurion said or wrote during the Holocaust or about the Holocaust. Many examples could be cited: the November 1942 speech to the Elected Assembly; the March 1943 speech given at the Hamahanot Ha'olim youth movement conference; the January 1944 speech at the Mapai Council; and, most notably, the July 1944 speech delivered on Herzl Day, which reflected the anger and pain of those years.[42]

Ben-Gurion expressed heartfelt feelings even in restricted, operational settings. Such settings are businesslike arenas for the transmission of information, planning an operation, and for postoperational decisions or analysis. Flowery language is alien to such settings, since it obfuscates the pertinent discussion, resulting in more direct mode of expression. Moreover, the speaker usually assumes that his words will not be made public. Consciously or unconsciously, he views the closed conversation as a refuge from the need to project a false image of himself.

Ironically, the restricted operational settings did not provide Ben-Gurion with a place where he could reveal his sensitivity or even sentimentalism. This is noticeable in the following: instructions to Jewish Agency emissaries in the United States and Britain; remarks he made at the Mapai Center in February 1943; remarks to the chief rabbis Isaac Herzog and Ben-Zion Meir Uziel against the background of the fierce controversy that erupted in the Yishuv over the "Teheran Children" affair (June 1943); and remarks to representatives of the Agricultural Workers' Federation shortly afterward. These are just a few of the settings in which Ben-Gurion's profound feelings during the Holocaust were revealed.[43]

It is clear that in any such investigation one cannot exclude the person behind the leader, the sense of anxiety behind the power, the inner pain beneath the frozen exterior. They are an essential supplement to any systematic and orderly description of Ben-Gurion's active, operational involvement in rescue operations. If Ben-Gurion and his colleagues had rent their clothing, covered their heads with ashes, and sat lamenting on the steps of the rabbinate or the high commissioner's residence; if they had not let a day go by without protesting against what was happening in Europe—these would still not have been considered an appropriate substitute for the practical action demanded of the leader of the nation and his colleagues in confronting a challenge like the Holocaust. At the same time, the emotional aspect completes the portrait of the leader, the leadership, and even the historical period.

An accurate and systematic weighing and enumeration of Ben-Gurion's statements in all types of settings would demonstrate that he was not indifferent or aloof in his attitude toward the Holocaust and the Diaspora. He thought of the "Diaspora" as a collective term for brothers and sisters, parents and relatives who were in mortal danger. Throughout the war Ben-Gurion expressed his personal feelings to varying degrees. Alongside the general, cold, restrained statements one finds expressions of pain and warmth. The Holocaust did not slip past Ben-Gurion and he did not avoid studying and discussing it and its repercussions. It influenced his actions and his decisions and he reacted to it with expressions of horror, pain, and alarm. In general, Ben-Gurion was a leader who radiated power, stability, and courage—necessary qualities for the Zionist revolution—

but these attributes did not render him insensitive or alienated.

Thus, even if one adopts the questionable method of research that tries to draw qualitative conclusions from a quantitative examination of an issue such as this, the results will oblige the researcher to abandon the stereotypical image of Ben-Gurion and to acknowledge the sensitive aspect of his personality. However, the very notion of counting statements involves distortion. For example, it should be recalled that many links in the rescue and aid operations during the Holocaust were secret, and that any superfluous word spoken about them could result in bloodshed. Consequently, economy of speech and restricting secret information to a very small circle would greatly affect any tabulation of statements.

It should also be remembered that British censorship was sensitive to anything that might, in its view, lead to unrest in the Yishuv, and its "scissors" certainly must have reduced the number of statements on the Holocaust. And what about the silent language of gestures and secret signs, which can reflect and express what thousands of words in a myriad of documents cannot? Unfortunately, the researcher is constrained to reflect the experience only through written and verbal documentation that passing reality has left behind.

Although Ben-Gurion was capable of delivering hour-long speeches and wrote exhaustively, at times he tended to express matters of great significance with absolute brevity. He was in London on 7–8 May 1945 when the news arrived that the war in Europe had ended and that Germany had surrendered. From his window he watched Londoners cheering in the streets. Ben-Gurion confided to his diary in one brief entry the depth of his feelings and the intensity of that historic moment for the free world and for the Jewish people: "Victory Day, sad, very sad." At that very moment this quintessentially secular and reticent person felt impelled to refer to his ancient Jewish roots, committing to his diary the

following verse from Hosea (9:1): "Rejoice not, O Israel, for joy, as other people."[44]

THE STEREOTYPE AND ITS ROOTS

In addition to the question of what the Yishuv did to save European Jewry during the Holocaust, there is also considerable interest in the question of why public personalities—scholars and, in general, many Jews in Israel and abroad—felt that the Yishuv and its leadership did practically nothing to rescue their brethren during the Holocaust. Having clearly established that this was an erroneous assumption one is obliged to investigate its sources.

There is a wide range of feelings and claims, from those who believe that the Yishuv did nothing—arguing that it realized the task was beyond its abilities and therefore concentrated on building up the Yishuv and, subsequently, the Jewish State—to those who believe that both in their words and deeds the Yishuv and its leadership turned their backs on the Diaspora in its hour of need. One of the claims made is that they abandoned European Jewry for a political reward promised by Britain to the Zionist movement after the war, on condition that the Zionists would not "disturb" Britain during the war. The gist of the various other claims is that the Yishuv abandoned the Diaspora. Such claims were already being made during the war and are still being uttered as I write these lines.[45] I shall therefore attempt to uncover the source of this negative stereotype.

The answer lies partly in the fact that research and public debate on the Holocaust in Israel and the rest of the world ranged from absolute mystification to absolute relativization of an event of major significance in the history of humanity, and especially in the annals of the Jewish people and the State of Israel. The two tendencies disqualify their proponents from debate and contention. The mystification and relativization of the Holocaust have become almost "natural." Even less fateful events than the Holocaust have already awakened a spectrum of similar attitudes. Frequently stereotypical statements mask gross ignorance, obviating the need to deal with complex historical issues and making do with a pat solution to the fundamental methodological difficulties that characterize historical debate as a branch of knowledge.

Debate concerning the attitude of the Yishuv leadership toward European Jewry during the Holocaust period also suffers from these tendencies. In the early fifties it had already overstepped the boundaries of discussion of an important historical issue grounded in a particular context and set of circumstances—the Jewish Yishuv in Palestine during the Second World War—and soon became a tool in the ideological struggle to establish the image of the State of Israel. It was included in public thinking and scholarly debate concerning the degree of "cleanliness" of the Zionist revolution and the legitimacy of the State of Israel.

Among the accusations against the Zionist state that are still being bandied about are its sinful birth; its colonialism, militarism, and particularism; its tribalism; its innate irrationality and chauvinism; its leaders' indifference and wickedness and their injustice toward Palestinian Arabs, Oriental Jews, and women. From this plethora of accusations arose the claim that the Zionist movement and its leaders, the source of all this evil, cut themselves off from their brethren during the Holocaust and coolly manipulated the survivors by turning them into a social, political, and military instrument to attain their goals. Consequently, the Zionist leaders were not only indirectly partners in the slaughter of six million but were personally responsible for the "murder" of the seventh million.

We have here a phenomenon involving the extraction of historical debate from its past context, its repositioning on unfounded assumptions, and its enshrinement in the present, with implications for the future. It now lacks the necessary foundation for a relevant discussion of

how the Yishuv and its leadership coped with the Holocaust of European Jewry. To serve their own ends, those who propel scholarly and public debate in such directions foment the natural tension between "archaeological" and "historical" truth, according to Ahad Ha'am's definition. They encourage the disinclination to make use of facts, or to examine them as much as possible in an agreed upon manner. This tendency has long since moved way beyond a valid or invalid interpretation of the facts. All the camps in the Israeli public, including the intellectual and political elites, use the Holocaust for a variety of political ends. Remarkably enough, the use of findings on the Holocaust even preceded the findings themselves.[46]

This phenomenon perfectly illustrates that history is indeed a kind of "unending dialogue between the present and the past," as the British historian E. H. Carr so tellingly expressed it. The more blazing the discussion on the "present," as well the debate on the future, or the ideal for the future, were more questions about the degree of legitimacy and "cleanliness" of the Zionist revolution were swept into this discourse. The more the debate was harsh and painful so the significance of the discussion of the findings diminished.

This phenomenon may be compared with the demand for political correctness in the United States. The derivation of this moralizing approach in the United States was so devoid of any connection with basic facts that it aroused ridicule even among outspoken liberals. So it is in Israel, where several of those debating the issue of Zionism and the Holocaust simply ignore facts that don't support their positions. According to them, their interest lies exclusively in "feelings," "images," and "motivations."[47]

The necessity to reflect the facts from the standpoint of the present clouds their consciousness. The mediation of concepts, aspirations, and fears of our time prevent them from grasping the simple truth that rescue efforts during the Holocaust failed primarily because all the big rescue plans were extremely complex politically and logistically, and because the Jewish people were helpless.

First of all, the Jews residing in that "other planet" were helpless. But the Jews in the free world, including those in Palestine, suffered from political and operational impotence and were therefore incapable of rescuing masses of Jews. There is no way to convey to present-day readers the sheer complexity of the operations and the profound significance of that helplessness at every level. Allowing for major differences, one might point out that even a superpower like the United States found it extremely difficult to rescue a handful of hostages from its embassy in Teheran. One might therefore derive an answer to the question of how to bridge the gap between our findings and the negative stereotype in the lines of development of that "dialogue" between present and past. From our current vantage point it is very difficult to comprehend why the big rescue operations were destined to fail, and it is even more difficult to plumb the depths of the helplessness of the Jewish people at the time of the Holocaust.

A second explanation for the gap lies in one of the principal subjects of this book, namely, undercover activity. It should come as no surprise that documentation in this area is rare, encoded, and has come to light only fairly recently. Consequently, it has remained far removed from the consciousness of researchers and the public. The erroneous impression that nothing at all was done grew stronger following the failure of most of the rescue efforts.

The fact that prominent rescue activists remained silent and that rescue operations failed also gave rise to the claim that the Yishuv only allocated junior-level staff for rescue activities. Combined with this argument was an evaluation of the mindset of these people and the Palestinocentric attitude. According to this argument, the Yishuv was immersed in its own needs and preoccupations (settlement, defense, growth), and, since the rescue effort was not a necessity or of interest to the Yishuv, it was entrusted to a junior team. The top-ranking, experienced individuals were assigned to other functions.

As we have seen, nothing could be further from the truth. Before and after the Second World War—and even in the early years of the state—people like Meirov-Avigur, Golomb, Zaslani-Shiloah, Epstein-Ealth, Kollek, Avriel, Schind, Bader, and Pomeranz-Hadari were engaged in such Palestinocentric matters as arms, security, and intelligence. They were among the most prominent and savvy people in various Yishuv organizations and the Zionist movement. And it was these very same people who were involved in rescue efforts! Those who led such groups as the Rescue Committee were indeed drawn from the second and third rank, but only because the Rescue Committee was not an important body. The failure of rescue efforts was not the result of an incompetent team having been assigned. The attempts failed even though the Yishuv's best people were sent on such missions. It is difficult to accept, let alone comprehend, this fact. Historians do not, as a rule, speculate as to "what would have happened if . . . ?" but the historian who encounters such an issue as the negative stereotype of Ben-Gurion and the Yishuv can permit himself a moment of mental laxity and nonetheless ask: What would have happened had those intensive efforts I have described ended differently? For example, what would have happened if every year on the twentieth day of Tamuz (Herzl Day) the central squares of Tel Aviv and other Israeli cities and towns had been filled with hundreds of thousands of survivors from Hungary, Romania, Slovakia, and Greece, standing there alongside their children and grandchildren? There is no doubt that such imaginary city squares would have compensated for the lack of documentation and would have given rise to a different historiography—which is precisely what would have happened, the assumption goes, if the Yishuv's efforts to rescue the Jews of Europe had succeeded. At any rate, the real city squares cry out in their emptiness, and the pain is liable to cloud one's thinking.

It must be stressed that the poor results of the rescue plans are not a reflection of the half-hearted efforts of the Yishuv or its disinclination to rescue. It may be apposite, in such cases, to extend the scope of historical and moral judgment to encompass intentions, but perhaps we are not permitted to go to such lengths. There is simply no remedy for the deep regret that a considerable portion of the rescue operations did not succeed and that so few were saved. This painful fact does not justify accusations against those who tried to rescue Jews, but it has motivated not a few later critics, who reason that if they did not succeed in their rescue attempts, they did not try sufficiently hard. The logical flaw is obvious..

Additional explanations for the fact that another negative stereotype was a well-assimilated lie, it would appear, may be found in its easy association with the "discourse" between present and past, a type of "many-sided discourse" involving public groups perceived as promulgating the negative stereotype associated with Ben-Gurion. Their interpretation of the facts was helped by Ben-Gurion's ideological attitudes, which were not necessarily connected with the Holocaust. It also relied on principles of action typical of his leadership. An example of such an interpretation has been presented with respect to his two unfortunate statements. His image as an ostensibly all-powerful leader also contributed to the conclusion that many more Jews were not saved because he wasn't interested in them. This image developed mainly in the fifties, a decade that molded the Jews of Israel into a political nation. This image was were bound up with the severe crises that also fostered the acceptance of the negative stereotype.

The negative stereotype fitted very easily into the conceptual framework whose development and nurturing Ben-Gurion himself contributed to. He was considered the leading standard-bearer espousing the "negation of the Diaspora." This principle, the product of the Haskalah movement's legacy, was an important element in Ben-Gurion's Zionist outlook. What could be more simple than the negation of the Diaspora and, as a direct and immediate consequence, its abandonment. It is more complicated to explain how it was possible to advocate this principle of "the negation of the Diaspora" and, at the same time, to believe that everything possible must be done to help those Jews who chose to live in the Diaspora.

In a "smooth" conceptual construction, it is relatively easy to resolve the contradictions by means of an all-purpose explanation, which attributes the failure of most of the rescue efforts to the fact that the action taken was inappropriate to the dimension of the catastrophe; in more extreme cases the failure was attributed to the "Zionist" outlook of Ben-Gurion and his colleagues, who rejected any plan that was not connected with Palestine.

Those who put forward such arguments ignored the fact that most of the Jews in Palestine were young and had European roots; most of them, including the Yishuv leaders, had left behind parents, brothers and sisters, and other relatives. Even if, in the eyes of their Yishuv associates, they were completely "assimilated" or irreparably tied to the Jewish exile (Diaspora), this does not mean that the leaders of the Yishuv would neglect their suffering and loss. Despite this fact, the accusers did not hesitate to draw a shocking but utterly unfounded connection between the negation of the Diaspora and its abandonment.

The negative stereotype was also fueled by the public's difficulty in believing that the Zionist movement and its leadership had not anticipated this kind of a profound change in the "rules of the game" and were therefore not prepared for the magnitude of the Holocaust. How could they be surprised, one wondered, when their own Zionist prognosis had been so horribly confirmed. Despite all the angry words and the lack of expectation concerning the extended life of the Diaspora, the Zionists never conceived that the Jews of Europe would undergo such a massive extermination. When Menahem Begin, Natan Yalin-Mor, and Moshe Kleinbaum-Sneh left their communities and came to Palestine, they believed that before them lay a period of war and separation and no more. Even if they had held a deep-seated belief that the Jews of Europe should immigrate to Palestine, this would not have led them to deduce from this "we warned you, and since you didn't listen, then you deserve to go up in smoke." The difficulty of the Jews of the free world, including Zionist "Diaspora negators," to interpret early accounts of the extermination has been discussed in great detail.

Evaluating rescue efforts based on their results served also to provide convenient raw material for the building of a negative stereotype. Although we are all familiar with the saying "for everyone who saved one soul in Israel, it is as if he had saved a whole world," nevertheless it is hard to comprehend how so few were rescued. The number of survivors or the success rate of the rescue efforts seem completely unrealistic when compared to the six million who perished. The number of children rescued with great effort is pitifully small. The stereotype made it possible—and still makes it possible—to bridge this terrible gap. It provides a convenient explanation that serves as a refuge from the torment of embarrassment and even supplies a guilty party in the "vicious" persona of Ben-Gurion.

The demonization of Ben-Gurion is actually helped by the fact that, several years later, he led a successful enterprise despite opposition and difficulties. His status changed from that of leader of a minority in a land under foreign rule to leader of a national revolution that succeeded in establishing a state shortly after such a horrifying cataclysm. This fact served as the foundation for the assertion that when the "grand wizard" wished, he could succeed; he wanted a state and established one. From this assertion one could extrapolate the opposite: if Ben-Gurion did not succeed in rescuing Europe's Jews during the Holocaust, it was simply because he had no interest in saving them. The demonization of Ben-Gurion is therefore an essential element in the logically flawed argument referred to earlier.

Another facet of this stereotype stems from Ben-Gurion's image as a pragmatic, powerful, and businesslike leader, which no one has contested. Ben-Gurion was capable of making patently cruel decisions. Hence the tendency to ascribe to him the tough decisions made during the Holocaust. In the view of his harshest critics, it is "just like him" to make cold-blooded decisions, and so this is how he acted. Here, too, the flawed reasoning is apparent, leading those who accept it to attribute to Ben-Gurion attitudes he never held. When the Yishuv was compelled to choose between focusing on the building of a national home in Palestine and allocating most of its resources to operations that stood practically no chance of success, it was "fitting" for a leader like Ben-Gurion to make the difficult decision not to waste resources on such "futile steps." In truth, the complete opposite was true: Ben-Gurion asserted in the most unequivocal manner that Yishuv leaders had to try and save Jews even when their chances of succeeding were one in a million.

The bitter political confrontations that erupted when the State of Israel was first established and that continued during the early years of its development also contributed to the creation of the negative stereotype and even strengthened its hold on the public. Ben-Gurion was a central figure in these confrontations. Frequently such controversies deviated from the political sphere and focused on the roots of the Jewish revival in Palestine. Questions were raised concerning the struggle of European Jews and the Jews of Palestine against the Nazis; relations among the Yishuv leadership, the Zionist movement, and the British during the war; and moral issues of heroism and resistance versus cowardice and collaboration.

Furthermore, the acceptance of the negative stereotype was preceded by other bitter arguments less frequently associated with the Holocaust. One, the "Season," involved conflicting attitudes between the majority in the Yishuv and right-wing Revisionists with respect to Britain's immigration and rescue policies during and following the Holocaust. Another argument was concerned with who had caused Britain to leave Palestine. These did not produce the stereotype, but they created a favorable climate for its acceptance and growth.

The violent controversy surrounding the reparations agreement with the former West Germany, as well as the military and diplomatic links tied to it, marked a turning point in this multilayered confrontation. One highlight was the "Kasztner trial" (which as a matter of fact was the "Grünwald trial"). That trial was perhaps the determining factor in the establishment of the negative stereotype. The suit brought against Kasztner's accusers was also a watershed in the history of the State of Israel. That trial marked the beginning of a systematic erosion in the standing of Mapai. Its internal squabbles and confrontations with others over its activities during the Holocaust, Kasztner's mistakes during the trial (which was manna to attorney Shmuel Tamir), Ben Hecht's book *Perfidy*—all these contributed to creating the negative stereotype.

Concerning the phenomenon of the ultra-Orthodox polemic against Ben-Gurion and the Zionist movement during the Holocaust, which deserves fuller treatment elsewhere, suffice it to say that blaming the Zionists was apparently one way in which the ultra-Orthodox contended with the impotence of its leadership in confronting the Holocaust, which was a severe blow to the faithful followers of the god of Israel [in Hebrew: *Shlomei Emunei Israel*]. Ironically, in retrospect their accusations crowned the Zionist movement and elevated it in the eyes of the Jewish people. At any rate, the ultra-Orthodox also played a not inconsiderable part in the creation of the negative stereotype.

Other factors contributing to the creation of the negative stereotype can only be assumed, but with little fear of exaggeration. It is certainly possible that one such factor was the public's increasing weariness with Ben-Gurion's revolutionary leadership, which was inflexible. He did not realize that the people had grown tired of such buzzwords as "tension," "readiness," "pioneering mobilization," and "Zionist mission." Following the declaration of independence and the war of independence, the climax of the Zionist revolution, the Israeli public wanted to begin living the ordinary life. It consequently was inclined to attribute to the aging, unbending, pedantic leader "crimes" that would permit the public to rid itself of him.

Many Israelis wanted to see ousted the man who, following the Holocaust, had, as it were, steamrolled the establishment of a state and reduced the Zionist ideal—which had been forged in a war of independence involving many fatalities—to a prosaic daily struggle to maintain a state that was not at all "the exemplary state" Ben-Gurion and his opponents had hoped for. Some other Israelis actually renounced his call to struggle against the state's moral "weaknesses" and to renew efforts to elevate the image and strengthen the moral fiber of the State of Israel so that it could serve as a role model. Ben-Gurion did not adapt to the transition of the Yishuv/Jewish state from a revolutionary-utopian society to one lacking such a significant foundation.

Other factors contributing to the creation of Ben-Gurion's negative stereotype were his directness, his courage, and his sincerity, which he used to chastise the public. These attributes aroused opposition and facilitated the work of those desiring to be rid of him. Ben-Gurion was faced with a people's desire to "go home" and rest after years of mobilization. The selfish tendency to "take care of one's own" that characterizes postrevolutionary periods demands legitimacy and historical and philosophical depth for itself. Herein lies one of the profoundest sources of Ben-Gurion's negative stereotype and that of the Yishuv under his "pio-neering" leadership during the Holocaust period: the public's need to smash its own old image and to reconstitute it, combined with the need to justify a retreat from a way of life, one of whose fundamental traits was public service. This tension preceded the current argument between those who seek to examine and accept only what is worth adopting from global culture and those who fear that if Israeli society does not adopt all the "achievements" of the West, the fruit of the Israeli revolution will remain sparse, poor, backward, and decadent.[48]

It is also possible that the development of Ben-Gurion's negative stereotype satisfied the need for a "purifying sacrifice." Perhaps this process of Israel's veering away from the aging "founding father" of its political society is bound up with a need to sacrifice a scapegoat in order to expiate the guilt feelings over those killed in the extermination camps. The intensity of the attachment to the negative stereotype becomes even clearer if one takes into account the wish for a "purifying sacrifice" to dispel the feelings of anger and pain that accompanied the exodus of the Jews from the ruins of Europe following the terrible experience of the Holocaust and, more recently, after a War of Independence with its painful price.[49] Perhaps it was necessary for the

Israelis who were followers of Ben-Gurion to sacrifice the "king" who had ostensibly sacrificed his brethren in Europe to forge a state.

A number of powerful factors combined to create the negative stereotype of the Yishuv and Ben-Gurion and his leadership: an ideological concept—the "negation of the Diaspora"—was presented as a valid moral basis for nonintervention, as was the contradiction, marked by inaction, between Zionism and rescue; a practical factor—the inability of such a small and poor society as the Yishuv to shoulder the burden of two such immense enterprises as rescue and establishing a state—led to the accusation that the Yishuv chose to abandon the rescue and to focus on the building of an infrastructure for the state; a leader who projected the public image of a tough personality, a man capable of making difficult decisions in times of crisis; a terrible numerical gap between survivors and slaughtered for which no rational explanation was sufficient—an anachronism that provided "explanations" as required; later political struggles and the psychological residue resulting from the building of a nation; and discourse with the past in a reality of continuing debate about the future moral shape of the state. Will this negative stereotype continue its hold in the future? We shall have to wait and see.

Notes

8. "A One-in-a-Million Chance"

1. Memorandum titled "from Joel's words," 11.6.44, GCD, ABG; JAE, 14.6.44, CZA; U.S. Consul, Istanbul, to Foreign Office, 13.6.44, 1344, 862/20200/6, NA; Shalom Rosenfeld, *Criminal Case 124/53*, 81–84; Yehuda Bauer, "Joel Brand Mission," *Yalkut Moreshet*, no. 26 (November 1978), 25, 49–52; Vago, "Intelligence Aspects of the Joel Brand Mission," 89–90; Bauer, "Joel Brand Mission," *The Holocaust*, 148–191.
2. U.S. Vice Consul to Foreign Office, Squires's memo, 17.6.44, NA, OSS, RG 84; Rubin, *Istanbul Intrigues*, 196–197 [English].
3. JAE, 25.5.44, CZA; Bauer, "Joel Brand Mission," *The Holocaust*, 148; Porat, *The Blue and the Yellow Stars of David*, 189.
4. Joel Brand, *On Behalf of Those Condemned to Death* (Tel Aviv: Aynot, 1960). See also Yehuda Bauer, "Joel Brand Mission," *Yalkut Moreshet No. 26* (November 1978): 23–60; Bauer, "Joel Brand Mission," *The Holocaust*, 148–191; Vago, "Intelligence Aspects of the Joel Brand Mission," *Yad Vashem Studies* 10 (1974): 81–93; Bela Vago, "The British Government and the Fate of Hungarian Jewry in 1944," 205–223 [English]; David Hadar, "The Allies' Attitude Toward the Joel Brand Mission," *Molad* 4 (27), nos. 19–20 (229–230) (May–June 1971), 112–125; Wasserstein, *Britain and the Jews of Europe*; Kedem, "The Political Activity of Chaim Weizmann in the Second World War"; Penkower, *The Jews Were Expendable* [English]; H. Feingold, "The Roosevelt Administration and the Effort to Save the Jews of Hungary" [English]; R. L. Braham, *Eichmann and the Destruction of Hungarian Jewry* (New York: Twayne, 1961) [English]; Porat, *The Blue and the Yellow Stars of David*, 188–211; MEMOIRS, TESTIMONIES, AND DOCUMENTS: Barlas, *Rescue During the Holocaust*; Bader, *Sad Missions*; Avriel, *Open the Gates!*; Hirschmann, *Lifeline to the Promised Land* [English]; Joel and Hansi Brand, *Satan and the Soul*, ed. Gepner; Biss, A., *A Million Jews to Save: Check to the Final Solution* (London: Hutchinson, 1973) [English]; Gideon Hausner, *The Chief Prosecutor of the Israeli Government Against Adolf Eichmann*, vol. 2, *Testimonies* (Jerusalem: Center for Explanation, 1974); Israel Kasztner, *The Truth of Kasztner: A Report on the Hungarian Rescue Committee, 1942–1945*, reported by Dr. Israel Kasztner, trans. Binyamin Gat Rimon (Tel Aviv: Association to Perpetuate the Memory of Dr. Israel Kasztner, 1981); Arthur D. Morse, *While Six Million Died* [English]; Rosenfeld, *Criminal Case 124/53*; Amos Elon, *Timetable* (New York: Doubleday, 1980) [English].
5. BG, Mapai Secretariat, 22.2.44, LPA.
6. Bauer, "Joel Brand Mission," *Yalkut Moreshet*, 25; Bela Vago, "Hungarian Jewry's Leadership," in *The Leadership of Hungarian Jewry During the Holocaust*, eds. Gutman Israel, Bela Vago, Livia Rothkirchen (Jerusalem: Yad Vashem, 1976), 61–76; Kasztner, *The Truth of Kasztner*, 60–61; for a recent discussion, see Bauer, *Jews for Sale?*, 152–153 [English].
7. BG, Mapai Secretariat, 22.2.44, LPA; Bauer, "Joel Brand Mission," *Yalkut Moreshet*, 25; JAE, 26.3.44, CZA; BG, Mapai Secretariat, 9.4.44, LPA.
8. 22.3.44, S25/178, CZA, cited in Gilbert, *Auschwitz and the Allies*, 184.
9. BGD, 23.3.44, ABG; JAE, 26.3.44, CZA.
10. Moshe Dax and others to BG, Dobkin, and Kaplan, 23.4.44, correspondence, ABG.
11. Gruenbaum to Weiss, copy to BG, 8.5.44, S44/471, CZA; Dobkin to JAE, copy to BG, 25.5.44, S44/679, CZA, copy to Kaplan in S53/1569, CZA; Bader to Palestine, 1.5.44, S26/1287, CZA; Rabbi Taub, Zurich, to Rabbi Herzog, copy to BG and Kaplan, 12.5.44, correspondence, ABG; Vago, "The British Government and the Fate of Hungarian Jewry in 1944," 205–223 [English]; Penkower, *The Jews Were Expendable*, 187 [English]; Porat, *The Blue and the Yellow Stars of David*, 188.
12. JAE, 9.4.44, 21.5.44, CZA; Rabbis Herzog and Uziel to the Orthodox Patriarch, Istanbul, 21.5.44, S53/1612, CZA; Rabbis Herzog and Uziel to Roosevelt and Churchill, 22.5.44, S44/679, CZA (a copy of the telegram was sent to BG's office on 30.5.44); Gruenbaum to L. Yaffe, New York, 22.5.44, correspondence, ABG. Appeals were also sent to different union organizations in the United States, the World Jewish Congress, the United Nations, the Vatican, and others.
13. Gruenbaum, JAE, 2.4.44, CZA; Kasztner, *The Truth of Kasztner*, 63–64, 67; Rubin, *Istanbul Intrigues*, 142–143, 172 [English].
14. JAE, 2.4.44, CZA.
15. Ibid.
16. Bauer, "Joel Brand Mission," *Yalkut Moreshet*, 24; Hadari, *Against All Odds*, 203.
17. Avriel, *Open the Gates!*, 179–180; Elon, *Timetable*, 74–85.
18. S25/1678, CZA, according to Martin Gilbert, *Auschwitz and the Allies*, 212; Avriel, *Open the Gates!*, 178–180; cable no. 794, FO 371,W8465 42758, PRO.
19. A conversation with Prof. Ze'ev Hadari-Pomeranz, 29.5.89; cf. Barlas, *Rescue During the Holocaust*, 120; Shertok's report, 27.6.44, London, Z4/14870, CZA.
20. 19.5.44, correspondence, ABG (the letter was written in a little notebook in small letters); Barlas, *Rescue During the Holocaust*, 114–115.

21. For a different version, see Elon, *Timetable,* 97–99.

22. JAE, 25.5.44, CZA.

23. Ibid.; Porat, *The Blue and the Yellow Stars of David,* 188; Bauer, "Joel Brand Mission," *Yalkut Moreshet,* 24–25.

24. Bauer, *Jews for Sale?,* 151–153 [English].

25. Ibid., 165 [English]; Pomeranz, JAE, 25.5.44, CZA.

26. JAE, 25.5.44, CZA; Shertok's report, 27.6.44, London, Z4/14870, CZA; Rosenfeld, *Criminal Case 124/53,* 81–84; Bauer, "Joel Brand Mission," *Yalkut Moreshet,* 25, 49–52; Vago, "Intelligence Aspects of the Joel Brand Mission," 82ff.

27. JAE, 25.5.44, CZA; Avriel, *Open the Gates!,* 174–179.

28. JAE, 25.5.44, CZA; Porat, *The Blue and the Yellow Stars of David,* 191; Bader, *Sad Missions,* 103; Barlas, *Rescue During the Holocaust,* 113; British Ambassador, cable no. 794, FO 371/42758, PRO; Barlas to friends in Budapest, 5.7.44, correspondence, ABG; memorandum on developments in Istanbul, 17.6.44, NA, OSS, RG 84; Squires's memo, 5.6.44, NA, OSS, RG 84; Eiga Shapira to Ehud Avriel, 2.6.44, S25/22684, CZA; eavesdropping report on Barlas's cable to Shertok, 21.5.44, NA, OSS, RG 226, entry 120, box 27, folder 171; Bauer, *Jews for Sale?,* 175 [English].

29. JAE, 25.5.44, CZA; Gruenbaum's urgent cable to Stephan Weiss and Nahum Goldmann, 25.5.44, S53/1569, CZA.

30. Bauer, "Joel Brand Mission," *Yalkut Moreshet,* 40–41; Shertok's report, 27.6.44, London, Z4/14870, CZA; JAE, 29.5.44, CZA.

31. Harold MacMichael to the Colonial Office Secretary, 26.5.44, no. 683, Top Secret, FO 371/42758, PRO; other addressees included the ambassador in Ankara and the resident minister in Cairo; the letter is also cited in Cabinet Papers (hereafter CAB) 95/15/152; MacMichael to Steinhardt, 26.5.44, P12/25, Yad Vashem Archive; Shertok's report, 27.6.44, London, Z4/14870, CZA.

32. JAE, 29.5.44, CZA; Shertok's report, 27.6.44, CZA; Barlas, *Rescue During the Holocaust,* 120–121.

33. JAE, 29.5.44, CZA.

34. Barlas, Ankara, to BG, 25.5.44, correspondence, ABG.

35. "Meir" [Palestine office in Istanbul] to "friends" [JAE and others], 27.5.44, correspondence, ABG.

36. Avriel, *Open the Gates!,* 181; Bader, *Sad Missions,* 102–104; Rosenfeld, *Criminal Case 124/53,* 54, 57.

37. Rosenfeld, *Criminal Case 124/53,* 53–54; Avriel, *Open the Gates!,* 182.

38. 29.5.44, S26/1251, CZA; Barlas to "friends" in Budapest, 5.7.44, correspondence, ABG; Bader, *Sad Missions,* 104–105; Brand, *On Behalf of Those Condemned to Death,* 124–125; Avriel, *Open the Gates!,* 181–183; Bader to Pomeranz, 10.6.44, D.1.1720, MAGH, according to Bauer, "Joel Brand Mission," *Yalkut Moreshet,* 38.

39. Elon, *Timetable,* 153–154; JAE, 4.6.44, CZA; Barlas to "friends" in Budapest, 5.7.44, correspondence, ABG; Kasztner to friends, 31.8.44, S25/8907, CZA; Kasztner, *The Truth of Kasztner,* 113; see Bader's notes for 1944, MAGH. I thank Dr. Eli Tzor of Yad Ya'ari for bringing this to my attention.

40. Porat, *The Blue and the Yellow Stars of David,* 193–194.

41. Shertok's report, 27.6.44, Z4/14870, CZA; Bauer, "Joel Brand Mission," *The Holocaust,* 148–186.

42. Bader, *Sad Missions,* 105; Bader's letters to Pomeranz, 27.5.44, 10.6.44, according to Bauer, "Joel Brand Mission," *Yalkut Moreshet,* 37–38; Avriel, *Open the Gates!,* 182-183; Rosenfeld, *Criminal Case 124/53,* 55, 62–64; Vago, "Intelligence Aspects of the Joel Brand Mission," 81.

43. JAE, 4.6.44, CZA; "Alarme for saving the rement," Jerusalem, 6.6.44, *The Documents Book,* 355–356.

44. Brand, *On Behalf of Those Condemned to Death,* 130–132; Bader, *Sad Missions,* 105; Rosenfeld, *Criminal Case 124/53,* 58; Avriel, *Open the Gates!,* 183.

45. JAE, 14.6.44, CZA; Shertok's report, 27.6.44, London, Z4/14870, CZA; Brand, *On Behalf of Those Condemned to Death,* 129–131; Avriel, *Open the Gates!,* 181–185; Rosenfeld, *Criminal Case 124/53,* 55–65; Bader, *Sad Missions,* 105.

46. Bauer, "Joel Brand Mission," *Yalkut Moreshet,* 42–45; Wasserstein, *Britain and the Jews of Europe,* 250–252.

47. 27.5.44, FO 371/42758 ,W8626, PRO.

48. 31.5.44, CAB 95/15, PRO; Gilbert, *Auschwitz and the Allies,* 217; Wasserstein, *Britain and the Jews of Europe,* 251–254.

49. Conclusion No. 3, War Cabinet no.71, 1.6.44, PRO.

50. Wasserstein, *Britain and the Jews of Europe,* 255–258, 259–262.

51. Randall to Weizmann, 5.6.44; George Hall to Weizmann, 5.6.44; Weizmann to Eden, 6.6.44—all Weizmann Archive; BG, JAE, 4.6.44, CZA; Kedem, "The Political Activity of Chaim Weizmann," 256; Wasserstein, *Britain and the Jews of Europe,* 254–255; Hadar, "The Allies' Attitude Toward the Joel Brand Mission," 117; Bauer, "Joel Brand Mission," *Yalkut Moreshet,* 43.

52. Halifax to Foreign Office in Washington, 5.6.44, P12/25, Yad Vashem Archive; Shertok to JAE, 24.6.44, CZA; Hirschmann, *Lifeline to the Promised Land,* 106–107; Wasserstein, *Britain and the Jews of Europe,* 244ff.

53. Rubin, *Istanbul Intrigues,* 261–262 [English]; Gilbert, *Auschwitz and the Allies,* 224–225.

54. Bauer, "Joel Brand Mission," *Yalkut Moreshet,* 44; Gilbert, *Auschwitz and the Allies,* 224–225.

55. Gilbert, *Auschwitz and the Allies,* 224–225; Porat, *The Blue and the Yellow Stars of David,* 195–196; Wasserstein, *Britain and the Jews of Europe,* 252–262; Hadar, "The Allies' Attitude Toward the Joel Brand Mission," 112–119; Morse, *While Six Million Died,* 284; Hirschmann, *Lifeline to the Promised Land,* 106–108; Bader, *Sad Missions,* 103; Barlas, *Rescue During the Holocaust,* 116–117, 120.

56. Gilbert, *Auschwitz and the Allies,* 224–225; Porat, *The Blue and the Yellow Stars of David,* 195–196.

57. JAE, 14.6.44, CZA; Gilbert, *Auschwitz and the Allies,* 223, 225–227, 280–281.

58. Avriel, *Open the Gates!,* 185–186; Rosenfeld, *Criminal Case 124/53,* 360; Eshed, *Reuven Shiloah: The Man behind the "Mossad",* 74–75.

59. Shertok's report, 27.6.44, London, Z4/14870, CZA; JAE, 14.6.44, CZA; Barlas, *Rescue During the Holocaust,*

121–123; Rosenfeld, *Criminal Case 124/53*, 65; Avriel, *Open the Gates!*, 185–186..

60. JAE, 14.6.44, CZA; memorandum on Shertok-Brand conversation in Aleppo, 11.6.44, GCD, ABG (also in S26/1251, CZA).

61. Bauer, "Joel Brand Mission," *The Holocaust*, 151–153; Vago, "Intelligence Aspects of the Joel Brand Mission," 87–88.

62. Rubin, *Istanbul Intrigues*, 192 [English]; Bauer, *Jews for Sale?*, 129–130 [English]; Bar-Zohar, *Conspiracy*.

63. Kasztner to friends, 31.8.44, S25/8907, CZA.

64. Bauer, "Joel Brand Mission," *The Holocaust*, 151–153; Vago, "Intelligence Aspects of the Joel Brand Mission," 87–88.

65. Memorandum on the conversation, 11.6.44, GCD, ABG; JAE, 14.6.44, CZA; Livia Rothkirchen, "Clandestine Connections Between the Jewish Leaderships in Slovakia and Hungary," *Jewish Hungarian Leadership in the Holocaust* (Jerusalem: Yad Vashem, 1976), 129.

66. See discussion in chapter 9.

67. Joel Brand, Aleppo, 11.6.44, GCD, ABG; JAE, 14.6.44, CZA; Bauer, "Joel Brand Mission," *The Holocaust*, 157–158.

68. Brand, *On Behalf of Those Condemned to Death*, 98; Bauer, "Joel Brand Mission," *The Holocaust*, 157–158; Kasztner, *The Truth of Kasztner*, 86.

69. Burton Berry's letter to his superiors, 13.6.44, NA, OSS, RG 226, entry 94, box 554, folder 30; Vago, "Intelligence Aspects of the Joel Brand Mission," 89–90; Bauer, "Joel Brand Mission," *The Holocaust*, 160–163.

70. Joel Brand, Aleppo, 11.6.44, GCD, ABG; JAE, 14.6.44, CZA; Shertok's report, 27.6.44, Z4/14870, CZA; U.S. Consul in Istanbul to Foreign Office, 13.6.44, NA, OSS, RG 226, entry 94, box 554, folder 30.

71. Vago, "Intelligence Aspects of the Joel Brand Mission," 89–90; Bauer, "Joel Brand Mission," *The Holocaust*, 160–163; Rubin, *Istanbul Intrigues*, 182 [English].

72. Shertok told Brand that he had "already heard his story . . . twice, but he would like once more to hear a report of the developments directly from him." One source was Pomeranz and the other was probably Avriel, who reported to Shertok during the two days of waiting.

73. Joel Brand, Aleppo, 11.6.44, GCD, ABG; JAE, 14.6.44, CZA; Shertok's report, 27.6.44, Z4/14870, CZA; Bauer, "Joel Brand Mission," *Yalkut Moreshet*, 23–33; Berry's report and Squires's memo, 8.6.44, NA, OSS, RG 226, RG 84.

74. Eshed, *Reuven Shiloah: The Man behind the "Mossad"*, 74–75.

75. Brand, *On Behalf of Those Condemned to Death*, 133–135.

76. Elon, *Timetable*, 204.

77. JAE, 14.6.44, CZA; U.S. Consul, Istanbul, to Foreign Office, 13.6.44, NA, OSS, RG 226, entry 94, box 554, folder 30.

78. Memo from Stella Kleczkowsky, 15.4.44, NA, OSS, RG 226, entry E120, box 20, folder 099; Vago, "Intelligence Aspects of the Joel Brand Mission," 89–93; Bauer, "Joel Brand Mission," *Yalkut Moreshet*, 51-52; U.S. Consul, Istanbul, to Foreign Office, 13.6.44, NA, OSS RG 226, entry

94, box 554, folder 30; U.S. Consul, Istanbul, to Foreign Office, 13.6.44, NA, OSS, RG 226, entry 94, box 554, folder 30; Squires's memo, 8.6.44, NA, OSS, RG 84.

79. JAE, 14.6.44, CZA; Barlas, *Rescue During the Holocaust*, 124.

80. High Commissioner to Colonial Office, copies to ambassador in Ankara and resident minister in Cairo, 15.5.44, FO 371/42758, PRO; Barlas, *Rescue During the Holocaust*, 124–125; Shertok's report, 27.6.44, Z4/14870, CZA; Elon, *Timetable*, 205–208; Squires's memo, 8.6.44, NA, OSS, RG 84.

81. Squires's memo, 8.6.44, NA, OSS, RG 84.

82. Barlas, *Rescue During the Holocaust*, 124.

83. High Commissioner to Colonial Secretary, FO 371/42758, PRO; Randall to Halifax, W 8507, cable no. 4938, FO 371/42758, PRO; 2.6.44, minute, FO 371/42758, PRO—the last two according to Gilbert, *Auschwitz and the Allies*, 218–219.

84. JAE, 18.6.44, CZA.

85. Ibid.; cf. Porat, *The Blue and the Yellow Stars of David*, 199–200; Bauer, "Joel Brand Mission," *Yalkut Moreshet*, 37 40.

86. JAE, 18.6.44, CZA; JAE, 25.5.44, CZA; Steinhardt's report, 25.5.44, in *FRUS, 1944*, 1:1050, according to Hadar, "The Allies' Attitude Toward the Joel Brand Mission," 112–125; U.S. Consul, Istanbul, to Foreign Minister, 13.6.44, NA, OSS, RG 226, entry 94, box 554, NA, OSS, RG 226, entry 120, box 27, folder 171.

87. JAE, 18.6.44, CZA; High Commissioner to Colonial Secretary, 14.6.44, FO 371/42758, PRO.

88. JAE, 18.6.44, CZA.

89. Ibid.

90. JAE, 24.6.44, CZA; Shertok's report, 27.6.44, Z4/14870, CZA; Barlas, *Rescue During the Holocaust*, 125; Hirschmann, *Lifeline to the Promised Land*, 109–112, 117–126; Feingold, "The Roosevelt Administration," 236 [English]; Brand, *On Behalf of Those Condemned to Death*, 148–151; Burton Y. Berry, American Consul General, Istanbul, to Secretary of State, 13.6.44, NA, OSS, RG 226, entry 94, box 554, folder 30; Steinhardt to Pinkney Tuck, 20.6.44, NA, OSS, RG 84.

91. JAE, 24.6.44, CZA; Shertok's report, 27.6.44, Z4/14870, CZA; Hirschmann, *Lifeline to the Promised Land*, 109–115; N. Andronovitch to A.C. of S. Jerusalem, 2.6.44, NA, OSS, RG 226, entry E120, box 32, folder 221; Hirschmann memo, 22.6.44, NA, OSS, RG 84.

92. JAE, 24.6.44, CZA; Bader, Ankara, to his family, 29.6.44, MAGH.

93. JAE, 24.6.44, CZA; Barlas, *Rescue During the Holocaust*, 125; OSS Cairo, 28.6.44, NA, OSS, RG 226, entry E120, box 32, folder 222.

94. Shertok's report, 27.6.44, Z4/14870, CZA, 8–9; H. Mac-Michael to Colonial Secretary, 26.5.44, FO 371/42758, PRO.

95. Shertok's report, 27.6.44, Z4/14870, CZA, 8; summary of Dobkin's and Schwartz's conversation, 4–7.8.43, S26/1080, CZA.

96. Shertok's report, 27.6.44, Z4/14870, CZA, 8–9; David Niv, *Battle for Freedom: The Irgun Zvai Leumi* (Tel Aviv: Klausner Institute, 1973), 4:134–141.

97. Bader's weekly review, 25.6.44, S25/22465, CZA; Hirschmann, *Lifeline to the Promised Land*, 109–127.

98. Bauer, *American Jewry and the Holocaust*, 259–261 [English]; Steinhardt to Tuck, 20.6.44, NA, OSS, RG 84; Shertok's report, 27.6.44, Z4/14870, CZA.

99. OSS Palestine branch's memo, 27.8.44, 4; Magnes to Poul Baerwald, 22.6.44, NA, OSS, RG 226, entry E120.

100. Hirschmann, *Lifeline to the Promised Land*, 126–127; Bader's weekly review, 25.6.44, S25/22465, CZA; Shertok's report, 27.6.44, Z4/14870, 8, CZA; Kaplan, JAE, 28.7.44, CZA; Hirschman addendum, 22.6.44, NA, OSS, RG 84.

101. JAE, 24.6.44, CZA.

102. Ibid.

103. JAE, 25.6.44, CZA; Shertok to Dobkin, Lisbon, 16.6.44, S26/1253, CZA.

104. 15–20.6.44; Walker to Lord Moyne, Colonial Office, 17.6.44; Randall, 19.6.44—all FO 371/42758, PRO; Elon, *Timetable*, 231.

105. Hankey, 20.6.44, FO 371/42758, PRO.

106. 21.6.44, FO 371/42758, PRO.

107. Hall to Weizmann, 22.6.44, FO 371/42758, PRO; U.S. Consul to Foreign Office, 13.6.44, NA, OSS, RG 226, entry 94, box 554, folder 30.

108. Randall to Weizmann, 23.6.44, Z4/15202, CZA (also includes Shertok's cable and report to Weizmann).

109. Randall to Weizmann, 24.6.44, Z4/14870, CZA; Bauer, "Joel Brand Mission," *Yalkut Moreshet*, 46; British Foreign Office memorandum, 26.6.44. The cables that arrived from Istanbul were the third source.

110. Agronsky's report, BGD, 6.7.44, ABG; Weizmann to Hall, 23.6.44, Z4/15202, CZA; Elon, *Timetable*, 231.

111. Shertok, London, to Kaplan, 28.6.44, correspondence, ABG.

112. Hall's conversation with Weizmann and Shertok on 30.6.44, according to Porat, *The Blue and the Yellow Stars of David*, 202–203.

113. Shertok to BG, 30.6.44, Z4/14870, CZA; JAE, 2.7.44, CZA; JAE, 9.7.44, CZA; Shertok to BG, through the Palestine Chief Secretary, 7.7.44, correspondence, ABG; Bauer, *Jews for Sale?*, 187 [English].

114. Agronsky's report, BGD, 6.7.44, ABG; Shertok to Leo Cohen, 5.7.44, correspondence, ABG; BG, JAE, 9.7.44, CZA; Gelber, *Growing a Fleur-de-Lis*, 1:53, 261; Kollek, *One Jerusalem*, 47.

115. BGD, 6.7.44, ABG; Gruenbaum to Barlas, 28.6.44, correspondence, ABG.

116. Shertok to BG, through Palestine Chief Secretary, 7.7.44, correspondence, ABG; Bauer, *Jews for Sale?*, 187 [English].

117. JAE, 2.7.44, CZA; Bader to Venja, 10.6.44, correspondence, ABG.

118. BG, JAE, 2.7.44, CZA; Zaslani's cable to Kollek, 28.6.44, correspondence, ABG. The message was sent from Istanbul on 25.6.44; Kasztner to Istanbul Palestine Office, German, 29.6.44, correspondence, ABG; Bader to Kasztner, Budapest, 29.6.44, correspondence, ABG; Kasztner, *The Truth of Kasztner*, 67, 107.

119. Rubin, *Istanbul Intrigues*, 182–187; Avriel to Zaslani, 3.11.43, S25/22685, CZA; author's 1994 conversation with Kollek in Keren's offices in Jerusalem.

120. Rubin, *Istanbul Intrigues*, 187 [English].

121. Bauer, *Jews for Sale?*, 136–137 [English].

122. Ibid., 140, 196–197 [English].

123. Shlomo Aronson and Richard Breitman, "The End of the 'Final Solution'?: Nazi Plans to Ransom Jews in 1944," *Central European History*, 25, no. 2 (1992), 194–203 [English].

124. Zaslani's cable to Kollek, 28.6.44, correspondence, ABG.

125. JAE, 2.7.44, CZA; Barlas to Gruenbaum, 25.6.44, S26/1284, CZA.

126. JAE, 2.7.44, CZA; Bader to Venja, 10.6.44, correspondence, ABG.

127. See, e.g., Bader to Venja, 10.6.44, correspondence, ABG; Hirschmann, *Lifeline to the Promised Land*, 136–137; N. Andronovitch to A.C. of S. Jerusalem, 2.6.44, NA, OSS, RG 226, entry E120, box 32, folder 221; BG's cable to Sharett, 2.7.44, correspondence, ABG (also in Z4/14870, CZA).

128. Bader to BG, 8.7.44, correspondence, ABG.

129. JAE, 18.6.44, CZA; Barlas to Gruenbaum, 25.6.44, S26/1284, CZA; Gruenbaum's answer to Barlas, 28.6.44, correspondence, ABG; Y. Kleinbaum to British Airways, 16.6.44, S25/22681, CZA; Eiga Shapira to Ze'ev Schind, 22.6.44, S25/22681, CZA.

130. BG's cable to Shertok, 2.7.44, correspondence, ABG (also in Z4/14870, CZA); Istanbul Palestine office to "friends" in Budapest [German] 5.7.44, correspondence, ABG.

131. Porat, "Ben-Gurion and the Holocaust," 306–307.

132. 17.7.44, NA, OSS, RG 226, entry E120, box 27, folder 174; the document is also in NA, OSS, RG 226, entry 108, box 55, together with other reports.

133. Bader's weekly review, 25.6.44–1.7.44, S25/22460, CZA.

134. Hirschmann addendum, 22.6.44, NA, OSS, RG 84; Hirschmann to Magnes, ibid.

135. Hirschmann memo, 22.6.44, NA, OSS, RG 84.

136. Bader's weekly review, 25.6.44–1.7.44, S25/22460, CZA.

137. Ibid.

138. Ibid.; Hirschmann addendum, 22.6.44, NA, OSS, RG 84; Hirschmann to Magnes, 22.6.44, ibid.; Ehud Avriel to Eiga Shapira, 29.6.44, S25/22681, CZA; Kaplan's report upon his return from Turkey, JAE, 28.7.44, CZA; Kasztner, *The Truth of Kasztner*, 113.

139. Bader to BG, 8.7.44, correspondence, ABG.

140. Ibid.

141. Ibid.; Barlas to "friends" in Budapest, 5.7.44, ibid.

142. Memorandum from Istanbul, 10.7.44, GCD, ABG; Bader to Kasztner, 29.6.44, correspondence, ABG; Magnes's memo and report, 13.7.44, correspondence, ABG; cf. Avriel, *Open the Gates!*, 186–187; Kasztner to Bader, 15.7.44, correspondence, ABG.

143. Memorandum from Istanbul, 10.7.44, GCD, ABG; memorandum from Istanbul, 8.7.44 [English], GCD, ABG.

Based on the issues covered in this memo, it appears that the correct date should be 12 or 13 July.

144. Rubin, *Istanbul Intrigues*, 195–200 [English]; Shertok's report from London, 27.6.44, Z4/14870, 2; Squires's memo, 8.6.44, Ankara, NA, OSS, RG 84.

145. Bauer, *Jews for Sale?*, 205–221 [English]; Paul L. Rose, "Joel Brand's 'Interim Agreement' and the Course of Nazi–Jewish Negotiations, 1944–1945," *Historical Journal*, 34, no. 4 (1991), 910ff.

146. Barlas to "friends" in Budapest, 5.7.44, correspondence, ABG; Bader, *Sad Missions*, 104–105; Brand, *On Behalf of Those Condemned to Death*, 124–125; Avriel, *Open the Gates!*, 181–183; Bader to Pomeranz, 10.6.44, D.I.1720, MAGH, according to Bauer, "Joel Brand Mission," 26, 38; According to Rose, the agreement only arrived in Budapest on 7 July. I believe that this was the second agreement, which was cabled to Vienna on 30 June.

147. Bauer, "Joel Brand Mission," *The Holocaust*, 120, Rose, "Joel Brand's 'Interim Agreement,'" 912 [English]; cf. Rose, 910.

148. JAE, 2.7.44, CZA; Bader to Venja, 10.6.44, correspondence, ABG; Kasztner to Istanbul Palestine Office, 29.6.44, correspondence, ABG; Bader to Kasztner, Budapest, correspondence, ABG

149. Rose ("Joel Brand's 'Interim Agreement,'" 914 [English]), who determined that there was only one agreement, which only reached Budapest in July, describes what I refer to as Intermediate Agreement B as a message. It should be noted that even such an interpretation gives that kind of change a degree of importance.

150. Bader to BG, 8.7.44, correspondence, ABG; Barlas to "friends" in Budapest, 5.7.44, correspondence, ABG; Rose, "Joel Brand's 'Interim Agreement,'" 914 [English].

151. For a fully documented, fascinating description, see Bauer, *Jews for Sale?*, chaps. 7–9 [English].

152. The strained relations between the Abwehr and the SD included the former's reservations concerning the SD's lack of professionalism and devotion to Nazi ideology. On the other hand, the SD doubted the ideological loyalty of many of the Abwehr's members. Canaris protected those Abwehr members who, like him, had reservations about Hitler. Before the war he even tried to warn the West—through the Vatican—of Hitler's aggressive tendencies.

153. Rubin, *Istanbul Intrigues*, 179 [English].

154. Rose, "Joel Brand's 'Interim Agreement,'" 915 [English].

155. Bader to BG, 8.7.44, correspondence, ABG; Barlas to "friends" in Budapest, 5.7.44, correspondence, ABG.

156. Rubin, *Istanbul Intrigues*, 195–200 [English]; Shertok's report, 27.6.44, Z4/14870, CZA, 2; Squires's memo, 8.6.44, Ankara, NA, OSS, RG 84.

157. Dobkin's report, JAE, 21.9.44, CZA; Dobkin's report, Mapai Secretariat, 24.9.44, LPA; BG's and Shertok's cables, through the Palestine Chief Secretary, 2, 4–5, 7 July 1944; Shertok to BG, 13.7.44; Bader to BG, 8.7.44; Dobkin to the British ambassador in Portugal, 12.7.44; Venja and Bader to the JAE, 23.7.44—all in correspondence, ABG.

158. Dobkin's report, JAE, 21.9.44, CZA; Dobkin, JAE, 26.3.44, CZA.

159. Dobkin's report, JAE, 21.9.44, CZA.

160. Kasztner to Bader, 15.7.44, correspondence, ABG; Barlas to "friends" in Budapest, 5.7.44, correspondence, ABG.

161. On the cables, see Z4/14890; see also Kasztner's and Krausz's proposals for action; Goldmann to Weizmann, 1.7.44, Z6/1/16, CZA.

162. Sharett to BG and Goldmann, 6.7.44, Z4/14870, CZA (memorandum also in GCD, ABG).

163. 6.7.44, Z4/14870, CZA (also contains minutes of the meeting).

164. Ibid.; BG, JAE, 9.7.44, CZA; BG's cable to Shertok, 13.7.44, Z4/14870, CZA.

165. BG's speech at "Herzl Day" in Jerusalem, 10.7.44, SA, ABG.

166. BG to Shertok, 13.7.44; BG to Shertok, 13.7.44, through the Palestine Chief Secretary, Magnes's memorandum, 13.7.44—all in correspondence, ABG (also in S25/1682, CZA); see also Porat, "Ben-Gurion and the Holocaust," 307.

167. Shertok to Randall, 14.7.44, correspondence, ABG.

168. Shertok's cable to BG, through the Palestine Chief Secretary, 17.7.44, FO 371/42809, PRO (also in 14.7.44, correspondence, ABG, and 14.7.44, Z4/14870, CZA).

169. Report on Shertok's conversation with Randall and Henderson, 14.7.44, Z4/14870, CZA; Barlas, *Rescue During the Holocaust*, 118, 126–127.

170. Churchill to Eden, 11.7.44, according to Gilbert, *Auschwitz and the Allies*, 277–278.

171. Shertok to BG, 14.7.44, FO 371/42809, PRO.

172. JAE, 16.7.44, CZA.

173. Ibid.; cable no. 343, 16.7.44; BG to Shertok, Magnes's memo, 13.7.44; Venja and Bader to JAE, 23.7.44—all in correspondence, ABG.

174. JAE, 16.7.44, CZA.

175. Sharett to Leo Cohen, the source of the leak in Ankara, 24.7.44, correspondence, ABG; Gruenbaum and Kaplan, JAE, 23.7.44, CZA; Dobkin, JAE, 21.9.44, CZA; Wasserstein, *Britain and the Jews of Europe*, 261–262. The question of who first leaked the information has been investigated by several researchers and is irrelevant to my discussion. The Allies blamed each other, but the leak served them all.

176. Eiga Shapira to friends in Istanbul, 26.7.44, S25/22681, CZA; Gruenbaum, JAE, 23.7.44, CZA; Barlas to JAE, 23.7.44, correspondence, ABG; Schind, Histadrut Executive Committee Secretariat, 6.9.44, ILMAL; Shertok, JAE, 20.10.44, CZA; Zionist Actions Committee, 19.11.44, CZA.

177. Gruenbaum, JAE, 23.7.44, CZA; Barlas to JAE, 23.7.44, correspondence, ABG; Schind, Histadrut Executive Committee Secretariat, 6.9.44, ILMAL; Shertok, JAE, 20.10.44, CZA; Zionist Actions Committee, 19.11.44, CZA.

178. BG's speech at "Herzl Day" in Jerusalem, 10.7.44, SA, ABG.

179. This was an extremely complex relationship and included many instances of cooperation and real help on the part of BG.

180. JAE, 23.7.44, CZA; JAE, 16.1.44, CZA; *Davar,* 15.8.44.
181. JAE, 23.7.44, CZA.
182. Bauer, *Jews for Sale?,* 181 [English]; Gilbert, *Auschwitz and the Allies,* 287, 289–298; Wasserstein, *Britain and the Jews of Europe,* 263–264.
183. Shertok to Leo Cohen, 24.7.44, correspondence, ABG; Shertok to Randall, 14.7.44, Z4/14840, CZA; Randall to Shertok, 15.7.44, CZA; Shertok to Leo Cohen, copy to BG, 21.7.44 (received 23.7.44), correspondence, ABG.
184. Venja and Bader to JAE, 23.7.44, correspondence, ABG.
185. "Meir" (Yishuv office in Istanbul) to "Artzi" (Palestine), copy to BG, 29.7.44, correspondence, ABG; Kasztner to friends, 31.8.44, S25/8907, CZA; Venja and Bader to JAE, 3.8.44, through the Polish Consulate in Jerusalem, correspondence, ABG.
186. Hirschmann, *Lifeline to the Promised Land,* 127–129; Barlas, *Rescue During the Holocaust,* 133, 327; 28.7.44, P12/25, Yad Vashem Archive; Dobkin to the British ambassador in Lisbon, 12.7.44, correspondence, ABG; Dobkin's report, JAE, 21.9.44, CZA.
187. Shertok, London, to Leo Cohen, Jerusalem, 20.7.44, cited in an American intelligence report, 30.8.44, NA, OSS, RG 226, entry 191, box 3; Kaplan's report, JAE, 28.7.44, CZA.
188. See chapter 4: "Shalom Adler-Rudel's Mission to Sweden," 183–194.
189. The cable, which reached Jerusalem on 1.7.44, was intercepted by American Intelligence. See NA, OSS, RG 226, entry E120, box 27, folder 171, 5.
190. JAE, 6.8.44, CZA.
191. Adler-Rudel to JAE, Jerusalem, 14.9.44; Bader to Adler-Rudel, 28.9.44; Adler-Rudel to Bader, 29.9.44; Bader to Adler-Rudel, 30.9.44; Bader to Adler-Rudel, 3.10.44—all in A140/347, CZA.
192. Menachem Bader, Istanbul, to JAE, 30.9.44, S53/1603, CZA, secs. 1 and 3.
193. Shertok, London, to Leo Cohen, Jerusalem, 20.7.44, quoted in an American intelligence report, 30.8.44, NA, OSS, RG 226, entry 191, box 3. See also other cables sent to Bader regarding the Brand affair in OSS, Washington, to Macfarland, Istanbul, 26.10.44, NA, OSS, RG 226, entry 088, box 609; Director OSS, Washington, to Macfarland, Istanbul, 3.11.44, NA, OSS, RG 226, entry 088, box 609; Macfarland, Istanbul, to Director OSS, Washington, 13.11.144, NA, OSS, RG 226, entry 134, box 299, folder 1661; 21.6.44, NA, OSS, RG 226, entry 134, box 299, folder 1660; American attaché in Turkey to Washington, 24.9.44, NA, OSS, RG 226, entry 120, box 27, folder 175; JAE, 28.7.44, CZA.
194. Kleist testimony, 21.2.46, NA, OSS, RG 226, entry 125, box 29, folder 407; Aronson and Breitman, "The End of the 'Final Solution'?," 192–193 [English]; Bauer, *Jews for Sale?,* 168 [English].
195. Kleist testimony, 21.2.46, NA, OSS, RG 226, entry 125, box 29, folder 407.
196. Aronson and Breitman, 'The End of the 'Final Solution'?," 192 [English].
197. Bauer, *Jews for Sale?,* 168, 225 [English]; Aronson and Breitman, "The End of the 'Final Solution'?," 201–203 [English].
198. Adler-Rudel's personal archive, memorandum of meetings with German officials in Stockholm, 19.1.45, A140/231, CZA; Adler-Rudel, "A Chronicle of Rescue Efforts," 236–238 [English].
199. Adler-Rudel's memorandum, 19.1.45, A140/231, CZA; for a different version regarding Kleist, see Adler-Rudel, "A Chronicle of Rescue Efforts," 236-238 [English]; Bader, Istanbul, to JAE, sec. 3, 30.9.44, S53/1603, CZA.
200. Aronson and Breitman, "The End of the 'Final Solution'?," 179, n. 7 [English].
201. Dobkin's report, JAE, 21.9.44, CZA; Hirschmann, *Lifeline to the Promised Land,* 129; Kaplan, JAE, 23.7.44, CZA; Yehuda Bauer, "Negotiations Between Saly Mayer and SS Representatives in 1944–1945," *The Holocaust: Historical Aspects,* 192 ff.; Aronson and Breitman, "The End of the 'Final Solution'?," 192, 201 [English].
202. Shertok, London, to Leo Cohen, Jerusalem, 20.7.44, quoted in an American intelligence report, 30.8.44, OSS, NA, RG 226, entry 191, box 3; see n. 77.
203. Brand, Rescue Committee presidency meeting protocol, 16.10.44, S26/1238, CZA; Brand, Mapai Center, 17.10.44, according to Porat, *The Blue and the Yellow Stars of David,* 209–210; see also answers by Golomb, Kaplan, Neustadt, and Dobkin in Mapai Center, 17.10.44, LPA; Joel and Hansi Brand, *Satan and the Soul,* 73–77; Brand, *On Behalf of Those Condemned to Death,* 168–170, 174ff. The explanations Brand was given following his release from jail did not always satisfy him.
204. Friling, "Changing Roles," 405–431 [Hebrew]; Friling, "Meeting the Survivors: Ben-Gurion's Visit to Bulgaria, December 1944," 175.
205. Gruenbaum to Ehrenpreis, 24.7.44; Storch to Leibovitz, for the Rescue Committee, 11.8.44; Linton to Cohen, 6.10.44; Storch to Gruenbaum, 10.2.45; Storch to JAE, passed to Gruenbaum, 10.2.45—all in S26/1277, CZA; Lichtheim to Gruenbaum, 22.2.45, S26/1232, CZA; Lichtheim to Gruenbaum, 24.2.45, S26/1232, CZA; Gruenbaum to Storch, 22.1.45, C4/434, CZA; Gruenbaum to Ehrenpreis, 17.10.44, A140/347, CZA; Gruenbaum to Lichtheim, 21.2.45, S53/1591, CZA.
206. Kasztner, *The Truth of Kasztner,* 114–115, 127–132, 147–148, 156–157, 160–168; Bauer, *Jews for Sale?,* chaps. 11–12 [English]; Bauer, "Negotiations Between Saly Mayer and SS Representatives in 1944–1945," 192–219.
207. Bauer, "Negotiations Between Saly Mayer and SS Representatives in 1944–1945," 192–194, 207.
208. Ibid., 196.
209. Ibid., 211.
210. Ibid., 213–214; Lichtheim to Gruenbaum, 24.2.45, S26/1232, CZA.

211. Bauer, "Negotiations Between Saly Mayer and SS Representatives in 1944–1945," 216–217.

212. Ibid., 203.

213. Kaplan's report upon his return from Turkey, JAE, 28.7.44, CZA, 9, 10.

214. Leo Cohen to BG, Avriel's cable, 22.8.44, correspondence, ABG; 24.8.44, ibid. Message was also passed on to Shertok abroad.

215. Leo Cohen to Shertok, London, 24.8.44, correspondence, ABG.

216. Joel Brand, *On Behalf of Those Condemned to Death*, 165–166; Joel and Hansi Brand, *Satan and the Soul*, 98–99; report, November 1944, NA, OSS, RG 226, entry E120, box 32, folder 221, 2; Leo Cohen to BG, Avriel's cable, 22.8.44, correspondence, ABG; Leo Cohen to Shertok, London, 24.8.44, correspondence, ABG; Dobkin's report, JAE, 21.9.44, CZA; Hirschmann, *Life-line to the Promised Land*, 129; Kaplan, JAE, 23.7.44, CZA; Aronson and Breitman, "The End of the 'Final Solution'?," 199–203 [English]; Kasztner to friends, 31.8.44, S25/8907, CZA, secs. 9–10.

217. Adler-Rudel, "A Chronicle of Rescue Efforts," 238 [English]; Felix Kersten, *The Kersten Memoirs* (London: Hutchinson, 1956) [English]; Folke Bernadotte, *The Fall of the Curtain: Last Days of the Third Reich* (London: Cassell, 1945) [English]; Hugo Valentin, "Rescue and Relief Activities on Behalf of Jewish Victims of Nazism in Scandinavia," *YIVO Annual* 8 (1953), 224–251 [English].

218. For a detailed description of this communication, see Bauer, *Jews for Sale?*, 102–105 [English].

219. Storch to Gruenbaum, 22.2.45, S26/1232, CZA; Storch to Adler-Rudel, 27.3.45, A140/232, CZA; Storch to Weiss, Goldmann, and Tartakover, 27.3.45, A140/232, CZA.

220. Storch to Adler-Rudel, Weiss, Goldmann, and Tartakover, 31.3.45, A140/232, CZA.

221. Norbert Masur, *A Jew Talks with Himmler* (Tel Aviv: Israel-Sweden Friendship Association, 1985), 9, 15–28.

222. Norbert Masur's memorandum concerning his trip to Berlin, Top Secret, Stockholm, 23.4.45, A140/232, CZA; Adler-Rudel's notes on Masur memo, 30.4.45, A140/232, CZA; *Evening Standard* (London), 16.5.45; Adler-Rudel's note, n.d., A140/232, CZA; unsigned, Stockholm, to Gruenbaum, 6.5.45, S26/1277, CZA; Masur, *A Jew Talks with Himmler*, 15–28; Bauer, *Jews for Sale?*, 247–248 [English].

223. Kaplan's report, JAE, 28.7.44, CZA; Leo Cohen to Shertok, London, copy to BG, 3.8.44; Reiss to JA, copy to BG, 7.8.44; Linton to Cohen, copy to BG, 13.10.44—all correspondence, ABG; Lichtheim's cable to Gruenbaum, 24.2.45, S26/1232, CZA.

224. Masur, *A Jew Talks with Himmler*, 15-28.

225. JAE, 25.5.44, CZA.

226. JAE, 18.6.44, CZA.

227. For example, it is unclear where it was decided that Brand would set off for Turkey from Aleppo; how it was decided to send interim agreements A and B or to share the matter with Britain and the United States; or who decided on the change in position regarding opening negotiations on stopping transports to the death camps.

228. Ze'ev Tzahor, "'The Mossad Le Aliyah Bet': The Source of Its Authority," *Cathedra*, no. 39 (April 1986), 162–178; Porat, *The Blue and the Yellow Stars of David*, 210–211.

229. On the JDC-JAE agreement, see chapter. 5, 231–238; Tuvia Friling, "Istanbul, June 1944: The Intriguing Proposal to Menahem Bader," *Iyunim Bitkumat Israel: Studies in Zionism, the Yishuv, and the State of Israel* 4 (1994), 241ff.

230. Kaplan, JAE, 23.7.44, CZA; Dr. Eliash, JAE, 10.9.44, CZA; Rosenfeld, *Criminal Case 124/53*, 58, based on Avriel's testimony.

231. JAE, 18.6.44, CZA.

232. JAE, 25.5.44, 29.5.44, and 18.6.44, CZA.

233. Porat, *The Blue and the Yellow Stars of David*, 211.

234. JAE, 23.7.44 and 23.9.44, CZA.

235. BGD, 6.7.44, ABG.

236. Bauer, "Joel Brand Mission," *The Holocaust*, 23–60; Vago, "Intelligence Aspects of the Joel Brand Mission," 81–94; Porat, *The Blue and the Yellow Stars of David*, 386; Squires's memo, 8.6.44, NA, OSS, RG 84.

237. Rosenfeld, *Criminal Case 124/53*; Joel and Hansi Brand, *Satan and the Soul*; S. Nakdimon, "On Joel and Hansi Brand's Book *Satan and the Soul*," *Herut*, 5.7.60; Bauer, "The Kasztner Affair: The Historical Truth and the Political Use," *Ha'aretz*, 25.5.82; S. Fox, "The Kasztner Affair Is Back," *Ma'ariv*, weekend supplement, 24.5.85 and 31.5.85.

238. Tuvia Friling, "David Ben-Gurion and the Catastrophe of European Jewry, 1939–1945" (Ph.D. diss., Hebrew University of Jerusalem, 1991), 364–399.

239. Brand, *On Behalf of Those Condemned to Death*, 163; Elon, *Timetable*, 330; Kollek to Avriel, 14.8.44, correspondence, ABG.

240. Brand, *On Behalf of Those Condemned to Death*, 165–166; Joel and Hansi Brand, *Satan and the Soul*, 98–99.

241. Eiga Shapira (department secretary) to Ehud Avriel, Istanbul, 28.8.44, S25/22681, CZA.

242. Teddy Kollek, JA Political Department to Rescue Committee, 21.11.44, correspondence, ABG; Joel Brand to JAE, 7.12.44, S44/679, CZA; Brand's memo 11.9.44, S44/679, CZA; post-factum testimonies: Brand to Kaplan, copy to BG, 18.12.45, CZA; Eiga Shapira to "friends" in Istanbul 8.6.44, S25/22681, CZA; Gelber, *Growing a Fleur-de-Lis*, 490–492.

243. Kollek to friends in Istanbul, 17.8.44; Kollek to Ehud, 24.8.44; Kollek to Avriel (through Reed), 14.8.44—all in S25/22681, CZA; unsigned to "Avigayil," 1.12.44, file 14/59, Haganah Archive; to Gavriel (Hayim), infiltration file, 3.10.44, S25/8885, CZA; conversation with Raphael, 26.10.44, S25/8885, CZA; Kollek to Avriel, 2.11.44, S25/22516, CZA.

244. Unsigned cable to Lt. Col. Hunloke, 1.12.44, S25/22459, CZA.

245. Eiga Shapira to "friends" in Istanbul, 8.6.44, S25/22681, CZA.

246. Kollek to "friends" in Istanbul, 17.8.44, S25/ 22681, CZA; Brand, Rescue Committee presidency protocol, 16.10.44, S26/1238, CZA; Brand, Mapai Center, 17.10.44, according to Porat (see n. 29); Brand, *On Behalf of Those Condemned to Death*, 168–170; Joel and Hansi Brand, *Satan and the Soul*, 73–77, 174ff.

247. Avriel, *Open the Gates!*, 176–182; Brand, *On Behalf of Those Condemned to Death*, 109–113; Mapai Center, 17.10.44, LPA; Brand's report, 23.1.45, 25–27, S26/1190ab, CZA, according to Porat, *The Blue and the Yellow Stars of David*, 189–190, 210; Bader, *Sad Missions*, 100–102; Barlas, *Rescue During the Holocaust*, 113–115.

248. BG to Yehoshua Kasztner, 2.2.58, correspondence, ABG; Yehoshua Kasztner to BG, 2.2.58, correspondence, ABG; response and resolutions of Zionist Actions Committee in *Davar*, 12.9.44.

249. Barlas, *Davar*, 21.9.44; Kollek, *One Jerusalem*, 63; Bader, *Sad Missions*, 100; Porat, *The Blue and the Yellow Stars of David*, 189–190; Biss, *A Million Jews to Save*, 54 [English]; Kasztner, *The Truth of Kasztner*, 101.

250. 7.11.44, correspondence, ABG; JAE, 16.7.44, CZA; cable also in NA, Jerusalem, telegram no. 97, 840.48 Refugee S/7–1144, according to Martin Gilbert, *Auschwitz and the Allies*, 277–278; BG to Goldmann for Roosevelt, 11.7.44, War Refugee Board Papers, New York, according to Bauer, "Joel Brand Mission," *Yalkut Moreshet*, 60.

251. S25/1682, CZA, according to Gilbert, *Auschwitz and the Allies*, 277–278; Bauer, "Joel Brand Mission," *Yalkut Moreshet*, 53–54; Porat, "Ben-Gurion and the Holocaust," 307.

9. Bombing to Deter and Stultify

1. Walter Laqueur, *The Terrible Secret*, 156, 157, 171; Eshkoli-Wagman, "The Palestine Jewish Leadership's Stand on the Rescue of Europe's Jews," 93.

2. Bernard Wasserstein, *Britain and the Jews of Europe*, 299–305 [English].

3. Ibid., 299; Molotov's announcement, *Volzhiskaya Kommuna*, 16.10.42; report of U.S. embassy in Moscow to Washington, 16.10.42, NA, 740.00 116, European War, 1939 614; to Foreign Minister of Czech government-in-exile, 14.10.42.

4. JAE, 24.11.42, 6.12.42, CZA; Mapai Secretariat, 25.11.42, LPA.

5. Dr. Joseph to Emergency Committee, New York, 25.11.42, S26/1144 and S26/1289, CZA; JAE, 24.11.42, CZA.

6. Dr. Senator and Dr. Rupinn, JAE, 29.11.42, CZA; U.S. embassy in Moscow to Foreign Minister, 16.10.42, 655, NA, 740.00 116, European War, 1939 614.

7. Mapai Secretariat, 25.11.42, LPA; JAE, 6.12.42, CZA; BGD and Joseph's diary, 26.1.43, Diaries Section, ABG.

8. "To the Human Conscience," speech delivered at a special Elected Assembly gathering, 30.11.42, SA, ABG. See also Ben-Gurion, *In the Battle*, 3:116; and "The Mapai Information Center," no. 172 (Tel Aviv: 4.12.42).

9. BG, JAE, 6.12.42, CZA. See also Dobkin, Senator's, and Sprinzak's words.

10. "Avi Amos" [Ben-Gurion] to Arthur Lourie for Felix Frankfurter, 8.12.42, correspondence, ABG.

11. BG to Berl Locker, 8.12.42, correspondence, ABG; U.S. ambassador in London to Foreign Minister, 7.12.42, 660, NA, 740.00 116, European War, 1939.

12. BG at a gathering of Mapai activists, 8.12.42, SA, ABG.

13. Kirshenberg and Glickson to BG, 10.12.42, correspondence, ABG.

14. Blumberg to BG, Jerusalem, 27.11.42, correspondence, ABG.

15. Stephen Arnold and Maivsky to BG, 30.11.42, correspondence, ABG.

16. Declaration in S26/1236, CZA; Wasserstein, *Britain and the Jews of Europe*, 172–173 [English].

17. BG, Gruenbaum, Joseph, Dobkin, JAE, 20.12.42, CZA; Eshkoli-Wagman, "The Palestine Jewish Leadership's Stand," 94; *The Documents Book*, 336; Winant to Foreign Minister, 11.12.42, NA, 740.00 116, European War, 1939 660.

18. Wasserstein, *Britain and the Jews of Europe*, 174–176, 300–301 [English].

19. Ibid., 176.

20. Action Committee for Saving the Jews of Europe, 10.12.42, CZA; JAE, 20.12.42, CZA.

21. JAE, 10.1.43, CZA.

22. JAE, 24.1.43, CZA.

23. BG at Mobilization and Rescue Fund Convention, Tel Aviv, 11.1.43, SA, ABG; *Davar*, 12.1.43, 17.2.43.

24. Wasserstein, *Britain and the Jews of Europe*, 305–307 [English]; Gilbert, *Auschwitz and the Allies*, 142 [English]; BG at Mobilized Youth convention, 6.4.43, SA, ABG.

25. Gruenbaum, Zionist Actions Committee, 18.2.43, CZA; Y. Kleinbaum to the Czechoslovkian, Hungarian, and Yugoslavian immigrants' associations, and to the Belgian consul, 17.2.43, correspondence, ABG; Steinhardt to Barlas, 3.4.43, correspondence, ABG; JAE, 28.2.43, CZA; Mapai Secretariat, 30.3.43, LPA; JAE and Mapai Secretariat, 27.4.43, LPA.

26. JAE, 26.9.43, CZA; Gruenbaum's report upon his return from South Africa, Zionist Actions Committee, 14.11.43, CZA; Elected Assembly, 13.6.43, *The Documents Book*, 343–344; Gruenbaum's speech at a writers convention, quoted in Yitzhak Gruenbaum, *On Destruction and Holocaust Days, 1940–1946* (Jerusalem: Haverim, 1946), 124; Wasserstein, *Britain and the Jews of Europe*, 301–302 [English].

27. Announcement in S26/1236, CZA; Wasserstein, *Britain and the Jews of Europe*, 295 [English]; Gilbert, *Auschwitz and the Allies*, 158–160 [English].

28. Wasserstein, *Britain and the Jews of Europe*, 299 [English].

29. Gilbert, *Auschwitz and the Allies*, 143 [English]; Ze'ev Schind, Mapai Secretariat, 15.12.43, LPA.

30. Gruenbaum at a special session of the Elected Assembly for Rescue, 12.1.44, *The Documents Book*, 352; Yitzhak

31. Gruenbaum, "First of All the Massacre Must Be Stopped," *Hazman*, 28.1.44; Gruenbaum, "And Again on the Same Issue," *Hazman*, 14.2.44.

31. Dr. Joseph to Shertok, 22.3.44, correspondence, ABG; Shertok to Joseph, 27.3.44, correspondence, ABG, copies to BG; JAE, 26.3.44, CZA; Roosevelt announcement, 23.3.44, S26/1236, CZA; *Davar*, 26.3.44; 24.3.44, NA, 740.0011 EW 39/1368.

32. Wasserstein, *Britain and the Jews of Europe*, 296–297 [English]; Sompolinsky, "The Anglo-Jewish Leadership," 162; Gilbert, *Auschwitz and the Allies*, 185–186 [English].

33. Gruenbaum's speech at the Elected Assembly, 19.4.44 (as well as his speech on 12.4.44), quoted in Gruenbaum, *On Destruction and Holocaust Days*, 85, 81–83; Wasserstein, *Britain and the Jews of Europe*, 300–301[English].

34. Shertok's report, Mapai Center, 8.5.44, LPA, 24; Barlas to JA, 5.5.44, correspondence, ABG; Gruenbaum to Weiss, 8.5.44, correspondence, ABG.

35. This issue was not discussed at JAE meetings on 25.5.44 or 29.5.44; Porat, *The Blue and the Yellow Stars of David*, 212; Rabbi Binyamin's note to Shertok, 25.5.44, S26/1251, CZA; Rabbi Binyamin, *Ha'aretz*, 9.6.44, and *Bamishor*, 29.6.44; see Morgenstern, "The Rescue Committee's Actions During 1943–1945," 87; Gruenbaum's cable to Shertok, 29.5.44, quoted in Gilbert, *Auschwitz and the Allies*, 219–220 [English]; Gruenbaum to Reiss in London, 30.5.44, S26/1232, CZA.

36. Report on Gruenbaum's and Pinkerton's conversation in 2.6.44 and 7.6.44, GCD, ABG (also in S26/1232, CZA); two cables from Bratislava dated 16.5.44 and 23.5.44, according to Gilbert, *Auschwitz and the Allies*, 236–237 [English].

37. JAE, 11.6.44, CZA.

38. Ibid.; Elon, Timetable, 196–202 [English]; Shabtai B. Beit-Zvi, 'Was Ben-Gurion Against Bombing Auschwitz?," *Ma'ariv*, 1.8.80.

39. Porat, *The Blue and the Yellow Stars of David*, 213–214.

40. Ibid., 214–215; Gilbert, *Auschwitz and the Allies*, 231–239. [English].

41. Porat, *The Blue and the Yellow Stars of David*, 214–215; Gruenbaum to Kubowitzky, 11.6.44, A127/544, CZA.

42. 1.6.44, S44/543, CZA.

43. Cable no. 761, FO 371/42758, W9647, PRO; Gilbert, *Auschwitz and the Allies*, 229 [English].

44. Rescue Committee presidency protocol, 18.6.44, S26/1238a, CZA; Rescue Committee plenum, 29.6.44, S26/1238a, CZA; Gruenbaum to Barlas, 21.6.44, S26/1284, CZA; Rescue Committee presidency, 10.10.44, S26/1284, CZA.

45. Livia Rothkirchen, *The Destruction of Slovakia's Jews*, 36; Gilbert, *Auschwitz and the Allies*, 231ff. [English]; Erich Kulka, "Five Escapes from Auschwitz," *Yalkut Moreshet*, no. 3 (December 1964), 23–38; Porat, *The Blue and the Yellow Stars of David*, 215–217; D. S. Wyman, "Why Auschwitz Was Never Bombed," *Commentary* 5 (May 1978), 37–46 [English]; Penkower, *The Jews Were Expendable*, 185ff. [English]; Avraham Fox, *I Called and There Was No Answer: Weissmandel's Cry During the Holocaust* (Jerusalem: privately printed, 1983), 126–127.

46. Gruenbaum to Shertok and Weiss, 27.6.44, Z4/14870, CZA; Gruenbaum to Shertok, 29.6.44, Z4/14870, CZA; Gruenbaum to Schwartzbart and Reiss, 19.6.44 and onward, A127/544, CZA; Yitzhak Gruenbaum, "The Mercy Overcome," *Hazman*, 26.6.44; Hebrew Writers' Union to British Writers' Union, 4.7.44, S26/1251, CZA; Pinkerton to Gruenbaum and Hall's reply, 23.6.44, S26/1232, CZA.

47. Agronsky's report, BGD, 6.7.44, ABG; Shertok's cable to BG, 30.6.44, Weizmann Archive (also in Z4/14870, CZA); report on the conversation with Eden, 6.7.44; Weizmann and Shertok's memorandum to Eden, 6.7.44; Shertok's cable to BG and Goldmann, and Shertok's memo, 11.7.44—all CZA. The memo is also cited in Barlas, *Rescue During the Holocaust*, 293–295; a testimony was attached to the memo, published by Jewish Telegraph Agency, 9.7.44, Z4/14870, CZA; report of meeting with Hall, Weizmann, and Shertok, 30.6.44, FO 371/42807 WR49G, PRO.

48. JAE, 2.7.44, CZA; Gilbert, *Auschwitz and the Allies*, 255 [English].

49. Randall to Shertok, 15.7.44, Z4/14870, CZA; Gilbert, *Auschwitz and the Allies*, 267–272; Wasserstein, *Britain and the Jews of Europe*, 311–313 [English]; Kedem, "The Political Activity of Chaim Weizmann in the Second World War," 254–255; Vago, "The British Government and the Fate of Hungarian Jewry in 1944," 216–217 [English].

50. Wasserstein, *Britain and the Jews of Europe*, 311–312 [English]; Wyman, "Why Auschwitz Was Never Bombed," 37–46 [English]; Penkower, *The Jews Were Expendable*, 193ff. [English]; Feingold, "The Roosevelt Administration and the Effort to Save the Jews of Hungary," 223 [English]; Barlas, *Rescue During the Holocaust*, 293; Gilbert, *Auschwitz and the Allies*, 238–244 [English]; Porat, *The Blue and the Yellow Stars of David*, 217.

51. JAE, 16.7.44, CZA; Lauterbach to Linton, 20.7.44, Weizmann Archive; Kedem, "The Political Activity of Chaim Weizmann," 250–251.

52. Z4/14870, CZA; Gilbert, *Auschwitz and the Allies*, 278–280 [English].

53. Shertok to Gruenbaum, 21.8.44, S26/1232, CZA; 13.9.44, S26/1251, CZA.

54. Gruenbaum to Barlas, 31.8.44, S53/1569, CZA; Gruenbaum, Rescue Committee, 3.10.44, S26/1238b, CZA; Gruenbaum's speech at Zionist convention, 28.11.44, cited in Gruenbaum, *On Destruction and Holocaust Days, 1940–1946*, 169 [Hebrew].

55. Eliash's report of his visit to Istanbul, JAE, 10.9.44, CZA; Linton to Foreign Office, 16.8.44, Z4/15202, CZA; 16.8.44, FO 371/42814 WR49/3/9, PRO; Shertok to JAE, 18.8.44, S25/1678, CZA; 29.7.44, S53/1569, CZA; Kedem, "The Political Activity of Chaim Weizmann," 225–257; Porat, *The Blue and the Yellow Stars of David*, 218; Wasserstein, *Britain and the Jews of Europe*, 305–315 [English]; Vago, "The British Government and the Fate of Hungarian Jewry in 1944," 216–217.

56. Law to Weizmann, 1.9.44, Z4/15202, CZA; Kedem, "The Political Activity of Chaim Weizmann," 255–258; Wasserstein, *Britain and the Jews of Europe,* 307–317 [English].

57. Randall to Shertok, 15.7.44, FO 371/42807 WR102/3/48, PRO; Epstein, 3.9.44, S25/286, CZA; Barlas, "Meetings in Constantinople," 61; Wyman, "Why Auschwitz Was Never Bombed," 40 [English]; Gilbert, *Auschwitz and the Allies,* 255–256 [English]; Gruenbaum to Shertok, 13.9.44, received at the Foreign Office on 22.9.44, FO 371/42818, PRO; Gruenbaum to Stalin, 18.1.45, S26/1232, CZA.

58. Lichtheim to JAE, end of September 1944, S53/1569, CZA; Wasserstein, *Britain and the Jews of Europe,* 301–303 [English]; Gilbert, *Auschwitz and the Allies,* 325 [English]; Porat, *The Blue and the Yellow Stars of David,* 218–219.

59. Rescue Committee secretary (on Gruenbaum's behalf) to BG and Shertok, on Gruenbaum's cables to Roosevelt, Churchill, and Stalin, 29.1.45; Gruenbaum's cables to Roosevelt, Churchill, and Stalin, 1.2.45; Gruenbaum to Goldmann, Locker, Schwartzbart, and Sommerstein, 2.2.45; Pinkerton to Gruenbaum, 10.4.45—all S26/1144, CZA; Wasserstein, *Britain and the Jews of Europe,* 308–310, 310–312, 316–317, 348–349 [English].

60. Wyman, "Why Auschwitz Was Never Bombed," 83–92 [English]; see also Wyman, *The Abandonment of the Jews* [English]; Wasserstein, *Britain and the Jews of Europe,* 301–303 [English]; Gilbert, *Auschwitz and the Allies,* 339–341 [English]; Penkower, *The Jews Were Expendable* [English].

61. BG to Nahari, 10.6.65, quoted in Bar-Zohar, *Ben-Gurion,* 1:430; Beit-Zvi, *Post Zionism,* 424–425; Porat, *The Blue and the Yellow Stars of David,* 218–220; Wasserstein, *Britain and the Jews of Europe,* 319–320 [English].

10. At the Edge of the Abyss

1. Porat, *The Blue and the Yellow Stars of David,* 72–73.

2. Mordechai Berger, *The Mobilization and Rescue Fund* (Jerusalem: Taxes Museum, 1970), 73; Kaplan to BG, 10.8.42, S53/209, CZA.

3. Neustadt, Zionist Actions Committee's budgetary committee, 11.1.43, S26/1235-1, CZA.

4. Porat, *The Blue and the Yellow Stars of David,* 91–92.

5. Barlas, Rescue Committee, 3.10.44, S26/1268, CZA; summary of Rescue Committee expenses, S26/1266, CZA; Kaplan, JAE, 15.10.44, CZA; Rescue balance sheet, English, 8.2.44, GCD, ABG; *The Yishuv Economy Book,* ed. M. Ettinger (Tel Aviv: National Council, 1947), 79; Dalia Ofer, "The Activities of the Jewish Agency Delegation in Istanbul in 1943," in *Rescue Attempts During the Holocaust,* 447–449 [English].

6. Porat, *The Blue and the Yellow Stars of David,* 91–92.

7. Nir, "The Rescue Committee in Istanbul," 363–364.

8. Menahem Bader's personal archive, MAGH, "mission summary," 4.

9. Ibid.

10. Ibid.; Bader to Venja Pomeranz and Ze'ev Schind, 11.6.43, D.1.713, MAGH.

11. *Rescue Committee Report to the Twenty-third Zionist Congress* (Jerusalem: Jewish Agency Publication, 1947), 14.

12. Teveth, "The Black Hole," 188.

13. See, e.g., Shaul Meirov to Berl Katzanelson, 2.5.39, file 47/67; Eliyahu [Golomb] to Dov [Hos], 25.7.37, file 47/70—both Haganah Archive.

14. Kaplan, Mapai Secretariat, 10.2.43, LPA; Shertok, Mapai political committee, 3.5.43, 3, LPA; Teveth, *Ben-Gurion: The Burning Ground,* 690–692, 832 [English]; Kaplan to BG, 8.11.34, S53/209a; Reiss to BG, 29.4.36, S44/58; BG to the Zionist organizations in Latin America, 24.3.36, S44/57; Golomb to BG, 27.11.39, S53/49; Leib Yaffe to BG, 18.1.40, S44/47; Shertok to BG in U.S., 2.7.42, S53/209; Kaplan to BG, 6.7.42; BG, New York, to Kaplan, 8.7.42—all CZA; BGD, 19.7.42, ABG.

15. See chapter. 11.

16. Joseph, JAE, 20.12.42, CZA; Dr. Joseph to Palestine immigration officer, 18.12.42, correspondence, ABG; Porat, *The Blue and the Yellow Stars of David,* 74.

17. Mapai Secretariat, 9.12.42, LPA; JAE, 13.12.42, 14.12.42, 20.12.42, 24.1.43, CZA; see chap. 5, "The Slovakia Plan and the Europa Plan," 307–342; Porat, *The Blue and the Yellow Stars of David,* 174–188.

18. JAE, 13.12.42, CZA; meeting of JAE Committee for Child Immigration, 14.12.42, CZA.

19. JAE, 13.12.42, CZA.

20. Arye Bahir, Levi Shkolnik (Eshcol), Mapai Secretariat, 23.12.42, LPA.

21. BG, Mapai Secretariat, 23.12.42, LPA; BG, Mapai Secretariat, 29.12.42, LPA.

22. See chapter 5 for a general discussion of the Transnistria Plan. Here I deal only with the plan's budgetary aspects.

23. Kaplan, JAE, 23.12.42, CZA; Mapai Secretariat, 23.12.42, LPA.

24. See chapter 11.

25. JAE, 23.12.42, CZA; JAE, 13.12.42, CZA.

26. Mapai Secretariat, 23.12.42, LPA; JAE, 23.12.42, CZA.

27. This sum has to be compared, e.g., with the JAE's budget (which was then 1.15 million Palestinian pounds) and the cost of rescue plans previously mentioned.

28. Zionist Actions Committee Budgetary Committee, 11.1.43, S26/1235-1, copy to BG; JAE, 24.1.43 and 31.1.43; Schwalb to Barlas, copy to BG, 12.1.43, S26/1235; Schwalb to Dr. Goldin; Histadrut Executive Committee Budgetary Committee, 10.1.43 and 17.1.43; Zionist Actions Committee, 18.1.43; Histadrut Executive Committee, 31.12.42 and 27–28.1.43, S26/1235-1; Lauterbach, JA Organization Department, to JAE, copy to BG, 12.1.43; Lichtheim to Zionist Executive, 7.1.43, National Council, 17.1.43—all CZA; Remez, Histadrut Executive Committee, 31.12.42, ILMAL; Histadrut Executive Committee Secretariat, 21.1.43, 27.1.43, 28.1.43, ILMAL.

29. Remez, Mapai Secretariat, 10.2.43, LPA; Kaplan and Histadrut delegation meeting, 22.1.43; Zionist Actions Committee, 21.1.43, ILMAL; Kaplan, JAE, 24.1.43, CZA.

30. Neustadt, Mapai Secretariat, 10.2.43, LPA.
31. Meir, *My Life,* 139–141 [English].
32. Golomb, Mapai Secretariat, 10.2.43, LPA; Bader, Histadrut Executive Committee, 11.2.43, ILMAL.
33. Aharonovitz, Mapai Secretariat, 10.2.43, LPA; Kaplan, Mapai Secretariat, 10.2.43, LPA.
34. Kaplan, Mapai Secretariat, 10.2.43, LPA.
35. BG, Mapai Secretariat, 10.2.43, LPA.
36. JAE, 21.2.43, CZA; Mapai Center, 24.2.43, LPA.
37. Yehieli-Schechter was here referring to the ban by the Allies, announced in the summer of 1942, on the transfer of monies to occupied territories for fear that it might fall into enemy hands. On the Allies' warning, see also Bader on the Transnistria Plan, Histadrut Executive Committee, 11.2.43, ILMAL.
38. Mapai Center, 24.2.43, LPA.
39. Ibid.
40. BG, JAE, 28.2.43, CZA.
41. Ibid. This was BG's first meeting as chairman after his return to the JAE.
42. On Kaplan's "shooting an arrow in the dark," see Bader, *Sad Missions,* 60; JAE, 28.3.43, CZA; Rescue Committee, 28.3.43, S26/1237, CZA; Mapai Secretariat, 30.3.43, LPA.
43. Kaplan, JAE, 28.3.43, CZA; Kaplan, Rescue Committee, 28.3.43, S26/1237, CZA; Kaplan, Mapai Secretariat, 30.3.43, LPA.
44. Kaplan, JAE, 28.3.43, CZA; Kaplan, Mapai Secretariat, 30.3.43, LPA.
45. JAE, 4.4.43, CZA; JAE, 27.4.43, CZA.
46. JAE, 27.4.43, CZA; Shertok, Zionist Actions Committee, 18.5.43, CZA.
47. See, e.g., Zionist Actions Committee, 18.5.43, CZA.
48. Hartglas, 24.4.43, S26/1232, CZA (also in S26/1235, BG's copy); Morgenstern, "The Rescue Committee's Actions During 1943–1945," 72–73.
49. JAE, 18.4.43, CZA; Porat, *The Blue and the Yellow Stars of David,* 81.
50. Bader, Zionist Actions Committee, 18.5.43, CZA; Bader was visiting Palestine during May and spoke before the Histadrut Executive Committee on 13.5.43 and the Rescue Committee on 17.5.43.
51. Remez, Zerubavel, Reiss, Zionist Actions Committee, 18.5.43, CZA; see chapter 5, 212–238 on the Slovakia Plan; Porat, *The Blue and the Yellow Stars of David,* 174–188.
52. Gruenbaum, Zionist Actions Committee, 18.5.43, CZA; no response from BG to that criticism has turned up.
53. Venja Pomeranz and Ze'ev Schind, Istanbul, to BG, 25.5.43, correspondence, ABG (also in S6/5552, CZA); Pomeranz and Bader to JAE, 6.8.43, S25/22522, CZA; Bader to Hakibbutz Ha'artzi Secretariat, 14.9.43, file 50/9, Haganah Archive, Israel Galili's Archive; unsigned to "dear friends," 18.9.43, file 50/9, Haganah Archive, Israel Galili's Archive; unsigned to JAE for Dobkin, Jerusalem, 18.9.43, S25/22522, CZA; Bader to Hakibbutz Ha'artzi Secretariat, 17.9.43, file 50/9, Haganah Archive, Israel Galili's Archive; Bader, Istanbul, 1.10.43, S25/22522, CZA.

54. Pomeranz and Bader to JAE, 6.8.43, S25/22522, CZA.
55. Gruenbaum, JAE, 13.6.43, 15, CZA.
56. Bader to Barlas, 11.6.43, D.1.713m, MAGH.
57. Ibid.
58. Ibid.
59. Ibid.
60. Ibid.; Kaplan, JAE, 6.6.43, CZA.
61. Reiss, Zionist Actions Committee, 24.6.43, CZA.
62. Gruenbaum, Zionist Actions Committee, 24.6.43, CZA.
63. Ibid.; JAE, 16.5.43, 6.6.43, CZA; see chapter 11.
64. Porat, *The Blue and the Yellow Stars of David,* 82–83; untitled, 6.5.43, S53/1617, CZA.
65. Zionist Actions Committee, 24.6.43, CZA; rescue expense report, 26.5.43, S53/1604, CZA; JA Finance Department to Kaplan, 31.5.43, S53/1604, CZA.
66. Gruenbaum and Dobkin, Zionist Actions Committee, 24.6.43, CZA; JAE, 10.5.43, 20.6.43, and 27.6.43, CZA.
67. Zionist Actions Committee, 6.6.43, CZA.
68. Ibid.
69. Kaplan, Zionist Actions Committee, 6.6.43, CZA.
70. Ibid., 6.6.43, CZA.
71. Bader, *Sad Missions,* 71; Kaplan, JAE, 27.6.43, CZA.
72. Histadrut Executive Committee Secretariat, 22.7.43 and 5.8.43, according to Porat, *The Blue and the Yellow Stars of David,* 83–84.
73. Suprasky, Zionist Actions Committee, 1.9.43, CZA.
74. Venja, Bader, and Ze'ev to JAE, Rescue Committee and Histadrut Executive Committee, 3.8.43, S26/1240, CZA; Mapai Center, 24.8.43, LPA.
75. Venja Pomeranz, Mapai Center, 24.8.43, LPA; Moshe Dax to friends, Bratislava, 6.5.43, file 50/9, Haganah Archive; 6.6.43, LPA; "Malkiel" [Meirov-Avigur], Istanbul, to friends, 27.5.43, LPA.
76. BG, Mapai Center, 24.8.43, LPA.
77. Kaplan and Shertok (see his report in the JAE, 22.8.43, and in Zionist Actions Committee, 1.9.43) made no distinction between the various kinds of rescue; JAE, 12.9.43, CZA; Barlas, JAE, 4.10.43.
78. Mapai Center, 24.8.43, LPA; in Mapai Secretariat documentation there is a gap of more than a month (between 18.8.43 and 6.10.43), and there is no documentation on debates in the Mapai Secretariat from 24.8.43 to mid-September.
79. JAE, 5.9.43, 12.9.43, CZA; Rescue Committee, 7.9.43, S53/1617, CZA; 13.9.43, S53/612, CZA; *The Documents Book,* 346; Emmanuel Harosi, ed., *The Fund-raising Book* (Tel Aviv: Mobilization and Rescue Fund, 1951), 97; Berger, *The Mobilization and Rescue Fund,* 65; Porat, *The Blue and the Yellow Stars of David,* 85.
80. For debates on BG's resignation and the resulting crisis in the Executive, see JAE, 26.10.43, 31.10.43, 7.11.43, 14.11.43, 22.11.43, 28.11.43, 30.11.43, 5.12.43, and 12.12.43, CZA; Mapai Center, 1.12.43, 8.12.43, LPA.
81. Shertok, JAE, 18.11.43, CZA; JAE, 21.11.43, CZA; Mapai Center, 1.12.43, LPA.
82. Barlas, JAE, 10.10.43, CZA; Kaplan, JAE, 24.10.43, CZA; Porat, *The Blue and the Yellow Stars of David,* 86.

83. JAE, 24.10.43, 20.12.43, CZA; Histadrut Executive Committee Secretariat, 12.10.43, CZA; National Council, 6.12.43, CZA.

84. Bader, *Sad Missions*, 86; Kaplan, JAE, 20.12.43, CZA; Histadrut Executive Committee, 30.12.43, ILMAL; Ze'ev Schind, Mapai Secretariat, 15.12.43, LPA.

85. Porat, *The Blue and the Yellow Stars of David*, 87.

86. JAE, 19.12.43, CZA; Porat, *The Blue and the Yellow Stars of David*, 87.

87. JAE, 24.10.43 and 17.10.43; JAE, 9.11.43; JAE, 28.11.43—all CZA.

88. JAE, 4.10.43; JAE, 22.8.43; Shertok's report, Zionist Actions Committee, 1.9.43—all CZA.

11. Financing Aid and Rescue Activity in Liberated Europe

1. Porat, *The Blue and the Yellow Stars of David*, 87; National Council, *Davar*, 2.2.44.

2. JAE, 13.2.44, CZA; National Council Executive, 24.1.44, CZA; Rescue Committee, 10.2.44, S26/1239, S25/1237, CZA; Histadrut Executive Committee Secretariat, 26.1.44, 1.2.44, ILMAL.

3. Porat, *The Blue and the Yellow Stars of David*, 88–89.

4. JAE, 26.3.44, CZA; Committee of Five, from Poalei-Zion members for helping Hungarian Jews, to BG, Dobkin, and Kaplan, 23.4.44, correspondence, ABG.

5. JAE, 26.3.44, CZA; Dobkin to BG, 30.4.44, correspondence, ABG.

6. JAE, 26.3.44, CZA; BG, JAE, 9.4.44, CZA.

7. BGD, 23.3.44, ABG; Mapai Center, 24.8.43, LPA.

8. JAE, 9.4.44, CZA.

9. See chapter 12, 704–725.

10. Gruenbaum, JAE, 11.6.44, CZA; Kaplan, JAE, 18.6.44, CZA; Dobkin and Haft, Histadrut Executive Committee Secretariat, 14.6.44, according to: Porat, *The Blue and the Yellow Stars of David*, 89.

11. Shaul Meirov's report, Histadrut Executive Committee Secretariat, 19.4.44, ILMAL.

12. Ibid.

13. Ibid.

14. See chapter 8, 6–10, this volume.

15. JAE, 25.5.44, CZA.

16. Ibid.

17. Venja Pomeranz had left for Palestine before the emissaries were informed that there were two missions—those of Grosz and Brand.

18. See chapter 8, 663–668.

19. JAE, 4.6.44, CZA.

20. Kaplan's report, JAE, 28.7.44, CZA; Shertok's report, 27.6.44, London, Z4/14870, CZA; Hirschmann addendum, 22.6.44, memo, 27.8.44, 4, NA, OSS, RG 84, ibid, entry E120, 22.6.44.

21. Dobkin's report, JAE, 21.9.44, CZA; Dobkin's report, Mapai Secretariat, 24.9.44, LPA; 8.7.44, correspondence, ABG; Dobkin to British ambassador in Portugal, 12.7.44, ABG; Venja and Bader to JAE, 23.7.44, ABG; BGD, 6.7.44, ABG; Agronsky's report, 1.7.44, Z6/1/16, CZA; Porat, *The Blue and the Yellow Stars of David*, 291, n. 81; Gruenbaum

22. and Dobkin to Ehrenpreis, June-July 1944, S26/1251, CZA; Gruenbaum, JAE, 27.10.44, CZA.

22. See Gutman and Drechsler, eds., *The Remnants, 1944–1948;* Nathaniel Katzuver, "From Freedom to Revolt: Hungarian Jews Facing a Changing Government, 1945–1948," in Gutman and Drechsler, eds., 103–126; Jan Anchell, "Holocaust Survivors in Romania," 127–148 [Hebrew]; Shalom Cholevsky, "Partsans and Ghetto Fighters: An Active Feature among the Holocaust Surivors," in Gutman and Drechsler, eds., 223–231; Israel Gutman, "The Remnants: Problems and Clarification," in Gutman and Drechsler, *Rehabilitation and Political Struggle* 461–479.

23. "Meir" (the Yishuv's office in Istanbul) to friends, 27.5.44, received in Jerusalem 13.6.44, correspondence, ABG.

24. Venja Pomeranz , Histadrut Executive Committee Secretariat, 14.6.44, ILMAL (see also Meirov and Zisling); Kaplan, JAE, 18.6.44, CZA; Porat, *The Blue and the Yellow Stars of David*, 89–90.

25. Kaplan, JAE, 18.6.44, CZA; unsigned note, 27.6.44, GCD, ABG.

26. JAE, 11.6.44, CZA; Gruenbaum, JAE, 25.6.44, CZA; Gruenbaum to Leib Yaffe, New York, 22.5.44, S26/1232, CZA; JAE, 18.6.44, CZA.

27. JAE, 18.6.44, CZA.

28. Kaplan, JAE, 23.7.44, CZA; Kaplan's report, Rescue Committee, 28.7.44, copy to BG, GCD, ABG.

29. Rescue Committee, 28.7.44, GCD, ABG.

30. JAE, 23.7.44, CZA; Rescue Committee, 28.7.44, GCD, ABG.

31. Dr. Emil Sommerstein, Moscow, to JAE, 24.8.44, correspondence, ABG; the JA to Dr. Sommerstein, Moscow, 27.8.44, correspondence, ABG; *Davar,* 31.8.44, 6.2.45; JAE, 31.7.44, 6.8.44, 27.8.44, and 28.9.44, CZA; JAE, 14.9.44, CZA; Sheffer to Barlas, 28.6.44, S26/1283, CZA; Magnes's request, 12.9.44, file 748, JANY.

32. Tuvia Friling, "Meeting the Survivors: Ben-Gurion's Visit to Bulgaria, December 1944," *Studies in Zionism* 10, no. 2 (autumn 1989), 175–195 [English].

33. JAE, 17.12.44, CZA; BGD, 4.12.44, ABG; Friling, "Meeting the Survivors: Ben-Gurion's Visit to Bulgaria, December 1944," 178.

34. JAE, 17.12.44, CZA.

35. Ibid.

36. Kashlass, *The History of Bulgaria's Jews*, 100.

37. BGD, 10.12.44, ABG.

38. JAE, 17.12.44, CZA; Zvi Maimon (BG's secretary) to BG, 14.1.45; BG to Avriel, 17.1.45; BG's address to Hungarian Jews, 19.1.45—all correspondence, ABG; BGD, 6.12.44, ABG.

39. BGD, 4.12.44 and 11.12.44, ABG; JAE, 17.12.44 and 31.12.44, CZA; Kashlass, *The History of Bulgaria's Jews*, 123–126; JAE, 13.10.44, CZA; Shertok to Leo Cohen, 6.10.44, correspondence, ABG.

40. BGD, 10.12.44, 11.12.44, ABG.

41. BGD, 5.12.44 and 6.12.44, ABG; JAE, 17.12.44, CZA; Mapai Secretariat, 14.12.44, LPA; Moshe Mossek, "The

Struggle for Leadership among the Jews of Bulgaria, Following the Liberation," in *Eastern European Jewry: From Holocaust to Redemption, 1944–1948,* ed. Benjamin Pinkus (Sede Boker Campus Press: Ben-Gurion University of the Negev, 1987), 202–209.

42. Mapai Secretariat, 14.12.44, LPA; JAE, 17.12.44, CZA.

12. The Jewish Agency Budget and Fund-raising Appeals in Palestine

1. JAE, 13.12.42, CZA.
2. JAE, 20.12.42, CZA.
3. Ibid.
4. Rescue Committee, 11.1.43, S26/1235-1, CZA; Budget Committee of the Zionist Actions Committee, 11.1.43, copy to BG, S26/1235-1, CZA.
5. Zionist Actions Committee, 18.1.43, CZA.
6. Kaplan to Schwartz, 26.12.42, S53/198, CZA; Kaplan to Kirschner, 2.5.43, S53/104, CZA.
7. The Jewish Agency budget consisted of two parts: the "regular" budget (budget A), based on Palestine Foundation Fund (PFF) funding; and the "extraordinary" budget (budget B), funded by income derived from loans, donations, and so forth. Efforts were made to include in the regular budget essential activities that the leadership did not wish to make contingent upon unpredictable income.
8. JAE, 5.11.43, 12.12.43, 19.12.43, 26.12.43, 2.1.44, and 6.2.44, CZA; Zionist Actions Committee, 14.3.44, CZA.
9. JAE, 12.12.43, CZA.
10. Fishman-Maimon, JAE, 12.12.43, CZA.
11. Gruenbaum, Zionist Actions Committee, 3.1.44, CZA, and Kaplan; Gruenbaum, Rescue Committee, 16.12.43 and 2.1.44, S26/1237, CZA; JAE, 16.1.44, CZA.
12. JAE, 16.1.44, CZA, and Dobkin, Kaplan, and Senator; Rescue Committee, 19.1.44, 26/1237, CZA; Ben-Zvi to Gruenbaum, 17.1.44, correspondence, ABG; Elected Assembly announcement, 12.1.44, *The Documents Book; Davar,* 13.1.44.
13. JAE, 26.12.43, CZA; JAE, 2.1.44, CZA; Dobkin, Zionist Actions Committee, 14.3.44, CZA.
14. Zionist Actions Committee, 3.1.44, CZA.
15. JAE, 2.1.44, CZA.
16. Zionist Actions Committee, 3.1.44, CZA, Neustadt, Suprasky, Ya'ari, Rabbi Neifeld; Zionist Actions Committee, 14.1.44, budget approval session, CZA.
17. JAE, 5.11.43, CZA.
18. JAE, 12.12.43, CZA, afternoon session.
19. JAE, 19.12.43, CZA.
20. Ibid.
21. Ibid.; Rosenblum, Zionist Actions Committee, 14.3.44, CZA.
22. JAE, 5.11.43, 2.1.44, CZA.
23. Gelber, *Growing a Fleur-de-Lis,* 1:12, 15; interview with Eliyahu Sacharov, 7.10.86, file 80/162/p/1, Haganah Archive.
24. Yitzhak [Kleinbaum] to Ehud, 30.8.44, S25/22681, CZA.
25. JAE, 5.11.43, CZA.

26. JAE, 24.10.43, CZA; BG, Zionist Actions Committee, 14.3.44, CZA.
27. Gruenbaum, JAE, 5.11.43, CZA.
28. Zionist Actions Committee, 14.3.44, CZA.
29. JAE, 20.12.42, CZA, secs. "JAE Budget for 1943" and "The Jewish Situation in Europe"; Gruenbaum and Kaplan, JAE, 27.12.42, CZA.
30. Porat, *The Blue and the Yellow Stars of David,* 79–80.
31. Joint meeting of Rescue Committee and Mobilization and Rescue Fund presidency, 8.2.43; see Berger, *The Mobilization and Rescue Fund,* 55; *The Fund-raising Book,* 84.
32. Kaplan, Mapai Secretariat, 10.2.43, LPA; cf. Porat, *The Blue and the Yellow Stars of David,* 79–80.
33. JAE, 24.1.43, CZA; Zvi Maimon to Dr. Aharon Bart, 26.11.42, S44/445, CZA.
34. Mapai Secretariat, 10.2.43, LPA, and Kaplan; Kleinbaum to Ben-Zvi, National Council, 17.2.43, S26/1240, CZA; National Council to Rescue Committee, 19.2.43, S26/1240, CZA; Keren Hayesod publications on behalf of the JAE, *Davar,* 19.2.43.
35. Remez, Golda, Aharonovitz, Neustadt, Golomb, and Fromkin, Mapai Secretariat, 10.2.43, LPA.
36. Mapai Secretariat, 10.2.43, LPA; National Council, *Davar,* 11.2.43.
37. JAE, 14.2.43, CZA; Rescue Committee, 1.2.43, S26/1239, CZA.
38. JAE, 14.2.43, CZA, and Remez.
39. JAE, 14.2.43, CZA; Rescue Committee, 14.2.43, S26/1241, CZA; Mobilization and Rescue Fund presidency, 1.2.43, S26/1241, CZA; Kaplan, Mapai Secretariat, 10.2.43, LPA.
40. Mapai Center, 24.2.43, LPA; Menahem Bader, *Sad Missions,* 57; JAE, 28.2.43, CZA; Rescue Committee, 28.2.43 and 4.3.43, S26/1237, CZA; Rescue Committee, 23.3.43, S26/1239, CZA; Kaplan to Hoofein, 26.2.43, S53/56, CZA; Dr. Kortz to BG, 6.12.42, S44/456, CZA.
41. Yitzhak Arditi to BG, 24.2.43, correspondence, ABG.
42. Y. Klinove to BG, 14.1.43, S44/2b, CZA; BG at Mobilization and Rescue Fund Convention, Tel Aviv, 11.1.43, SA, ABG.
43. JAE, 18.4.43, CZA; Porat, *The Blue and the Yellow Stars of David,* 81; Dr. George Halpern to BG, 6.4.43, and Zvi Maimon to Halpern, 7.4.43—both S44/445, CZA.
44. Zionist Actions Committee, 24.6.43, CZA; see also chapter 10, n. 64.
45. To JAE and Mobilization and Rescue Fund presidency, BG acknowledgment, 18.5.43, S44/448, CZA.
46. According to Dobkin, the Yishuv supplied 113,000 Palestinian pounds in the first five months of 1943, consisting of 45,000 from the recruitment fund, 25,000 as a special allocation from Jewish Agency funds (totaling 70,000), with the remaining 43,000 taken from the Jewish Agency's own budget. This sum did not include an additional allocation of 45,000 Palestinian pounds, 25,000 of which was probably an advance payment that could be viewed as a "lost debt."
47. Zionist Actions Committee, 24.6.43, CZA.
48. Ibid.; Kaplan, JAE, 27.6.43, CZA; JAE, 26.9.43, S53/1604, CZA.

49. Zionist Actions Committee, 24.6.43, CZA; JAE, 27.6.43, CZA.

50. Brudny-Bareli, JAE, 5.9.43, CZA.

51. JAE, 5.9.43, CZA, joint meeting of JAE, Mobilization and Rescue Fund, and National Council representatives; 7.9.43, S53/1617, CZA; 23.9.43, S53/612, CZA.

52. JAE, 12.9.43, CZA; JAE, 5.9.43, CZA, Bart, Dobkin and Shertok; Berger, *The Mobilization and Rescue Fund*, 64: Shertok to Safety Board, 13.9.43; PFF national board to BG, 19.8.43 and 8.9.43, S44/56, CZA; BG, 13.10.43, S44/56, CZA.

53. Porat, *The Blue and the Yellow Stars of David*, 85.

54. Ibid., 85–86; *The Documents Book*, 346; *The Fund-raising Book*, 97; Berger, *The Mobilization and Rescue Fund*, 65.

55. Industrialists and businessmen for the Mobilization and Rescue Fund gathering, Jerusalem, 23.9.43, Minutes of Meetings, ABG; Abraham Haft to Kaplan, 19.9.43, S53/1612, CZA; Y. Botkovsky to BG, 22.9.43, S44/471, CZA; Zvi Maimon to Mobilization and Rescue Fund, 8.10.43, CZA; BG to Hanoch Shpigel, CZA.

56. Industrialists and businessmen for the Mobilization and Rescue Fund gathering, Jerusalem, 23.9.43, Minutes of Meetings, ABG; Venja Pomeranz and Menachem Bader, Istanbul, to JAE, 6.8.43, S25/22522, CZA; Istanbul to Kibbutz Secretariat, 14.9.43, file 50/9, Israel Galili Archive, Haganah Archive; Istanbul to "dear friends," 18.9.43, Israel Galili Archive, Haganah Archive.

57. BG, Industrialists and businessmen for the Mobilization and Rescue Fund gathering, Jerusalem, 23.9.43, Minutes of Meetings, ABG; also Schmorak and Bart.

58. Schmorak and Bart, Industrialists and businessmen for the Mobilization and Rescue Fund gathering, Jerusalem, 23.9.43, Minutes of Meetings, ABG; Istanbul to "dear friends," 18.9.43, file 50/9, Israel Galili Archive, Haganah Archive.

59. Industrialists and businessmen for the Mobilization and Rescue Fund gathering, Jerusalem, 23.9.43, Minutes of Meetings, ABG; BG, Zionist Actions Committee, 1.9.43, CZA.

60. Yitzhak Brudny-Bareli, JAE, 5.9.43, CZA.

61. *Davar*, 12–13.9.43.

62. JAE, 15.9.43, CZA.

63. *Davar*, 16.9.43.

64. Ibid., 16.9.43, 17.9.43, 20.9.43, 21.9.43, 22.9.43, 24.9.43, 26.9.43, 4.10.43, 6.10.43, and 8.10.43; Kaplan, Jerusalem Workers Council convention, 25.9.43, S53/12a, CZA.

65. Porat, *The Blue and the Yellow Stars of David*, 85–86; *Davar*, 17.10.43; JAE, 20.10.43, CZA; Kollek to friends, 1.11.43, S25/22685, CZA.

66. Kaplan, JAE, 12.12.43, CZA; Porat, *The Blue and the Yellow Stars of David*, 86.

67. Dr. Bart to David Remez, 28.11.43, according to Berger, *The Mobilization and Rescue Fund*, 64.

68. Porat, *The Blue and the Yellow Stars of David*, 86.

69. The Histadrut Executive Committee Secretariat, 18.11.43, according to Porat, *The Blue and the Yellow Stars of David*, 86.

70. Porat, *The Blue and the Yellow Stars of David*, 86 [Hebrew]; JAE, 10.10.43, CZA; JAE, 18.11.43, 21.11.43, CZA; Shertok, JAE, 22.8.43, CZA.

71. Porat, *The Blue and the Yellow Stars of David*, 86; JAE, 12.3.44 and 19.3.44, CZA; Schmorak, Industrialists and businessmen for the Mobilization and Rescue Fund gathering, Jerusalem, 23.9.43, Minutes of Meetings, ABG; Venja and Bader to JAE, 8.10.43, S53/1603, CZA.

72. Kaplan and Dobkin, JAE, 20.12.43, CZA; Kaplan and Schmorak, Industrialists and businessmen for the Mobilization and Rescue Fund gathering, Jerusalem, 23.9.43, Minutes of Meetings, ABG; Lederer, JAE, 5.9.43, CZA; Moshe Aram, Histadrut Executive Committee Secretariat, 5.8.43, according: Porat, *The Blue and the Yellow Stars of David*, 86–87.

73. Dr. Emil Schmorak to BG, 3.7.44, S44/448, CZA.

74. S. Gintzberg to BG, 5.10.44, S44/448, CZA; National Board for the Jewish Soldier to JAE, 16.10.44, CZA.

75. Gruenbaum, JAE, 13.2.44, CZA; National Council Executive, 24.1.44, CZA; Rescue Committee, 1.2.44, S26/1237, CZA; Rescue Committee, 10.2.44, S26/1239, CZA; Histadrut Executive Committee Secretariat, 26.1.44, CZA; joint meeting protocol, 7.2.44, according to Porat, *The Blue and the Yellow Stars of David*, 88.

76. *Davar*, 29.3.44; BG, *Davar*, 3.4.44; Gruenbaum to BG, 20.2.44, S44/471, CZA.

77. *Davar*, 31.3.44, 2.4.44, 4.4.44, 10.4.44, 12.4.44, and 17.4.44; Porat, *The Blue and the Yellow Stars of David*, 89.

78. BG, JAE, 12.3.44, CZA.

79. Porat, *An Entangled Leadership:* The Yishuv and the Holocaust 1942–1945 (Tel Aviv: Am Oved, 1986) [Hebrew], 157.

80. Kaplan, JAE, 3.9.44, 15.10.44, 27.10.44, and 10.12.44, CZA; Kaplan, Rescue Committee protocol, 15.1.45, S26/1238b, CZA.

81. Kaplan, Rescue Committee protocol, 15.1.45, S26/1238b, CZA.

13. Fund-raising Campaigns Abroad

1. "Rescue Operations—Stockholm" [English], 15.1.45, A140/179, CZA.

2. BGD, 17.9.42, ABG; BGD, 24.7.42, ABG; BG to Paul Baerwald, 31.7.42, Palestine, file 747, JANY; Miriam Cohen to Moshe Levitt, JDC secretary, 31.7.42, Palestine, file 747, JANY; BG to Kaplan, 6.8.42, S53/193, CZA; Kaplan and Shertok to BG, 6.8.42, S53/193, CZA.

3. Baerwald to BG, New York, 7.8.42, file 747, JANY; Moshe Levitt to JA Immigration Department, 21.8.42, S6/4639, CZA, according to Porat, *The Blue and the Yellow Stars of David*, 94; Kaplan to BG, 10.8.42, S53/209b, CZA; BG to Kaplan, with copies to Simon and Viteles, JDC personnel in Jerusalem, 16.8.43 and 23.8.43, S53/198, CZA.

4. Dobkin, Mapai Secretariat, 24.11.42, LPA.

5. JAE, 13.12.42, CZA; JAE Committee for Child Immigration, 14.12.42, Minutes of Meeting, ABG; BG, JAE, 20.12.42, CZA; BG, JAE, 27.12.42, CZA.

6. JAE Committee for Child Immigration, 14.12.42, Minutes of Meeting, ABG; Kaplan, JAE, 24.2.43, CZA; Gruenbaum, Zionist Actions Committee, 18.1.43, CZA; Zionist Actions Committee, 2.2.43, CZA.

7. Kaplan's report, Mapai Secretariat, 30.3.43, LPA; Schechter-Yehieli, Mapai Center, 24.2.43, LPA; Bader, *Sad Missions,* 69–70; Kaplan, Mapai Secretariat, 10.2.43, LPA; JAE, 28.3.43, CZA.

8. Magnes to Paul Baerwald, 14.5.43, Palestine, file 748, JANY.

9. Ibid.

10. Bader, *Sad Missions,* 69–70; Fromkin, Histadrut Executive Committee, 26.5.43, ILMAL.

11. Zionist Actions Committee, 24.6.43, CZA, and also Dobkin; Barlas, *Rescue During the Holocaust,* 28.

12. Menachem Bader to Venja Pomeranz and Ze'ev Schind, 11.6.43, D.1.713, MAGH.

13. Dobkin and Schwartz, summary of conversations, 8.8.43, GCD, ABG; JAE, 4.8.43 and 7.8.43, CZA.

14. Bauer, *Jews for Sale?,* 76–77 [English]; Herbert Katzky interview by Menachem Kaufman, 30.3.76, Institute of Contemporary Jewry, Hebrew University of Jerusalem, Oral Documentation section, 16, 24.

15. Viteles to Dr. Schwartz, Lisbon, 10.10.43, file 748, JANY.

16. National Council, Rescue Committee, 9.8.43, CZA; Zionist Actions Committee Secretariat, 12.8.43, ILMAL; *Davar,* 11.8.43.

17. Bauer, *American Jewry and the Holocaust,* 223 [English]; Bauer, *Jews for Sale?,* 76–77 [English].

18. National Council, Rescue Committee, 9.8.43, CZA; Zionist Actions Committee Secretariat, 12.8.43, ILMAL.

19. JAE, 8.8.43, 1.8.43, and 15.8.43, CZA; JAE, 19–20.12.43, CZA; Dobkin to Schwartz, with copies to BG, Schmorak, and Shertok, 5.8.43, correspondence, ABG.

20. Shertok to Goldmann, 30.8.43, S25/73, CZA, according to Porat, *The Blue and the Yellow Stars of David,* 97.

21. JAE subcommittee, 12.9.43, CZA; Evellinn Morisey to Louis Rossner, 10.11.43; Mereminsky to David Remez, 14.11.43; Levitt, JDC, to Histadrut Executive Committee, 16.11.43; Levitt, New York, to Joseph Schwartz, Lisbon, 24.11.43—all JDC, file 748, JANY.

22. Schwartz-Dobkin agreement, 8.8.43, GCD, ABG; Joseph Schwartz to Henry Viteles, Jerusalem, a message to Kaplan, 7.12.43, JDC, file 748, JANY.

23. Schwartz to Viteles, 7.12.43, JDC, file 748, JANY; cable also in S53/1614, 14.12.43, CZA; Kaplan, JAE, 19.12.43, CZA.

24. JAE, 17.10.43, 9.11.43, 28.11.43, and 30.1.44, CZA; Gruenbaum, JAE, 28.11.43, CZA; Dobkin, Histadrut Executive Committee Secretariat, 29.12.43, ILMAL; JAE, 9.11.43, CZA; Rescue Committee, S26/1235-1, CZA; Moshe Yishai to Immigration Department, Rescue Committee, 23.11.43, S26/1237, CZA; Bauer, *American Jewry and the Holocaust,* 214–216 [English]; Porat, *The Blue and the Yellow Stars of David,* 98–99.

25. JAE, 9.1.44, 30.1.44, CZA.

26. Kaplan, JAE, 30.1.44, CZA; JAE, 9.1.44, CZA; Joseph Schwartz, Lisbon, to Dobkin, copies to BG and Shertok,

2.4.44 (received in Jerusalem 5.4.44), correspondence, ABG; JAE, 18.6.44, CZA.

27. Bader, *Sad Missions,* 92.

28. Minutes of Meeting between JDC personnel and Kaplan, 22.5.44, Jerusalem, file 748, JANY.

29. Barlas to Gruenbaum and Kaplan, 6.6.44, S26/1232, CZA; Histadrut Executive Committee Secretariat, 14.6.44, ILMAL; Porat, *The Blue and the Yellow Stars of David,* 99–100.

30. Pinkney Tuck to Magnes, for Hirschmann, 22.6.44, NA, RG 84.

31. JAE, 18.6.44, CZA.

32. Herbert Katzky interview, 32–33.

33. Magnes and Gruenbaum, JAE, 16.7.44, CZA.

34. Kaplan, JAE, 23.7.44, CZA; Kaplan's report, Rescue Committee, 28.7.44, S26/1238a, CZA; report, 28.7.44, GCD, ABG.

35. JAE, 16.7.44, CZA, JDC to JAE, 20.7.44, GCD, ABG.

36. Kaplan, JAE, 16.7.44, CZA.

37. JAE, 23.7.44, CZA; Rescue Committee, 28.7.44, CZA.

38. Ibid.; since there are no diary entries in BGD from 20.7.44 to 10.10.44, it is hard to tell if BG met Schwartz.

39. JAE, 23.7.44, CZA.

40. Meeting at Viteles's house, 23.7.44; Dr. Magnes to Dr. Schwartz, 24.7.44; Dr. Magnes to Paul Baerwald, New York, 25.7.44—all file 748, JANY; *Davar,* 24.8.44; Bauer, *American Jewry and the Holocaust,* 185 [English].

41. Magnes's report, JAE, 16.7.44, CZA; Dobkin's report, JAE, 21.9.44, CZA; Dobkin's report, Mapai Secretariat, 24.9.44, LPA; BG's cable to Shertok, 2.7.44, correspondence, ABG.

42. Dobkin's report, JAE, 21.9.44, CZA.

43. Dobkin to BG, 28.9.44, correspondence, ABG; Dobkin to Gruenbaum, 28.9.44, CZA.

44. Dobkin to Kaplan, through the American consul in Jerusalem, 1.7.44, S25/22681, CZA.

45. Levitt to Passman, Jerusalem, through the American consul in Jerusalem, 11.10.44, file 748, JANY.

46. John Pehle, War Refugee Board director, Washington, to Levitt, JDC New York, 19.10.44, file 748, JANY.

47. Gruenbaum, JAE, 20.10.44, CZA.

48. Gruenbaum, JAE, 27.10.44, CZA, 26.10.44, S53/1614, CZA; Zagagi to Kaplan, 1.9.44, S53/1604, CZA; see also unsigned note in S53/1604.

49. Kaplan to Robert Pilpel, Lisbon, 15.10.44, S26/1253, CZA; summary of meeting, 30.10.44, S26/1239, CZA; Dobkin, *Davar,* 6.2.45.

50. Levitt, New York, to Passman, Jerusalem, 10.11.44; JDC's report, 17.11.44; memorandum no. 2664, 2.10.44; memorandum no. 2657—all file 748, JANY; Barlas, Rescue Committee, 3.10.44, CZA.

51. Kaplan, Jerusalem, to Avriel, Istanbul, 19.10.44, S25/22681, CZA.

52. BGD, 11.12.44, ABG; *Davar,* 8.3.45; BGD, 25.10.45, 29.10.45, ABG.

53. Summary of meeting between JDC and JAE representatives, 14.2.45, S44/37b, CZA; Barlas to Gruenbaum, 1.3.45,

S26/1284, CZA; Goldmann to Dobkin, 10.1.45, correspondence, ABG.

54. Rescue Committee protocol meeting, 15.1.45, S53/1613, CZA; Dobkin's announcement, *Davar*, 6.2.45.

55. Shimoni, "The South African Jewish Community and the Zionist Movement," (2) 95.

56. BG, JAE, 28.2.43, CZA.

57. JAE, 26.9.43, CZA.

58. Pincus, South Africa, to BG, Jerusalem, 26.5.43, correspondence, ABG; South African Jewish War Appeal to BG, 29.5.43, correspondence, ABG (see also cables in S53/1606, CZA); Kaplan to Maimon, 31.5.43, correspondence, ABG.

59. BG to JAE members, n.d., S44/69b, CZA; Bader to Pomeranz and Schind, 11.6.43, D.1.713, MAGH.

60. JAE, 25.7.43; Shertok, Zionist Actions Committee, 1.9.43, 7; Gruenbaum's report, Zionist Actions Committee, 14.11.43; JAE, 26.9.43—all CZA.

61. Gruenbaum to JAE, copy to BG, 13.8.43, correspondence, ABG.

62. Gruenbaum to JAE, copy to BG, 26.8.43, correspondence, ABG; Dobkin to Gruenbaum, South Africa, 27.8.43, S26/1255, CZA; Gruenbaum, Johannesburg, to JAE, copy to BG, 1.9.43, correspondence, ABG; Shimoni, "The South African Jewish Community and the Zionist Movement," 321; Gruenbaum, Zionist Actions Committee, 14.11.43, CZA; Gruenbaum, JAE, 26.9.43, CZA.

63. Kirschner, JAE, 26.9.43, CZA; Gruenbaum, Zionist Actions Committee, 3.1.44, CZA.

64. JAE, 26.9.43, CZA.

65. Zionist Actions Committee, 14.11.43; JAE, 26.9.43 and 24.10.43; Gruenbaum, Rescue Committee, 23.11.43, S26/1237; Gruenbaum, Zionist Actions Committee, 3.1.44—all CZA.

66. Zionist Actions Committee, 3.1.44, CZA; JAE, 26.9.43, CZA.

67. Zionist Actions Committee, 3.1.44, CZA.

68. Suprasky and Kaplan, Zionist Actions Committee, 3.1.44, CZA; Rescue Committee presidency, 1.11.43, S26/1237, CZA; from London to friends, 1.11.43, correspondence, ABG; Kollek to friends, 1.11.43, S25/22685, CZA.

69. Zionist Actions Committee, 3.1.44, CZA; Rescue Committee presidency, 1.11.43, S26/1237, CZA.

70. Levin, Mapai Secretariat, 26.7.44, LPA.

71. Zionist-Socialist party secretary, South Africa, to BG, 14.2.44, correspondence, ABG.

72. Zionist Federation, South Africa, to JAE, 17.4.44 (two cables on same day); JAE to Zionist Federation, South Africa, 18.4.44; JAE to Zionist Federation, South Africa, 20.4.44—all correspondence, ABG.

73. Kirschner, Johannesburg, to Kaplan, Jerusalem, copy to BG, 2.5.44, correspondence, ABG; Gittlinn and Herbstein to JAE, 3.5.44, copy to BG, correspondence, ABG; South African Jewish War Appeal to Kaplan, 5.6.44 and 9.6.44—both S44/679, CZA.

74. BGD, 4.5.44, ABG; Shertok's report, JAE, 7–8.5.44, CZA; "Monetary Allocations for Immigration," JAE, 8.6.44, CZA.

75. Gruenbaum, 11.5.44, S6/4587, CZA, according to Porat, *The Blue and the Yellow Stars of David*, 103; Rescue Committee, 18.6.44, S26/1238a, CZA.

76. Zionist Federation, South Africa, to JAE, 12.7.44, correspondence, ABG; JAE to Zionist Federation, South Africa, copy to BG, 24.7.44, correspondence, ABG.

77. Kirschner, South Africa, to BG, 3.8.44; BG to Kirschner, 6.8.44; Ethel Haimann to Kirschner, 7.8.44; Kirschner to Dr. Joseph, 10.8.44—all correspondence, ABG.

78. Report of a meeting between Smuts and Joseph, 24.8.44, GCD, ABG; Abrahamson, South Africa, to Dr. Joseph, copy to BG, 12.9.44, correspondence, ABG; Zionist Federation, South Africa, to JAE, copy to BG, 13.9.44, correspondence, ABG; Dov Joseph to Kaplan, 30.8.44, S53/1606, CZA.

79. Oserin, South African Jewish War Appeal, to JAE, copy to BG, 8.9.44, correspondence, ABG.

80. Oserin, South African Jewish War Appeal, to JAE, copy to BG, 10.10.44, correspondence, ABG; JAE to Jewish War Appeal, 18.10.44, correspondence, ABG; South African Zionist Federation to Kaplan, 14.9.44, S53/1606, CZA; Kaplan to Jewish War Appeal, 11.12.44, S53/1606, CZA; Gruenbaum, Zionist Actions Committee, 3.1.44, CZA.

81. Porat, *The Blue and the Yellow Stars of David*, 105–107; Fishman, JAE, 21.5.44, CZA; Schmorak, JAE, 21.5.44, CZA; JAE, 11.6.44, CZA; Dobkin, Histadrut Executive Committee Secretariat, according to Porat, *The Blue and the Yellow Stars of David*, 105–107; Kaplan to Nicolay Kirschner, 2.5.43, S53/104, CZA.

82. BG, Kaplan and Gruenbaum's meeting with the chief rabbis, Jerusalem, 24.6.43, Minutes of Meetings, ABG.

83. JAE, 16.5.43, 30.5.43, CZA; Dr. Goldmann to Shertok, correspondence, ABG; JAE, 6.6.43, CZA; Moshe Shenfeld, ed., *The Teheran's Children Accuse: Facts and Documents* (Bni-Brak, 1971), 60–61.

84. JAE, 30.5.43, CZA.

85. Gruenbaum, Shapira, Rabbi Fishman, Kaplan, JAE, 30.5.43, CZA; Geula Bat-Yehuda, *Rabbi Maimon* (Jerusalem: Rabbi Kook Institute, 1979), 494. The author is Rabbi Fishman-Maimon's daughter.

86. Summary of meeting between Polish minister (plus his secretary) and Gruenbaum and Schmorak, copy to BG, 28.6.43, GCD, ABG; Berl Locker to JAE, 6.7.43, correspondence, ABG.

87. JAE, 6.6.43; report to BG, S44/479; Kaplan to Dr. Gravovsky, 4.7.44, S53/1613; M. Zagagi to Kaplan, 1.9.44, S53/1604—all CZA.

88. JAE, 31.1.43, CZA; Dr. Joseph's dairy, 22–25.1.43, 1, 12–13, Diaries Section, ABG; cf. Porat, *The Blue and the Yellow Stars of David*, 103–104; Kaplan to Ruth Eliav, 12.3.44, S53/1591, CZA.

89. Ruth Eliav's reports to Kaplan and Gruenbaum, Rescue Committee, February-March 1943, S26/1261 and S53/2118, CZA.

90. JAE, 11.4.43, CZA.

91. JAE, 6.6.43, CZA.

92. Kaplan's report upon his return from Egypt, JAE, 6.6.43, CZA; Zionist Actions Committee, 24.6.43, CZA (see also Dobkin).

93. Bader to Pomeranz and Schind, 11.6.43, sec. 15, D.1.713, MAGH.

94. Kaplan, Senator, and BG, JAE, 12.3.44, CZA; Kaplan to Ruth Eliav, 12.3.44, S53/1591, CZA.

95. Gruenbaum, Zionist Actions Committee, 3.1.44, CZA; Gruenbaum, Rescue Committee, 19.1.44, S26/1237, CZA; Kaplan to Leon Kastro, Cairo, 26.3.44, CZA.

96. Dobkin, Rescue Committee, 15.1.45, S53/1613, CZA; cf. Porat, *The Blue and the Yellow Stars of David*, 104–105; Sima Gureli to Kaplan, 1.2.44, S53/1591, CZA; Kaplan to Ovadia Salem, Cairo, 24.8.44, S53/1591, CZA.

14. Money Transfers

1. Kaplan, Mapai Center, 24.8.43, LPA; Kaplan, Zionist Actions Committee, 14.3.44, CZA; Kaplan to Kirschner, 2.5.43, S53/104, CZA.

2. JAE, 25.4.44, 18.6.44, 26.11.44 and 10.12.44; Zionist Actions Committee, 18.5.43; Kaplan, Zionist Actions Committee, 14.3.44; Kaplan to Kirschner, 2.5.43, S53/104; JAE, 6.6.43—all CZA; Mapai Secretariat, 27.4.44, LPA.

3. Shertok's report, JAE, 25.4.43, CZA; Mapai Secretariat, 27.4.43, LPA; JAE, 16.5.43 and 6.6.43, CZA.

4. JAE, 25.7.43, CZA; NA, OSS, RG 226, 25.7.44, Palestine Labor Movement, Histadrut Finances, message from Albert R. Epstein, New York, to Brudny and Remez, Workers Bank, Tel Aviv.

5. Dobkin and Gruenbaum, Zionist Actions Committee, 24.6.43, CZA.

6. Rubin, *Istanbul Intrigues*, 57, 212, 213 [English]; to JAE, for Dobkin, 18.9.43, S25/22522, CZA; Alexander Pott, *A School for Spies* (Tel Aviv: Ma'arachut, 1959), 103–108; Hirschmann, *Lifeline to the Promised Land*, 135—137.

7. Kaplan, Zionist Actions Committee, 14.3.44, CZA; Aharon Remez interview by Yoav Gelber, 4.8.78, OD, tape 442, ABG; Zvi Livne, *On an Economic Mission: The American Palestine Trading Corporation History* (Tel Aviv: Tarbut VeChinuch, 1964).

8. Rivlin, Amir, and Stempler, eds., *Parachutists of Hope*, 24.

9. Cairo trip (23.4-2.5), report from the Cairo trip (2.5.44), S25/8885, CZA; Infiltration Committee, 21.5.44, S25/890, CZA; see note. 25 herein.

10. N. Fowler-Smith to Mr. Zaslani, 21.11.44, S25/8907, CZA; Infiltration Committee, 26.10.44, S25/8885, CZA; Rivlin, Amir, and Stempler, eds., *Parachutists of Hope*, 160–161.

11. Lyova Gukovsky, Arye Fichman, and Dov Harari, *Letters from the Lion's Den: The Rescue Parachutists,* Mordechai Rishfi, ed. (Kibbutz Beit-Oren, n.p., 1971), 38.

12. N. Fowler-Smith to Mr. Zaslani (details provided by Squadron Leader R. S. Taylor) 21.11.44, S25/8907, CZA.

13. Zaslani to Reed, 28.3.44, S25/8909, CZA.

14. Cairo trip (23.4-2.5), report from the Cairo trip (2.5.44), S25/8885, CZA.

15. Sereni to friends, 8.4.44, S25/8896, CZA; 31.7.44, S25/8884, CZA (also in English in S25/22681, CZA); report of a meeting in Jerusalem with Rafael, 3.9.44, S25/8889, CZA.

16. Zaslani to Squadron Leader Reed, M.L.O.-R.A.F.-H.Q., Jerusalem, 13.1.44, S25/8909, CZA; Zaslani to Reed, 28.3.44, S25/8909, CZA; summary of meeting, 7.5.43, S25/8884, CZA; JA Political Department to Teddy Kollek, 25.6.43, S25/22685, CZA; see n. 10.

17. To friends in Istanbul, 22.3.44, S25/8884, CZA.

18. Zaslani, temporary receipt, 17.5.44, S25/8909, CZA.

19. NA, OSS, RG 226, entry 108, box 54, 25.5.44.

20. N. Fowler-Smith to Mr. Zaslani, 21.11.44, S25/8907, CZA; Bader, weekly review, 25.6.44–1.7.44, S25/22465, CZA; Venja and Menachem to JAE, 6.8.43, S25/22522, CZA.

21. "A Short History of S.M.9 (the Middle East)—Balkans Operations," Top Secret, in Rivlin, Amir, and Stempler, eds., *Parachutists of Hope*, 130–164; Schind and Avriel to Kollek, 6.10.43, S25/22685, CZA; Kollek to friends (Schind and Avriel), 11.10.43, S25/22685, CZA; Avriel to Zaslani, 19.10.43, S25/22685, CZA; Gukovsky to Venja, 4.1.44, in Gukovsky, Fichman, and Harari, *Letters from the Lion's Den,* 61.

22. Intelligence report—Romania, 9.5.44, S25/8903, CZA; Yanko Skarlet, "A Pioneer Testimony," in Rishfi, ed., *Letters from the Lion's Den,* 39–40, 62–63, 73–76.

23. Intelligence report—Romania, Lyova [English], May 1944, S25/8903, CZA.

24. Dov to Zvi, 25.5.45, S25/10118, CZA; H. to Teddy Kollek, 17.4.45, S25/8907, CZA; Teddy Kollek to B. Nevill, 26.4.45, S25/8907, CZA; These documents reflect the methods used for transferring money and the accounting practices employed by those individuals in Jerusalem, Istanbul, and Romania, on the one hand, and by the British espionage group (under Tony Simmonds), on the other.

25. Infiltration Committee, 26.10.44, S25/8885, CZA; see also n. 9.

26. Venja to Moshe, Dov, and David, 18.3.45, file 14/61a, Haganah Archive; Shalom to Ehud, 3.5.45, S25/22516; Kadmon to JA, 31.10.45, S25/8909, plus the following attachment: Infiltration Committee expense account for August-September 1945; Ehud to Miriam, 12.5.45, S25/22516; Dov to Zvi, 25.5.45, S25/101118; Zvi to Dov, 2.3.45—all CZA.

27. Ehud to Reuven, 18.12.43, S25/22685, CZA; Ehud from Poland to Kibbutz Secretariat, 14.9.43; Ehud to friends, 18.9.43; Bader to Kibbutz Secretariat members, 1.10.43—all file 50/9, Israel Galili Archive, Haganah Archive; Bader, weekly review, 25.6.44–1.7.44, S25/22465, CZA; Rubin, *Istanbul Intrigues,* 57 [English].

28. Kollek to Yitzhak Gruenbaum, copy to Kaplan, 1.4.45, S25/8909, CZA.

29. Hadari, *Against All Odds,* 350–351.

30. Avneri, "A Mystery—Escape from Greece," *Davar,* 6.5.83.

31. Nancy Habberfield's money receipt; Squadron Leader Reed to Zaslani, 10.1.44, S25/8909, CZA; 6.1.44, S25/8908, CZA.

32. Chaim to Danny, 10.7.44, S25/8884, CZA.
33. Avneri, "A Mystery—Escape from Greece."
34. Unsigned to Ehud, 1.6.44, S25/22684 [English]; a receipt for 2,200 Palestinian pounds in Teddy Kollek's name, 4.6.44, S25/22681; unsigned to friends, 8.6.44—all CZA.
35. Rubin, *Istanbul Intrigues*, 148 [English]; Infiltration Committee, 26.10.44, S25/8885; Cairo trip (23.4-2.5), report from the Cairo trip (2.5.44), S25/8885; Pinkerton to Zaslani, 12.5.44, passing along cable dated 10.5.44 from American consulate in Istanbul for "Ben-Yehuda" [Meirov], S25/22203; Zaslani to Pinkerton for "Ben-Yehuda," through Seager-Avriel, 9.8.44, S25/22681; Y. Kleinbaum to Pinkerton, from Kaplan to Avriel, through Seager, 8.9.44, S25/2268; receipt for 2,200 Palestinian pounds in Teddy Kollek's name, 4.6.44, S25/22681—all CZA.
36. Kollek, *One Jerusalem*, 40–42; Kollek interview by Yigal Donyets, 6.6.79, OD, ABG.
37. Pott, *A School For Spies*, 103–108; Bauer, *The Holocaust*, 196.
38. Schind to Kollek, 6.10.43 and 9.10.43, S25/22685, CZA. I was unable to determine if Jonas was Paulos Mastidas, who is mentioned by Venja Pomeranz in his book *Against All Odds* (61) Mastidas, a banker of Greek origin who went by the code name "Mercury," had various connections with the Yishuv emissaries and with British and American espionage groups.
39. Schind to Z[aslani], 22.10.43, S25/22685, CZA.
40. Kollek to friends, 11.10.43, S25/22685, CZA.
41. Schind to Z[aslani], 22.10.43, S25/22685, CZA; Schind to Kollek, 22.10.43, S25/22685, CZA.
42. Ibid.
43. Schind and Avriel to Kollek, 14.10.43, S25/22685, CZA.
44. Kollek to friends, 25.10.43, S25/22685, CZA.
45. Ibid.; Schind to Kollek, 25.10.43; Teddy to friends, 22.11.43—both S25/22685, CZA.
46. Kollek to friends, 1.11.43, S25/22685, CZA.
47. Ibid.
48. Ze'ev Schind to Teddy, Istanbul, 14.11.43, S25/22685, CZA.
49. Teddy to friends, 22.11.43 and 30.11.43, S25/22685, CZA.
50. Ze'ev Schind to Teddy, Istanbul, 14.11.43, S25/22685; Teddy to friends, 22.11.43, S25/22685; to Zaslani, 29.9.43, S25/8903—all CZA.
51. Teddy to friends, 22.11.43, S25/22685, CZA.
52. Ehud to Teddy, 5.11.44, S25/22516, CZA; T. Kollek to Mr. O.T. Steger, 23.11.44, S25/22516, CZA; Dov to Reuven, Zvi, and Teddy, 26.11.44, S25/10118, CZA; to "Meir," 15.12.44, file 14/59, Haganah Archive; from Ehud and Hanna, 15.12.44, file 14/61a, Haganah Archive; Miriam to Ehud, 28.12.44, S25/22516, CZA.
53. "Meir" to "Artzi," 12.11.44, file 14/62, Haganah Archive; Teddy to Ehud, 16.11.44, S25/22516, CZA; "Meir" to "Artzi," 17.11.44, S53/1619, CZA; unsigned to "Artzi," 15.12.44, file 14/59, Haganah Archive; "Meir" to "Artzi," 16.12.44, file 14/62, Haganah Archive.
54. Unsigned to "Artzi," 15.12.44, file 14/59, Haganah Archive; Ehud to Teddy, 23.12.44, S25/22516, CZA; Piko

Levi from Ehud Avriel, 26.12.44, file 14/62, Haganah Archive; from "Meir," Istanbul, 30.12.44, file 14/798, Haganah Archive (also in S53/1619, CZA).
55. Venja Pomeranz and Ze'ev Schind, Istanbul, to BG, 25.5.43, correspondence, ABG (also in S25/22685, CZA, and in file 14/798, Haganah Archive). Copies were sent to Kaplan, Remez, Golda Meir, and Neustadt.
56. Kollek, *One Jerusalem*, 55; Magnes's report of his visit to Istanbul, Rescue Committee protocol, 14.7.44, 9, 10–14, CZA; Rubin, *Istanbul Intrigues*, 209, 210, 213, 217, 218 [English]; Eliahu Epstein's journal of a visit to Turkey, 23–26.3.43, S53/230, 16, CZA (also in GCD, ABG).
57. Kollek, *One Jerusalem*, 55.
58. Eban, *Life Story*, 48.
59. Message from Reuven, Eiga Shapira's notes, 22.7.43, S25/22487, CZA, and a bill dated 16.3.42. (also in S25/22439 and S25/22434); British payments re: the Interrogations Office action, and March 1942 bill, to Reed, 16.4.42, ibid.; NA, OSS, RG 226, 25.7.44, Palestine Labor Movement, Histadrut Finances, message from Albert R. Epstein, New York, to Brudny and Remez, Workers' Bank, Tel Aviv; Friling, "Under a Magnifying Glass," 592–604; NA, OSS, RG 226, entry 108, box 51, G2675.
60. Pinkerton to "Ben-Yehuda" (Meirov-Avigur) and Zaslani, 6.5.44, S25/22203 and S25/22681, CZA; M. to friends, 19.5.44, correspondence, ABG.
61. Pinkerton to "Ben-Yehuda" and Zaslani, letter forwarded for them from "Meir" (Palestine office in Istanbul), 6.5.44, S25/22203, CZA; Kleinbaum, on Ben-Yehuda's name, to Pinkerton, for Ehud and "Meir," Istanbul, 9.5.44, S25/22203, CZA.
62. Pinkerton to "Ben-Yehuda" and Zaslani, 6.5.44, S25/22203, CZA; Kleinbaum to Pinkerton for Ehud and "Meir," Istanbul, 9.5.44, S25/22203, CZA; Herbert Katzky interviewed by Menahem Kaufman, 30.3.76, Institute of Contemporary Jewry, OD, 27.
63. Pinkerton to Zaslani, letter forwarded to him from Istanbul, 12.5.44, S25/22203 (also in S25/22681), CZA; Zaslani to Reed, 12.5.44, S25/22203, CZA.
64. Notes of a phone conversation with Pinkerton, 17.5.44, S25/22203, CZA (also 19.5.44); Y. Kleinbaum to Pinkerton, cable payment, 18.5.44, S25/22681, CZA; M. to friends, 19.5.44, correspondence, ABG.
65. Y. Kleinbaum to Pinkerton, for Avriel, through Seager, 27.5.44, S25/22681 and 22684, CZA [English and Hebrew].
66. Report of a conversation with Rafael, sec. 9, 28.5.44, S25/8885, CZA.
67. "Meir" to "Artzi," 24.6.44, S25/22681, CZA.
68. Mayer-Stephany, London, to Kaplan, Jerusalem, 29.6.44, S53/1613, CZA; Kleinbaum to Pinkerton, for Kaplan, through Seager and Schind, 6.7.44, S25/2261, CZA, attached, Dobkin to Kaplan, through the American consulate, 1.7.44, S25/22681.
69. NA, OSS, RG 226, entry 88, box 495, 27.10.44, from Saint-Bucarest.
70. Kollek, *One Jerusalem*, 60.

71. Ibid., 59.

72. Ibid., 60–61.

73. Ibid., 61.

74. Hirschmann, *Lifeline to the Promised Land,* 76–81.

75. NA, OSS, RG 226, entry 88, box 495, 27.10.44, from Saint-Bucarest; Ofer, *Escaping the Holocaust,* 250–251 and n. 32.

76. Histadrut Executive Committee, 9.3.43, ILMAL; W. Schevenels to Executive Committee, General Federation of Jewish Labor in Eretz Israel, 26.9.43; Fund-raising report, 26.9.43; Schevenels to Dov Hos, 31.8.43; to Dov Hos and BG, 25.9.43, 6913; Schevenels to Dov Hos, London, 20.9.43—all IV-104-49-2-96B, LPA.

77. Schevenels to Dov Hos, London, 9.10.43, IV-104-49-2-96B, LPA (also 19.10.43).

78. Dov Hos to Schevenels, 2.9.43; report of International Council meeting, 11.10.43; Dov Hos to Zionist Actions Committee Secretariat, 21.9.43—all file 66/2, Haganah Archive; Schevenels to Histadrut Secretariat, 28.9.43, IV-104-49-2-96B, LPA; Dov Hos to Zionist Actions Committee Secretariat, 23.10.43, file 66/2, Haganah Archive; Hoover Institute Archives "on War, Revolution and Peace," Stanford University, Palo Alto, California, Schevenels/S, box 10, folder FSI; Szold to Schevenels, 21.10.41, ibid.; Schevenels's answer, 17.2.43, box 12, folder FSI; Golda to Schevenels, 16.10.42, ibid.—all Hoover Institute Archives.

79. Hayim Golan, *The Israel Mereminsky Diaries, 1941–1945* (Ramat Effal: Yad Tabenkin, 1995), 16, 27, 43–44, 48, 68.

15. Funding Aid and Rescue Operations

1. Porat, *The Blue and the Yellow Stars of David,* 91–92; JAE, 5.11.44, 26.11.44, 3.12.44. In part of those meetings BG was absent, because his visit to Bulgaria.

2. Menahem Bader to Hakibbutz Ha'artzi Secretariat, 17.9.43, MAGH.

3. Kaplan and Gruenbaum, JAE, 15.10.44; Shapira, JAE, 3.12.44; JAE, 10.12.44—all CZA.

4. See also JAE budgetary discussions for 1945, which contain many aspects typical of previous discussions, e.g., the usual pressure to increase budgets for departments not involved in rescue. "Budget A" allocated 1.7 million Palestinian pounds, whereas "Budget B" allocated 1.2 million.

5. BG at the third students' convention, 12.1.44, SA, ABG.

Conclusion

1. Teveth, *Ben-Gurion: The Burning Ground,* 409–410 [English].

2. Avizohar, *The Struggle for Zionism,* 17; Shabtai Teveth, "Ben-Gurion and the Holocaust Failure," *Ha'aretz,* 10.4.87; Yoav Gelber, "Zionist Policy and the Transfer Agreement, 1933–1935," *Yalkut Moreshet,* no. 17 (February 1974), 1:97–152; no. 18, (November 1974), 2:23–100.

3. Friling, "What Was the United States' Real Intention at the Evian Conference?" 217–228; Teveth, "The Black Hole," 114–115.

4. Teveth, *Ben-Gurion: The Burning Ground,* 449–451 [English].

5. Ben-Gurion, *Memoirs,* 3:105.

6. Israel Kolatt, "The Debate Over Partition Within the Labor Movement," in *Studies in the Palestine Partition Plans, 1937–1947,* ed. Meir Avizohar and Isaiah Friedman (Sede Boqer: Ben-Gurion University in the Negev Campus Press, 1984), 40–54.

7. Mapai Council, 5–8.3.44, LPA.

8. Forty-third Histadrut Council, session 3, 9.4.41, ILMAL; BG at General Zionists meeting, Tel Aviv, 10.4.41, Minutes of Meetings, ABG.

9. BGD, 11.8.41 and 10.11.41, ABG.

10. BG at Elected Assembly convention, 30.11.42, SA, ABG; BG at gathering of Mapai activists, 8.12.42, SA, ABG.

11. Gilbert, *Auschwitz and the Allies,* 134–135 [English].

12. Ben-Gurion, *In the Battle,* 3:121–122.

13. JAE, 12.9.43, CZA.

14. Shertok's (Sharett's) report, JAE, 27.4.43, CZA.

15. BGD, 17.8.45, ABG; Friling, "Changing Roles," 450–480 [English].

16. Matityahu Mintz, "The Building of Eretz Israel and the Work in the Present: A Concept of Unity Versus the Actuality of Contradiction," *Zionism,* no. 9 (1984), 147–155.

17. Ali Shaltiel, "Ben-Gurion: Struggles from Within and Without," *Ha'aretz,* 29.5.87.

18. Yael Yishai, "Leaders' Resignations and Their Lesson," Migvan, 1, no. 5 (1976), 39–42.

19. Bar-Zohar, *Ben-Gurion,* 279–302.

20. BG, Zionist Actions Committee, afternoon session, 1.9.43, CZA, 4, 5.

21. Minutes of Meetings, 5.10.42, ABG, 1.

22. Porat, *An Entangled Leadership,* 11. This document is of special significance, being foreign and external, related neither to Ben-Gurion nor Zionism.

23. BG to Frankfurter, 8.12.42, correspondence, ABG; BG, Mapai Center, 24.2.43, LPA.

24. BG, JAE, 23.7.44, CZA, 12; BG, JAE, 23.4.44, CZA, 3.

25. BGD, 29.1.40, ABG; BG, Mapai political committee, 3.5.43, LPA; Gruenbaum, Zionist Actions Committee, afternoon session, 18.5.43, CZA, 1; Kaplan, 18.5.43, ibid; Mapai Secretariat, 30.3.43, LPA.

26. This is clear from the way the three operated; see also Shertok, Mapai political committee, 3.5.43, LPA.

27. Among Kaplan's secret missions were his trips to Istanbul in February-March 1943 and July 1944, missions to Cairo, and meetings in Palestine with senior British officials. Rescue plans were always discussed on these occasions.

28. Obvious examples of an "advance control" spearheaded by a member of the triumvirate are tied to large rescue plans, such as the three ransom plans and the children's rescue plan.

29. Eshed, *Reuven Shiloah the man Behind the Mossad,* 79; Ze'ev Hadari, "Ehud Avriel and His Times," in *Eastern European Jewry: From Holocaust to Redemption, 1944–1948,*

ed. Benjamin Pinkus (Sede Boqer Campus Press: Ben-Gurion University of the Negev / Sede Boqer Campus, 1987), 272, 273; JAE, 6.8.44, CZA, 5.

30. To Shaul [Meirov-Avigur] and Eliyahu [Golomb], 12.7.37, GCD, ABG; Meir, *My Life*, 137–140 [English].

31. BG, Mapai political committee, 3.5.43, LPA; Shertok, Zionist Actions Committee, 1.9.43, CZA, 12; CID (Criminal Investigation Department) Jerusalem second in command to the Palestinian general secretary, 11.11.43, GCD, ABG, from Kurzman archive; Hirschmann, *Lifeline to the Promised Land*, 73–75 [English].

32. JAE, 24.10.43, CZA, 1.

33. Porat, "Ben-Gurion and the Holocaust," (1987), 12:306–307; Ariel Horovitz, "Menahem Bader's Mission in Istanbul and the Contacts of 'Hashomer-Hatza'ir' with European Jewry," *Yalkut Moreshet*, no. 35 (April 1983), 153–202.

34. Zionist Actions Committee, 18.1.43, CZA.

35. Although a review of JAE protocols in late 1942 and early 1943 shows that no decision was reached on Slovakia, emissaries and other individuals acted as if someone had instructed them to begin examining various plans.

36. Bauer, *From Diplomacy to Resistance*, 123–124 [English]; Teveth, *The Road to May*, 177, 235.

37. Elazar Weinryb, *Historical Thought: The Philosophy of History* (Tel Aviv: Open University, 1987), 1:402–407, 410, 444.

38. BG, Mapai Center, 7.12.38, LPA.

39. "Rozka: Her Fight, Thought, and Character," ed. Yehuda Tovin, Levi Dror, and Joseph Dov, *Yalkut Moreshet* no. 45 (1988): 212–214; Teveth, "The Black Hole," 158–160.

40. Tuvia Friling, "The Zionist Movement's March of Folly and Tom Segev's 'The Seventh Million,'" *Journal of Israeli History* 16, no. 2 (1995), 133–158 [English]; Yehuda Bauer and Tuvia Friling, "Lo Tom Ve-Lo Segev, 'The Seventh Million' and Yoel Brand's Plan," *Iton 77* (May-June 1993), 160–161.

41. Tuvia Friling, "The Emotional Elements in Ben-Gurion's Relations to the Diaspora during the Holocaust," in *Organizing Rescue: Jewish National Solidarity in the Modern Period*, ed. I. Troen and B. Pinkus (London: Frank Cass, 1992), 191–221 [English].

42. BG at a youth gathering, 2–3.4.43, SA, ABG; Mapai Council, 15.1.44, LPA; Kibbutz Hameuhad convention, 19.1.44 and 10.7.44—all SA, LPA.

43. BG to Frankfurter, through Lourie, 8.12.42, correspondence; BG at gathering of industrialists and businessmen, 24.6.43, 13.7.43, and 23.9.43, Minutes of Meetings; BGD, 6.7.44—all ABG.

44. BGD, 7.5.45 and 8.5.45, ABG.

45. Editorial, *Hamashkif*, 6.8.44; M. Ya'ari, *Hashomer Hatza'ir*, 6.1.43; Goldmann, *Memoirs*, 186ff.; Beit-Zvi, *Post Zionism on Trial: A Study of the Factors that Caused the Mistakes Made by the Zionist Movement during the Holocaust*; Dan Kurzman, *Ben-Gurion: Prophet of Fire* (New York: Simon & Schuster, 1983) [English]; Tom Segev, *The Seventh Million: The Israelis and the Holocaust* (Jerusalem: Keter, 1991); Idith Zertal, "The Poisoned Heart: The Jews of Palestine and the Holocaust," *Tikkun* 2, no. 2 (1987), 47–50, 120–122 [English]; Jim Allen, *Perdition* (London: Ithaca Press, 1986) [English]; Friling, "David Ben-Gurion and the Catastrophe of European Jewry, 1939–1945," i–vi; see n. 40 above.

46. Friling, "David Ben-Gurion and the Catastrophe of European Jewry, 1939–1945," i–vi.

47. Moshe Zimmermann, "Fifty Years Later: The Holocaust's Influence on Cinema and Culture in Israel," (unpublished manuscript supplied by author); Shlomo Avineri, introduction to *What Is History?*, by E. H. Carr (Tel Aviv: Modan, 1986), 7–14.

48. Eliezer Schweid, "Zionism in 'Post-Zionist' Times," *Davar*, 24.6.94.

49. Dan Miron, *Face the Silenced Brother: Poetry of the War of Liberation* (Tel Aviv: Open University, 1992), 379.

Bibliography

ARCHIVES AND UNPUBLISHED SOURCES

BEN-GURION HERITAGE INSTITUTE ARCHIVES (ABG)

Diaries Section, Ben-Gurion's Diary; extracts from diaries of Dov (Bernard) Joseph; Reuven Shiloah (Zaslani); Eliahu Ealth (Epstein)
Correspondence Section
Minutes of Meeting Section
Minutes of Organization Section
General Choronological Ducuments Section (GCD)
Speeches and Articles Section (SA)
Newspapers Section
Subjects Files Section
Personal Archives Section: Ehud Avriel's Archive, Yehushua Cohen's Archive, Kurzman archive
Selected Collection from archives abroad

CENTRAL ZIONIST ARCHIVES, JERUSALEM (CZA)

BG Office, S44
Jewish Agency Executive Minutes (JAE), J1
Zionist Actions Committee Minutes, S25
Rescue Committee Protocols, S26
Kaplan's Office, S53
JA Political Department Files, S25
JA Immigration Department Files, S6
Zionist Federation, London, S4
Mobilization and Rescue Fund Files, J8
Adler-Rudel, Personal Archive, A140
Jewish National Fund (JNF) Files
Jewish Agency Political Deparment

ISRAEL LABOR PARTY ARCHIVES, BEIT BERL (LPA)

Minutes of Mapai Center meetings
Minutes of Mapai Secretatiat
Minutes of Mapai Office meetings

Minutes of Mapai Political Committee meetings
Minutes of Mapai Council meetings
Minutes of Mapai Conventions
Minutes of different gatherings

ISRAEL LABOR MOVEMENT ARCHIVES AT THE LAVON INSTITUTE (ILMAL)

Minutes of Histadrut Executive Committee
Minutes of Histadrut Executive Secretariat
Minutes of Histadrut Council
Minutes of Histadrut Conventions

BET LOHAMEI HAGETAOT ARCHIVE

Venja Pomeranz Collection at the Illegal Immigration Research Center, Ben-Gurion University, courtesy of Venja Pomeranz
Moreshet Archive, Ya'ari Center, Givat Haviva (MAGH)
Menahem Bader, Personal Archive

YAD VASHEM ARCHIVE, JERUSALEM

HAGANAH ARCHIVE, BET GOLOMB, TEL AVIV

WEIZMANN ARCHIVE, REHOVOT

PUBLIC RECORDS OFFICE, LONDON (PRO)

Admirality (ADM)
Cabinet Papers (CAB)
Colonial Office (CO)
Foreign Office, Political (FO 371)
War Office (WO)

NATIONAL ARCHIVES, UNITED STATES (NA)

War Refugee Board
Office of Strategic Services (OSS), RG 226, 80, 84, 86
European War 740, 548.G1

Joint Anti-Fascist Refugee Committee, 811, 862, 111, 500

Office of War Information (OWI)

DWIGHT D. EISENHOWER LIBRARY, ABILENE, KANSAS

Pre-Presidential File, 1943–1945
Combined Chiefs of Staff, 1943–1945
General W. B. Smith, 1942–1945

HARRY S TRUMAN LIBRARY, INDEPENDENCE, MISSOURI

White House Central Files, Official File, 1945

BRANDEIS UNIVERSITY, WALTHAM, MASSACHUSETTS

American Jewish Historical Society Archives

DONOVAN ARCHIVES, CARLISLE, PENNSYLVANIA

Hoover Institution Archives, Stanford University, Stanford, California
Walther Schevenels Papers

AMERICAN JEWISH HISTORICAL SOCIETY (AJHS)

P-134, box 104-10, box 122-4; P-248, box 107-1
Stephen Wise Collection

ZIONIST ARCHIVES, NEW YORK (ZANY)

Ben-Gurion Files and Newspapers

JDC ARCHIVES, NEW YORK (JANY)

Palestine, file 763, 770, 747, 748.
Minutes of the Emergency Committee for Zionist Affairs

BUND ARCHIVE, NEW YORK, NEWSPAPER SECTION

American Jewish Archives, Cincinnati
World Zionist Congress to John Winant, 18.2.42,

ORAL DOCUMENTATION, OD

Ehud Avriel, Miriam Cohen-Taub, Robert Szold, Emanuel Neumann, Ruth Eliav-Klieger, Anshel Reiss, Aharon Remez—all interviewed by Yigal Donyets; Aharon Remez—interviewed by Yoav Gleber, Ben-Gurion Heritage Institute, Verbal Documentation Department.
Moshe Agami-Averbuch—interviewed by Aharon Kaidar, Institute of Contemporary Jewry, Hebrew University of Jerusalem.

DAILY NEWSPAPERS AND JOURNALS

Davar
Ha'aretz
Haboker
Hazman
Hamashkif
Haolom
Hapoe Hatzair
Hatzoffe
New Palestine
Der Tag
Parverts

SECONDARY SOURCES

Allen, Jim. *Perdition: A Play in Two Acts.* Atlantic Highlands, N.J.: Ithaca Press, 1987 [English].
Anchell, Jan. "The Romanian Holocaust Survivors under Full Communist Rule, August 1944–December 1947." *She'erit Hapleta (The Remnants), 1944–1948: Rehabilitation and Political Struggle, Proceedings of the Sixth Yad Vashem International Historical Conference,* ed. I. Gutman and A. Drechsler, 127–148. Jerusalem: Yad Vashem, 1990 [Hebrew].
———. "Deportation Plans for Romanian Jewry, in Documentation," *Yad Vashem Studies,* No. 16 (1985): 299–332 [Hebrew].
———. "Holocaust Survivors in Romania in Transition to a Full Communists Regime," *American Jewish Yearbook* (1946–1947) [English].

Aronson, Shlomo. "On Different Types of Political Leaders." *In the Political Arena.* Jerusalem: N.p., n.d. [Hebrew].

———. *Hitler, the Allies, and the Jews.* Cambridge: Cambridge University Press, 2004 [English].

Aronson, Shlomo, and Breitman, Richard. "The End of the 'Final Solution' Nazi Plans to Ransom Jews in 1944." *Central European History* 25.2 (1992): 194–203 [English].

Avichay, Avraham. *David Ben-Gurion: A State Shape.* Jerusalem: Keter, 1974 [Hebrew].

Avineri, Shlomo, ed. *David Ben-Gurion: A Leader of the Labour Movement.* Tel Aviv: Am Oved, 1988 [Hebrew].

Avizohar, Meir, "Ben-Gurion's Militant Strategy for the Creation of A Jewish State," *Studies in the Palestine Partition Plans, 1937–1947,* ed. Meir Avizohar. 95–127. Sede Boqer: Ben-Gurion University of the Negev Press, Sede Boqer Campus, 1984 [Hebrew].

———. "Ben-Gurion's Visit to the D.P. Camps and his National Outlook in the Aftermath of World War II," Eastern-European Jewry—from Holocaust to Redemption, 1944–1948, ed. Benjamin Pinkus, 253–270. Sede Boqer: Ben-Gurion University of the Negev Press, Sede Boqer Campus, 1987 [Hebrew].

———. *The Struggling Zionism: Preface to Ben-Gurion's Diary and Memories, 1939.* Sede Boqer Campus: Ben-Gurion Research Center, 1985 [Hebrew].

Avneri, Arieh L. "A Mystery—Escape from Greece." *Davar,* May 6, 1983 [Hebrew].

Avni, Shmaya. "On the Transnistria Plan." *Yalkut Moreshet* No. 30 (November 1980): 199–203 [Hebrew].

Azaryhu, Maoz. *State Rituals: Independence Celebrations and Eternalizing the Memory of the Fallen, 1948–1956.* Sede Boqer: Ben-Gurion Research Center, Sede Boqer Campus, 1995 [Hebrew].

Bar-Zohar, Michael. *Ben-Gurion.* Tel Aviv: Am Oved, 1975–1977 [Hebrew].

———. *Ben-Gurion: A Political Biography.* Jerusalem: Keter, 1980 [Hebrew].

———. *Ben-Gurion: The Man Behind the Legend, Biography.* Tel Aviv: Ministry of Defense, 1986 [Hebrew].

———. *Conspiracy—Hitler's Jewish Spy.* Jerusalem: Keter, 1992 [Hebrew].

Bat-Yehuda, Geula. *Rabbi Maimon.* Jerusalem: Rabbi Kook Institute, 1979 [Hebrew].

Bauer, Yehuda, *American Jewry and the Holocaust: The American Jewish Joint Distribution Committee, 1939–1945.* Detroit: Wayne State University Press, 1981 [English].

———. *Flight and Rescue: Brichah.* New York: Random House, 1970 [English].

———. *From Diplomacy to Resistance.* Philadelphia: Jewish Publication Society, 1970 [English].

———. "From Biltmore to Paris—The Holocaust Influence on Zionist Policy 1942–1946." *The Sixth World Congress for Jewish Studies,* Vol. 2. Jerusalem: World Union of Jewish Studies, 1976 [Hebrew].

———. *The Holocaust—Some Historical Aspects, The Institute of Contemporary Jewry.* Tel Aviv: Hebrew University of Jerusalem, 1982 [Hebrew].

———. "Jewish Foreign Policy during the Holocaust." *Ha'aretz,* 10.4.83 [Hebrew].

———. "Jewish Parachutists during the Holocaust." *Monthly Review* No. 10 (October 1979): 30–36 [Hebrew].

———. *Jews for Sale? Nazi-Jewish Negotiations, 1933–1945.* New Haven: Yale University Press, 1994 [English].

———. "Joel Brand Mission." *Yalkut Moreshet,* No. 26 (November 1978): 23–60 [Hebrew].

———. "The Kastner Affair: The Historical Truth and Political Use." *Ha'aretz,* 25.5.82 [Hebrew].

———. *My Brother's Keeper: A History of the American Jewish Joint Distribution Committee, 1929–1939.* Philadelphia: Jewish Publication Society, 1974 [English].

———. "The Negotiations between Saly Mayer and the Representatives of the SS in 1944–1945," *Rescue Attempts during the Holocaust,* Proceedings of the Second Yad Vashem International Historical Conference, Jerusalem, April 8–11, 1974, 5–46, New York: New York: Ktav Publishing House, 1978 [English]. [Hebrew; Jerusalem: Yad Vashem, 1977].

———. "Parashutists and the Defense Plan," *Yalkut Moreshet,* No. 1 (November 1963): 86–95 [Hebrew].

Bauer, Yehuda and Tuvia Friling. "Lo Tom Ve-Lo Segev, The Seventh Million and Yoel Brand's Plan," *Iton 77,* No. 160–161 (May-June 1993) [Hebrew].

Beit-Zvi, Shabtai B. *Post-Zionism on Trial: A Study of the Factors That Caused the Mistake Made by the Zionist Movement during the Holocaust.* Tel Aviv: Zahala, 1991 [Hebrew].

———. "Was Ben-Gurion Against Bombing Auschwitz?" *Ma'ariv,* 1.8.80 [Hebrew].

Ben, Yosef. *Greek Jewry in the Holocaust and the Resistance, 1941–1944.* Edited with the assistance of the Institute of the Salonika Jewry Research Center. Tel Aviv: Salonika Jewry Research Center, 1985 [Hebrew].

Ben-Gurion, David. *Ben-Gurion Looks Back in Talks with Moshe Pearlman.* London: Weidenfeld & Nicholsoson, 1965 [English].

———. *Memories.* ed. Meir Avizohar. Tel Aviv: Am Oved, 1987.

Berger, P. L. and T. Luckmann. *The Social Construction of Reality: A Treatise in Sociology of Knowledge,* New York: Doubleday, 1967 [English].

Biss, A. *A Million Jews to Save: Check to the Final Solution.* London: Hutchinson, 1973 [English].

Bondy, Ruth. *The Emissary: The Life and Death of Enzo Sereni.* Tel Aviv: Am Oved, 1973 [Hebrew].

Braham, Randolph. L. *Eichmann and the Destruction of Hungarian Jewry.* New York: Twayne Publishers, 1961 [English].

———. *The Politics of Genocide—The Holocaust in Hungary.* New York: Columbia University Press, 1981 [English].

———. *The Tragedy of Hungarian Jewry.* New York: Institute for Holocaust Studies of the City University of New York, 1986 [English].

Brener, Uri. *To an Independent Jewish Army: Hakibbutz Hameuhad in the Haganah, 1939–1945.* Tel Aviv: Hakibbutz Hameuchad, 1985 [Hebrew].

Breuer, William B. *The Secret War with Germany.* Novato, Calif.: Presidio Press, 1988 [English].

Bronovsky, Yaakov. *The Knowledge and Imagination Sources.* Tel Aviv: Am Oved, 1983 [Hebrew].

Brown, A. C. *Bodygard of Lies.* London: W. A. Allen, 1976 [English].

Browning, C. R. *The Final Solution and the German Foreign Office.* New York: Holmes & Meier, 1978 [English].

———. "Nazi Resettlement policy and the search for a Solution to the Jewish Question, 1939–1941," *German Studies Review* 9.3 (Fall 1986): 497–519 [English].

Burns, James McGregor. *Roosevelt: The Lion and the Fox.* New York: Harcourt Brace, 1956 [English].

Canaan, Chaviv. *Two Hundred Days of Anxiety: Palestine Facing Rommel.* Tel Aviv: n.p., 1974 [Hebrew].

———. "The Yishuv in Eretz-Israel during the Second World War." *Massuah* No. 4 (April 1976): 134–162 [Hebrew].

Carr, E. H. *What Is History? Shlomo Avineri's Introduction.* 7-14. Tel Aviv: Modan, 1986 [Hebrew].

Cholevsky, Shalom. "The Partisans and the Ghetto Fighters—An Active Feature among the Holocaust Survivors." *She'erit Hapleta (The Remnants), 1944–1948: Rehabilitation and Political Struggle, Proceedings of the Sixth*

Yad Vashem International Historical Conference, ed. I. Gutman and A. Drechsler, 231–233. Jerusalem: Yad Vashem, 1990 [English and Hebrew].

Cohen-Shany, Shmuel. *Paris Operation: Intelligence and Quiet Diplomacy in a New State.* Tel Aviv: n.p., 1994 [Hebrew].

Cookridge, E. H., and Spiro, E. *Inside SOE: The Story of Special Operations in Western Europe 1940–45.* London: Arthur Baker, 1966.

Dawidowicz, Lucy S. *The War against the Jews, 1933–1945.* New York: Penguin Books, 1977 [English].

Dinor, Ben-Zion, and Shaul Avigur, eds. *The "Haganah" Book.* Tel Aviv: Am Oved, 1972.

Doron, A., "The 23 Seamen Mystery," *Maariv,* 2.12.88 [Hebrew].

Dotan, Shmuel. *The Struggle for Eretz-Israel.* Tel Aviv: Defense Ministry, 1982 [Hebrew].

Dworzecki, Meir, "The International Red Cross and Its Policy vis-a-vis the Jews in the Ghettos and Concentration Camps in Nazi-Occupied Europe," *Rescue Attempts during the Holocaust.* Proceedings of the Second Yad Vashem International Historical Conference, Jerusalem, April 8–11, 1974, 71–110. New York: Ktav Publishing House, 1978 [English].

Elam, Yigal. *An Introduction to Zionist History.* Jerusalem: Lewin-Epstein, 1972 [Hebrew].

Elon, Amos. *The Israelis: Founders and Sons.* New York: Schocken, 1971.

———. *Timetable.* Garden City, N.Y.: Doubleday, 1980 [English].

Engel, David. "The Polish Government-in-Exile and the Holocaust: Stanislaw Kot's Confrontation with Palestinian Jewry, November 1942–January 1943." *Selected Documents, Poland* 2 (1987) [English].

———. "The Yishuv during the Second World War as Reflected in Polish Diplomatic Reports." *Zionism,* No. 12 (1987): 401–424 [Hebrew].

Eppler, Elizabeth E. "The Rescue Work of the World Jewish Congress During the Nazi Period." *Rescue Attempts during the Holocaust.* Proceedings of the Second Yad Vashem International Historical Conference, Jerusalem, April 8–11, 1974, 47–70. New York: Ktav Publishing House, 1978 [English]. [Hebrew; Jerusalem: Yad Vashem, 1977].

Erez, Yehuda, "Ben-Gurion Was Not Writing an Autobiography." *Keshet* (summer 1975) [Hebrew].

Eshed, Haggai. *Reuven Shiloah, the Man behind the Mossad: Secret Diplomacy in the Creation of Israel.* London: Frank Cass, 1997.

Eshkoli-Wagman, Hava. "The Palestine Jewish Leadership's Stand on the Rescue of Europe's Jews." *Yalkut Moreshet,* No. 24 (October 1977) 87–116 [Hebrew].

———. *Silence: Mapai and the Holocaust, 1939–1942.* Jerusalem: Yad Yizhak Ben-Zvi 1994 [Hebrew].

———. "Transnistria Plan: An Opportunity for Rescue or a Deception," *American Jewry during the Holocaust,* ed. Seymour Maxwel Finger, 237–260. New York: Holmes and Meier, 1984 [English].

Ettinger, Amos. *Blind Jump: The Story of Shaike Dan.* New York: Cronwall Books, 1992 [English].

Even-Zohar, Itamar. "The Emergency and Crystallization of Local and Native Hebrew Culture in Eretz-Israel, 1882–1948." *Cathedra,* No. 16 (July 1980): 165–189 [Hebrew].

———. "The Hebrew Israeli Literature—an Historical Model." *Hasifrut,* No. 33 (1973): 427–440 [Hebrew].

Feingold, H. L. *The Politics of Rescue.* New Brunswick, N.J.: Rutgers University Press, 1970 [English].

———. "The Roosevelt Administration and the Effort to Save the Jews of Hungary." *Hungarian-Jewish Studies* 2 (1969): 211–253 [English].

Ford, Corey. *Donovan of OSS.* Boston: Little, Brown, 1970 [English].

Fox, S. "The Kasztner Affair Is Back." *Ma'ariv*, weekend supplement, 24.5.85, 31.5.85 [Hebrew].

Friedman, S. S. *No Haven for the Oppressed*. Detroit: Wayne State University Press, 1973 [English].

Friling, Tuvia. "Ben-Gurion and the Holocaust of European Jewry, 1939–1945: A Stereotype Re-examined." *Yad Vashem Studies* 17/18 (1987): 199–232 [English and Hebrew].

———. "Ben-Gurion and the Rescue of Jewish Children from the Balkan Countries, 1942–1943." *Yalkut Moreshet*, part 1: No. 38 (December 1984): 31–54 [Hebrew]; part 2: No. 41 (June 1986): 119–137 [Hebrew].

———. "Meeting the Survivors: Ben-Gurion's Visit to Bulgaria, December 1944." *Studies in Zionism*, Vol. 10, No. 2. 1989, 175–195 [English].

———. "The 'Boys' in Istanbul, Jerusalem and the 'Parallel System.'" 23rd Annual Scholars' Conference, The University of Tulsa, Oklahoma, March 1992. *Proceedings from the Annual Scholars' Conference*, CD-ROM, 1996–1997.

———. "Changing Roles: Ben-Gurion's Conception of the Yishuv—She'erit Hapleta Relations, 1942–1945." *She'erit Hapleta (The Remnants), 1944–1948: Rehabilitation and Political Struggle, Proceedings of the Sixth Yad Vashem International Historical Conference*, ed. I. Gutman and A. Drechsler, 405–480. Jerusalem: Yad Vashem, 1990 [English].

———. "Clandestine Co-operation—the Paratroopers—the Plan for Jewish Defense in Europe." *The Paratroopers*, ed. S. Stempler, 111–145. Yad Tabenkin-Efal: n.p., 1995 [Hebrew].

———. "The Distorted Stereotype about D. Ben-Gurion and the Holocaust." *Iyunim Bitkumat Israel: Studies in Zionism, the Yishuv and the State of Israel* 7 (1997): 219–238 [Hebrew].

———. "The Emotional Elements in Ben-Gurion's Relations with the Diaspora during the Holocaust." *Organizing Rescue: Jewish National Solidarity in the Modern Period*, ed. I. Troen and B. Pinkus, 191–221. London: Frank Cass, 1992 [English].

———. "Istanbul, June 1944: The Intriguing Proposal to Menahem Bader." *Iyunim Bitkumat Israel: Studies in Zionism, the Yishuv and the State of Israel* 4 (1994): 229–277 [Hebrew].

———. "Nazi-Jewish Negotiations in Istanbul in mid-1944." *Holocaust and Genocide Studies* 13, no. 3 (Winter 1999): 405–436 [English].

———. "Under a Magnifying Glass." *Iyunim Bitkumat Israel: Studies in Zionism, the Yishuv and the State of Israel* 4 (1994): 592–604 [Hebrew].

———. "What Was the United States' Real Intention at the Evian Conference?" *Ha-Uma, Quarterly* 68 (September 1982): 217–228 [Hebrew].

———. "The Zionist Movement's March of Folly and the Seventh Million." *Journal of Israeli History* 16.2 (1995): 133–158 [English].

Gal, Allon. *David Ben-Gurion—Preparing For A Jewish State, 1938–1941*. Sede Boqer: Ben-Gurion Research Center, Sede Boqer Campus, Ben-Gurion University of the Negev Press, 1985 [Hebrew].

Gelber, Yoav. "British and Zionist Policies in Palestine and the Possibility of a Jewish Revolt (1942–1944)." *Zionism* 7 (1981): 324–396 [Hebrew].

———. "Crystallizing the Jewish Yishuv in Palestine, 1936–1947." *The Jewish Yishuv in Palestine at the British Period*, ed. Moshe Lisak, Anita Shapira, and Gavriel Cohen, 303–464. Jerusalem: Bialik Institute, 1995 [Hebrew].

———. *Growing a Fleur-de-Lis: The Intelligence Services of the Jewish Yishuv in Palestine 1918-1947*, Vols. 1–2. Tel Aviv: Ministry of Defense, 1992 [Hebrew].

———. *Jewish Palestine Volunteering in the British Army during the Second World War*. Vol. 1: *Volunteering and its Role in Zionist Policy 1939–1942*. Jerusalem: Yad Yizhak Ben-Zvi, 1979 [Hebrew].

———. *Jewish Palestine Volunteering in the British Army During the Second World War.* Vol. 2: *The Struggle for a Jewish Army.* Jerusalem: Yad Yizhak Ben-Zvi, 1981 [Hebrew].

———. *Jewish Palestine Volunteering in the British Army During the Second World War.* Vol. 3: *The Standard Bearers, Rescue Mission to the Jewish People.* Jerusalem: Yad Yizhak Ben-Zvi, 1983 [Hebrew].

———. *Jewish Palestine Volunteering in the British Army During the Second World War.* Vol. 4: *Jewish Volunteers in British Forces.* Jerusalem: Yad Yizhak Ben-Zvi, 1984 [Hebrew].

———. "Zionist Policy and the Fate of European Jewry 1939–1942." *Yad Vashem Studies* No. 13 (1980) [Hebrew].

———. "Zionist Policy and the Transfer Agreement 1933–1935." *Yalkut Morshet,* part 1, No. 17 (January 1974): 97–152; part 2: No. 18 (November 1974): 23–100 [Hebrew].

Genizi, Chaim. *The Adviser on Jewish Affairs to the American Army and the Displaced Persons, 1945–1949.* Tel Aviv: Moreshet-Sifriat Hapoalim, 1987 [Hebrew].

———. "Non-Sectrarian Organizations in the USA and the Displaced Persons Problem, 1933–1945." *Yad Vashem Studies* 11 (1976): 127–171 [Hebrew].

Gilbert, Martin. *Auschwitz and the Allies.* London: M. Joseph, 1981 [English]. [Hebrew, 1988].

Gorni, Yosef. *Hachdut Haavoda Party, 1919–1930.* Tel Aviv: Hakibbutz Hameuhad, 1973 [Hebrew].

———. *Partnership and Conflict: Chaim Weizmann and the Jewish Labor Movement in Palestine.* Tel Aviv: Hakibbutz Hameuhad, 1976 [Hebrew].

Gorrevitz, David, Aharon Gertz, and Roberto Beki. *Immigration: The Yishuv and its Population.* Jerusalem: Jewish Agency Statistics Department, 1945 [Hebrew].

Gutman, Israel. *The Jews in Poland after the Second World War.* Jerusalem: Zalman Shazar Center, 1985 [Hebrew].

———. "The Remnants—Problems and Clarifications." *She'erit Hapleta (The Remnants), 1944–1948: Rehabilitation and Political Struggle, Proceedings of the Sixth Yad Vashem International Historical Conference,* ed. I. Gutman and A. Drechsler, 450–480. Jerusalem: Yad Vashem, 1990 [English and Hebrew].

Hadar, David. "The Allies' Attitude to Joel Brand Mission." *Molad,* Vol. 4 (27), No. 19–20 (229–230) (May–June 1971): 112–125 [Hebrew].

Hadari-Ramage, Yona. "A Glass of Water over a Burning Township." *Ha'aretz,* 3.10.86 [Hebrew].

Harheli, Shaul. *Turkey—The Land, History, and Politics.* Jerusalem: Reuven Mass Publishers, 1941.

Hausner, Gideon. *The Chief Prosecutor of the Israeli Government against Adolf Eichmann.* Vol. 2: *Testimonies.* Jerusalem: Center for Explanation, 1974 [Hebrew].

Heller, Joseph. "Weizmann, Jabotinsky and the Arab Question—the Peel Commission." *Zmanim—A Historical Quarterly* 2, No. 11 (March 1983): 78–91 [Hebrew].

Hever, Hannan. *Captives of Utopia: An Essay on Messianism and Politics in Hebrew Poetry in Eretz-Israel Between the Two World Wars.* Sede Boqer: Ben-Gurion Research Center, Sede Boqer Campus, 1995 [Hebrew].

Hilberg, R. *The Destruction of European Jews.* New York: Franklin Watts, 1973 [English].

Hindley, Meredith, "Negotiating the Boundary of Unconditional Surrender: The War Refugee Board in Sweden and Nazi Proposals to Ransom Jews, 1944–1945." *Holocaust and Genocide Studies* 10, No. 1 (Spring 1996): 52–77 [English].

Horovitz, Ariel. "Menahem Bader's Mission in Istanbul and the Contacts of 'Hashomer-Hatza'ir' and Occupied Europe Jewry." *Yalkut Moreshet* 35 (April 1983): 153–202 [Hebrew].

Horovitz, Dan, and Moshe Lissak. *From a Yishuv to A State: Palestine's Jews under British Rule.* Tel Aviv: Am Oved, 1977 [Hebrew].

Howarth, P. *Undercover: The Men and Women of the Special Operation Executive.* London: Routledge & Kegan Paul, 1980 [English].

Ilan, Amitzur. *America, Britain and Palestine.* Jerusalem: Yad Yitzhak Ben-Zvi, 1979.

Jones, R. V. *The Wizard War, British Scientific Intelligence, 1939–1945.* New York: Coward, McCann & Geoghegan, 1978 [English].

Kafkafi, Eyal. "On Ben-Gurion's Diary." *Mibifnim (From Within),* Vol. 46, No. 3 (May 1984): 391–396 [Hebrew].

Kaplan, Jonathan. "The Activities of the Bergson Group, a branch of the 'Irgun' in USA during World War II." *Yalkut Moreshet,* part 1: 30 (November 1980) 115–138; part 2: 31 (April 1981): 75–96 [Hebrew].

Kashlass, Hayim. *The History of Bulgaria's Jews,* Vol. 4. Tel Aviv: Davar, 1969 [Hebrew].

Katz, Yaakov, "The Holocaust—Was It Predictable?", Betfotzot Hagula, Vol. 17, No. 75/76, Winter 1975, 59–68 [Hebrew].

Katzuver, Nathanel. "From Freedom to Revolt—Hungarian Jews Facing a Changing Government, 1945–1948." *She'erit Hapleta (The Remnants), 1944–1948: Rehabilitation and Political Struggle, Proceedings of the Sixth Yad Vashem International Historical Conference,* ed. I. Gutman and A. Drechsler, 103–126. Jerusalem: Yad Vashem, 1990 [English & Hebrew].

Keren-Patkin, Nili. "Saving Jewish Children in France." *Yalkut Moreshet* 36 (December 1983): 101–150 [Hebrew].

Kimche, John, and David Kimche. *Secret Roads: The "Illegal" Migration of a People, 1938–1948.* Jerusalem: Jerusalem Post, 1956 [Hebrew].

Kolatt, Israel. "Ben-Gurion: The Character and the Greatness." *Molad,* Vol. 4 (27), No. 22 (232) (December 1971): 340–351 [Hebrew].

———. "The Debate on Partition Within the Labor Movement." *Studies in the Palestine Partition Plans 1937–1947,* ed. M. Avizohar and

J. Friedman, 40–54. Sede Boqer: Ben-Gurion University of the Negev Press, Sede Boqer Campus, 1984 [Hebrew].

———. *Fathers and Founders.* Tel Aviv: Hakibbutz Hameuhad, 1975 [Hebrew].

Kreitler, H., and S. Kreitler. *Psychology of the Arts.* Durham, N.C.: Duke University Press, 1972 [English].

Ksirer, Ernest. *Essay on Human Beings.* Tel Aviv: Am Oved, 1972 [Hebrew].

Kulka, Erich. "Five Escapes from Auschwitz." *Yalkut Moreshet* 3 (December 1964) 23–38 [Hebrew].

Kurzman, Dan. *Ben-Gurion—Prophet of Fire.* New York: Simon & Schuster, 1983 [English].

Laqueur, Walter. *The Terrible Secret: Suppression of the Truth about Hitler's "Final Solution."* Boston: Little Brown, 1981 [English].

Laqueur, Walter, and Richard Breitman. *Breaking the Silence: The Secret Mission of Eduard Schulte.* London: Bodley Head, 1986 [English]. [Hebrew: TA-Jerusalem, 1988].

Lavi, Theodore. *Romanian Jewry in the Second World War: Fight for Survival.* Jerusalem: Yad Vashem and Hitachdut Olei Romania, 1965 [Hebrew].

Lookstein, H. *Were We Our Brother's Keepers?* New York: Hartmore House, 1985 [English].

Lorberbaum, Abraham. "The Hebrew Press in Eretz-Israel in the Year 1942—An Intensive Silencing?" *Yalkut Moreshet* 39 (May 1985): 153–180 [Hebrew].

Masterman, Sir John. *The Double-Cross System in the War of 1939–1945.* New Haven: Yale University Press, 1972 [English]. [Hebrew, 1975].

Melman, Yossi, and Dan Raviv. *Every Spy a Prince: The Complete History of Israel's Intelligence Community.* Boston: Houghton Mifflin, 1991 [Hebrew].

Meroz, Tamar, and Reuben Pedatzur. "The Deal That Never Was." *Ha'aretz,* 29.4.84 [Hebrew].

Mintz, Matityahu. "The Upbuilding of Eretz-Israel and Work in the Present—A Concept of Unity Versus the Actuality of Contradition." *Zionism* 9 (1984): 147–155 [Hebrew].

Miron, Dan. *Face the Silenced Brother: The Liberation War's Poetry*. Tel Aviv: Open University, 1992 [Hebrew].

———. "Face the Crocodile Tears," *Efess Shataym* 2 (Winter 1993): 116–119 [Hebrew].

Molho, Michael, and Joseph Nehama. *The Destruction of Greek Jewry, 1941–1944*. Jerusalem: Yad Vashem, 1965 [Hebrew].

Morgenstern, Arye. "The Rescue Committee's Actions during 1943–1945." *Yalkut Moreshet* 13 (June 1971): 60–103 [Hebrew].

Morse, Arthur D. *While Six Million Died: A Chronicle of American Apathy*. New York: Ace Publishing, 1967 [English]. [Hebrew, 1972].

Mossek, Moshe. "The Struggle for the Leadership among the Jews of Bulgaria, Following Liberation." *Eastern-European Jewry—from Holocaust to Redemption, 1944–1948*, ed. B. Pinkus, 188–215. Sede Boqer: Ben-Gurion University of the Negev Press, Sede Boqer Campus, 1987 [Hebrew].

Mosskat, Arye. "Spain and Its Attitude to the Jews during Second World War." *Massuah* 5 (April 1977) [Hebrew].

Nakdimon, S. "On Joel and Hansi Brand's Book: *Satan and the Soul*." *Herut*, 5.7.60 [Hebrew].

Nedava, Joseph. "Prediction of the Holocaust." *Ma'ariv*, 14.5.84 [Hebrew].

Niv, David. *Battle for Freedom: The Irgun Zvai Leumi*, Vol. 4. Tel Aviv: Klausner Institute, 1973 [Hebrew].

Ofer, Dalia. *Escaping the Holocaust*. Oxford: Oxford University Press, 1990 [English].

———. "The Activities of the Jewish Agency Delegation in Istanbul in 1943." *Rescue Attempts during the Holocaust*. Proceedings of the Second Yad Vashem International Historical Conference, Jerusalem, April 8–11, 1974, 435–450. New York: Ktav Publishing House, 1978 [English]. [Hebrew; Jerusalem: Yad Vashem, 1977, 360–370].

Office of Strategic Services. *Official History*. New York, 1976 [English].

Ophir, Ephraim. "Was It Possible to Save 70,000 Jews of Transnistria." *Yalkut Moreshet* 33, (June 1982): 103–128. [Hebrew].

———. "The Transnistria Plan—Was It Possible?" *Anti-Semites' Research Center Journal* (Forthcoming) [Hebrew].

Oren, Elhannan. "Ben-Gurion's War Diary As a Historical Source." *Cathedra* 43 (March 1987): 173–192 [Hebrew].

Penkower, M. N. *The Jews Were Expendable*. Urbana: University of Illinois Press, 1983 [English].

Pinkus, Benjamin, ed. *Eastern-European Jewry—from Holocaust to Redemption, 1944–1948*. Sede Boqer: Ben-Gurion University of the Negev Press, Sede Boqer Campus, 1987 [Hebrew].

Porat, Dina. "Al-Domi—A Group of Intellectuals—and the Holocaust, 1943–1945." *Zionism* 8 (1983): 245–275 [Hebrew].

———. "Ben-Gurion and the Holocaust." *Zionism* 12 (1987): 293–314 [Hebrew].

———. *The Blue and the Yellow Stars of David*. Cambridge: Harvard University Press, 1990.

———. "Palestine Jewry and the Jewish Agency: Public Response to the Holocaust." *Vision and Conflict in the Holy Land*, ed. R. Cohen, 246–273. New York: St. Martin's, 1985 [English].

———. "The Weissmendal Affair as Discrediting." *Ha'aretz*, 13.5.84 [Hebrew].

Prister, Roman, and Yitzhak Gruenbaum. *Without Compromise*. Tel Aviv: Zmora Bitan, 1987 [Hebrew].

Reitlinger, G. *The Final Solution: The Attempt to Exterminate the Jews of Europe, 1939–1945*. New York: Thomas Yoseloff, 1968 [English].

Rivlin, Gershon, and Aliza Rivlin. *The Stranger Cannot Understand: Code-Names in the Jewish Underground in Palestine*. Tel Aviv: Ministry of Defense, 1988 [Hebrew].

Rivlin, Gershon, and Elhanann Oren, eds. *A War Diary*. Tel Aviv: Ministry of Defense, 1982 [Hebrew].

Rivlin, Gershon, Amir Rehavam, and Shmuel Stempler, eds. *Parachutists of Hope*. Tel Aviv: Ministry of Defense, 1995 [Hebrew].

Ronen, Avihu. "Halinka's Mission." *Yalkut Moreshet* 42 (December 1986): 55–80 [Hebrew].

Rose, Paul L. "Joel Brand's 'Interim Agreement' and the Course of Nazi-Jewish Negotiations 1944–1945." *Historical Journal* 34.4 (1991) [Hebrew].

Rosenfeld, Shalom. *Criminal Case* 124/53. Tel Aviv: N.p., 1955 [Hebrew].

Rothkirchen, Livia. "Clandestine Connections between the Jewish Leaderships in Slovakia and Hungary." *Jewish Hungarian Leadership in the Holocaust*, 118–134. Jerusalem: Yad Vashem, 1976 [Hebrew].

———. *The Destruction of Slovkia's Jews*. Jerusalem: Yad Vashem, 1961 [Hebrew].

———. "On the Policy of the Vatican and the 'Jewish Question' in 'Independent' Slovakia, 1939–1945." *Yad Vashem Studies*, Vol. 6 (1966): 23–46 [Hebrew].

Rubin, Barry. *Istanbul Intrigues*. New York: Pharos Books, 1992 [English].

St. John, Robert. *David Ben-Gurion: Unordinary Biography*. Jerusalem: Achiassaf, 1959 [Hebrew].

Sayx, Christopher. *From Balfor to Bevin: Struggles over Palestine*. Tel Aviv: Ma'arachut, 1966 [Hebrew].

Schweid, Eliezer. *Homeland and Land of Promise in the Israeli People's Thought*. Tel Aviv: Am Oved, 1979 [Hebrew].

———. "Zionism at a Post-Zionist Time." *Davar*, 24.6.94 [Hebrew].

Segev, Tom. "The Old Man and the Diary." *Ha'aretz*, supplement, 7.9.83 [Hebrew].

———. *The Seventh Million: The Israelis and the Holocaust*. New York: Hill and Wang, 1993.

Shcham, David. *The New Encyclopedia*, Vol. 1. Yedio Hacharonut, Tel Aviv, 1995 [Hebrew].

Shaltiel, A. "Ben-Gurion—Struggles from Within and Without." *Ha'aretz*, 29.5.87 [Hebrew].

Shapira, Anita. *Berl: The Biography of a Socialist Zionist*. Cambridge: Cambridge University Press, 1984.

Shechtman, Y. B. "The Transnistria Reservations." *Yivo Annual of Jewish Social Science* 8 (1953) [English].

Shepherd, Naomi. *Wilfrid Israel: German Jewry's Secret Ambassador*. Jerusalem: Bialik Institute, 1989 [Hebrew].

Shiloach, Zvi. "The Ben-Gurion Wickedness Legend." *Davar*, 28.7.94.

Shirer, William L., *The Rise and Fall of the Third Reich, A History of Nazi Germany*. New York: Simon and Schuster, 1960.

Slutsky, Yehuda. "The Yishuv in Palestine and the Aid to European Jews during the Holocaust." *The Jewish Positions during the Holocaust*. Jerusalem: N.p. 1970 [Hebrew].

———. *The "Haganah" Book*. Tel Aviv: Ma'arachut, 1964 [Hebrew].

Smith, R. H. *OSS: The Secret History of America's First Central Intelligence Agency*. Berkeley: University of California Press, 1972 [English].

Sompolinsky, M. "The Anglo-Jewish Leadership, the British Government and the Rescue Policy, 1944–1945." *Yad Vashem Studies* 13 (1980) [Hebrew].

Stern, Eliahu. "The Palestine Delegation in Istanbul and it Contacts with the Polish Jewry." *Yalkut Moreshet* 39 (May 1985): 135–153 [Hebrew].

Tal, U. "On the Holocaust and Genocide Research." *Yad Vashem Studies* 13 (1980) [Hebrew].

Tartakover, Arye. "Political Action in the U.S. for Polish Jewry during World War II." *Gal-Ed* 6 (1982): 167–184 [Hebrew].

Tenenbaum, Joseph. *Race and Reich: The Story of an Epoch.* Jerusalem: Yad Vashem, 1960 [Hebrew].

Teveth, Shabtai. *Ben-Gurion: The Burning Ground, 1886–1948.* Boston: Houghton Mifflin, 1987 [English]. [Hebrew, Vol. 3, 1987].

———. *Ben-Gurion and the Holocaust.* New York: Harcourt Brace, 1996 [English].

———. "Ben-Gurion and the Holocaust Debacle." *Ha'aretz,* 10.4.87 [Hebrew].

———. "The Black Hole." *Alpayim—A Multidisciplinary Publication for Contemporary Thought and Literature* 10 (1994): 111–195 [Hebrew].

———. *The Life of David Ben-Gurion,* Vol. 1. Tel Aviv: Schocken, 1976 [Hebrew].

———. "The Long Run Runner." *Yediot Hacharonot* supplement, 3.10.86 [Hebrew].

———. *Moshe Dayan: A Biography.* Tel Aviv: Schocken, 1971 [Hebrew].

———. *The Road to May.* Tel Aviv: Ministry of Defense, 1986 [Hebrew].

Tsamriyon, Tsemah. *Newspapers of the Jewish Holocaust Survivors in Germany as an Expression of Their Problems.* Tel Aviv: Organization of Bergen Belsen Survivors in Israel, 1970 [Hebrew].

Tydor-Baumel, Judith. "Commemorating the Holocaust by Communities and Individuals in the State of Israel." *Iyunim Bitkumat Israel: Studies in Zionism, the Yishuv and the State of Israel* 5 (1995): 364–387 [Hebrew].

Tzahor, Ze'ev. "Ben-Gurion Writes a Biography." *Keshet* (Fall 1974) [Hebrew].

———. "'The Mossad Le Aliya Bet'—The Source of Its Authority." *Cathedra,* No. 39 (April 1986): 162–178 [Hebrew].

Vago, Bela. "The British Government and the Fate of Hungarian Jewry in 1944." *Rescue Attempts during the Holocaust,* Proceedings of the Second Yad Vashem International Historical Conference, Jerusalem, April 8–11, 1974, 205–224. New York: Ktav Publishing House, 1978 [English]. [Hebrew; Jerusalem: Yad Vashem, 1977, 168–182].

———. "Hungarian Jewry's Leadership." *The Leadership of Hungarian Jewry during the Holocaust,* ed. I. Gutman, B. Vago, and L. Rothkirchen, 61–76. Jerusalem: Yad Vashem 1976 [Hebrew].

———. "Intelligence Aspects of the Joel Brand Mission." *Yad Vashem Studies* 10 (1974): 81–94 [Hebrew].

Valentin, Hugo. "Rescue and Relief Activities on Behalf of Jewish Victims of Nazism in Scandinavia." *YIVO Annual* 8 (1953): 224–251 [English].

Walltsh, R. *Doubts Regarding the Ben-Gurion's Myth through Time.* Tel Aviv: n.p., 1981 [Hebrew].

Wasserstein, Bernard. *Britain and the Jews of Europe 1939–1945.* London: Institute of Jewish Affairs; Oxford: Clarendon Press, 1979 [English].

Weinryb, Elazar. *Historical Thought—The Philosophy of History,* Vol. 1. Tel Aviv: Open University, 1987 [Hebrew].

Weissberg, Alex. *Advocate for the Dead: The Story of Joel Brand.* London: Andre Deutsch, 1958 [English].

Weitz, Yehiam. *Aware but Helpless: Mapai and the Holocaust, 1943–1945.* Jerusalem: Yad Yizhak Ben-Zvi, 1994 [Hebrew].

———. "The Holocaust Survivors as Seen By the Jewish Agency's Leadership, May 1945–November 1945." *Yalkut Moreshet* 29 (May 1980): 53–80 [Hebrew].

———. *The Man Who Was Murdered Twice.* Jerusalem: Keter 1995 [Hebrew].

Wyman, D. S., *The Abandonment of the Jews.* New York: Pantheon Books, 1984 [English].

———. "Why Auschwitz Was Never Bombed." *Commentary* 5 (May 1978): 37–46 [English]. [Hebrew, *Zmanim,* No. 6 (1981): 83–89].

Yahil, Chaim. "Palestine Jewry Delegation to the Jewish Survivors, 1945–1949." *Yalkut Moreshet* 30 (November 1980): 7–40 [Hebrew].

Yahil, Leni. *The Holocaust—the Fate of European Jewry.* Tel Aviv: Yad Vashem and Jerusalem: Schocken, 1987 [Hebrew].

———. *Test of a Democracy: The Rescue of Danish Jewry in World War II.* Jerusalem: Magnes Institute and Yad Vashem, 1966 [Hebrew].

Yelinek, Jeshayahu. "The Diaries of David Ben-Gurion, 1915–1929." *Zionism* 11 (1986): 403–412 [Hebrew].

Yishay, Yael. "Leaders Resignations and their Lesson." *Migvan,* Vol. 1, No. 5 (1975): 39–42 [Hebrew].

Zariz, Ruth. "The Rescue of the Jews from Holland through the Use of Immigration Certificates." *Yalkut Moreshet* 23 (April 1977): 135–162 [Hebrew].

Zertal, Idith. "The Mossad Le Aliya Bet as a Political Instrument of the Zionist Leadership." *The Ha'apala Contribution to the Struggle against the British 1945–1947,* ed. N. Bugner, A. Halamish, I. Zertal. Tel Aviv: Haganah Center, 1991 [Hebrew].

———. "The Poisoned Heart: The Jews of Palestine and the Holocaust." *Tikkun* 2.2 (1987): 47–50, 120–122 [English].

Zimmermann, Moshe. Introduction to "Fifty Years Later: The Holocaust Influence on Cinema and Culture in Israel." manuscript supplied by the author [Hebrew].

Zweig R. W. *Britain and Palestine during the Second World War.* London: Boydell Press for the Royal Historical Society, 1986 [English].

———. "British Policy on Immigration to Palestine during the Holocaust—The Last Stage." *Zionism* 8 (1983): 195–244 [Hebrew].

———. "Great Britain, the 'Haganah,' and the Fate of the White Paper." *Cathedra* 29 (September 1983): 145–172 [Hebrew].

MEMOIRS, TESTIMONIES, SPEECH COLLECTIONS, ARTICLES, AND LETTERS

Adler-Rudel, S. "A Chronicle of Rescue Effort." *Leo Baeck Institute Year Book* 11 (1966) [English].

Avigur (Meirov), Shaul. "Our Parachutists." *Magen Baseter* (Secret defense), ed. Z. Gilad, 194–197. Jerusalem: Jewish Agency Press, 1948 [Hebrew].

———. *With the Haganah Generation.* Tel Aviv: Ma'archut, 1970 [Hebrew].

Avriel, Ehud. *Open the Gates!* London: Weidenfeld & Nicolson, 1975 [English]. [Hebrew: Tel Aviv, 1976].

Azarya, Zvi. *We Bear Witness.* Tel Aviv: Yavne, 1970 [Hebrew].

Bader, Menahem. *Sad Missions.* Merhavia: n.p., 1954 [Hebrew].

Barlas, Chaim. *Rescue during the Holocaust.* Tel Aviv: n.p., 1975 [Hebrew].

———. "Meetings in Constantinople." *Massuah* 4 (April 1976): 125–133 [Hebrew].

Ben-Gurion, David. *BaMaaracha* (In the Battle). Tel Aviv: Mapai Press, 1947–1949 [Hebrew].

———. *MiMaamad LeAm (From Class to a Nation).* Tel Aviv: Ayanut, 1955 [Hebrew].

———. *Memoirs.* New York: World, 1970.

———. "On the Way to an Army and a State in Israel." *Davar* (1966) [Hebrew].

———. *The Renewed State of Israel.* Tel Aviv: Am Oved, 1969 [Hebrew].

Berdichev, Abba. *In the Struggle.* 1956 [Hebrew].

Berger, Mordhay. *The Mobilization and Rescue Fund.* Jerusalem: Taxes Museum, 1970 [Hebrew].

Bernadotte, Folke. *The Fall of the Curtain—Last Days of the Third Reich.* London: Cassell, 1945 [English].

Binyamin, Rabbi. "On What I Had Burst in the Yishuv Convention." *Ha'aretz,* 9.6.44 [Hebrew].

———. *Bamishor*, 29.6.44 [Hebrew].

Brand, Joel, and Hansi Brand. *Satan and the Soul*. ed. B. Gepner. Tel Aviv: "Ledori" Publishers, 1960 [Hebrew]

Brand, Joel. *On Behalf of Those Condemned to Death*. Tel Aviv: 1960 [Hebrew].

Churchill, Winston. *The Second World War*. Boston: Houghton Mifflin, 1948.

Dayan, Moshe. *Milestones: Autobiography*. Eidanim, Jerusalem, 1976 [Hebrew].

Dinor, Ben-Zion. *Remember: Notes On the Holocaust and its Lesson*. Jerusalem: Yad Vashem 1958 [Hebrew].

Dobkin, Eliyahu. *Immigration and Rescue during the Holocaust*. Jerusalem: Reuven Mass, 1946 [Hebrew].

Dulles, A. W. *Germany's Underground*. New York: Macmillan, 1947. [English].

Eban, Abba. *Life Story*. Tel Aviv: Sifriat Ma'ariv, 1978 [Hebrew].

Eisenhower, Dwight. "The Europe Liberation Campaign." *Ktavim* (1951) [Hebrew].

Elath, Eliahu. *San Francisco Diary*. Tel Aviv: Dvir, 1971 [Hebrew].

———. *The Struggle for Statehood, Washington: 1945–1948*. Tel Aviv: n.p., 1979–1982 [Hebrew].

Foller, J. P. *The Second World War*. Tel Aviv: Ma'archot, 1987 [Hebrew].

Fox, Avraham. *I Called and There Was No Answer: Weissmandal Cry during the Holocaust*. Jerusalem: self-published, 1983 [Hebrew].

Gilad, Zerubavel, ed. Magen Baseter (Secret Defense): The Underground Actions during World War II—Testimonies, Documents, and Plots. Jerusalem: Jewish Agency Press, 1949 [Hebrew].

Goldmann, Nahum. *Memories*. London: Wadenfeld & Nicolson, 1972 [Hebrew].

Golomb, Eliyahu. "Cooperating and Struggling with the Government." *Magen Baseter* (Secretly Defence), ed. Z. Gilad, 3–13. Jerusalem: Jewish Agency Press, 1948 [Hebrew].

Golan, Hayim, The Israel Mereminsky's Diaries, 1941–1945, Yad Tabenkin, Ramat Effal, 1995 [Hebrew].

Gruenbaum, Yitzhak. "And Again on the Same Issue." *Hazman*, 14.2.44 [Hebrew].

———. "The Annihilation Committees." *Haolam*, 26.11.42 [Hebrew].

———. Editorial. *Davar*, 26.11.42 [Hebrew].

———. "First of All the Massacre Must Be Stopped." *Hazman*, 28.1.44 [Hebrew].

———. "The Mercy Overcome." *Hazman*, 26.6.44 [Hebrew].

———. *On Distruction and Holocaust Days, 1940–1946*. Jerusalem: n.p., 1946 [Hebrew].

Gukovsky, Lyova [Yehuda Achishar]. *To Wherever I Was Called: Story of a Hebrew Parachutist*. Tel Aviv: Hakibbutz Hameuchad, 1955 [Hebrew].

Gukovsky, Lyova, Arye Fichman, and Dov Harri. *Letters from the Lions' Den: The Rescue Parachutists*, ed. M. Rishfi. Kibbutz Beit-Oren: n.p., 1971 [Hebrew].

Hacohen, David. *Time to Tell: An Israeli Life, 1898–1984*. New York: Cornwall Books, 1985 [Hebrew; Am Oved, Tel Aviv, 1974].

———. "The Cooperation Affair." *Magen Baseter* (Secret defense), ed. Z. Gilad, 39–50. Jerusalem: Jewish Agency Press, 1948 [Hebrew].

Hadari, Ze'ev Venja. *Against All Odds, Istanbul 1942–1945*. Tel Aviv: Israel Ministry of Defense, 1992 [Hebrew].

Hadari, Ze'ev. "Ehud Avriel and His Times." *Eastern-European Jewry—From Holocaust to Redemption, 1944–1948*, ed. B. Pinkus, 271–273. Sede Boqer: Ben-Gurion University of the Negev Press, Sede Boqer Campus, 1987 [Hebrew].

Hecht, Ben. *Perfidy*. New York: Julian Messner, 1961 [English]. [Hebrew: Tel-Aviv: self-published, 1970].

Hermesh, Hayim. *Operation Amsterdam:* Tel Aviv: The Liberal College after Dr. Furder, 1985 [Hebrew].

Hirschmann, Ira A. *Life Line to a Promised Land.* New York: Vanguard Press, 1946 [English]. [Hebrew: Jerusalem: n.p., 1974].

Horowitz, David. *The Development of the Palestinian Economy.* Tel Aviv: Bialik Insistute, 1944 [Hebrew].

———. *On a Newborn State's Mission.* Jerusalem: Schocken, 1951 [Hebrew].

Kasztner, Israel. *The Truth of Kasztner: A report on the Hungarian Rescue Committee, 1942–1945,* trans. B. Gat Rimon. Tel Aviv: Association for the Eternalizing the Memory of Dr. Israel Kasztner, 1981.

Kersten, Felix. *The Kersten Memoirs.* London: Hutchinson, 1956 [English].

Kollek, Amos, and Teddy Kollek. *One Jerusalem.* Tel Aviv: Sifriat Maa'riv, 1979 [Hebrew].

Ingersoll R. *Top Secret.* New York: Harcourt Brace and Co., 1946 [English].

Livne, Zvi. *On an Economic Mission: The American Palestine Trading Corp. History.* Tel Aviv: Tarbut VeChinuch, 1964 [Hebrew].

Locker, Berl. *In Survival and Revival Suffering: Notes and Selected Speeches.* Jerusalem: Bialik Institute, 1963 [Hebrew].

Masur, Norbert. *A Jew Talks with Himmler.* Tel Aviv: Israel-Sweden Friendship Association, 1985 [Hebrew].

Meir, Golda. *My Life.* Jerusalem: Steimatzky Agency, 1975.

Nadich, Judah. *Eisenhower and the Jews.* New York: Twayne, 1953 [English].

Neumann, [Oskar] Yirmiyahu. *In the Shadow of Death: Struggle to Rescue Slovakia's Jews.* Tel Aviv: Neumann Pub., 1992 [Hebrew].

Neustadt, Melekh. *The Annihilation Year.* Tel Aviv, 1944 [Hebrew].

Nicholas, H. G. [ed.]. *Washington Despatches, 1941–1945: Weekly Political Reports from the British Embassy.* London: Weidenfeld & Nicholson, 1981 [English].

On Holocaust Days: The "Hachalutz" Emissaries. Tel Aviv: Hakibbutz Hameuhad, 1940 [Hebrew].

Palgi, Yoel. *And Behold, a Great Wind Came.* Tel Aviv: Am Oved, 1977 [Hebrew].

Pott, Alexander. *A School for Spies.* Tel Aviv: Ma'arachut, 1959 [Hebrew].

Rattner, Yohanan. *My Life and I.* Jerusalem: Schocken, 1978 [Hebrew].

Reifer, Manfred. *The Death March.* Tel Aviv: Am Oved, 1946 [Hebrew].

Reiss, Anschel. *Davar,* 27.11.42 [Hebrew].

———. *In the Time Storms.* Tel Aviv: Am Oved, 1982 [Hebrew].

———. "On the Aid and Rescue Activities." *Holocaust and Revolt Research Papers,* ed. Nachman Blumental, 2:19–36. Jerusalem: Beit Lohamei HaGhettaot and Hakibbutz Hameuhad, 1952 [Hebrew].

"Ruz'ka: Her Fight, Cogitation, and Character." *Yalkut Moreshet,* Y. Tovin, L. Dror, J. Dov, ed. Tel Aviv: Mordechai Anilevitz Testimony House & Sifriat Poalim, 1988, 212–214 [Hebrew].

Sadeh, Yitzhak. "The 23 Seamen's Mission." *Magen Baseter* (Secret Defense), ed. Z. Gilad, Jerusalem: Jewish Agency Press, 1948, 89–93 [Hebrew].

Sharett, Moshe. *Political Diary, 1940–1942.* Tel Aviv: n.p., 1979 [Hebrew].

Tabenkin, Yitzhak. "In Bitter Loneliness." Parcel of Letters, No. 131, 22.1.43. Tel Aviv: Hakibbutz Hameuhad [Hebrew].

The Yishuv Economy Book. Tel Aviv: National Council Pub., 1947.

Vazelman, M. *Sign of Cain: On the Zionist Movement and the Jewish Agency's Omissions during the Holocaust, 1939–1945,* ed. M. Gerlik. Tel Aviv: n.p., n.d.

Vilensky, Emnuel, "The Haifa Interrogation Bureau." *Magen Baseter* (Secret Defense), Z. Gilad, ed. The Jewish Agency Press, Jerusalem, 1948, 178–192 [Hebrew].

Wise, S. *Challenging Years.* New York: G. P. Putnam, 1949 [English].

Weissmandel, Michael Dov. *From the Boundary: Memories from 1942–1945.* Jerusalem:

published by author's sons, 1960 [Hebrew].

Weizmann, Chaim. *Massa vaMaa's: Memories from the Life of an Israeli President.* Jerusalem: Schocken, 1949 [Hebrew].

———. "Palestine's Role in the Solution of the Jewish Problem." *Foreign Affairs* 1 (1942) [English].

Ya'ari, Meir. 'Facing the Disaster', Hashomer Hatza'ir Weekly, 6.1.43 [Hebrew].

PUBLISHED DOCUMENTS AND REPORTS BY ORGANIZATIONS

Atiash, Moshe. *The Documents Book of the National Council for Knesset Israel in Palestine, 1918–1948.* Jerusalem, National Council, 1963 [Hebrew].

The Chief Prosecutor of the Israeli Government against Adolf Eichmann. *Testimonies,* Vol. 2. Jerusalem, 1974 [Hebrew].

Documents Relating to the Palestine Problem, 1945. London: Jewish Agency for Palestine, 1945, 88–90 [English].

Ettinger, M., ed. *The Yishuv Economy Book, 1947.* Tel Aviv: National Council, 1947 [Hebrew].

Emnuel Harosi, ed. *The Fund-raising Book.* Tel Aviv: Mobilization and Rescue Fund, 1951 [Hebrew].

Foreign Relations of the United States. *Diplomatic Papers, 1943.* Vol. 1: *General, The British Commonwealth, The Far East (1960).* Washington, D.C.: GPO, 1960 [English].

B. Mintz and Y. Klausner, eds. *The Horror Book.* Jerusalem: Rescue Committee-Reuven Mass, Jerusalem, 1945 [Hebrew].

The Rescue Committee Report to the 23rd Zionist Congress. Jerusalem: Jewish Agency Press, 1947 [Hebrew].

Pinkas Hakehillot: Encyclopaedia of Jewish Communities: Romania. T. Lavie, A. Brushi (ed. Vol 1, 1970); J. Anchell, T. Lavie (ed. Vol 2, 1980). Jerusalem: Yad Vashem, 1969 [Hebrew].

Prager, Moshe. *Israel Destruction in Europe.* Ein-Harod: Hakibbutz Hameuchad, 1947 [Hebrew].

———. *The New Miry Pit: Polish Jewry in the Nazis Claws, Massada.* Tel Aviv: n.p., 1941 [Hebrew].

Shenfeld, Moshe, ed. *Teheran Children Accuse: Facts and Documents.* Bni-Brak: n.p., 1971 [Hebrew].

PH.D. DISSERTATIONS, MASTER'S THESES, AND UNPUBLISHED PAPERS

Friedman, Mordechai. "The Political Public Response of American Jewry to the Holocaust, 1939–1945." Dissertation, Tel Aviv University, Tel Aviv, 1984 [Hebrew].

Friling, Tuvia. "David Ben-Gurion and the Catastrophe of European Jewry, 1939–1945." Dissertation, Hebrew University, Jerusalem, 1991 [Hebrew].

———. "Ben-Gurion's Interaction in the Child Rescue and the Absorption Polemic." Master's thesis, Hebrew University, Jerusalem, 1982 [Hebrew].

Ginosar, Pinchas. "Ways of Relating to Eretz-Israel and its Reality in Hebrew Poetry." Master's thesis, Tel Aviv University, Tel Aviv, 1980 [Hebrew].

Halevi, Hayim Shalom. "The Effect of the Second World War on Demographic Traits of the Jewish Nation." Dissertation, Hebrew University, Jerusalem, 1963 [Hebrew].

Kedem, Menachem. "The Political Activity of Chaim Weizmann in the Second World War." Dissertation, Bar-Ilan University, 1979 [Hebrew].

Nir, Akiva. "The Rescue Committee in Istanbul: Contacts with Slovakia." Seminar paper, Institute of Contemporary Jewry, Hebrew University, Jerusalem, 1989 [Hebrew].

Nitzan, Sara. "The Political Polemic regarding the Teheran Children." Master's thesis, Hebrew University, Jerusalem, 1986 [Hebrew].

Ofer, Dalia. "Illegal Immigration to Palestine during the Second World War, 1939–1942." Dissertation, Hebrew University, Jerusalem, 1981 [Hebrew].

Patran, Gilla. "The Slovkian Jews 1938–1944: The Jewish Center UZ—Collaboration Organization or Rescue Organization." Dissertation, Hebrew University, Jerusalem, 1988 [Hebrew].

Porat, Dina. "The Role Played by the Jewish Agency in Jerusalem in the Efforts to Rescue the Jews of Europe, 1942–1945." Dissertation, Tel Aviv University, 1983 [Hebrew].

Shachan, Avigdor. "The Ghettoes of Transnistria, 1941–1944." Dissertation, Hebrew University, Jerusalem, 1980 [Hebrew].

Shapira, David. "The Emergency Committee As a Political Operational Arm of American Zionism. 1938–1944." Dissertation, Hebrew University, Jerusalem, 1979 [Hebrew].

Shimoni, Gideon. "The South African Jewish Community and Zionist Movement, 1910–1948." Dissertation, Hebrew University, Jerusalem, 1974 [Hebrew].

Sompolinsky, M. "The Anglo-Jewish Leadership, the British Government and the Holocaust." Master's thesis, Bar-Ilan University, 1977 [Hebrew].

Yablonka, Hanna. "Europa Plan." Master's thesis, Hebrew University, Jerusalem, 1984 [Hebrew].

Names Index

Subject Index